D1527948

A Generous and Merciful Enemy

C&C

CAMPAIGNS & COMMANDERS

GREGORY J. W. URWIN, SERIES EDITOR

CAMPAIGNS AND COMMANDERS

GENERAL EDITOR
Gregory J. W. Urwin, *Temple University, Philadelphia, Pennsylvania*

ADVISORY BOARD
Lawrence E. Babits, *East Carolina University, Greenville*
James C. Bradford, *Texas A&M University, College Station*
Robert M. Epstein, *U.S. Army School of Advanced Military Studies, Fort Leavenworth, Kansas*
David M. Glantz, *Carlisle, Pennsylvania*
Jerome A. Greene, *Denver, Colorado*
Victor Davis Hanson, *California State University, Fresno*
Herman Hattaway, *University of Missouri, Kansas City*
J. A. Houlding, *Rückersdorf, Germany*
Eugenia C. Kiesling, *U.S. Military Academy, West Point, New York*
Timothy K. Nenninger, *National Archives, Washington, D.C.*
Bruce Vandervort, *Virginia Military Institute, Lexington*

A Generous and Merciful Enemy

Life for German Prisoners of War
during the American Revolution

Daniel Krebs

To Kay and Ross,
I hope you un...
enjoy :)

University of Oklahoma Press · Norman

Library of Congress Cataloging-in-Publication Data

Krebs, Daniel, 1974–
  A generous and merciful enemy : life for German prisoners of war during
the American Revolution / Daniel Krebs.
     pages cm. — (Campaigns and commanders ; v. 38)
  Includes bibliographical references and index.
  ISBN 978-0-8061-4356-9 (hbk. : alk. paper) 1. United States—History—
Revolution, 1775–1783—Prisoners and prisons, German. 2. German
mercenaries—History—18th century. 3. United States—History—Revolution,
1775–1783—Participation, German. 4. Prisoners of war—United States—
History—18th century. 5. Prisoners of war—Germany—History—18th century.
6. Military prisons—United States—History—18th century. 7. Forced labor—
United States—History—18th century. 8. Indentured servants—United
States—History—18th century. I. Title.
  E268.K74 2013
  973.3'7143—dc23
                                                              2012041399

A Generous and Merciful Enemy: Life for German Prisoners of War during the American Revolution is Volume 38 in the Campaigns and Commanders series.

The paper in this book meets the guidelines for permanence and durability
of the Committee on Production Guidelines for Book Longevity of the
Council on Library Resources, Inc. ∞

Copyright © 2013 by the University of Oklahoma Press, Norman, Publishing
Division of the University. Manufactured in the U.S.A.

All rights reserved. No part of this publication may be reproduced, stored
in a retrieval system, or transmitted, in any form or by any means, electronic,
mechanical, photocopying, recording, or otherwise—except as permitted
under Section 107 or 108 of the United States Copyright Act—without the
prior written permission of the University of Oklahoma Press. To request
permission to reproduce selections from this book, write to Permissions,
University of Oklahoma Press, 2800 Venture Drive, Norman OK 73069, or
email rights.oupress@ou.edu.

1 2 3 4 5 6 7 8 9 10

To my parents
Without them, this would not have been possible

To Mariel
For all time, with love

Contents

Illustrations

Tables

Acknowledgments

I could not have written this book without the invaluable help of numerous teachers, colleagues, institutions, friends, and family. First and foremost, I want to thank my graduate advisor, James Van Horn Melton, Emory University, who enthusiastically accepted me as a student with a topic very different from his own research. He patiently struggled through my clumsy prose while I was trying to master a foreign language. His advice made this book, as it is based on my dissertation, a much better product. Over the years, Daniel Richter, McNeil Center for Early American Studies at the University of Pennsylvania, became both a mentor and friend who read and supported my research at various points of my career. An exhilarating year as Society of the Cincinnati & Friends of the MCEAS Dissertation Fellow at the McNeil Center enabled me to write much of my dissertation and benefit from many brilliant historians and fellow graduate students who selflessly shared their knowledge. After beginning the process of revising my dissertation, a Donald L. Saunders Postdoctoral Research Fellowship at the John Carter Brown Library at Brown University allowed me to take off a semester from teaching at the University of Louisville, finish research, and write an initial draft of the book. The fellows, staff, and archivists at the John Carter Brown Library, particularly its director, Edward Widmer, encouraged me to write a book that goes beyond merely compiling evidence for an argument. Bernhard Kroener, University of Potsdam, Germany, and the late Wilfried Bottke, University of Augsburg, Germany, initially gave me the confidence to pursue my doctorate in the United States and focus on military history.

Over the years, a number of grants and awards from many institutions have made research in various national and international archives possible. An agreement between the University of Augsburg and Emory University allowed me to spend a year in the United States as an exchange student. While I was in graduate school, Emory University provided me with a four-year fellowship for my Ph.D. studies and supported a trip to German and English repositories through a grant from its Fund for Internationalization. The David Library of the American Revolution, the German Historical Institute in Washington, D.C., and the Virginia Historical Society all made funds available to work in their and other collections. A Blair Rogers Major and James Russell Major Dissertation Award in Early Modern European History from the Department of History at Emory University was crucial for completing the writing process of my dissertation. A Research Initiation Grant from the University of Louisville, as well as travel funds from the History Department, enabled further research in Germany while I was preparing the book manuscript.

In every archive and library, I have met staff members and scholars whose advice and assistance made my work easier. I could not have succeeded without their help. In particular, I would like to thank the many archivists and librarians at the Bayerisches Hauptstaatsarchiv, the David Library of the American Revolution, Ekstrom Library at the University of Louisville, the Geheimes Staatsarchiv Preußischer Kulturbesitz, the Historical Society of Frederick, the Historical Society of Pennsylvania, the John Carter Brown Library and the John Hay Library at Brown University, the Lancaster County Historical Society, the Library of Congress, the Library of Virginia, the Maryland Historical Society, the Moravian Archives, the Landes- und Murhardsche Bibliothek der Stadt Kassel, the National Archives and Records Administration, the National Archives of the United Kingdom (Public Record Office), the Schlossbibliothek Ansbach, the Staatsarchive Bamberg, Marburg, Nürnberg, Wolfenbüttel, and Würzburg, the Stadtarchive Ansbach and Bayreuth, the Universitätsbibliothek Bayreuth, the Virginia Historical Society, Woodruff Library at Emory University, and the York County Heritage Trust.

I would be ungrateful, however, if I did not thank a number of people by name who have read all or parts of the dissertation and book manuscript, shared their own research, helped in preparing the manuscript for publication, allowed me to present and test my findings before fellow scholars, or patiently answered my questions even during the busiest times. Others are just very good and close friends whose companionship makes life and working in academia such a pleasure. I could not have written this book without you: Sutton Adams; Holger Afflerbach; Fred Anderson; Matthias Asche; Bill Campbell; my colleagues in the History Department at the University of Louisville, particularly Glenn Crothers; Ute Frevert; Holger Gräf; Lena Haunert; Candice Harrison; John Houlding; Stephan Huck; Lee Keeling; Adolf Lang; Wayne Lee; Horst Lochner; Don Londahl-Smidt; Katherine Ludwig; Nicole Mills; the participants at the Kentucky Seminar in Early American Studies, particularly Jane Calvert and Brad Wood; Werner Rieß; Kelly Ryan; Paul Springer; David Stewart; Sharon Strocchia; and Elizabeth Todd.

Very special thanks go to the entire team of Oklahoma University Press and its Campaigns and Commanders series. The series editor, Gregory Urwin, first approached me with the idea for this book. I am honored by the trust he placed in me and my research. Charles Rankin, editor-in-chief, saw the entire project through, from initial idea to the finished product. The manuscript readers gave excellent suggestions for much-needed improvements. Emily Jerman, manuscript editor, helped me navigate copy editing and proofreading and kept me on a very tight schedule. Lynn Carlson, GIS manager at Brown University, made both maps and endured my constant requests for changes. Jane Lyle, my copy editor, saved me from numerous mistakes and worked extremely hard, even very late at night, to improve my writing and narrative. This book would not be what it is without her efforts. From the bottom of my heart, thank you! Of course, all remaining errors are my own.

Over the years, my parents, Erni and Werner Krebs, supported me and my studies at all times, even when my career took me far away from home. It is finally done! My wife, Mariel, endured my long absences for research, and my frequent absent-mindedness at home. She always encouraged me, and pushed me hard to remove "moreover" as often from the text as possible. For this and her love, I owe her more than any words of gratitude could ever express.

A Note about Spelling, Terminology, and Currencies

German places and names in this study are given in their original spelling. An English translation of key German terms is given in parentheses or, if longer explanations were necessary, in the endnotes. All direct quotes from German primary and secondary sources were translated into English by the author. When numbers for various contemporary German currencies (*Thaler, Gulden,* etc.) are given, the approximate equivalent in British pounds (£), shillings (s.), and pence (d.) is provided. These calculations are based on the exchange rate of £3 for 24 *Gulden,* from the early eighteenth century, a period of relative financial stability. Colonists who fought and worked against the British motherland and its German auxiliaries between 1775 and 1783 are described as "revolutionaries" or "American revolutionaries." The term "Americans" was avoided in general reference to revolutionaries, as were the terms "rebels," from a British perspective, and "Patriots," from an American perspective. Colonists who fought on or otherwise supported the British side during the war are described as "loyalists." German soldiers who fought for the British following subsidy treaties concluded between their princes and George III from 1776 to 1783 are usually described as "subsidy soldiers" or "German auxiliaries." When the term "mercenaries" appears in those sections that discuss recruitment for these auxiliary forces, it is meant solely in the early modern sense of the word, to denote men who agreed to perform military service in exchange for some kind of monetary compensation, but not in its modern, largely derogatory meaning.

A Generous and Merciful Enemy

Introduction

As a soldier, you may rarely think about being captured. It is not a pleasant subject and assuming that it can happen only to the other guy is easy.
    —U.S. Army Training Circular 27-10-2, September 1991

This is a story about prisoners of war. It is a case study of the life and treatment of some 5,400 common German soldiers who found themselves in revolutionary American hands between 1776 and 1783. These prisoners were part of several large troop contingents, totaling about 37,000 soldiers, from six principalities in the Holy Roman Empire—Braunschweig-Wolfenbüttel, Hessen-Kassel, Hessen-Hanau, Waldeck, Ansbach-Bayreuth, and Anhalt-Zerbst—who had been hired by King George III to fight his thirteen rebellious colonies in North America. Unlike other powerful European empires, Great Britain did not maintain a sufficiently large standing army in the eighteenth century, so every major conflict involving the British required negotiations with other sovereigns for additional forces in exchange for money.[1]

Soldiers who lost in battle did not make good heroes. They are largely absent from traditional military history, which was aimed primarily at educating future military leaders, and thus focused only on the tactical, strategic, and operational parameters of conflict, ascribing little value to an examination of wartime captivity.[2] The advent of conscription and citizen armies during the American and French Revolutions also turned military service in the Western world into a national duty. Soldiers who surrendered or were captured were morally suspect, seen as not having given everything—including their lives, if necessary—for cause and country. No value could be derived from learning about men who had essentially failed their nation.[3] As a result of such predispositions in scholarship, key questions remained largely unanswered: How does fighting end during a battle? How do surrender and capture work? How should enemies who are captured in warfare be treated?

Because of their sheer numbers and the unparalleled brutality of the conflicts, prisoners of war from the U.S. Civil War, both world wars, and the Vietnam War have received considerable attention from historians on both sides of the Atlantic.[4] For the prerevolutionary period in North America, only Indian captives have attracted significant interest.[5] Legal historians were always concerned with prisoners of war, but their inquiries were naturally limited to the specific perspective of this subdiscipline.[6] The few academic publications that center their analysis on prisoners of war during the American Revolution focus mostly on American prisoners in British hands.[7] Little scholarship has been published on the fate of British or German prisoners of war in revolutionary hands.[8]

Recent studies on American prisoner-of-war policies since the American Revolution have made an excellent start toward remedying this omission.[9] However, there is more to wartime captivity than questions of policy. The experience of captivity for low-ranking common soldiers is as important as the decisions made at the top level of government and military leadership. Learning about the treatment and experiences of prisoners of war teaches us about society and its aspirations. It is only fitting to begin such an inquiry with the American Revolution and the War of Independence, the period that ushered in our modern understanding of government, the people, and warfare.

At times, German subsidy soldiers constituted as much as a third of the British army in North America during the American War of Independence, yet despite their large numbers and their importance for the crown's overall war effort, they have received comparatively little attention from scholars.[10] Indeed, only a few book-length studies on either side of the Atlantic have focused on these vital auxiliaries.[11] In Germany, research has concentrated primarily on the much-debated soldier trade and the rising criticism of this practice at the end of the eighteenth century.[12] German scholars have also shown a strong interest in the soldiers' view of the American Revolution.[13] In the United States, the lack of scholarship on German subsidy troops can be traced back to the nineteenth century. In writing the early history of the new nation, American historians were primarily concerned with explaining how the country was born out of a just war against the British motherland.[14] German auxiliaries usually appeared in such accounts only as the "foreign mercenaries" of Thomas Jefferson's Declaration of Independence.[15] Research on these neglected participants in the American Revolution can widen the story beyond the standard representation of a primarily Anglo-American struggle. The Atlantic world was not built exclusively around imperial Western European powers, Africa, and the Americas. The Holy Roman Empire, with its numerous larger and smaller states, was equally involved in these world-changing events.[16]

~

Written from the perspective of low-ranking common soldiers and noncommissioned officers, who have so often been relegated to anonymity, this study attempts to close some of these gaps in the historiography. Common soldiers take center stage and do not appear merely as "numbers, as sums in casualty lists," scarcely mentioned after the fighting.[17] This is history from the bottom up, taking us beyond laws, policies, parole, exchange agreements, and the fate of elite military leaders.[18]

From this perspective, it becomes apparent that the German prisoners posed major challenges for the revolutionaries, but they were not just a burden—more mouths to feed, more bodies to house and guard. Prisoners of war were also useful enemies, sometimes even human capital, and presented their captors with a number of opportunities.[19] Initially, communities that had to detain enemy soldiers could not see beyond the costs of prisoner treatment and looked desperately for ways to reduce, or even avoid, some of the expenses. But they soon discovered that they could use the prisoners to their benefit. For example, captive soldiers were often employed as prisoner-laborers. Adopted first on the local level, this practice soon spread to the state level and even to Congress. Hiring out prisoners of war enabled revolutionaries on all levels to handle large numbers of enemy captives despite an often chaotic governmental situation and inadequate resources.

Unfree labor in all forms was the norm in contemporary North America, so using captives as laborers was in keeping with this common New World experience.[20]

The prisoners, in turn, were eager to work because it enabled them to escape crowded housing and earned them additional food and money. It also accorded with their experiences as soldiers in garrison, where they practiced civilian trades to augment the often meager pay. Over the course of the conflict, prisoners of war were hired to work on farms in Pennsylvania, at saltworks in Maryland and ironworks in New Jersey, and for towns in New England. Their contributions became so valuable to the local economy that some communities protested when Congress later wanted to remove the captives to another area. After 1779, however, labor became less of a choice and more of a necessity for captured common soldiers. The American revolutionaries were plagued by massive financial problems in the later years of the war and could no longer ensure sufficient prisoner support.

But the revolutionaries used their enemy prisoners for much more than labor. According to Rüdiger Overmans, prisoners of war could fulfill various other functions for their captors: as hostages, bridges of communication, consumers, proof of military victories, objects of indoctrination, tools of propaganda, agents of social change, and even political instruments.[21] Rituals after the British surrenders at Saratoga and Yorktown turned the new prisoners into useful enemies by establishing the revolutionaries as legitimate belligerents in a new kind of conflict that was different from the usual dynastic or imperial struggle of the eighteenth century. Some of these rituals, modeled after ancient rites of passage, safely guided the vanquished into enemy hands; others humiliated German troops in order to strengthen revolutionary morale. Congress, General George Washington as the commander-in-chief of the Continental Army, and individual states repeatedly used the British and German captives as a bargaining chip in negotiations with the British regarding improved treatment of revolutionary prisoners of war. Both sides also made use of traditional prisoner exchanges or tried to recruit each other's captives. Because the prisoners continued to receive pay from their units, cash flowed into the American hinterland, fueling local economies. In 1778, prisoners of war were used by Congress in an attempt to exert financial pressure against the British Treasury by changing their supply system. And revolutionaries in Pennsylvania used enemy captives to increase their authority in less supportive parts of the state: when prisoners came to town, the revolutionary administration followed.

The German prisoners of war needed to be fed, housed, and clothed. Their captors were responsible for providing quarters and provisions, but clothing was customarily delivered along with their pay by their own army and sovereign. If any of those essential needs were not met, common soldiers quickly suffered and were compelled to seek a solution. This primarily meant working as prisoner-laborers for American employers. In the process, low-ranking soldiers were often able to play each side against the other, to their own advantage.

German and British prisoners of war were often treated differently by the American revolutionaries. The moment the first German subsidy troops set foot on North American soil in the summer of 1776, Congress drafted several messages designed to entice them to desert from British lines in exchange for land offers. Revolutionary leaders were convinced that these soldiers had been sent to North America against their will and were waiting for an opportunity to cast off their bonds and embrace American freedom and liberty. The German soldiers were fighting in North America only because their sovereigns had negotiated subsidy treaties with George III, and they could therefore be seen as victims of princely tyranny, much like the revolutionaries themselves. They might even be persuaded to stay and join the tens of thousands of German immigrants who had come across the Atlantic before the war.

When Pennsylvania militiamen captured a sizable group of German soldiers on Staten Island in the fall of 1776, they gave them a tour of Philadelphia before returning them to their units. They believed that these men would eagerly spread the story of American abundance among other German auxiliaries, thereby leading to additional desertions that would weaken the British army. Although American revolutionaries were fully convinced of the irresistible attractiveness of their land and ideas, desertion was a difficult decision for the German soldiers and prisoners. In Europe, a deserter could change his mind and return to his homeland, even after the war. This war, however, was being fought across the Atlantic, thousands of miles away from the Holy Roman Empire.

After the successful siege of Yorktown in 1781, the United States had essentially won its independence, but the new nation was also bankrupt and sorely lacking in manpower for its revolutionary forces. At that point, Congress decided to recruit German prisoners of war for the Continental Army. Those who were not inclined to fight for the revolutionaries could free themselves by paying a ransom. Soldiers who did not want to enlist and who did not have cash on hand for the ransom could sell themselves into indentured servitude. Before the war, servitude had paid for the passage of German immigrants across the Atlantic; now it paid for the passage of German prisoners out of captivity.

To understand fully what happened to common German soldiers as prisoners of war during the American War of Independence, it is necessary to know who they were. These subsidy soldiers were more than brutal foreign fighters or poor victims of princely tyranny; archival sources, case studies of several units, and available secondary literature reveal a picture that is much more complex. In early modern Europe, powerful states routinely hired troop contingents from other states to enlarge their armies.[22] Subsidy agreements allowed small states such as Hessen-Kassel and Ansbach-Bayreuth to play a larger role in European power politics, pay off debts, and build infrastructure. By the late eighteenth century, however, a new understanding of warfare and the military was emerging in Europe, and these treaties came under scrutiny and criticism. The use of purely professional soldiers, men who were foreign to both the location and the cause of a conflict, was increasingly considered problematic. The term "mercenary" took on a negative connotation, and the German subsidy troops in North America became an anachronism. They were recruited and sent into British service according to long-standing practices of early modern European warfare but fought in a conflict that opened an age of revolution and national conflicts.

Recruitment in the six principalities that sent subsidy troops into British service was conducted in two ways. Braunschweig-

Wolfenbüttel focused on recruiting mercenaries, preferably from other German territories, while Ansbach-Bayreuth and Hessen-Kassel relied on some form of conscription. Ansbach-Bayreuth used enrollment lists from which the army picked the most "dispensable" men for military service—those who contributed little, by contemporary standards, to the local economy and society. Hessen-Kassel, which sent the most German soldiers to North America, recruited through the canton system (*Kantonsystem*), modeled after Prussia's example, which assigned each unit a particular recruiting district (*Kanton*) and imposed service requirements on the male population. After the first contingents left for North America, however, these states also looked to mercenaries for replacement and reinforcement transports.

The men who boarded British transports to fight in North America were a motley mix of soldiers. Some were new recruits; others were veterans of many years' service. Some joined voluntarily to overcome a temporary crisis in their civilian life; others hoped to stay in the New World after the war. Most common soldiers were about twenty-four years old when they came to North America. They were overwhelmingly Protestant, either Lutheran or Reformed. They came from the lower strata of society but not necessarily from the very bottom. Only a few were married, but they often had partners and were concerned with the well-being of their families at home. Records from Braunschweig-Wolfenbüttel, Waldeck, and Hessen-Kassel show that soldiers had a portion of their pay sent directly to their wives, partners, children, siblings, or parents.

~

This study utilizes a number of surviving journals, letters, and memoirs written by captive common soldiers. These autobiographical accounts are difficult to locate and are often based on revised recollections after the war, but they provide fascinating insights into how these soldiers came to terms with what happened around them and how they saw and understood themselves within the wider world. The authors of these journals and letters did not merely record events as they happened; they always made choices about what to tell and how—in the process emphasizing

certain events while deemphasizing others, omitting some entirely, inventing occurrences to make a point, striving to present
a particular group in a certain light, or justifying and legitimizing particular actions. Sometimes they lied. Such decisions were
influenced by previous and current experiences, the amount of
information available, their language skills, the time at which they
were writing, and their anticipated readership.[23] In the case of Johannes Reuber from Hessen-Kassel, we have page after page of
detailed descriptions of campaigns and life in captivity. Johann
Conrad Döhla from Ansbach-Bayreuth gives precise numbers and
detailed information about the fate of others in his company. Johann Christoph Döhlemann, who rose from corporal to officer
during the war, wrote a number of letters to his parents.

Since only a few autobiographical sources written by low-
ranking soldiers are available, this analysis also relies on other,
mostly administrative sources. They consist of documents from
various military and civil institutions and personnel on both sides
of the Atlantic Ocean, including official reports sent to Europe,
the papers of the Continental Congress, orders from George Washington, petitions by local revolutionaries, and letters from local
committees and state assemblies. Some of these are what the German historian Winfried Schulze calls "ego-documents," sources
that, while not autobiographical in nature, provide information
about an individual's self-perception within a family, a community,
a country, or the larger society. Ego-documents can also reflect an
individual's relationship to a role in society. Such perceptions or
reflections often remain hidden or are available in only a rudimentary form.[24] For example, petitions submitted to the margrave
of Ansbach-Bayreuth, Karl Alexander, by relatives of soldiers sent
to North America who were applying for grain rations, firewood
distribution, or tax and debt relief also tell us about the soldiers,
their families, their social circumstances, and even their motives
for joining the army.

~

The following analysis is divided into three parts, each prefaced
with a story about one or more common soldiers and their experiences. Part I introduces the troops and their service for the

British crown during the Revolutionary War, concentrating on recruitment patterns and social composition. Part II examines how these men became prisoners of war, through either capture or surrender. One chapter focuses on Western traditions of warfare, customs, practices, and regulations since Greek and Roman antiquity because these became the basis for current laws such as the Geneva Convention Relative to the Treatment of Prisoners of War (1949) and were also most important for the era of the American Revolution. Part III, the main part of the book, focuses on the common soldiers' everyday lives and experiences in captivity. Several chapters cover prisoners of war from New England to Louisiana and even Havana, Cuba. The narrative centers on a few large groups of captives, those taken prisoner at Trenton in 1776, at Bennington and Saratoga in 1777, on the British transports *Molly* and *Triton* in 1779, and around Baton Rouge that same year, as well as at Yorktown in 1781. The last chapter follows the prisoners during their release from captivity and return to Europe but also looks at those who decided to stay in North America. The epilogue carries the prisoners' story to the almost-forgotten Treaty of Amity and Commerce concluded in 1785 between the United States and Prussia. It was the first treaty in Western legal history, albeit only a bilateral agreement, to include detailed regulations about the treatment of prisoners of war and resulted directly from the experience of captors and captives during the American War of Independence.

PART I

German Soldiers in British Service

Johannes Reuber was born in 1759 to Herrmann Reuber, a laborer, and his wife, Margarete, who died only a week after giving birth to their son. Johannes grew up in Niedervellmar, a small village about three miles north of Kassel, the capital of the Landgraviate of Hessen-Kassel in the Holy Roman Empire. (See map 1 for an overview of the German principalities with subsidy troops in British service between 1776 and 1783.) In 1787, Niedervellmar had only 357 inhabitants, most of them farmers. The village boasted many fine fruit trees and even exported some linen. Overall, as a contemporary observer noted, the villagers had achieved a modest degree of prosperity.[1]

Not yet seventeen years old in September 1775, Johannes was drafted into the *Landgrenadierregiment*, a regional militia unit of heavy infantry. As was common practice in eighteenth-century standing armies, he was soon released again on furlough. Life initially seemed to continue as usual for this young Hessian. New Year's Day in 1776, however, changed everything. The landgrave of Hessen-Kassel, Friedrich II, had signed a subsidy treaty with the British crown for 12,000 of his soldiers, and Johannes received orders to report back to his regiment and join Major Johann Jost Matthäus's company at Immenhausen, five miles north of Niedervellmar. Destined for British service, his militia unit was converted to a regular grenadier regiment, reinforced, fitted out, and vigorously drilled twice a day. On March 3, noncommissioned officers handed out ammunition and "everything else that was needed for war." Realizing that they would soon leave Hessen-Kassel, the soldiers were nervous, exchanging "wild looks." The next morning, the newly established Grenadier Regiment Rall, named after its commander, Colonel Johann Gottlieb Rall, was on its way to North America.[2]

In February 1777, Stephan Popp from the Franconian village of Dachsbach was also preparing to fight in North America. Popp was a veteran soldier in the Regiment Voit von Salzburg, named after its commander, August Voit von Salzburg, and one of two infantry regiments that the margrave of Ansbach-Bayreuth, Karl Alexander, had sent into British service as subsidy troops.[3] After news broke on February 2 of the unit's impending departure, family members came to the barracks in Bayreuth to say goodbye. The air, Popp noted in his journal, was filled with "groans and sighs" of grief, but he was excited because he wanted to see the world.[4] To reassure family members, relatives, and friends, on March 12 Karl Alexander established a special postal service in his *Expeditionsamt*, the government's official mail office, where anybody "who wanted to write" a soldier in North America could drop off or pick up letters free of charge every Monday and Thursday.[5]

That such comforting measures were necessary became obvious on March 10. That day, the margrave's subsidy troops for Great Britain were scheduled to leave from Ochsenfurt, a small town on the River Main, for Nijmegen in Holland, their place of embarkation for North America. After arriving on foot on the evening of March 9, the soldiers were placed on small riverboats in Ochsenfurt's harbor, where they spent an ostensibly calm night.[6] Early the next morning, however, several hundred soldiers defied orders and left their boats, gathering at the harbor. Quarrels broke out between common soldiers and their superiors. More men then came ashore. Some began making their way into the surrounding hills and vineyards. The officers sent *Jäger*, elite light infantry soldiers recruited among the prince's trusted hunters and foresters, after them. Suddenly shots were heard, and a full-fledged skirmish broke out. Several men fell wounded, and order broke down completely. A mutiny was in full swing.[7] Fourier Carl Wilhelm Meyer, a noncommissioned officer responsible for supplies, later wrote that this was the first full-scale revolt he "had witnessed in his entire life." The soldiers "rose against their sovereign prince and superiors and, against all laws of nature and reason, refused to obey orders," with the result that "force . . . had to be used."[8] The officers regained control only at the end of the day. Karl Alexander hurried to the scene during the night and spoke to his men early in the morning of March 11. Concerned about their conduct, he stayed with them all the way to Holland. More than two hundred soldiers had taken part in the uprising, with twenty-five having deserted.[9]

During the British muster upon arrival in Holland, however, the Ansbach-Bayreuth soldiers made a very good impression. Colonel Charles Rainsford, the British commissary for embarking foreign troops, wrote to Secretary of State Henry Howard, Earl of Suffolk, that the margrave's infantry regiments were "two of the finest Battalions of foreign Troops I ever saw, young, tall, well appointed, and in excellent Condition."[10] Later that spring, Lieutenant Colonel George Osborn, responsible for the muster of subsidy troops in North America, reported to George Germain, Viscount Sackville, the secretary of state for America, that the Ansbach-Bayreuth units had arrived in "perfect good order."[11]

Other German subsidy soldiers received much less praise. In 1777, Osborn had numerous complaints about some troops from Waldeck. Many of them were too young or too short, or they lacked training and experience.[12] In Holland that same year, Rainsford found some Hessen-Kassel reinforcements to be a "very unequal Body of Men." Some were too old, and some were even missing an eye. He claimed to have accepted them only because he did not want to "turn them loose" in the country.[13]

~

Reuber's conscription, Popp's excitement upon leaving for North America, the mutiny in Ochsenfurt, and the complaints about the Waldeck troops and Hessen-Kassel reinforcements evoke questions about these German auxiliaries. Where did they come from? How many were conscripts like Reuber or veteran professionals like Popp? Who was recruited, and how? What motivation did they have to join an army destined for British service in North America? How old were they? Did they have family? What was their financial situation? Did the soldiers in Ochsenfurt revolt because they wanted to avoid service in North America? To address such questions, the first chapter in this part examines the subsidy treaties concluded with the British crown by Braunschweig-Wolfenbüttel, Hessen-Kassel, Hessen-Hanau, Ansbach-Bayreuth, Waldeck, and Anhalt-Zerbst and looks at the controversies surrounding those agreements. The second chapter analyzes recruitment patterns. How did young men in Braunschweig-Wolfenbüttel, Hessen-Kassel, and Ansbach-Bayreuth become soldiers? Who was drafted? Who was recruited as a professional soldier? How were these troops perceived by the revolutionaries, and how did they understand themselves and their service for the British in North America? Moving beyond patterns and principles, the final chapter in this first part uses case studies from Braunschweig-Wolfenbüttel, Hessen-Kassel, and Ansbach-Bayreuth to shed light on the social composition of German auxiliaries between 1776 and 1783.[14]

CHAPTER 1

Subsidy Treaties

Unlike other powerful European states, Great Britain never kept a large standing army. The English Civil War of the seventeenth century had cemented in the public mind a fear of the corrupting power of a paid professional military force.[1] Therefore, when hostilities broke out with thirteen North American colonies in the spring of 1775, it was clear that the crown needed additional soldiers. Like his predecessors, George III looked to other states to enlarge his army, using subsidy treaties, an arrangement under which one contracting party provided funds to another in exchange for soldiers or other military efforts.[2] Such agreements were common in early modern Europe—so common that "auxiliaries" is a more appropriate term for the troops than "subsidy soldiers." Contemporary armies were international institutions composed of servicemen from various regions and territories. Subsidy treaties quickly brought large numbers of trained and equipped soldiers to the front, at a relatively low cost. Over time, long-standing relationships, even alliances, developed between states that repeatedly negotiated such agreements. Hanover, particularly after the accession of Prince-Elector Georg Ludwig to the British throne in 1714, regularly sent large parts of its army into British service.[3] Zweibrücken's men were an integral part of the French army by the end of the eighteenth century, and German auxiliaries served not only with the British in North America but also in the Regiment Royal Deux-Ponts, part of General Jean-Baptiste de Vimeur, Comte de Rochambeau's French expeditionary force at Yorktown in 1781.[4] Prussia and Austria also used subsidy treaties to enlarge their already massive military establishments, particularly after

1740, when their decades-long contest for dominance in Central Europe began.

In 1775, Great Britain sent Hanoverian units to Gibraltar and Minorca, hoping to free up British troops there for service in North America.[5] After the revolutionaries' invasion of Canada, however, it became clear that many more troops were needed. The court at St. James then approached Russia with a proposal for a subsidy treaty. This agreement would ensure that all auxiliaries came from a single state so that the British army would not have to be cobbled together from various contingents, with the attendant problems of communication, command structure, and logistics. Because of their foreign culture and language, Major General Henry Clinton was convinced that Russian soldiers in North America would also be less likely to desert.[6] However, Catherine II did not want to send her soldiers so far away and claimed that she could not spare the large number of troops that George III desired.[7]

The British were forced to look elsewhere. As so often before, they found enough soldiers among a number of small German principalities in the Holy Roman Empire. Back in the winter of 1774/75, the British envoy, Colonel William Fawcett, had already spoken to emissaries from Hessen-Kassel about the possibility of a subsidy treaty.[8] For several decades, Hessen-Kassel had been closely associated with Great Britain and the so-called soldier trade (*Soldatenhandel*). Indeed, by August 1775, most officials in Hessen-Kassel fully expected that their entire army of 12,000 men would soon enter British service. Theirs was one of the best-trained, most readily available, and largest fighting forces on the European continent.[9]

Subsidy Treaties

The first subsidy treaty, however, was signed with the principality of Braunschweig-Wolfenbüttel. In January 1776, Duke Karl I and his prince hereditary, Karl Wilhelm, agreed to make available 3,964 infantrymen and 336 dragoons. (See table 1 for British subsidy treaties with German principalities between 1776 and 1783.) Over the following years, Braunschweig-Wolfenbüttel also sent numerous reinforcements. By 1783, more than 5,000 auxiliaries from this territory had served for the British.[10]

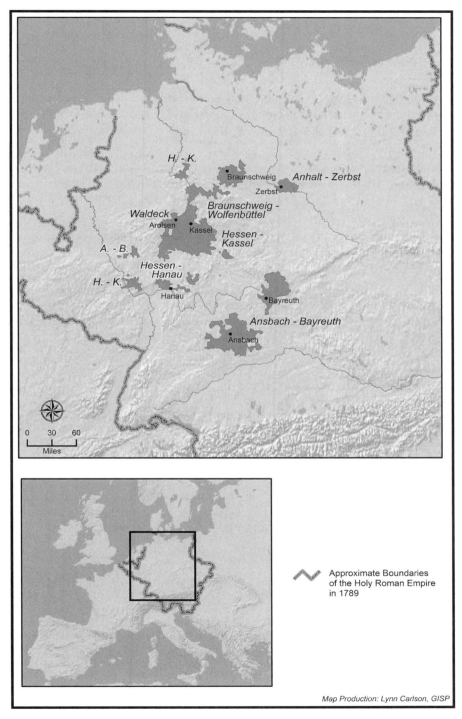

Map 1.   German Principalities with Subsidy Troops in North America, 1776–1783

21

In February 1776, shortly after concluding the agreement with Braunschweig-Wolfenbüttel, Fawcett signed the long-awaited treaty with Friedrich II of Hessen-Kassel. It was the most lucrative of all such treaties for a German principality in this conflict. The British backdated the agreement to January 15, making more subsidies available to speed up recruitment. Indeed, almost the entire Hessen-Kassel army entered British service and left for North America in April and June: four grenadier battalions, fifteen infantry regiments, and two *Jäger* companies, totaling 12,000 men.[11] By 1782, seven replacement and reinforcement transports had brought the number of soldiers from this principality who served in North America to about 20,000.[12]

On February 5, 1776, neighboring Hessen-Hanau, a small principality ruled by Wilhelm IX, son of Friedrich II and the prince hereditary of Hessen-Kassel, agreed to send one infantry regiment into British service.[13] Under the command of Colonel Wilhelm Rudolf von Gall, this unit left Willemstad in the Netherlands with 729 soldiers, more than the contracted number of 688.[14] On April 25, Britain negotiated for an additional artillery company of 120 soldiers under the command of Major Georg Päusch.[15] One year later, on February 10, 1777, Wilhelm IX and the British crown signed yet another treaty, for a *Jäger* corps of 412 men.[16] Finally, in January 1781, Hessen-Hanau agreed to create a *Freikorps* (corps of light infantry) with 830 soldiers.[17] Including replacements and reinforcements, this small principality sent 2,422 men into British service. In light of these many subsidy treaties, later nationalistic German historians decried Hessen-Hanau's ruler as one of the worst petty princes in the Holy Roman Empire. Friedrich Kapp, for instance, characterized him as a "groveler without a will of his own."[18]

On April 20, 1776, Prince Friedrich Karl August of Waldeck agreed to send 670 soldiers from one infantry regiment to North America as auxiliaries. Like other territories in the Holy Roman Empire, this tiny principality—Waldeck had only 36,642 inhabitants in 1777—had first offered its soldiers in November 1775.[19] Since two other Waldeck regiments were already serving as auxiliaries for the Dutch, it took longer than expected to raise another unit. To the dismay of the British, the 3rd Infantry Regiment arrived late for embarkation at Bremerlehe on May 30, and did not leave a stellar impression.[20] A roster compiled at Portsmouth three weeks later listed a total of 758 Waldeck soldiers, organized into one grenadier company and four musketeer companies.[21] Including reinforcements and replacements, 1,220 men served with this unit in North America during the Revolutionary War.[22]

In Ansbach-Bayreuth, on February 1, 1777, Karl Alexander's first minister, Carl Friedrich von Gemmingen, agreed to a subsidy treaty with Fawcett for two infantry regiments, one *Jäger* company, and an artillery unit.[23] Like Prince Friedrich of Waldeck, Margrave Alexander had offered his troops to London in 1775, but it was 1777 before Ansbach-Bayreuth finally received the highly desired and lucrative treaty.[24] Great Britain was planning large offensives that year and needed more troops. A regiment was raised in each of the two parts of the principality, Brandenburg-Ansbach and Brandenburg-Kulmbach. At Nijmegen, 1,223 soldiers were mustered into British service.[25] Over the course of the war, a total of 2,386 Ansbach-Bayreuth auxiliaries served in North America, including several replacement and reinforcement transports as well as an enlarged *Jäger* corps.[26]

The last subsidy treaty between George II and a German principality was negotiated in October 1777 and took effect on April 23, 1778. Anhalt-Zerbst was initially supposed to deliver 1,100 soldiers for North America, but because of severe recruitment problems, only 625 left the Holy Roman Empire from Stade near Hamburg. Of the 828 recruits who had assembled in Anhalt-Zerbst, at least 334 deserted during the march toward the coast. A detour had made their trip longer because Prussia, fearing a war with Austria and Russia, had refused to allow the auxiliaries to march through its territory. En route to Stade, however, officers were able to enlist a number of men as partial replacements for the deserters.[27]

In explaining these subsidy treaties, it is insufficient to point only toward the princes' greed or their need to finance extravagant lifestyles. Rather, such agreements had become increasingly important in enabling smaller states in the Holy Roman Empire to keep relatively large standing armies, which in turn allowed their rulers to play a bigger role in European power politics. Standing armies were also a matter of pride, honor, and status.

Table 1.   British Subsidy Treaties with German Principalities, 1776–1783

Principalities	Treaties	Contracted Soldiers[a]	Total Number of Soldiers Sent into British Service[b]
Braunschweig-Wolfenbüttel	January 9, 1776	4,300	5,000
Hessen-Kassel	January 15, 1776	12,000	25,688
	November 29, 1776	805	
Hessen-Hanau	February 5, 1776	668	2,422
	April 25, 1776	128	
	February 10, 1777	412	
	January 15, 1781	830	
Waldeck	April 20, 1776	670	1,220
Ansbach-Bayreuth	February 1, 1777	1,200	2,386
Anhalt-Zerbst	April 23, 1778	600	1,160
Total		21,613	37,876

[a] The numbers in this column are drawn from National Archives/Public Record Office, Kew, England, HO 32/1; *HETRINA*; Kapp, *Soldatenhandel*, 268–69; and Lowell, *Hessians*, 12–15, 300.

[b] The numbers in this column include known replacements and reinforcement transports. Many of these soldiers never made it to North America but stayed on furlough or remained in garrison even though their unit was contracted to the British. The calculations are drawn from Atwood, *Hessians*, 254; Burgoyne, *Third English-Waldeck Regiment*, 242; Huck, "Soldaten gegen Nordamerika," 1; Kapp, *Soldatenhandel*, 269; Seehase, "Die hessischen Truppen"; Städtler, *Die Ansbach-Bayreuther Truppen*, 21.

Subsidy treaties not only paid for the soldiers but also secured respect for their sovereign among Europe's ruling elite.[28] Moreover, they pumped money into local economies. In the 1770s, for instance, Braunschweig-Wolfenbüttel and Ansbach-Bayreuth were still suffering from the destructive effects of the Seven Years' War and were burdened by debts. Karl I and his son in

Braunschweig-Wolfenbüttel eagerly signed the subsidy treaty with Great Britain in 1776 because it essentially averted the bankruptcy of the duchy.[29] Karl Alexander of Ansbach-Bayreuth, in turn, used the subsidies to create a central bank for his territories.[30] Other states, including Hessen-Kassel, started infrastructure projects. Contemporary observers pointed out that the subsidy treaties also affected dynastic relationships between the Hanoverian king in Great Britain and rulers such as Karl I, Friedrich II, and Karl Alexander. These principalities can be considered part of an eighteenth-century "Protestant System" that included most of the northern states in the Holy Roman Empire, Great Britain, Sweden, Denmark, and the Netherlands.[31]

During the long eighteenth century, from 1688 to 1815, warfare became increasingly globalized. The great imperial struggles between Great Britain and France in this period were fought in Europe, the Americas, Africa, and Asia. Auxiliaries hired through subsidy treaties were thrust into new worlds around the globe. At the same time that soldiers from Braunschweig-Wolfenbüttel, Hessen-Kassel, Hessen-Hanau, Waldeck, Ansbach-Bayreuth, and Anhalt-Zerbst served for the British in North America, two Hanoverian regiments went to India.[32] In writing the history of the Atlantic world, it is not enough to focus on the exchange of goods and free or forced migration. It is also necessary to take into account warfare, the expanding conflicts of this era, the soldiers who fought in these wars and were shipped back and forth across the oceans, and the profound effects of those wars back home.[33] In this imperial world of global reach, the Holy Roman Empire was not just a place from which tens of thousands of migrants went east and west; it was also a preferred recruiting ground for the British, French, and Dutch armies. When Karl Alexander opened that special post office in Ansbach, a distant world was suddenly brought very close. Events unfolding in faraway places had repercussions in parochial towns and villages such as Ansbach, Arolsen, Hanau, Hanover, Kassel, Wolfenbüttel, and Zerbst. The Holy Roman Empire was linked to the larger Atlantic world not only through trade and the exchange of goods and people, but also through subsidy treaties and the provision of soldiers for British, Dutch, and French imperial wars. The American War of Independence involved not only revolutionaries in Boston and Philadelphia and their British, French, Spanish, Dutch, and American Indian enemies and allies, but also Central Europe with the Holy Roman Empire and its many small states and principalities.

Criticism

Despite their long tradition and ubiquity, subsidy treaties were heavily criticized by German intellectuals and Enlightenment thinkers at the end of the eighteenth century. Friedrich Schiller portrayed German subsidy soldiers as innocent victims of greedy and tyrannical rulers who were interested only in luxuries for themselves and their mistresses. His 1784 drama *Kabale und Liebe* (Intrigue and Love) includes a famous scene in which an old servant brings Lady Milford, the prince's mistress, a collection of precious gemstones. When she asks him who paid for all the jewelry, the despondent response is that the prince sold 7,000 men, including the servant's sons, to the British as soldiers. These young men, the servant explains, "pay for everything." When some of the soldiers dared to question their service for the British, they were immediately shot. Horrified, the others then shouted in unison, "Hooray, let's go to America!"[34]

Less elegant but equally critical of the subsidy treaties was a play by Johann Krauseneck from 1777, staged just as the Ansbach-Bayreuth treaty went into effect. Titled *Die Werbung für England*, it tells the story of the Brawe family—a father, mother, and two daughters living in an unnamed principality—on the day before the recruits are supposed to leave for British service in North America. (Not incidentally, the family's name is pronounced like the German word *brav*, meaning "well-behaved" or "upright.") The family is about to be torn apart because the father, who is in his forties, has been conscripted into the army and is scheduled to leave for North America, despite having fought with distinction in the Seven Years' War and subsequently led a respectable life as a farmer. Fritz Knauf, the son of Brawe's well-to-do neighbor and madly in love with Lise, one of Brawe's daughters, has been conscripted, too. Mrs. Brawe, confronted with the prospect of losing her husband and future son-in-law, exclaims in anger,

It's wrong! It's cruel! Is the prince not ashamed? . . . Does he feel anything? Is he not bothered at all . . . by driving so many fathers, mothers, brides into despair? Oh, those hard, inhuman hearts of the rulers. . . . So, we educate and bring up our sons as servants to a rich people, to protect a country that has nothing to do with us?[35]

In the end, it is Brawe's old commander from the Seven Years' War, Captain Stromberg, who saves both Brawe and Fritz. He offers the recruitment officer two other soldiers in exchange for them. The play concludes with a play on words when Brawe says, "Blessed would be those states in which all princes thought like Captain Stromberg." Stromberg answers, "And their subjects would only be *Brawe*."[36]

Another influential critic of subsidy treaties was Johann Gott-fried Seume. His autobiographical works *Spaziergang nach Syrakus* (A Stroll to Syracuse), from 1803, and *Mein Leben* (My Life), published posthumously in 1813, attacked German princes in a powerful way, setting the tone for decades to come. In particular, Seume accused the Hessen-Kassel army of abducting him while he was traveling through the territory as a student in 1782 and then impressing him into military service for the British in North America. Only the war's end in the spring of 1783, he implies, saved him from death in a foreign land.[37]

Although this account is heart-wrenching, it is not true. Historian Inge Auerbach and others have pointed out that Seume was actually seeking a career in the military when he traveled through Hessen-Kassel in 1782. He was not en route to Paris as a student, as he later claimed, but wanted to enroll in the well-known French artillery school in Metz. Instead of continuing on to Metz, it seems that he took the opportunity offered by Hessen-Kassel's engagement in North America and joined the military voluntarily. Arriving in Halifax with one of the last Hessian reinforcement transports, he was actually disappointed to have lost the opportunity to distinguish himself in combat and become an officer. Seume was genuinely dismayed that the Peace of Paris had abruptly ended his military career.[38] He began criticizing the "soldier trade" only after he was disappointed with Napoleon's coup d'état in 1799. In his mind, one monarch in France had merely replaced another. This "return to the normalcy of despotism" prompted a reexamination of earlier positions, leading him and others to question the Holy Roman Empire's entire societal and political system. Small German principalities, with their long history of subsidy treaties, now looked like the worst examples of tyranny in the ancien régime—symbolic of everything that had gone wrong in Europe. Even worse, over the next years these states often sided with Napoleon in exchange for territorial gains or other promises, weakening a "national" German resistance movement against French invasions.[39]

Criticism of the Hessen-Kassel and Ansbach-Bayreuth subsidy treaties with Great Britain also reflected contemporary discussions about German patriotism and military service. The years between 1760 and 1850 were a time of momentous change in Germany, aptly termed the *Sattelzeit* by Reinhart Koselleck (an allusion to someone crossing a mountain saddle). Early modern notions of the relationship between sovereigns, states, and society began to disappear during this period, and modern concepts were formulated and established. Numerous contradictions remained, however, and the new order was not yet fully in place. The *Sattelzeit* also brought increasing criticism of absolutist standing armies, particularly their practice of recruiting professional soldiers—mercenaries—for dynastic wars, and recognition of a pressing need for reform. Political and military leaders were convinced that soldiers became motivated, reliable, and enthusiastic only when they were fighting for a true cause and their homeland, not just for money. This was the thinking behind the French *levée en masse* of 1793, the Jourdan Law of 1798, and German "citizen and national soldiers" during the Wars of Liberation against Napoleon. The nation as an ideal and an idea transformed all notions of statehood, sovereignty, society, citizenship, and the military.[40]

Some of these convictions were already in evidence during the American War of Independence, particularly in relation to the various subsidy treaties between German states and the British crown. In 1776, for instance, pondering different ways to recruit subsidy troops for the British, the prince hereditary of Braunschweig-Wolfenbüttel, Karl Wilhelm Ferdinand, stated that a freeborn man, "if not used entirely to defend the fatherland," cannot "be lawfully forced to take up arms against the inhabitants in Canada."[41] On the one hand, he welcomed the subsidy treaty because it supported the debt-ridden principality and its economy. On the other, he believed that sovereigns could call on their subjects only for the defense of the "fatherland." This contradictory position reflected an intellectual climate in which it was progressively more difficult to justify subsidy treaties and hire out one's standing army. Even though "fatherland" denoted only one's local state and territory, and a German "nation" existed only as an idea, soldiers were no longer supposed to serve "foreign" powers. Unlike Hessen-Kassel and Ansbach-Bayreuth, Braunschweig-Wolfenbüttel tried to overcome such contradictions, at least partly, by not recruiting subsidy soldiers through conscription.

Later in the nineteenth century, German historians criticized the subsidy treaties, especially those of the American War of Independence, from an outspoken nationalistic perspective. Friedrich Kapp and others viewed such agreements as the worst possible example of German particularism. For them, the treaties were not a legitimate attempt by small states to play a role in European power politics, or a way for the "Third Germany" to remain relevant next to powerful Austria and Prussia, or merely a controversial but useful means to pay off debts and boost regional economies. Rather, the treaties showed that rulers such as Friedrich II and Karl Alexander cared more about their own petty interests (and coffers) than about the larger German nation and society. Even worse, these agreements actually bolstered small territories and slowed German unification efforts under Prussian leadership.[42]

New ways of thinking about the nation and military service were also at the heart of a pamphlet published in 1778 by the later French revolutionary Honoré-Gabriel Riqueti, Comte de Mirabeau. He condemned the Germans as "mercenaries and satellites" of their rulers because they had allowed themselves to be sent off across the Atlantic in foreign ships, "packed together like cattle," to fight a people "who had not done them any harm." The revolutionaries, on the other hand, were defending their property and their homeland. They were fighting a just war against foreign invaders, "spit out by the ocean" onto their shores.[43] The court of

Friedrich II considered these lines so damning that Martin Ernst von Schlieffen, first minister and negotiator of the 1776 subsidy treaty, was tasked to write a rebuttal, which was published in 1782. In his response to Mirabeau's accusations, Schlieffen stressed that the British subsidies had enabled Friedrich II to lower taxes for his subjects and build new villages, schools, and hospitals. Moreover, the treaty with George III was merely another expression of a long-standing alliance among Protestant powers in Europe, forged in many previous struggles against the Catholic powers France and Austria.[44]

Other German princes with auxiliaries in British pay also felt compelled to defend their agreements against mounting criticism. In the case of Ansbach-Bayreuth, they openly appealed to the soldiers and their families. When the principality's two infantry regiments and *Jäger* company left Ansbach on March 7, 1777, an official song was published that reflected concern for the fears of parents and families, while also providing a suitable rationale for the soldiers' service in America:

Was wir iezt thun hat seiner Seits	What we are doing now,
Der Britte längst gethan	The Briton has done long before.
Er sah den stolzen Gallier	He saw the proud Gaul
Uns Tod und Knechtschaft drohn;	Threatening us with death and servitude;
Und Grosmutsvoll kam er daher	And he came generously
Befreite uns davon.	To liberate us.
Auf wilden Wellen nahten sich	Through rough waters,
Die Helfer, Teutschm Strand:	Our supporters approached German shores:
Und wie ein Gott vom Himmel, stieg	And like God from heaven,
Ihr König selbst ans Land!	Their king himself stepped onto land.
Georg erschien: Ihm folgete	George appeared, soon followed,
Die Waffen in der Hand	Weapons in hand,
Der Stolz der Brittischen Armee	Pride of the British army,
Sein Sohn, Held Cumberland!	His son, the hero Cumberland!

Und alle Fochten voller Wuth	And all fought full of rage
Germania! Für Dich;	Germany! For you;
Erfochten drauf mit Tod und Blut	Through death and blood,
Dir Freyheit und den Sieg.	They fought for freedom and victory.
Ha! Solchen Freunden beyzustehn,	To stand beside such friends,
Mit glühendem Gesicht	With faces gleaming,
Auf ihre Feinde loszugehen	To fight against their enemies,
Ist Edler Teutschen Pflicht.[45]	Is a noble German's duty.

Any criticism of the subsidy treaty with Great Britain, in other words, was misguided. Karl Alexander and his subjects were obligated to support George III in North America because the British army had previously come to the rescue of Ansbach-Bayreuth. During the War of the Austrian Succession and the Battle of Dettingen in 1743, King George II and the Duke of Cumberland had defeated the French. In 1777, the time had come for Ansbach-Bayreuth to repay the favor and support Great Britain in North America.[46]

Newspapers and calendars in Ansbach-Bayreuth disseminated the same message. The *Bayreuther Neuer Zeitungs-Calender*, a combination of almanac, newspaper, and calendar, was a widely distributed source of information, particularly in rural areas. In 1778, it announced that subsequent issues would include news from the troops in North America because "country folk, who do not read a newspaper," did not know enough "about the reasons for sending the two Regiments Bayreuth and Ansbach of His Serene Highness to America in His Majesty's, the King of Great Britain's service." Many "subjects still believe . . . unjustified rumors" about this conflict and the principality's involvement. Instead, the publication emphasized, every inhabitant should remember how George II, as "protector of the Protestant religion," had defended the Holy Roman Empire and Ansbach-Bayreuth against the French. For this sacrifice, the principality's inhabitants should be "eternally grateful" and should now support Great Britain and George III. Besides, the calendar added rather pragmatically, Ansbach-Bayreuth soldiers in British service were "well supplied and paid."[47]

Mercenaries?

The British subsidy treaties covering tens of thousands of German soldiers naturally concerned American revolutionaries—militarily, of course, but also politically.[48] Although such agreements were routine in European warfare, the revolutionaries viewed these auxiliaries, which had nothing to do with the original causes of the conflict and did not even come from the British motherland, as embodying everything that was wrong with the military, society, and the relationship between sovereigns and citizens in the British Empire. The German soldiers were part of a European standing army filled with subservient subjects and professional soldiers, so the auxiliaries were decried as mercenaries. The *Pennsylvania Evening Post* wrote on March 30, 1776, after receiving the first news of the subsidy treaties, that these Germans had "neither property nor families to fight for" and had "no principle, either of honour, religion, public spirit, regard for liberty, or love of country."[49] Ironically, such sentiments also led leading American revolutionaries to conclude that these soldiers could easily be enticed to desert. For instance, Arthur Lee, revolutionary envoy to Spain and Prussia, reported in 1776 from London that Friedrich II of Hessen-Kassel was a dishonest man who sent only the worst of his soldiers to North America. They could easily be persuaded to leave the British side if "proper offers are made."[50] Other revolutionaries harbored more conflicted opinions and ascribed a double role to these men. Mercy Otis Warren, for instance, viewed the German soldiers both as "barbarous strangers" who were assisting the British in their unjust attempt to subjugate the colonies and as pitiful "slaves" who were suffering under European despotism just as the American colonists were. In other words, these men were as much victims as perpetrators.[51]

The label "mercenaries" sticks to these soldiers to this day, with all its negative connotations (figure 1).[52] Yet what did the term actually mean in the late eighteenth century? Following the American and French Revolutions, commentators in the nineteenth and twentieth centuries defined mercenaries as soldiers who fought only for money, who made a profession out of committing violent acts, and who had no connection to either the causes or the

Figure 1.   Cartoon Denouncing British Subsidy Treaties

A contemporary cartoon criticizing the British subsidy treaties with German principalities. In addition to the enormous costs of these agreements, the crown is also denounced for hiring Hessian soldiers, whom contemporaries repeatedly accused of extreme brutality in warfare. Courtesy of the John Carter Brown Library, Brown University, Providence, R.I.

location of a military conflict.[53] To apply this definition to soldiers before or during this period of change, however, is problematic at best. For example, pay is not a legitimate criterion for distinguishing between mercenaries and citizen soldiers during the American War of Independence. After all, soldiers on both sides were paid, or were supposed to be paid, one way or another. All armies of the early modern period, moreover, were international institutions. It did not matter to a prince or sovereign in Europe where his soldiers were from—as long as they fought loyally and obeyed orders. Under such definitions, all armies fighting in the Revolutionary War would have to be regarded as mercenary forces, including the Continental Army.

American revolutionaries and later historians were able to denounce German auxiliaries as mercenaries while celebrating their own forces as citizen soldiers because society, not the soldiers' actions or the way they were recruited, trained, and fought, assigned troops their place in the political, societal, and cultural fabric of a state. European commentators from the sixteenth and seventeenth centuries, for instance, distinguished only between soldiers who fought and campaigned as part of a military organization and those who did not. In other words, all that contemporaries cared about was whether a soldier was part of a regular, state-controlled army; it was immaterial whether he hailed from the same region or from somewhere far away, or whether he was paid for his actions.

The Anglo-American discourse of republicanism, and ideas of civilian society discussed among Central Europe's middle class (*bürgerliche Gesellschaft*) in the eighteenth century, fundamentally challenged this understanding.[54] By the end of the eighteenth century, a soldier who regularly committed violent acts solely to make a living set himself far apart from the other citizens (*Bürger*) of a state. Indeed, he constituted a major threat to society. Once a "subject" had become a "citizen," only citizen soldiers fighting for a common, greater good, and out of altruistic motives, deserved recognition as legitimate warriors.[55] When the need to defend the achievements of the American and French Revolutions against outside enemies made it necessary for the newly established citizenry to create permanent large-scale military forces, the entire nation had to be mobilized and had to give all, if necessary, to support the fight. Under these circumstances, a soldier's use of violence was considered legitimate and laudable only for the benefit of the nation. A professional soldier fighting in alien service, however, became entirely unacceptable—he was a mercenary. This new understanding of military service, based on service for one's nation rather than for a princely sovereign, also allowed states and armies to pay their soldiers without exposing them to accusations of mercenary behavior. These *national* soldiers made fighting and the use of violence their profession, but they did so as citizens in the service of the nation.[56] Serving for a foreign army or state, on the other hand, was now considered high treason.[57]

～

The German auxiliaries who were sent to North America from 1776 to 1783 were caught between two opposing concepts. Coming from standing armies in the supernational Holy Roman Empire, they embodied traditional notions of military service and recruitment. However, they fought in a war that led to a very different understanding of their profession, society, and government. From this perspective, it did not matter that American revolutionaries and citizens retreated quickly from the *rage militaire* of 1775 and 1776 and that the Continental Army looked remarkably similar to regular European standing armies by 1783, complete with a number of high-profile foreign officers and international units.[58] The ideal had remained intact. In national memory, it was Americans coming together as citizen soldiers who had won the Revolutionary War—not professional soldiers who expected to be paid for their service.[59] German auxiliaries were always viewed as a foreign element in the war. They were mercenaries who were not fighting for a cause or a nation, or as citizens. But there was a chance for redemption. As Mercy Otis Warren stated, German auxiliaries of the British could be understood not just as barbarous strangers but also as victims of princely tyranny. With "proper offers," as Arthur Lee recommended, they could choose to be freed from their bonds and become respectable soldiers and valuable members of revolutionary American society.

CHAPTER 2

Recruitment Patterns

By the eighteenth century, standing armies in early modern Europe had become large professional establishments.[1] Peacetime armies sometimes had as many as 200,000 soldiers in service, at least in such powerful states as France, Austria, and Russia.[2] The costs of war—human, financial, and economic—rose to unprecedented levels. In fact, an early modern arms race unfolded over the course of this century.[3] Small states in the Holy Roman Empire such as Hessen-Kassel, Braunschweig-Wolfenbüttel, Brandenburg-Ansbach, and Waldeck did not have the resources to keep up with Prussia, Austria, or even midsize states such as Bavaria. After the unification of Bavaria and the Palatinate in 1777, the combined Wittelsbach army counted about 22,430 men on paper (about 19,900 were effectives).[4] Yet smaller states made every effort to follow the trend, turning at least parts of their military establishments into permanent forces and increasing the number of soldiers in their service. These enlarged armies could often be financed only through subsidy treaties. A table from 1790 listing the ratio of soldiers to population for several territories in the Holy Roman Empire shows the great efforts all states made to build and keep large standing armies. Austria recruited about one soldier for every sixty-four subjects, Saxony about one for every seventy-three. In Prussia, the rising military power of the European continent in this century, the ratio was one for thirty-two. Strikingly, Hessen-Kassel's ratio was one for thirty-three. Counting Hessen-Kassel's various militia and garrison units, the so-called *Landmiliz-* and *Garnisonsregimenter,* one in every fifteen Hessen-Kassel males served in some kind of military unit at some point in their lives.[5]

This meant that Hessen-Kassel in 1776 fielded a regular army of 12,000 and militia or garrison units of equal size. This buildup had begun in 1673, under Landgrave Karl, when the principality established three standing cavalry companies and eleven infantry companies. By 1683, it had a regular paid army of 6,000 soldiers. Over the course of the Seven Years' War, the principality enrolled as many as 24,000 men into its army and sent regiment after regiment to England as auxiliaries.[6] In Brandenburg-Ansbach, the first standing infantry regiment was established in 1682.[7] By 1724, the principality's capital, Ansbach, had barracks for its troops, and a separate church for the soldiers was added in 1726. The city also included housing for the hussars and *Jäger* as well as a military hospital—an impressive array of military facilities for a city of only 5,000 inhabitants.[8]

States in the Holy Roman Empire used two major recruitment systems to fill the ranks of their standing armies in the eighteenth century. Either they hired mercenaries—men who became, at least temporarily, professional soldiers (*Söldnerwerbung*)—or they employed various forms of conscription (*Dienstverpflichtung*), including militia service, selective enlistment by enrollment lists (*Enrollierungslisten*), and the canton system (*Kantonsystem*), which assigned recruitment districts to particular units.[9] German principalities with auxiliaries in British service between 1776 and 1783 used both approaches in many variations. Braunschweig-Wolfenbüttel, for example, relied solely on the recruitment of mercenaries, while Ansbach-Bayreuth used enrollment lists. Hessen-Kassel made extensive use of the canton system.

There was much overlap as well as many exceptions and exemptions. Friedrich II of Hessen-Kassel and Karl Alexander of Ansbach-Bayreuth used both basic recruiting systems during the war, sometimes simultaneously and sometimes separately. Once their initial contingents left for North America in 1776 and 1777, respectively, the two sovereigns ordered that only mercenaries, particularly foreigners, should be used for reinforcements and replacements. That way, they hoped to protect their local economies from additional demographic loss while still benefiting from the subsidy payments. In April 1777, Karl Alexander explicitly ordered his officials to capture and enlist every vagrant in his territories who was less than thirty years old and taller than five feet four inches.[10] By the fall, Adjutant General Karl Georg von Schlammersdorf could exult in having recruited 145 men for the army, all foreigners.[11] Rewards encouraged local authorities to enlist as many foreign males as possible. Depending on the height of the recruits, for instance, officials in Ansbach-Bayreuth were offered up to twenty-four *Gulden* per soldier (£3 12 s.). Some districts in Ansbach-Bayreuth even had the liberty to offer recruits contracts with a fixed term of six to eight years (*Kapitulationen*) and were told to point out how excellent the pay was in British service.[12]

Recruitment of Mercenaries

In the most basic use of the term, a mercenary was someone willing to serve in an army for pay. Recruiters from a number of territories were stationed in cities and towns or traveled throughout the Holy Roman Empire. Once a recruit signed a contract and arrived at his new unit, he received a bounty. This sum was usually the main draw for the initial signature. The terms of the contracts varied, as did the bounties paid to each recruit. Recruiters generally focused their efforts on large imperial cities such as Cologne, Frankfurt, and Ulm, where many free inhabitants lived.[13] When the need for troops was particularly pressing, before a conflict or after severe losses on a campaign, recruiters readily enlisted people on the margins of early modern society: vagrants, runaway serfs, and petty criminals. They also hired deserters from other armies without hesitation; after all, these men were already trained and drilled soldiers. Having previously broken an oath, deserters naturally were often eyed with suspicion or had to meet certain criteria. In 1739, for instance, Protestant Brandenburg-Ansbach specifically prohibited the recruitment of deserters from Catholic territories such as Bavaria and France.[14]

Not much was expected from the average recruit beyond being tall enough and reasonably healthy. Before the outbreak of the War of the Austrian Succession in 1740, Brandenburg-Ansbach, for instance, required only that new recruits be between seventeen and forty years old and "not infirm."[15] Height was important, both for reasons of appearance and to facilitate the use of long smoothbore muskets. Recruits also had to have sufficient teeth to bite open their musket cartridges, and they had to be intelligent enough to understand and execute orders. Even these few standards were stretched when recruits were needed quickly or when few eligible young men were available. At the end of the War of the Austrian Succession, Brandenburg-Ansbach officials enlisted all the vagrants they could find, "without regard to their height."[16]

The low standards and the fact that recruitment campaigns often targeted men on the margins led contemporaries and many historians to denounce early modern armies as comprising the dregs of society. Only the most brutal discipline, so the narrative went, could keep such lowly people under control—and that was much needed for linear tactics anyway. Recent research, however, has shown that early modern armies did not function this way.[17] Lowering the standards too far brought in unwilling and unfit soldiers, prone to desertion, who then weakened the overall combat strength of individual units. Contemporary noncommissioned officers and officers were very much aware of this problem. Also, because armies still operated under *Kompaniewirtschaft* and *Regimentswirtschaft* (independent financial administration), officers who disregarded basic standards for new recruits would have to repay any losses from desertion or stolen equipment. Naturally, then, they sought men who showed promise as good, well-behaved soldiers. At the same time, such concerns gave recruits considerable influence when it came to negotiating contracts and the conditions of their service. Some among the rank and file even blackmailed their officers with threats of mass desertion.[18]

Of course, recruiters regularly used pressure, trickery, and even physical violence in their efforts. It is difficult, however, to determine with any certainty how many soldiers were coerced or forced into military service. How much force was involved when a recruit signed up drunk after enjoying free alcohol? Did criminals or deserters who received a pardon in exchange for military service act voluntarily? Did a farmer's son who had no prospect of inheriting land join an army voluntarily? The categories for such assessments are difficult to define.[19] What, for instance, did the margrave in Brandenburg-Ansbach mean when he told officials in 1712 to use "helpful words of encouragement" when recruiting?[20]

Some policies of eighteenth-century mercantilist states were intended to broaden the pool of possible recruits. Hessen-Kassel's *Hufen-Edikt* of 1773 forbade the long-standing practice of partible inheritance. Over generations, this practice had resulted in land plots of less than three acres—too small to sustain a family. The new law, coming on the heels of an agrarian crisis in 1770 and 1771, restricted the subdivision of land to the size of one *Hufe* (about eighteen acres). Because it was strictly enforced, this measure saved the poorest peasants from steady decline and deepening poverty. At the same time, it pushed younger children out of the village, even out of the principality, and many young males into the army.[21]

Some recruits enlisted not out of necessity but rather as a career choice. In Ansbach-Bayreuth, Johann Christoph Döhlemann, a veteran soldier in the company of Captain Ludwig Heinrich von Erckert in the Regiment von Eyb from Brandenburg-Ansbach, eagerly left with the troops for North America in 1777. Others might be fearful at the prospect of fighting in such distant lands, he wrote in his journal, and might even fake injuries to be released from the campaign, but he was excited.[22] Only during war, he knew, was a quick promotion possible. Ultimately, it did not matter to him whether he fought fifteen hours or fifteen hundred miles away. He could hardly wait to put "a bridle into the gob of the rebels" in North America.[23]

Döhlemann's parents, however, were alarmed to learn that he would be leaving Europe as a soldier. In a letter written just a few weeks before his son's departure, Joachim Döhlemann mourned on February 9, 1777, "What terrible . . . news for us parents. . . . Hot tears ran down our cheeks upon this revelation." As a minister, Joachim had some influence at court and tried to have his son released. He was surprised to discover that Johann wanted to go to North America and that the army had not pressured him into this decision.[24] Johann assured them that it would be relatively easy for him to become an officer in America. Even if this "turns out to be impossible," he wrote, "those who come back . . . will receive . . . good positions as civil servants. . . . Being a soldier in garrison is no challenge; one also has to experience a campaign."[25] For Johann, then, the war in North America was a chance for upward social mobility. Indeed, it was no longer impossible for a commoner to become an officer. At the same time, he was moved by his parents' concerns. He repeatedly begged for their blessing. When he finally received it, he wrote back with a sigh of relief, "Now that you have resigned yourself to my fate, it is much easier for me to travel to America."[26] Döhlemann would not be disappointed. Within a few months after the Ansbach-Bayreuth units arrived on Staten Island in June 1777, he was made corporal, and by February 1778 he had become a second lieutenant.[27]

Braunschweig-Wolfenbüttel was one of three principalities with auxiliaries in British service that relied solely on mercenary soldiers for their contracted units.[28] In the subsidy treaty, Karl I promised to deliver four infantry regiments with five companies each, one regiment of dragoons with four squadrons (dismounted), one grenadier battalion with five companies, and one light infantry battalion with one *Jäger* and four grenadier companies. General Friedrich Adolph Freiherr von Riedesel was to command these forces, and he lost no time in starting the recruitment campaign, even before final negotiations were completed. This was possible because the British had promised to pay for Braunschweig-Wolfenbüttel's recruitment efforts even if no agreement was ultimately reached.[29]

Rather than establish entirely new units, Riedesel suggested that existing regiments be divided, with those smaller groups to become the basis for the enlarged corps. Soldiers from fourteen existing companies formed the core of thirty-two new companies in the Regiments von Rhetz, von Riedesel, Prinz Friedrich, and von Specht as well as the dragoons and the light infantry Battalion von Barner. This way, 1,742 men were already available in Braunschweig-Wolfenbüttel, and only 2,071 fresh recruits were needed—plus servants and other necessary camp followers. Because Karl I and his son had vowed not to send native subjects (*Landeskinder*) to North America, those men were exchanged for foreigners from other units that were not leaving for British service. For instance, the Regiment von Riedesel replaced seventy-three subjects with an equal number of foreigners in the Regiment du Corps.[30] As several surviving muster rolls reveal, it was already sufficient to own, or expect to own, a house or work a *Kothof* or a *Brinksitzerstelle* (small farms) in order to be considered eligible for replacement by a foreigner.[31] This system expanded the army instead of creating new units, made the entire process faster, and promised greater combat strength. As Riedesel said in a letter, "The corps thus has some cohesion. One knows the officers and noncommissioned officers as well as a number of other people."[32]

Once the plan was in place, actual recruitment began. On December 7, 1775, eight officers and forty noncommissioned officers were sent out into the Holy Roman Empire. They received additional pay and a bounty of 2 *Thaler* (9 s.) for each recruit. Following common practice, they went into large imperial cities such as Nuremberg, Frankfurt, Cologne, Bremen, Hamburg, Lübeck, and Mühlhausen. From there, groups of noncommissioned officers fanned out into smaller imperial cities and territories in the surrounding area.[33] In addition to these stationary recruiters, several officers traveled around the Holy Roman Empire to enlist young men. Private enterprisers, mostly former officers, also attempted to find recruits in exchange for a bounty. Additionally, officials in Braunschweig-Wolfenbüttel were instructed to persuade resident foreigners or unemployed and unpropertied laborers to join the army.[34] Following mercantilist principles, valuable members of society, including married, self-sufficient farmers, master craftsmen, *Bürger* (lawful citizens in a town), and other taxpaying subjects, could not be recruited. If such basic principles were observed, recruitment campaigns actually enjoyed some support from the larger population. Tensions flared only when officers recruited indiscriminately.

To recruit on foreign soil, it was necessary to get permission. If a recruitment campaign was meant to enlist soldiers for a power outside the Holy Roman Empire, the emperor had to be informed. Fearing potential problems because of this stipulation, Cologne and Aachen denied Braunschweig-Wolfenbüttel permission to recruit there for the war in North America. In such cases, states regularly engaged in clandestine recruitment.[35] If permission was granted, recruiters usually worked out of a recruitment "office," most often a tavern, and hung a uniform jacket outside the door to inform passersby about who was seeking soldiers and for what branch. Normally, there was more than one recruitment campaign under way in any given city. Recruiters thus competed for the best recruits. Prussia's recruiters were present almost everywhere and often paid a higher bounty than other states—up to 100 *Thaler* (£22 10 s.).[36]

Initially, Braunschweig-Wolfenbüttel recruiters probably tried to hide the fact that their units were destined for North America and announced only that they would serve for Great Britain. Mentioning North America, because of its distance, might have deterred some recruits. Yet the British 60th Regiment also recruited in the Holy Roman Empire and made it clear from the start that its soldiers would serve across the Atlantic.[37] It was no secret that George III was fighting a war in North America, and almost everyone knew where these soldiers would be headed. Some recruits were actually attracted by this prospect.

It was no accident that recruitment "offices" were usually located in a tavern. Like other recruiters at the time, Braunschweig-Wolfenbüttel officers and noncommissioned officers frequently used alcohol to facilitate the process. Sometimes force was used, too. However, as Ralf Pröve and others have made clear, such cases were the exception rather than the rule. At most, 5 percent of recruits ended up in the military by force—despite what Seume, Schiller, and other contemporary writers and critics of the subsidy treaties later claimed.[38]

Financial incentives, especially the bounty that the men received upon entering military service, were the most important motivation for enlistment. In the case of Braunschweig-Wolfenbüttel, between 6 and 15 *Thaler* (£1 7 s.–£3 7 s. 6 d.) was offered, depending on the height of the recruit. Only part of the money was paid up front. Recruits received the balance after examination by a barber or company surgeon and once they had actually arrived at their new unit. To prevent desertion, recruiters tried to avoid the recruits' homelands when marching them toward their destination and always kept them under guard. If a recruit ran away, the recruiters had to defray the costs. Recruiting parties also collected men at regional assembly points before sending them off in larger groups. Blankenburg, for instance, was the assembly point for all Braunschweig-Wolfenbüttel recruits enlisted in and around Nuremberg and Mühlhausen.[39]

Joining an army was not always an irreversible decision. For many who enlisted for only a fixed period (*Kapitulanten*), it was a way to weather an economic crisis. A significant number of men in early modern German society seem to have served in the military more than once.[40] Among Braunschweig-Wolfenbüttel recruits, for instance, we find a number of men who had evaded Hessen-Kassel's conscription but enlisted voluntarily in one of Riedesel's regiments for several years.[41]

Braunschweig-Wolfenbüttel allowed soldiers who were subjects to have some of their pay withheld for family members. Among Riedesel's corps leaving for North America, 1,111 common soldiers and 328 officers, noncommissioned officers, and staff members requested that funds be directed to someone in their household. Common soldiers typically ordered about 3 *Groschen* (5 d.), about 10 percent of their pay, to be distributed to individual family members each month, while officers reserved more, as much as 90 *Thaler* (£20 5 s.) in the case of General von Riedesel. At the start of 1781, to put these numbers into perspective, there were about 1,721 subjects among the Braunschweig-Wolfenbüttel soldiers in North America, despite the duke's plans to the contrary. Roughly 83 percent of these men had a percentage of their pay withheld for family members.[42] Waldeck and Hessen-Kassel had similar systems.[43]

But money was not the only reason for joining an army. Some soldiers thirsted for adventure. Others were mercenaries in the classic sense and had made soldiering their profession.[44] Some wanted to escape feudal rule or the pressures caused by Europe's population increase during the eighteenth century.[45] In Braunschweig-Wolfenbüttel, convicts could receive pardons if they joined the military; some criminals were drafted merely "because it was in the public's interest" to remove them from civil society.[46] Sometimes the reason for joining an army was more personal. Adolph Schulze from Sachsen-Weimar was forty-five years old and owned a small house, yet he enrolled as a company surgeon with the Braunschweig-Wolfenbüttel troops bound for North America because he "could not get along with his wife and son-in-law." Before leaving, he bequeathed the house to his daughter.[47]

Braunschweig-Wolfenbüttel recruits, like other German auxiliaries, also enlisted because they wanted to emigrate.[48] The war in North America offered a rare opportunity to circumvent the imperial prohibition against emigration.[49] Granted, the risks of a military campaign and sea travel were high, but so were the risks faced by other migrants at the time. The contemporary perception, moreover, was that North America was a land where limitless economic opportunities awaited newcomers.[50] Such prospects must have been very appealing for young men who were already considering military service for financial reasons. However, we have no more than anecdotal evidence to substantiate the claims of past historians that the designated area of operations was a motivating factor for recruitment, particularly among the lower classes.[51] Hessen-Kassel soldiers who had a *Kapitulation* were allowed to remain in North America after the war. Such promises were often made during recruitment, particularly for reinforcement and replacement transports later in the war.[52]

These findings do show that the recruits who enlisted as mercenaries were not generally oppressed subjects of princely tyranny but rather regular employees at the lower end of the social spectrum whose primary concern was supporting themselves and their families. Hasty marriage ceremonies were often conducted right before the troops left for North America. The *Braunschweiger Anzeigen* listed nine weddings among common soldiers for February 17, 1776, and another twenty-three for March 13.[53] Once it became known in Hessen-Kassel that most army units would soon leave for North America, Field Chaplain Heinrich Kümmel received numerous requests to conduct marriages for soldiers who wanted "to secure female companionship in the perils ahead."[54] In Bayreuth, sixty-six common soldiers in the Regiment Voit von Salzburg, 14 percent of the unit's common soldiers, got married in the Church of St. Georgen between February 4 and February 27, 1777; the regiment left town on February 28.[55] Wrote the pastor, "The reason why so many soldiers were allowed to get married . . . was that His Serene Highness, our Prince, had given our troops, as well as those from Ansbach, into English pay, to march them to America and there to help the English against their rebellious colonies."[56]

Many of these ceremonies undoubtedly legalized long-standing partnerships. Soldiers wanted to secure support such as pay, housing in barracks, and bread rations for their female partners who remained behind.

Recruitment by Conscription

The earliest versions of conscription had appeared during the fifteenth and sixteenth centuries in some territories and cities of the Holy Roman Empire.[57] Brandenburg-Kulmbach established its first militia units between 1460 and 1480. They were meant to function as auxiliaries in cases of emergency, during border conflicts, in policing the principality or transferring criminals, and when the regular army needed support in capturing vagabonds. During the Thirty Years' War, local militia forces were converted to state militias, defending the principality together with regular units.[58]

As the German term for these units, *Ausschuss* (selected group), suggests, they comprised only chosen males in any given region. Examining them from a nineteenth- or twentieth-century perspective, with a universal draft for national armies in mind, is problematic. Soldiers for these forces were often selected by lot, but men called up for militia service could often avoid it by hiring substitutes. In fact, members of entire professions, cities, or regions—collectively called *Stände* (estates) in the Holy Roman Empire—managed to avoid service altogether or negotiated exemptions. By the end of the seventeenth century, tavern owners in Bayreuth, for instance, could dodge service in the city's militia by providing the army with a certain quantity of gunpowder.[59]

Recruitment policies underwent a major change in Brandenburg-Kulmbach during the first half of the eighteenth century. Increasingly, the principality's rulers called directly on their subjects for military service. By 1738, all the districts in Margrave Friedrich's territory were required to compile enrollment or muster lists (*Enrollierungslisten*) of male subjects between seventeen and thirty years old. Officers were ordered to muster those men they deemed most capable for a new state militia regiment under the margrave's command (*Land-Regiment*).[60] Although this unit was disbanded in 1752, every male subject of military age in the principality continued to be listed and assessed with regard to whether he would be obligated for military service. Each year, an officer went through the lists and mustered all unmarried men between the ages of sixteen and thirty.[61] Any young man who did not want to be called up had to apply for a release. Such releases (*Freyschein*) were granted, for instance, when a man got married, if he became infirm, or if he was simply not tall enough. If parents wanted to send their sons away as apprentices, they first had to obtain a leave of absence (*Urlaubsschein*). If a young man wanted to leave the principality for an extended period of time, he needed a travel pass (*Wander-Pass*). Men who were recorded in the muster lists were forbidden, under penalty of property confiscation, to sign up with other armies as mercenaries.[62]

Enforcement of these rules was difficult, and numerous exemptions were granted. Individuals had rights (or duties) based on their particular status as subjects, citizens of a town, and members of guilds or other social and professional groups (*Stände*). The absolutist state of the seventeenth and eighteenth centuries was not an all-powerful authority that controlled and regulated everybody's life. In the two principalities that became Ansbach-Bayreuth, after 1769 young men could go away to work or learn a trade outside the territory without obtaining a leave of absence. They could also get married and establish a household without first requesting permission. Others obtained a travel pass, exempting them from military service, without ever leaving the principality. Some cities granted releases from military service for only a fixed period, others indefinitely.[63]

Recruitment by conscription regularly took a back seat to considerations of mercantilist principles. Young men in Brandenburg-Kulmbach and Brandenburg-Ansbach were assessed as either dispensable (*entbehrlich*) or indispensable (*unentbehrlich*) for the local economy and community. Whenever possible, only dispensable men were sent off to the army. In 1775, when Colonel Johann Heinrich von Seybothen was ordered to undertake the "enrollment business" in Brandenburg-Kulmbach, the members of the

Bayreuth city council were directed not only to note in their lists whether or not a man was dispensable, but also to explain their reasoning. Karl Alexander obviously did not want to let too many potential soldiers slip away because of local concerns.[64]

Such orders did not deter the city from attempting to negotiate with the margrave about potential conscripts. On February 6, 1777, just weeks before the two Ansbach-Bayreuth infantry regiments departed for North America, Bayreuth's legal counsel, Johann Georg Tröger, wrote a circular to the cities of Kulmbach, Hof, Wunsiedel, Neustadt a. d. Aisch, Münchberg, and Kreuth, the remaining members of the old *Landschaft* (an ancient body of representatives). The *Landschaft* had to act quickly, Tröger stressed, if those citizens or sons of citizens who were married or worked as master craftsmen were to be relieved from military service in North America.[65] A master joiner in Kulmbach, who should have been considered indispensable, had been granted an official discharge but had not yet been released. Such cases made Tröger and others nervous. Fearing the prospect of involuntary military service in North America, a number of young men had fled Kulmbach.[66]

Neustadt a. d. Aisch notified Tröger that four citizens needed to be rescued from service in North America. In exchange, the city offered five others whom it regarded as utterly dispensable. They included Peter Heyd, a baker without baking rights, and Johann Prekk, a "vagabonding writer" whose only goal in life was to "waste away his days."[67] Other cities reported indispensable men who had been called up for military service. Münchberg and Hof, for instance, reported five such men, and Wunsiedel another four. With these names in hand, Tröger protested at the court in Ansbach and received assurances that the margrave's governor in Bayreuth, Karl Freiherr von Seckendorf, would discharge every man deemed indispensable by the *Landschaft*, provided that there were "suitable replacements"—men who were at least five feet four inches tall.[68] Hof responded to this good news on February 16, 1777, reporting that the city had dispatched six men for exchange. Admittedly, these replacements did not meet the height requirements, and they actually had been rejected before, but they were still considered good enough for British service.[69]

One of the indispensable men from the *Landschaft* was Johann Conrad Döhla from Wunsiedel. He had been in the Ansbach-Bayreuth army for eight years when Karl Alexander signed the subsidy treaty with Great Britain in 1777. Wunsiedel argued that Döhla should be discharged before the troops left for North America so that he could help his father, Conrad Döhla, who was the leaseholder of the local brickworks. The elder Döhla also owned a brickworks in his hometown of Zell. Wunsiedel feared that without his son's help, the father might go back to Zell, and Wunsiedel would lose not only the brickworks but also "a particularly skillful" craftsman. Adam Holper, a friend of Johann Conrad Döhla's from Münchberg, was also listed as indispensable by his hometown. Adam was the son of a master butcher, Georg Heinrich Holper, and had been enrolled in the army since October 16, 1776.[70] In 1777 he was needed at home, Münchberg argued, because his older brother had left for Hungary several years earlier, and his parents could no longer take care of the house on their own.[71]

Local concerns led Wunsiedel, Münchberg, and other cities to negotiate with the margrave for the release of individual soldiers. Such action was not motivated by fear for the men's safety or opposition to the war, but rather by worries about the economy and whether the soldiers' families might become a financial burden to the community. During two weeks in February 1777, the *Landschaft* in Brandenburg-Kulmbach attempted to have at least twenty-eight men discharged while offering twenty-two others in exchange. Despite Seckendorf's promise, however, these efforts met with little success: the available sources show that Döhla, Holper, and at least twelve other men from the *Landschaft* went to North America anyway.[72] Karl Alexander was more interested in having enough soldiers on hand than in keeping cities and communities content. Döhla seemed not to mind. In his detailed journal about the war in North America, he did not even mention his hometown's efforts to have him released from the army. Befitting the veteran soldier that he was, his entry for February 28 noted: "In the morning, at 7 o'clock, our . . . regiment . . . marched out of the barracks. . . . Thus, we took up . . . our profession in another part of the world."[73]

Undoubtedly faced with numerous such disputes when recruiting through enrollment lists, authorities in Ansbach-Bayreuth successively enlarged the pool of possible recruits over the second half of the eighteenth century. In 1762, Ansbach still ordered only unmarried sons of citizens and subjects to assemble for muster.[74] By 1775, Bayreuth was requiring every "suitable and dispensable young man" to appear.[75] In 1778, with the majority of the army serving in North America and with another large European war, the Bavarian War of Succession, on the horizon, Adjutant General von Schlammersdorf wanted to muster all citizens and subjects in the principality, including *Hintersassen, Schutzverwandte,* and *Hirten-Söhne,* who did not even enjoy full rights as citizens and subjects.[76] In 1779, he also called up for muster all men who had previously received a travel pass or had otherwise been furloughed.[77]

Hessen-Kassel went a step further than Ansbach-Bayreuth's enrollment lists in 1762 when it installed a canton system based on the Prussian model.[78] Each regiment in the army was assigned a particular district for conscription. In general, conscripts served for twenty-four years. In peacetime, however, about thirty men in each company were regularly furloughed to work in other trades, as hired laborers, or on family farms. There was a "constant coming and going" of soldiers within any given unit.[79] In each canton, local authorities rather than the regiments selected and distributed recruits. As in Ansbach-Bayreuth, communities in Hessen-Kassel sought to retain some influence over who was called up for military service in their district.[80] On January 30, 1776, just before Hessen-Kassel and Great Britain concluded their subsidy treaty, General Karl von Bose, one of Friedrich II's ministers, ordered the Brigade von Mirbach, which included the Regiments von Knyphausen, von Loßberg, and Rall, to discharge all soldiers from the village of Immenhausen who had been conscripted without the prior knowledge of the district's chief administrative officer (*Landrat*) or who were considered indispensable by their local communities. Only men who were considered dispensable by the locals were to be taken, even if they did not meet the height requirement.[81] Young men in Hessen-Kassel were labeled "dispensable" if they "were not needed at home" and their departure "did not hurt farming or other crafts and trades."[82]

Such policies were also concerned with establishing and maintaining a well-ordered state (*Policey*).[83] In this understanding of early modern society in the Holy Roman Empire, any man who did not contribute to the social economy of a state, city, or other territory had to be removed and put to use elsewhere, with the military often the most obvious choice. This way, military recruitment also interfered less with regular labor needs. When Anton Grübler from Marburg, who was around sixteen years old, beat his mother in 1781, he was immediately conscripted into the army and shipped to North America. In 1782, Anton's mother also accused her husband of "hard drinking and a most dissolute lifestyle." The city council acted as quickly as in Anton's case and sent Grübler Sr. to Ziegenhain, the central collection point for recruits. When a master cooper named Bender from Marburg apparently beat his wife and was sentenced to jail in August 1782, the city let him know right away that if it happened again, he would go to North America as a conscript.[84]

Various *Stände* in Hessen-Kassel were exempt from the canton system. For instance, subjects whose net worth exceeded 250 *Thaler* (£56 5 s.) or who owned a house or larger farm did not have to serve in the army. Knightly territories and all major cities (Kassel, Marburg, Rinteln, Ziegenhain, and Rheinfels) in the principality were also exempted from conscription, as were sons of landed families, apprentices and journeymen in all kinds of trades, students, miners, men who sold cooking pots, men who hauled salt, servants at the court, and even all liveried servants of the nobility. Of course, clergy could not be recruited, and married men with families could also stay home.[85] As a result, Hessen-Kassel technically conscripted only young men who had no voice in the *Landtag* (the body of representatives for the various estates in the principality), men who were unable to pay the tax that supported the army (*Kontribution*), and men in rural areas who were not needed for sustaining or increasing agricultural production.[86]

Establishing the canton system did not mean that militia forces in Hessen-Kassel were disbanded. On the contrary, they were reformed and converted into garrison regiments, to be used for temporary service in cases of emergency, for defensive measures such as manning fortresses, and for guard and other policing duties.[87]

In peacetime, soldiers from garrison regiments were drilled only once a year, between mid-May and mid-June, after the fields were sown and before the hay was harvested.[88] During the American War of Independence, many garrison regiments were divided into two battalions. One went to North America, and the other stayed in Hessen-Kassel. The oldest and most infirm soldiers—or those whom local communities decided they could not spare—were transferred into the latter battalion and remained at home. Unfortunately for many soldiers in these units, such principles were often violated. We find numerous men with families or with established households in units bound for North America between 1776 and 1783.[89]

For Hessen-Kassel, or at least those parts of the population who were actually affected, the canton system proved to be a massive burden during the American War of Independence. Charles Ingrao estimates that about 12 percent of all able-bodied male adults in this principality served at some point in a unit contracted by the British.[90] Because of the *Hufen-Edikt* and the way the canton system was structured, recruitment put a particular strain on rural areas. Those regions suffered significant labor shortages after 1776 and struggled with poverty. Farmers around Marburg, for instance, repeatedly protested that conscription took away much-needed farm laborers and second-born sons.[91] In some districts, potential recruits left the principality altogether to avoid conscription. Reports from Schmalkalden even spoke of "mass flights." Officials in Sontra, located in the northern part of the principality, described how young men on furlough attempted to leave the district "under all kinds of trivial pretexts."[92] The district around Marburg acknowledged in February 1776 that the required number of recruits could not be found because so few men showed up for muster. The city had to enroll several subjects whom they would have considered indispensable under normal circumstances.[93]

It is certain that principalities such as Hessen-Kassel and Ansbach-Bayreuth sent many unwilling soldiers into British service, but not whether these unwilling recruits were opposed to serving for the British in North America or were simply unhappy about having to join the army. What is obvious is that German princes who signed subsidy treaties with the British between 1776 and 1783 were concerned first and foremost with establishing their units at a low cost and as quickly as possible. Whether the goal was to hire mercenaries or enlist conscripts, all recruitment efforts targeted those parts of the population judged dispensable to the local economy and community under mercantilist principles. These groups usually included younger sons of poorer farmers, the unemployed in cities, vagrants, foreigners, people on the margins, and deserters from other armies. But in any given unit there was always a core of professional soldiers and others who had joined more or less voluntarily, whether out of financial considerations, because they wanted to advance a career, or in hopes of weathering a crisis in their lives.

In light of such findings, the mutiny by Ansbach-Bayreuth soldiers in Ochsenfurt on March 10, 1777, was probably not motivated by the men's unwillingness to serve for the British in North America, as contemporaries and some later historians claimed. It likely had more to do with a labor dispute between military employees and their employer.[94] Stephan Popp reported in his journal that after reaching Ochsenfurt, the troops immediately embarked on the ships and stayed there during the night, singing "spiritual songs" and praying devoutly. Nevertheless, it was a difficult situation because they had to "stand all night": there was not enough room on the boat for everyone to lie down.[95] The next morning, Popp heard "loud voices . . . mainly from where the Ansbach troops stayed." The members of that regiment disembarked and went back onshore, shouting angrily that they were "honest soldiers" who should not be confined on boats like "scoundrels." At this point, the men in Popp's regiment also disembarked. Wine sellers from Ochsenfurt promptly appeared and began peddling their goods.[96] The men soon began drinking heartily and started several fires to prepare meals. Popp's account now becomes confusing. Apparently, *Jäger* were posted around the infantry with orders not to let anyone run away. This angered the infantrymen, and fights broke out between them and the *Jäger*. In the ensuing melee, according to Popp, thirty infantry soldiers were wounded or killed. The chaos lasted until Karl Alexander arrived from Ansbach the next morning and calmed the soldiers down by inquiring about their grievances. "There were many," Popp emphasized.

"One man wanted this, another one wanted that." The margrave apparently tried to address all the problems, and the soldiers finally went calmly back onto the ships. He even made sure to give them two more ships so that they "would not lie that close together." In other words, Popp makes clear that the mutiny began over various grievances, particularly a lack of room on the boats. It turned violent only after the *Jäger* boxed in the infantrymen. When the margrave took the soldiers' concerns seriously, the situation was immediately resolved.[97]

Other sources confirm Popp's account. Johann Conrad Döhla emphasizes that the men debated intensely about their miserable situation on the crowded ships during the night before the mutiny.[98] The city council in Ochsenfurt observed that after the soldiers embarked in the evening of March 9, they immediately began complaining about how little room they had.[99] Shipmaster Olnieger from Ochsenfurt reported that the Bayreuth soldiers were already agitated when they arrived in Ochsenfurt's harbor. They told him that they had been promised a payment of 24 *Kreuzer* (1 s.) but had received only 15 *Kreuzer* (9 d.), and not even their proper rations of "meat, wine, and beer." The angry soldiers threatened to "burn the ship, drill a hole in it, and shoot dead and beat the boatmen." They made it clear that they would keep their word only if the officers kept theirs.[100]

Through the mutiny, then, the common soldiers communicated their grievances, negotiated terms, and forced their superiors to accept a new basis for their future relationship in North America.[101] Karl Alexander grasped the seriousness of the situation and immediately rushed to the scene. As Christian von Molitor, a Bayreuth officer from Company von Seitz, wrote later, "At night at 12 o'clock, His Serene Highness arrived on the staff-ship, examined the companies of both regiments, promised the people all mercy and received in return the assurance of further loyalty."[102] Of course, the margrave's main concern at the time was to receive the British subsidies. For that, he needed to bring well-ordered and disciplined troops to the field. He was probably more ready than usual in Ochsenfurt to heed his soldiers' demands. When Karl Alexander walked through the ranks of his soldiers on March 11, 1777, and spoke to them individually, he may even have gone beyond usual measures by allowing *Gnaden-Ertheilungen* later that year—gifts of grain or debt relief distributed to the families of the same troops who had mutinied at Ochsenfurt.[103] One of these soldiers, Johann Radler, may have been telling the truth when he later wrote to his mother from North America that the "Margrave had promised me that you shall receive two *Malter* grain each year."

~

By the eighteenth century, it was essential for even the smaller states in the Holy Roman Empire to build up and maintain standing armies. Forced to conclude subsidy treaties with other European countries for the needed funds, the various principalities used both contracts and compulsion to draw in recruits. Some men joined the army enthusiastically, while others were forcibly enrolled or turned to military service as a stopgap measure, seeing it as their best or only option for making it through difficult financial circumstances. The German auxiliaries who served for the British between 1776 and 1783 were thus a mix of professional soldiers, volunteers, and conscripts. It is inaccurate to condemn these men as mercenaries or as the dregs of eighteenth-century society. It is equally wrong to see them as victims who were sold off to North America by tyrannical prices. As subsidy troops, however, they were an anachronism, caught up in an age of transformation and change.

CHAPTER 3

Social Composition

With regard to the social composition of the subsidy troops, some information is available on units established through recruitment of mercenaries (Braunschweig-Wolfenbüttel), the canton system (Hessen-Kassel), and enrollment lists (Ansbach-Bayreuth). For the Hessen-Kassel Company von Dechow, for example, details about 121 common soldiers can be found in a company roster that survived in the scrapbook of Captain d'Armes Jeremias Kappes as well as the *HETRINA*, a comprehensive list of Hessen-Kassel, Hessen-Hanau, and Waldeck auxiliaries compiled at the state archive in Marburg.[1] In 1776, Company von Dechow was commanded by Major Karl Friedrich von Dechow. In September 1777, after Dechow's death at Trenton, Lieutenant Colonel Karl Philipp von Heymel took command of the remaining soldiers in this company as well as newly arrived recruits from Hessen-Kassel. From October 1780 to July 1782, Captain Ludwig von Löwenstein headed the unit. Major Georg Wilhelm Biesenrodt took command when the company returned to Europe in 1783.[2] Knowing so much about the common soldiers in a unit is significant because these men, together with most of the Regiment von Knyphausen, were defeated at Trenton on December 26, 1776, and remained in American captivity until the summer of 1778. One year later, in September 1779, many soldiers in the same unit, now led by Heymel, were captured again when their transports to Canada, the *Molly* and *Triton*, were damaged in a storm and subsequently taken by American privateers. That time they stayed in captivity until 1783.

For the Ansbach-Bayreuth Company Tritschler von Falckenstein, there is a roster of 332 soldiers who entered or left the unit between 1783 and 1793. Of those, 280 were common soldiers.[3] Among all the troops from Ansbach-Bayreuth in the last quarter of the eighteenth century—those who fought in North America, were in Dutch service, or participated in the French Revolutionary Wars—only this single company roster survived.[4] Company Tritschler was established on November 22, 1783, although its commanding officer, Captain Christian Carl Tritschler von Falckenstein, had led a *Jäger* unit in North America after 1781.[5] Detailed information about Ansbach-Bayreuth soldiers who actually campaigned in North America is thus very limited. In covering a period of ten years, this roster offers a rare overview over a span of time and not just a mere snapshot. In total, twenty-five men from Company Tritschler served in North America. Of those, ten were officers, seven were noncommissioned officers, and another seven were common soldiers.

Troops

All German units sent to North America between 1776 and 1783 fought as infantry soldiers. Even the few mounted troops hired by the British, such as the Braunschweig-Wolfenbüttel dragoons and several *Jäger* units, usually fought on foot.[6] Although artillery units are often listed separately when marching out of their garrison or in captivity, they were commonly distributed with their guns among infantry regiments.[7] *Jäger* were light infantry soldiers who conducted reconnaissance missions or engaged in partisan warfare and skirmishing.[8] Initially these soldiers were recruited from foresters and hunters. They often received extra pay and better equipment, such as rifles rather than muskets. Later in the war, because of rising casualties and British demands, more soldiers without any special background became *Jäger*, and the overall quality of these specialized forces seems to have declined. German commanders, for instance, simply transferred regular infantry soldiers into *Jäger* companies or distributed regular recruits among the *Jäger*.[9]

   Other infantry units came as regular field regiments or garrison troops. Usually they fought in long lines, three men deep. Marching toward the enemy, the soldiers attempted to discharge their muskets in a volley at close range, to increase the impact and break the enemy's front.[10] Men from garrison and militia regiments were often not professional soldiers; they trained for only a few weeks in late spring and early summer. Officers and noncommissioned officers in these units were often older soldiers who had been transferred from other units. When ordered to march with the regular army, as Reuber's journal shows, these units had to be drilled hard to make them fit for active duty. With notable exceptions such as the Regiment Rall, most garrison or militia regiments were used to man posts, forts, and cities such as Halifax, New York, Savannah, and Charleston.[11]

Pay and Possessions

Recruitment patterns suggest that most common soldiers came from the lower strata of late eighteenth-century society, and many turned to military service only because of financial need. The war in North America, as the *Bayreuther Neuer Zeitungs-Calender* pointed out, promised to be comparatively lucrative. Common soldiers in Ansbach-Bayreuth usually earned about 5 *Thaler* (£1 2 s. 6 d.) per month (see table 2).[12] In comparison, a contemporary servant to a noble family at the time earned between 1 and 1½ *Thaler* (4 s. 6 d.–6 s. 9 d.) per month. Soldiers usually made additional money through plundering and prize money. As a result, several common Ansbach-Bayreuth soldiers who died in North America left behind relatively large sums. Artilleryman Heidner, for instance, left behind 25 *Gulden* 12 *Kreuzer* (£3 15 s. 7 d.). Private Kern had 32 *Gulden* (£4 15 s. 12 d.) when he died, and Servant Beyser from the artillery left behind 9 *Gulden* 12 *Kreuzer* (£1 7 s. 7 d.).[13] A year after the war ended, in 1784, Barthold Koch, a noncommissioned officer, received prize money from the sale of French ships taken in the James River on October 22, 1780. He and other noncommissioned officers received 3 *Thaler* (13 s. 6 d.), while common soldiers made 1½ *Thaler* (about 6 s. 9 d.).[14]

By 1779, Hessen-Kassel soldiers had been able to leave 600,000 *Thaler* (£135,000) behind for their families.[15] Braunschweig-Wolfenbüttel subjects were also able to leave large sums, as were Waldeck soldiers. Sergeant Christoph Emde from the Waldeck

Table 2.   Pay Scale (per Day) for Selected Ranks among
Ansbach-Bayreuth Troops

Rank	Pounds	Shillings	Pence
Colonel	1	4	0
Major		15	8
Captain		10	0
First Lt.		4	8
Chaplain		6	8
Sergeant		1	6
Corporal		1	0
Drummer		1	0
Fifer		1	0
Private			8
Tent Servant			8

Source: "Pay for Ansbach-Bayreuth Soldiers," New York Public Library, Bancroft
Collection, no. 65, item 136.

regiment ordered a payment of 5 pounds 5 shillings to his wife.
Private Claude Crieur ordered 3 pounds 1 shilling for his wife in
1777 and 1 pound in 1778. In 1782, Wilhelm Berghöfer, a grenadier, sent 2 pounds 3 shillings to his daughters.[16] Similarly, a
Hessen-Kassel soldier from the Regiment von Huyn wrote to his
parents in 1777, "Please be so kind as to write to me, how things
are, and write to me, whether the money arrived that was sent to
Germany from America. There was a lot of money sent to Germany and I want to send you some money, too."[17]

At the other end of the spectrum, Charles Ingrao learned from
studying the property and possessions of 1,279 Hessen-Kassel deserters between 1777 and 1789 that a vast majority of them, 1,043
men, owned or expected property with less than 50 *Thaler* in
value (£11 5 s.). In other words, these soldiers were so poor that
they could probably never accumulate the necessary 300 to 1,000
Thaler to buy a plot of about 20 to 30 *Acker* (one *Hufe*) and sustain life as independent farmers.[18] In Ansbach-Bayreuth, *Gnaden-
Ertheilungen* took care of some of the neediest soldiers and their
families.[19] These were special aid packages granted by Margrave

Karl Alexander in the form of grain rations, tax deductions, and debt remissions; they went beyond regular food distributions or the common practice of providing quarters for the wives and children of soldiers in the barracks. However, only the families of soldiers who were sent to North America with the first contingent in March 1777 were eligible for such aid, and only seventy-nine of those cases are available for analysis today. It is unclear whether those were all the petitions submitted or merely those that survived in the archives.[20]

Most petitions came from parents or wives. They included day laborers, laundrywomen, shepherds, veteran soldiers, weavers, stokers, and farmhands. One was a bankrupt wheelwright, another a shoemaker down on his luck. All feared that they would lose support from their sons or husbands because of the war in North America. For instance, Johann Mittermeyer wrote in May 1782 that he had lost hope that he would "ever receive support or help" from his son again. Although he asked for one *Simra* of grain for subsistence and one *Klafter* of wood for heating and cooking, he received only a half *Simra* of grain and one *Klafter* of wood.[21] Mothers who applied for the *Gnaden* often had two or even three sons in the army and were occasionally truly desperate. The wife of Private Winter petitioned in May 1779. Upon examining her situation, the Ansbach-Bayreuth infantry headquarters, which decided on the aid packages, found out that she had not received room in the barracks and got no bread rations, and she had already "pawned all her clothing and possessions" to feed herself and the children.[22]

Most petitioners asked for grain and wood, but a few also requested tax, rent, or debt relief. The typical distribution for financial relief was 20 to 25 *Gulden*. Tax relief ranged between 10 and 15 *Gulden*. That was about as much as a servant earned in one year. The amount of grain granted to each successful petitioner varied between a half *Simra* and two *Simra* per year. Considering that a *Simra* in Ansbach-Bayreuth weighed about 220 kilograms (485 pounds) and that an average adult ate between 200 and 400 kilograms of bread per year, the *Gnaden-Ertheilungen* provided only minimum subsistence.[23] The amount of grain granted to the petitioners also depended on the number of people in the household.

Eva Maria Schmidt, for instance, was a widow from Schallhausen. Two of her sons were serving in America, while another was a day laborer in Sulz. She received only a half *Simra* of grain. The Schauer daughters, however, received two *Simra* of grain and six *Klafter* of wood for cooking and heating. Both of their brothers served in the Ansbach-Bayreuth military; one was a corporal in North America, the other a sergeant in Ansbach.[24]

Karl Alexander's authorities declined several petitions because the applicants did not seem needy enough. Anna Mayer from Markt Stefft stated that she was plagued by debt and could no longer pay her taxes, but her claim was rejected. The authorities coolly told her that she still had some possessions that she could sell to support herself and pay off her debts. The mere fact that one of her sons was a soldier in North America, while another was an apprentice and a third one a fisherman, was not grounds for the petition. Moreover, the authorities stated, Mayer's first son had actually joined the army voluntarily and earned additional pay as a *Jäger*.[25]

Age

Soldiers' ages can tell us a lot about an army. Key insights can be gained not only from their ages at a given moment, such as during a battle or a campaign or when they were captured, but also from their entry ages: how old they were when they entered military service. It can be even more helpful to look at soldiers' length of service before they embarked on a campaign or fought a battle. Unfortunately, available sources do not always provide all this data. Surviving muster lists and company rosters may give only the soldiers' years of birth, or their ages when they entered the unit or when the list was compiled. Moreover, because many soldiers in the eighteenth century did not know exactly when they were born, records are often riddled with mistakes, and all numbers have to be viewed with caution.

In 1776, when the Hessen-Kassel campaign in North America began, the average age of the common soldiers in Company von Dechow was twenty-four. The youngest soldier in this unit was Johannes Kühn, who was sixteen. He had been transferred on

February 1 from the company of Captain Georg Wilhelm von Biesenrodt. Kühn was wounded in the Battle of White Plains in October 1776 and died of illness in 1783. The company's oldest common soldier, Ludwig Erdmann, arrived with reinforcements in 1777 at age fifty-nine. Erdmann was born in Rabenau, Hessen-Darmstadt, and was recruited as a foreign mercenary following Friedrich II's order regarding all such transports after 1776.

There is insufficient data from the Company Tritschler roster to enable a calculation of the soldiers' average age; it provides only the rank and file's entry ages. The 279 men for whom we have data were twenty-eight years old on average when they entered the company. Compared with previous data on Hessen-Kassel troops, such numbers suggest that most of these soldiers had some kind of prior military experience. Indeed, further data from the roster shows that at least 185 soldiers of all ranks in this company had been in other units, usually also from Ansbach-Bayreuth, for an average of 6.5 years before coming under Tritschler's command. The longest-serving soldier was First Lieutenant Johann Ernst Prechtel, who had been in the Ansbach-Bayreuth military for twenty-nine years when he entered Company Tritschler in 1786.[26]

In Company von Dechow, seventy-nine common soldiers (65.3 percent) had been in Hessen-Kassel military service for some time before the American War of Independence. Most of the soldiers in Jeremias Kappes's list (figure 2) entered military service after 1769.[27] On average, common soldiers in this company seem to have served for about four years before leaving for North America in 1776. Most men in this unit, therefore, must have entered the army following adolescence and the establishment of the canton system in 1762. We also see a spike in 1773, the year in which the *Hufen-Edikt* was enacted.

These results are confirmed by findings for two Braunschweig-Wolfenbüttel units, the Regiments von Specht and Prinz Friedrich. The respective average age in these two units was thirty and thirty-one for 1776, when the regiments left their garrison for North America. As with Company Tritschler, this did not mean that only old men had enrolled for this principality or campaign. Rather, these were veteran soldiers. Their entry ages indicate that most of them were about twenty when they joined the military.

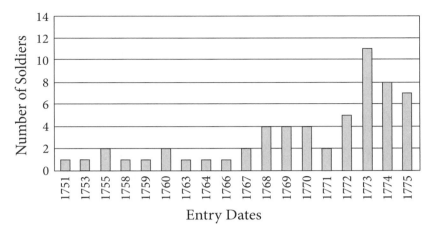

Figure 2.   Prior Military Service of Common Soldiers in Company von Dechow

Source: "Notizbuch des Captain d'Armes Jeremias Kappes," Landes- und Murhardsche Bibliothek der Stadt Kassel, Tgb. Nr. 77/76.

In other words, they were professional soldiers who went into the army immediately after or even during training for other trades. Most young men in the Holy Roman Empire started learning their trades around age fourteen, after Confirmation or First Communion, and then spent about three years in apprenticeship before becoming journeymen.[28]

Some of the most experienced soldiers who left Braunschweig-Wolfenbüttel for North America in 1776 had seen service since the Seven Years' War. These seasoned veterans were the backbone of the enlarged corps that went into British service. On average, new recruits for later reinforcement transports from Braunschweig-Wolfenbüttel were twenty-four or twenty-five, about the same age as the men from Company von Dechow in 1776. These were soldiers who had signed up during wartime, knowing full well that they would have to go to North America and into battle. They had obviously avoided enlisting as long as possible while attempting to make a living in other professions. For them, the army was likely a last resort of some kind. Entering military service during peacetime, by contrast, was an easier decision. As these findings show, it is impossible to discern a major difference based on age between units established by some form of conscription and those formed through mercenary recruitment.[29]

Regional Origins

Examining where German auxiliaries lived in the Holy Roman Empire gives us an idea about how the various recruitment principles worked in practice. Contemporaries in the eighteenth century considered a soldier's origins, particularly whether or not he was a foreigner, to be an important indicator of his reliability on campaign and in battle. A foreigner, it was assumed, would not be as good and loyal a soldier as someone who had a connection by birth to the territory and its sovereign. Such beliefs about foreigners' motivation and combat strength anticipated the establishment of national armies during the American and French Revolutions.[30]

Not surprisingly, only four men in Company von Dechow were foreigners to Hessen-Kassel, and they seem to have been reinforcements recruited after the spring of 1776. At the time, however, "foreigner" merely might have meant someone who was not a subject but a farmer from another region, a laborer from a neighboring territory, a fellow villager who had another sovereign or paid taxes to another prince, or simply someone who was not recorded as a *Kantonist*, a subject mustered and assigned to a certain recruitment district. Nationality, in other words, mattered little when it came to establishing and maintaining an army. One of the "foreigners" in the company came from nearby Saxony. Another, Antonius Steinhausen, was born in Günzburg a. d. Donau in the tiny southern principality of Burgau. Ludwig Erdmann was born in Hessen-Darmstadt, and Philipp Walter in the Hessian Ritterschaft, small neighboring territories ruled by individual nobles.[31] Most of the remaining 117 soldiers in the unit recorded their birthplaces as the rural areas around Ziegenhain and Schönstein in Hessen-Kassel, the regiment's canton district.

When Hessen-Kassel soldiers during the American War of Independence are examined as a whole, the numbers are striking.[32] The *HETRINA*, which lists 25,688 Hessen-Kassel soldiers who served at some point in a unit hired out to the British crown, suggests that a total of 4,868 men (21 percent) were foreigners. Yet a full 87 percent of them actually came from other German-speaking states. Most of these soldiers joined the Hessen-Kassel military after 1776, when Friedrich II ordered that only foreigners be recruited as replacements and reinforcements for his troops in North America. In the Grenadier Battalions von Block, von Linsingen, von Minnigerode, and Köhler, as well as the Garrison Regiment von Huyn, for instance, only 7 foreigners joined in 1776, but 186 arrived in 1777.[33]

While such comprehensive numbers cannot be provided for Ansbach-Bayreuth, an examination of Company Tritschler yields additional insights. Between 1783 and 1793, only twenty-eight men in this unit were foreigners (8.7 percent); twenty-five of them were common soldiers. A close look at the territories recorded for these foreigners shows that almost all of them came from neighboring territories in the same region. Seven soldiers came from the Prince-Bishopric of Bamberg and Würzburg, five from various knightly territories in the region, and four from the nearby imperial city of Nuremberg. The foreigner Andreas Schertzer listed his hometown as Fürth, a nearby territory of the prince-bishop of Bamberg and Würzburg, but he also claimed to be a subject of Karl Alexander in the district of Cadolsburg.

Prussian official Rudolf Friedrich Culemann made similar observations in 1796, when Prussia took control of Ansbach-Bayreuth. Examining local recruitment practices, he discovered no fewer than "nine different rulers and dominions" for subjects in the village of Ergersheim—located between the prince-bishopric's capitals Bamberg and Würzburg, on one side, and the imperial cities of Nuremberg and Rothenburg, on the other. Two other subjects of Karl Alexander lived in the village of Mönchsontheim, but all other inhabitants actually belonged to the Monastery of Obrach. Still, every young man in this town was eventually mustered within the Ansbach-Bayreuth district of Uffenheim. Similarly, some inhabitants in Ermezhofen belonged to Ansbach, while others enjoyed "the protection and patronage of the Barons of Seckendorf," but everybody was mustered for Uffenheim in Ansbach-Bayreuth. A soldier from such territories, then, could live in the same community as the other soldiers in his unit but still be counted as a foreigner in the muster rolls.[34]

The picture for Braunschweig-Wolfenbüttel units looks different—but not as different as might be expected from the original recruitment plans.[35] Karl I explicitly wanted to avoid recruiting native subjects (*Landeskinder*) because he was convinced that he could not force them into military service for a foreign nation on a different continent. Yet when the Regiments Prinz Friedrich and von Specht left Braunschweig-Wolfenbüttel in 1776, they contained a surprisingly low percentage of foreigners (table 3).

More than half of Braunschweig-Wolfenbüttel's soldiers in 1776 came from within the territory, seemingly contradicting the duke's professed concern for his native subjects' welfare. Upon closer examination, however, these numbers actually reinforce that concern. After the Seven Years' War, the size of the army was reduced significantly. To provide some financial security for his subjects, Karl I tried to keep as many of them in service as possible. When the American War of Independence broke out in 1775 and Great Britain negotiated with Braunschweig-Wolfenbüttel for auxiliaries, there was not enough time to replace all the subjects with new foreign recruits before embarkation for North America. Instead, the number of natives in some units was reduced over the course of the war. For instance, only about 10 percent of all recruits sent to the Regiments Prinz Friedrich and von Specht after 1776 were native subjects. Nevertheless, as in other territories with British subsidy troops, the label "foreigner" in Braunschweig-Wolfenbüttel often meant merely that a soldier had another German sovereign, usually Hanover or Prussia. In total, seventy-nine different states were represented in these units. On average, foreign soldiers were born about 150 miles away from Wolfenbüttel. Born farthest away, and clearly an exception, were Leopold Conrade and Johann Müller from Riga in Estland. We do not know how far such men had already migrated before enlisting in the Braunschweig-Wolfenbüttel army. Overall, however, these numbers show that Braunschweig-Wolfenbüttel went against the prevailing trend and successively increased the number of foreigners

Table 3. Foreigners in Braunschweig-Wolfenbüttel Units, 1776

Regiment	Foreigners (%)	Native Subjects (%)	Unknown (%)
Dragoons	30.5	60.9	8.6
Prinz Friedrich	39.9	54.8	5.3
Specht	34.3	59.0	6.7
Total	34.9	58.2	6.9

Source: Huck, "Soldaten gegen Nordamerika," 101, 103, 106, 303.

in its army between 1776 and 1783. While Karl I may have been prompted to such action by the controversy over the subsidy treaties, he may also have been attempting to preserve valuable native subjects for the principality.

Religious Denominations

Most northern territories in the Holy Roman Empire of the eighteenth century were Lutheran or Reformed, while most of the southern states were Catholic. As might be expected from a unit recruited in Hessen-Kassel, 112 of the 121 common soldiers in Company von Dechow were members of the Reformed Church (92.6 percent). The other nine were Lutherans. In the Ansbach-Bayreuth Company Tritschler, on the other hand, the vast majority of soldiers (91.7 percent) were Lutherans, in keeping with this territory's religious affiliation. Only fifteen soldiers in this unit were Catholics, and only four were members of the Reformed Church. Of the Catholics, seven came from the Catholic territory of Sayn-Altenkirchen in the western part of the Holy Roman Empire, which was also ruled by Karl Alexander of Ansbach-Bayreuth.[36] Again, one might expect different numbers and a wider mix of denominations from units established by mercenary recruitment in Braunschweig-Wolfenbüttel. However, once again 91 percent of all soldiers were Lutherans. Over the course of the war, increased recruitment of foreigners caused these numbers to drop, but only slightly. Unlike national origin, religion was apparently important in the early modern armies of the Holy Roman Empire: in any given unit, one denomination dominated the others by about nine to one.[37]

Yet it is important not to overgeneralize. When Karl Alexander sent his troops to North America in 1777, they were accompanied by a Catholic priest, the former Jesuit Franz Piret. In a letter to Prince-Bishop Adam Friedrich von Seinsheim of neighboring Bamberg and Würzburg, the margrave explained that it was necessary to send Piret with his troops because "so many Catholics" were among his rank and file.[38] The sources needed for checking the religious affiliation of Ansbach-Bayreuth auxiliaries for the British between 1777 and 1783 are missing, so it can only be assumed that Karl Alexander deemed the number of Catholics in his units high enough to warrant sending along a priest. He may also have understood the importance of religious practice and rituals for fostering a sense of community in a unit. A number of Braunschweig-Wolfenbüttel soldiers in Canada expressed unease about the fact that they, as German Protestants, had been sent to campaign with Catholics. Such opinions, the officers feared, might actually lead some soldiers to feel closer to the American enemies, who were fellow Protestants, than to their Catholic allies.[39]

Trades

Many recruits had acquired skills before entering an army or worked in some capacity while on furlough or in garrison. In Company von Dechow, 25 out of 121 common soldiers (20.1 percent) were listed with a civilian trade. Just over half of them were tailors or shoemakers. Other occupations included linen weavers, millers, smiths, joiners, cloth makers, and carpenters. Most soldiers with a trade were older than nineteen, an indication that they had learned these skills before entering the army.

In Company Tritschler, by contrast, 172 out of 332 men listed a civilian trade (51.8 percent). A vast majority of them, 160 men (93 percent), were rank and file. This much higher number is actually comparable to the numbers from other units in Saxony in 1742 (46.7 percent), the imperial city of Frankfurt in 1732 (38 percent), and the Swabian Imperial Circle in the eighteenth century (55 to 65 percent).[40] They are lower, however, than the Prussian numbers from the canton district in Prenzlau, where 96 percent of all enlisted men claimed a civilian trade. This indicates that many soldiers worked while on furlough.[41] The numbers for Company von Dechow are low because not only garrison units but all regular Hessen-Kassel regiments left one of their two battalions behind when they departed for North America in 1776. Efforts were made to transfer those soldiers who had a trade or were otherwise considered valuable to the local economy into the battalion that stayed at home.

In all examined units, the rosters listed a variety of skills for the soldiers. Forty-one different trades were represented in Company Tritschler, sixty-two in the Braunschweig-Wolfenbüttel units.[42] A large majority of soldiers with trades—111 men out of 172 in Company Tritschler—did work that provided for the basic human needs of food, construction, and clothing. These numbers roughly correspond to data found for early modern European society as a whole (table 4).[43]

As this data and the figures from table 4 indicate, armies in this period looked for certain skills among their recruits. Carpenters were useful for building field and siege works. Shoemakers and tailors were needed for making uniforms. Among the soldiers in Company Tritschler who did not work in food-, housing-, or clothing-related trades, there were sixteen smiths of various kinds (9.3 percent) and men with expertise in transportation (coach builders, wheelwrights, saddlers, harness makers) and in metal and wood (fitters, turners, coopers, and needle makers). Moreover, there were musicians, barbers, scribes, printers, miners, wig makers, even tobacco cutters—all trades that were necessary to operate an army in the field.[44] At the same time, in Companies von Dechow and Tritschler and the three Braunschweig-Wolfenbüttel units, a large number of soldiers had trades that had become less profitable over the course of the early modern period, particularly textile workers. More often than not, wandering journeymen became vagrants after finishing their training as weavers, tailors, and shoemakers. Military service was often the only available way for a man to overcome such a crisis and earn a living for himself and his family.[45]

Table 4.   Food-, Construction-, and Clothing-Related Trades among
Soldiers in Company Tritschler, 1783–1793

Trades	Number of Soldiers
Food	23 (13.4%)
Millers	3
Butchers	9
Bakers	3
Cooks	4
Brewers	4
Construction	36 (20.9%)
Carpenters	11
Bricklayers	2
Stonemasons	3
Masons	19
Glaziers	1
Clothing	52 (30.2%)
Weavers	14
Linen weavers	2
Stocking makers/weavers	4
Cloth makers	1
Shoemakers	9
Master tailors	1
Tailors	17
Hat makers	1
Furriers	3
Total	111 (64.5%)

Source: Tritschler, "Grundliste der löbl. Hauptmann von Tritschlerischen
Compagnie," Staatsarchiv Nürnberg, Rep 107/III, Nr. 118.

As Ralf Pröve has shown for Göttingen in Hanover during the
first half of the eighteenth century, many professional soldiers
in garrison worked simultaneously in civilian trades, both inside
and outside the barracks. Common soldiers in Hanover were paid
about 2 *Thaler* (9 s.) per month, but they were charged 21 *Groschen* 6 *Pfennig* (2 s. 9 d.) per month for uniforms and underwear,

medical services, and their unit's recruitment efforts. Thus their net pay was approximately 1 *Thaler* 14 *Groschen* 2 *Pfennig* per month (6 s. 3 d.)—about as much as a mason or carpenter journeyman earned in one week. To survive, in other words, soldiers needed additional income, particularly if they had families. Some found work inside the barracks as tailors, shoemakers, and hat makers for officers or fellow soldiers; others sought jobs on the outside. These *Pfuscher* (botchers)—a term that did not necessarily describe the quality of their work but marked them as working outside regular guild structures—labored as masons, carpenters, tailors, or shoemakers. Towns with army garrisons usually forbade such labor by soldiers, but the local population often preferred the soldiers' services because they worked more quickly and cheaply. Skilled soldiers, including musicians, surgeons, dyers, and carpenters, were in high demand. Even unskilled soldiers could earn extra money through farm labor, textile work, or poaching. Some soldiers' wives illegally collected and sold firewood.[46]

Family

On average, 10 percent of the soldiers in Hessen-Kassel and Ansbach-Bayreuth were married. In Company Tritschler, 36 out of 332 men were listed as married (9.6 percent) at one time or another between 1783 and 1793. Of those, 23 were common soldiers. In Kappes's list for Company von Dechow, only 12 out of 121 common soldiers (10 percent) appear as married. Among 11 soldiers in this company who reached the ranks of noncommissioned officers during the war, 8 were married.[47] Reports for the Company du Corps of the Hessen-Kassel Regimentvon Loßberg in June 1783 note that there were 10 married men among 102 common soldiers (9.8 percent).[48]

In Company Tritschler, 32 of the married soldiers were long-serving veterans. On average, they had been in the army for 12.6 years before coming to the unit. These married veterans were the backbone of the unit; they were the most experienced and valuable soldiers and probably received permission to marry for that reason. Soldiers in the eighteenth century were considered part of a prince's "household," and a prince had to care for these "relatives" just as he had to care for the members of his immediate family or court. This thinking resulted in regulations that allowed wives of soldiers to live in the barracks or receive other support, and it enabled soldiers to have some of their pay sent back home to their families. But it also reduced a sovereign's willingness to allow his soldiers to marry.[49]

Among the Braunschweig-Wolfenbüttel units examined here, 23.1 percent of the soldiers in the Regiment von Specht and 17.1 percent of the dragoons were married in 1776. While these numbers are different from those for Companies von Dechow and Tritschler, they accord with the figures for other units in the Holy Roman Empire in this period. On average, between 17 and 25 percent of contemporary soldiers seem to have been married.[50] One reason for the lower numbers of married soldiers in Companies Tritschler and von Dechow may have been recruitment by way of conscription, as it focused on unmarried men. Another possibility is that the two principalities wanted to send fewer married men to North America because they were more valuable to the local economy and would leave behind unsupported women and children if they deserted.

In the Regiment Prinz Friedrich, 41 percent of all soldiers had a wife upon leaving Wolfenbüttel. The only explanation for such a high number is that this unit was particularly eager to add married soldiers to the ranks because they were usually also the most experienced soldiers. Moreover, they were also more loyal to their sovereign. We know that married soldiers in Braunschweig-Wolfenbüttel units had served for 15.2 years on average before going to North America, compared to 6 years for unmarried soldiers.[51] Surely the desire for experienced and loyal soldiers explains the weddings that were permitted just before the auxiliaries left for North America.

In Braunschweig-Wolfenbüttel, the majority of married soldiers, 56.1 percent, were noncommissioned officers. Apparently many of those men even took their wives to North America; Stephan Huck was able to identify at least 267 women among 6,042 military personnel. He estimates that about 8 percent of all Braunschweig-Wolfenbüttel military personnel were involved in a stable relationship and that their partners were camp followers.[52] The average soldier's household contained 1.98 persons, indicating that a soldier usually had a wife and one child. Soldiers do not seem to have had a lot of children. Such numbers might also be evidence of temporary relationships or marriages: "partnerships of convenience." Many foreign Braunschweig-Wolfenbüttel recruits from other territories left behind their wives and children when they went to North America—and thereby gave up any real chance to support them while away. This usually meant a permanent separation from any "family" they might have had.[53]

Additional numbers available for the camp followers and baggage trains of German auxiliaries show that Friedrich II of Hessen-Kassel allowed only six women per company to accompany the troops, including the wives of noncommissioned officers. Each regiment, therefore, could leave the Holy Roman Empire with a maximum of thirty women. At home, local districts were ordered to provide shelter for the women left behind who had no other home. However, the landgrave did allow his units to take along an unspecified number of "necessary sutlers."[54]

When the Hessen-Hanau regiment under Colonel von Gall left the port of Willemstad on March 25, 1776, it was accompanied by eighteen women, four children, eighteen servants, and four *vivandiers et bousher* (female sutlers and butchers). Together with the soldiers, musicians, and staff personnel, this made for a diverse array of people, males and females, military and civilian.[55] The Regiment von Knyphausen was mustered on March 27 at Bremerlehe with thirty-five servants and five *soliciteurs* (sutlers).[56] One year later, the Ansbach-Bayreuth regiments left their principality with between fifty-seven and sixty-two women in their baggage trains.[57] All armies of the early modern period required the support of baggage trains. These camp followers included women, children, traders, craftsmen, servants, wagoners, and many others. Between May 30 and June 24, 1782, for instance, the Regiment von Knyphausen in New York received rations for 391 men, 20 women, 18 children, and 7 drivers.[58]

∼

As the statistics show, the German subsidy troops who fought alongside the British in the American War for Independence varied widely with respect to their backgrounds and life experience.

Many were already military veterans when they joined the auxiliary units, whereas others had been conscripted or recruited in order to reach the troop strength required by their states' subsidy agreement with King George III. For young men without a gainful trade, or who had experienced a crisis in their civilian occupation, military service for the British was financially attractive despite the reality of having to cross the Atlantic and fight. In the summer of 1776, the first of these German auxiliaries disembarked in North America. Because they were professional troops fighting for pay rather than for a cause, they would soon find themselves in a unique position, receiving unique treatment: they would come to be viewed both as foreign soldiers of the worst kind and as victims of princely tyranny whom the revolutionaries could use to their advantage.

PART II

Into Captivity

A long, cold, and stormy night lay behind the soldiers from three Hessen-Kassel infantry regiments, some *Jäger*, and a few British dragoons stationed in the small town of Trenton, New Jersey, when they suddenly came under assault by revolutionary forces in the early morning hours of December 26, 1776.[1] Just after eight o'clock, about 5,000 American soldiers, having crossed the Delaware River during the night under cover of a roaring winter storm, launched a surprise attack on the town, along the Pennington and River Roads. Roughly 1,400 soldiers under command of Colonel Johann Rall were rudely awakened by musketry and cannon fire. They had not believed that a full-scale attack would be possible in such bad weather.[2]

Despite their shock upon seeing General Washington's men advancing that morning, the Hessen-Kassel outposts did not flee before the enemy but conducted a fighting retreat, sounding the alarm in Trenton and allowing their fellow soldiers to organize a hasty defense.[3] During the battle, the Grenadier Regiment Rall and the Fusilier Regiment von Loßberg attempted two counterattacks, one north from the town center along King Street, and one west from an apple orchard. Colonel Rall fell mortally wounded in the chaotic moments of close combat. The Fusilier Regiment von Knyphausen tried to join the other two regiments in their counterattacks but was eventually forced to attempt a retreat on a bridge over Assunpink Creek. Revolutionary forces, however, had already overwhelmed the few guards there and closed this escape route. Under fire from both sides of Assunpink Creek, the Regiment von Knyphausen rushed toward another ford, only to find it occupied by the enemy as well. Surrounded, with many of their officers already killed or wounded, the Hessen-Kassel soldiers accepted their fate, gave up resistance, and were taken prisoner. Only about 350 men managed to escape toward Bordentown; 84 were wounded, and 22 were killed in action, including Colonel Rall and Major von Dechow, the acting commander of the Regiment von Knyphausen.[4] As best as can be determined from the records, 848 common Hessen-Kassel soldiers marched into American captivity after the battle.[5] Following a devastating series of setbacks that began with the loss of Long Island in the summer of 1776, the revolutionaries had finally won a victory against their seemingly invincible European adversaries. In fact, some historians argue that the success at Trenton that year saved the revolutionaries from ultimate defeat.[6]

Johannes Reuber, in Company Matthäus, was afraid after his unit was taken prisoner. He had no idea how the revolutionaries would treat him and his fellow auxiliaries in captivity—and the events unfolding around them over the next hours and days were not reassuring. As he later recounted in his journal, the Continentals immediately moved the captives across the icy Delaware River into Pennsylvania. In Newtown, they threw the common soldiers and noncommissioned officers into a "dreadful prison" and fed them through a hole in the roof.[7] In Reuber's opinion, they were treated like animals. Tired, cold, and exhausted, he wrote, "We really hoped to have some peace and quiet at last."[8]

However, his wish was not granted. Only a few days later, on December 30, the revolutionaries led their new prisoners to Philadelphia. There they paraded the captives on Market, Front, and Walnut Streets. The Hessen-Kassel soldiers were greeted by an angry mob outside of town. During the parade, they were pushed, shoved, and shouted at. Reuber knew that the guards had orders to lead them "through the entire city" so that everybody could see them.[9] Another captive, Captain d'Armes Kappes, summarized aptly, "We became a spectacle for the entire city."[10] Not even the officers escaped the humiliating treatment. Lieutenant Andreas Wiederholdt was happy to ride into the city in a covered wagon; otherwise, he "would have been pelted with dirt."[11] Over the course of the afternoon, the situation became more dangerous as more and more citizens threatened the captives. The guards had to abort the parade and marched their frightened prisoners into the city's barracks for their own protection.[12]

~

Focusing on common German soldiers, the next two chapters examine how fighting ended and captivity began for the vanquished during the American War of Independence. Too often, military historians have written about soldiers only before and during campaigns, ignoring what happened after combat. For the victors, this was a time of joy and relief over their success and survival. For the vanquished, it was an unsettling period of uncertainty. Would they be attacked, robbed, harassed, or even killed? How long would they remain in enemy hands? Defeated soldiers were introduced to a new existence and status in society. What happened in those first minutes, hours, and days of captivity merits further attention. The ostensibly simple transformation from soldiers into prisoners of war could indeed become complicated and dangerous.

The fourth chapter will briefly explain the evolving standards of prisoner-of-war treatment in Western warfare until the American War of Independence. Then, because it would be impossible to examine every campaign, battle, and skirmish that produced British or German prisoners of war between 1775 and 1783, the fifth chapter will concentrate on a few key examples to study the two fundamental ways in which a soldier could become a prisoner of war: capture or surrender. The examples were not chosen at random but had an enormous impact on the eventual outcome of the war and resulted in large numbers of common German prisoners of war in revolutionary hands. Further analysis in this study will repeatedly return to one or another of these groups of captives.

CHAPTER 4

Prisoners of War in Western Warfare

The term "prisoner of war" acquired precise legal meaning only in the twentieth century, following the First and Second Hague Peace Conferences of 1899 and 1907 and the Geneva Conventions of 1929 and 1949.[1] Before then, belligerents in Western warfare regulated their behavior through a set of customary rules, the laws of war, rooted in ancient Greek and Roman warfare, Christian teachings, and medieval traditions of knightly battle.[2] Enforcement of such customs was difficult. In fact, the laws of war worked only if armies made them part of their military regulations—the Articles of War during the early modern period, field manuals and rules of engagement in modern times. Usually, only the principle of reciprocity ensured that belligerents adhered to basic standards of behavior when approaching defeated enemies. Moreover, acceptable treatment of defeated enemies, particularly in the early modern period, depended greatly on how much authority a sovereign or state actually wielded over its soldiers. The more disciplined the troops were, the more likely it was that their opponents would accept defeat. Soldiers were far more likely to surrender when they knew that the victors would treat them decently.[3]

The Ancient World

Ancient Greeks did not have a specific term for prisoners of war. They called them "enemies taken with a spear," a description based on actual events on the battlefield, where hoplites arranged in a phalanx usually thrust spears, their main weapon, at their opponents.[4] Captured enemies became the personal property of their captors and faced either death or enslavement.[5] Approximately one-fifth of Greek field battles ended with the captives' being enslaved, and another fifth resulted in the massacre of surviving enemies. Similarly, about one-third of all Greek sieges led to the enslavement of enemy soldiers, while about one-fourth ended in a mass killing. In wars with non-Greeks, however, few constraints existed. Following the Greek victories at Marathon in 490 B.C. and Plataea in 479 B.C., for instance, the surviving Persian soldiers were killed indiscriminately.[6]

The Greeks, like many later Western civilizations, considered captured soldiers spoils of war. If a prisoner was kept alive, his captors usually assigned him some calculable value in order to sell him as a slave. The Romans likewise thought of defeated enemies as "human booty."[7] These prisoners constituted a major labor source for Roman society. In fact, slavery was the most important economic institution in the Roman Empire, and warfare provided Romans with a steady supply of much-needed laborers. At the same time, Romans allowed individuals, families, or friends to buy the captives' freedom. Sometimes entire communities or cities were ransomed.[8]

Medieval Europe

In medieval Europe, from about A.D. 1000 to 1300, there were relatively few prisoners of war. Nobles fought as mounted or dismounted knights, and the customs of war and chivalry dictated that only their peers could be taken captive. The act established a quasi-contractual relationship between noble captives and captors, which bound both sides to certain obligations.[9] Financial gain, whether through conquest, plunder, or ransom, was often the primary motive behind wars in this period. Victors normally demanded a ransom of about one year's revenue from the prisoners' homeland. Until these funds were paid, which sometimes took years, the prisoners were confined either in a castle or in open custody, depending on the circumstances. Prisoners were also released on parole, allowed to leave custody if they gave their word of honor to abide by certain restrictions.

There were no fixed and enforceable standards for the treatment of knightly prisoners in this period. Contemporaries did not orient their conduct during war to canon law, the tradition of Roman civil law, the ancient model of Vegetius's *De re militari*, or other organizational regulations for armies. Only a "body of uncodified customs" existed, which dealt with matters such as siege warfare, truces, and ransom. The desire or need to gain financially from ransom payments ensured that large-scale killings of vanquished knights eventually became relatively rare, with occasional exceptions such as Agincourt in 1415. However, even such limited constraints did not apply to wars that were considered unjust, such as rebellions and heresies, or to wars against non-Christians. In those cases, unlimited violence against all enemies, including prisoners, was permissible.[10]

Although commoners were always present in large numbers on medieval battlefields, they were not acceptable opponents.[11] Knights did not consider foot soldiers, archers, miners, engineers, city militiamen, peasants, or other local volunteers worthy of much attention. In the eyes of the nobility, such men possessed no honor and thus could not be used for ransoming. They could not become true prisoners of war. These soldiers literally remain nameless in our sources.[12] After a battle or siege, commoners were often merely chased away or forced to repair walls or other buildings. Often, however, they were massacred wholesale, particularly when a garrison had defended a castle or city for a long time and had cost the victors added casualties.[13] The practice of enslavement, however, diminished because slavery was no longer the foundation of the economy and society in the Latin West.[14]

By the fourteenth century, as Maurice Keen points out, customary rules of wartime conduct evolved into the laws of war, amounting to "some sort of prototype of the Geneva convention, a branch of international law governing the conduct of war," at least as far as noble warriors were concerned.[15] The countless French wars of the period had turned warfare into a "large-scale commercial venture," necessitating further definition and expansion of previously existing customs, as well as efforts to enforce them. Because so many nobles tried to make a living through warfare, it became imperative for all sides to observe "the rules of the game."[16] A rising number of tracts on legal and ethical questions reflect these concerns. Most important was John of Legnano's *Tractatus de bello, de represaliis et de duello,* particularly after it was rewritten in the vernacular by Honoré Bonet as *L'arbre des batailles.*[17]

The strict distinction between worthy and unworthy opponents on the battlefield had become untenable. Armies of the fourteenth and fifteenth centuries included thousands of soldiers from the lower ranks who fought with longbows, crossbows, pikes, and, soon, firearms. A noble knight might now be killed or wounded by an arrow or bullet shot from a distance by a commoner, rather than in honorable combat with a peer. Of equal concern, nobles could now easily fall into the hands of a low-ranking enemy, something that had previously been inconceivable. In other words, even the new laws of war had not kept pace with the changes in weaponry and tactics and no longer sufficed for regulating fighting and captivity.[18]

Common soldiers of this period who were captured by the enemy faced hardship. Although their numbers and importance on the battlefield had steadily increased, armies had not yet developed standards for their treatment. One reason for this unfortunate situation was that medieval, late medieval, and early modern commentators were fixated on the theory of just war, *bellum iustum*. Under this theory, only wars initiated by legitimate governments were considered legal, and therefore they had to be conducted with restraint.[19] This focus allowed very little concern with how prisoners of war were to be treated, let alone made possible a more precise definition of this status.[20] Since it was also the domain of respected theologians arguing on the basis of a higher *ius divinum* (divine law), scholars in this period studied the *ius ad bello*, dealing with the causes of war, rather than the *ius in bello*, covering the conduct of war.[21]

It was Spanish and Italian writers such as Francisco Suarez, Francisco de Vitoria, Alberico Gentili, and, finally, Hugo Grotius who moved Western thinking about conflict and international relations away from the theory of just war. In *De jure belli ac pacis* (1625) Grotius stressed arguments based on natural law.[22] When he stated that all soldiers, "without exception, who have been captured in a formal public war become slaves from the time when they are brought within the lines," he meant to introduce such seemingly unrestricted power over prisoners into the law of nations so that "captors, mollified by so many advantages, might willingly refrain from recourse to the utmost degree of severity, in accordance with which they could have slain the captives."[23] Captors, in other words, should keep their prisoners alive and treat them decently, regardless of rank or status, simply because there was no need to kill them. Such reasoning based on natural law gave rights and duties to both sides in a conflict, whether or not it was a just war.

That kings and nobles began using mercenary forces during the later Middle Ages to establish or enlarge their armies also explains the contemporary lack of overall standards for the treatment of common prisoners of war. Sovereigns often had little control over these troops. A commander who could not enforce order among his own soldiers could hardly protect captured enemy troops. Problems with supply and pay not only led to mutinies and desertions but also resulted in looting of enemy territory and captives' being robbed. The sacking of cities, for instance, became common practice as the early modern period opened.[24] Initially, mercenaries were hired only for a campaign season rather than as permanent soldiers. Unemployed and unpaid mercenary bands roamed through Europe during the off-months, stealing food, harming the population, and causing other problems. Contemporary observers complained about a lack of rules in warfare in this era: anyone could kill or capture anyone.[25]

Early Modern Europe

Between the sixteenth and the eighteenth centuries, a new code of conduct gradually emerged on European battlefields. It followed examples set by medieval chivalry and was primarily supported by an aristocratic officer corps commanding standing armies. With warfare after the Hundred Years' War increasingly taking the form of an armed struggle between centralized states, prisoners of war began to be viewed as legitimate representatives of the enemy's regular armed forces, and their treatment improved. However, the large-scale religious warfare that spread across Europe in the sixteenth and seventeenth centuries brought major setbacks, as with the brutal destruction of Magdeburg in 1631 during the Thirty Years' War.[26]

Common soldiers who fell into the enemy's hands during this period were still considered human booty, and in principle their captors could demand a ransom. However, families of average soldiers rarely had enough money for such payments. Many soldiers demanded contracts requiring the captain to pay the ransom in the event of their capture. In practice, it was almost impossible to assign captives to individuals as booty because armies and battles had become so much larger since the introduction of gunpowder weapons to European battlefields.[27] This dilemma was resolved only after armies and warfare came under stricter state control. By the end of the sixteenth century, belligerents on the state level began negotiating binding treaties that regulated ransom payments and prisoner-of-war exchanges.[28] Spain and the Netherlands signed the first such treaty in 1599. These agreements, called cartels, usually stipulated that prisoners of war be exchanged man for man, rank by rank. If that was not possible, the two sides tried to negotiate payments based on the soldiers' monthly pay or exchange rates between higher- and lower-ranking soldiers. Prisoners of war were commonly freed without ransom at the conclusion of peace.[29]

In this era, all sides in a conflict felt pressured to negotiate cartels as soon as possible after the outbreak of hostilities, or even before. Equipping and training soldiers was expensive, and few states could afford to leave their men idle in enemy hands or attend to prisoners of war. Every state and army had a vital interest in exchanging captured soldiers as swiftly as possible. As a result, cartels became routine in the seventeenth and eighteenth centuries. If no cartel existed or could be negotiated, armies released common soldiers on parole rather than keep them for an extended period. Often, captors tried to enlist their captives into their own forces.[30] Communities charged with housing large numbers of prisoners of war, even briefly, faced serious supply shortages. Moreover, the captives' pay, which was desperately needed to supplement the meager rations, did not arrive regularly. Housing was always a problem, and diseases spread quickly. Under such circumstances, armies treated prisoners of war most humanely by finding some way to release them from captivity as soon as possible. It could even be dangerous to keep them for extended periods. Captives slowed down faster-moving mounted forces and sometimes even provided secret support for the enemy. Not surprisingly, problems with negotiating cartels usually arose only when one party considered the enemy too weak to be a threat or when the end of the war was near.[31]

Under these circumstances, belligerents had a real interest in limiting casualties among their prisoners. They needed these men for cartels and exchanges, so wholesale massacres became rare. If a besieged city or garrison held out for too long and cost the attackers added casualties, however, or if a victorious army had a breakdown in order, defeated enemies could still face brutal treatment. The newly established constraints and standards for the treatment for prisoners of war were not yet applicable in wars fought against ethnically different, non-Christian enemies such as the Ottoman Empire. Those campaigns sometimes turned into outright wars of extermination. When conflicts among Christian states showed similar signs of brutality, as during the War of the League of Augsburg, contemporaries described them as "Turkish wars."[32]

While in enemy hands awaiting exchange, parole, or ransoming, prisoners of war expected to continue receiving their pay, as well as clothing, shoes, and blankets delivered by their unit, army, or state. To provide and organize this support, both sides usually exchanged agents. Because of delays and financial difficulties, however, help remained sporadic at best. Nevertheless, the mere promise of pay and clothing helped to maintain the prisoners' loyalty. During the Thirty Years' War, if a captured soldier's officers failed to support him or did not at least attempt to negotiate for his freedom, he considered himself released from his oath of allegiance and entitled to enter the service of another army. Recent research has shown, however, that mercenary soldiers of the sixteenth and seventeenth centuries switched sides much less often than the stereotype suggests. Common soldiers seem to have regarded their unit as a true home, a protective social sphere. When prisoners of war switched sides and joined enemy forces, it was mostly because serious supply problems left them no other choice and cartels could not be negotiated. Once the supply situation improved, many of those soldiers tried to run away from their new army and rejoin their old units.[33]

Around the mid-eighteenth century, Enlightenment thinkers fully disconnected the justness of a war from its conduct. Warfare, they believed, had to be humanized, whether or not it began as a legitimate conflict.[34] The basic "principles of humanity," Emer de Vattel, the most influential military theorist of the period, stated in 1758, dictated that "all . . . enemies thus subdued or disarmed" must be "spared."[35] At the same time, captured enemy soldiers could now be "secured" so that the "enemy may be weakened."[36] Prisoner-of-war treatment became an integral part of warfare. The number of exchange and ransom cartels declined as states became better at retaining large numbers of enemy soldiers for longer periods.[37] After weighing the advantages and disadvantages of exchange and confinement, states more often opted for confinement, forcing the other side to replace the captured soldiers with fresh troops and thus divert funds and energy from campaigns. Moreover, after 1775, as the era of limited Western warfare came to an end, small professional armies were replaced by large national armies, composed of soldiers who fought for ideology rather than money. Warfare escalated, in both quantity and quality, once again threatening the well-being of prisoners of war. Not surprisingly, it was at this time that the first attempts were made to codify the customary laws of war into written treaty law.[38]

Improved standards of treatment for prisoners of war in the nineteenth and twentieth centuries came at a steep price. Legal scholars began distinguishing between lawful combatants and illegal fighters. Lawful combatants had to be treated well in captivity and could not be subjected to cruel conditions. Such restrictions did not apply to soldiers who were considered illegal combatants, namely rebels and other insurgents. During the American and French Revolutions, the unclear distinction between legal and illegal combatants was especially problematic as many civilians were drawn into the fighting. In the eyes of Vattel and other eighteenth-century commentators, civilians in war deserved the same protection accorded to prisoners of war. During the revolutionary wars in North America and Europe, however, civilians were often suspected of supporting rebel or other insurgent forces, and therefore suffered considerable abuse. As the levels of protection were increased for captured soldiers, the number of other people who were entitled to such protection became smaller.[39]

North America

American Indian societies regularly engaged in violent conflicts, both before and after contact with Europeans. After the establishment of European colonies in North America during the seventeenth century, wars erupted frequently between the newcomers and the Natives, mainly over land. In the following decades, Old World wars usually also led to conflicts in North America because major European powers such as Spain, France, and England possessed colonial empires across the Atlantic Ocean. The greatest of these imperial struggles was the Seven Years' War, fought in North America from 1754 to 1763 between Great Britain and France and their respective American Indian and European allies.[40]

This conflict revealed two ways in which North American warfare differed from contemporary European conflicts. First, wars were fought on a much smaller scale in North America than in Europe. Neither the colonists nor their American Indian allies and enemies had the manpower, firepower, logistics, or finances to lead large armies into battle. Second, the wars that European colonists conducted against American Indians were often wars of annihilation or "a small-scale version of total war in the forests."[41] From the very start of their colonial endeavor in the seventeenth century, the English colonists drew heavily on the experience gained during wars of conquest in Ireland during the sixteenth century. There the English had exhibited a brutality only rarely seen among Europeans, even in the darkest days of religious warfare. In fact, many of the English colonial leaders had fought in Ireland before coming to North America. Enemies captured during such conflicts met death more often than captivity. After 1588, for example, the English collected, registered, and then systematically killed the survivors of the Spanish Armada who had landed on the Irish coast. They feared that the Spanish sailors and soldiers might incite a revolt.[42]

By the second half of the eighteenth century, warfare against American Indians in North America was "exacerbated by racism."[43] Constraints that had evolved among Christian states and standing armies in Europe over the previous centuries did not apply to fighting on North American frontiers. Apart from the English wars in Ireland, only the long conflict between the Habsburg and Ottoman Empires involved such brutality. White colonists in North America regularly denied American Indian opponents the status of comrades-in-arms. The killing of prisoners was not an exception but the rule.[44] The colonists justified such behavior by claiming that they were fighting for survival against savage opponents. Particularly in New England, Protestant colonists maintained that it was the close alliances between American Indians and the Catholic French that were preventing their benign and peaceful expansion into the continent. As in early modern continental Europe, control over the use of violence slipped away "on the margins," the frontier between French Canada and British North America.[45] Under such circumstances, only the captivity of white colonists and soldiers, whether they were part of a militia force or members of a regular army, conformed to the norms and customs of European warfare.

In the course of these many wars, American Indians discovered that their Old World allies and opponents were willing to pay sizable ransoms for Euro-American captives. Between the 1680s and the 1760s, Canadian and French colonists in New France frequently purchased such prisoners, dealing either directly with American Indian captors or with their own government. Canadian purchasers used these ransomed captives as laborers to replace their own busy militiamen. Once the former prisoners, now indentured servants, had worked off the sum that was paid for their release, New France officially exchanged them as prisoners of war with the English colonists. American Indians in the Northeast became closely linked to New France through this trade in captives. Because such agreements also understood prisoners of war as booty and assigned them a monetary value, they accorded with European traditions. Their form and rules, however, were distinctly American. No parallel system existed in European warfare. A high demand for labor, it seems, as well as fear and disdain of American Indian societies, made servitude appear preferable to captivity in Native hands. As Ian K. Steele and other historians have noted, three different military cultures were at play in North America: Indian, European, and colonial American.[46]

When the thirteen English colonies in North America went to war against their motherland in 1775, they faced the worrisome prospect that the king, Parliament, and His Majesty's armies might regard captured revolutionaries as mere rebels—that is, illegal combatants—and treat them just as brutally as they had treated the Irish, Scottish Highlanders, Jacobites, and American Indians before. To a degree, these worries were justified. The colonies had taken up arms against a perfectly legitimate and lawful sovereign. Frederick Mackenzie, a captain in the 23rd Foot, the Royal Welsh Fusiliers, was convinced that every American revolutionary who was kept alive after capture would only further fuel the rebellion. In his opinion, all American prisoners of war should be hanged.[47]

To avoid being mistaken for a rebel force, the revolutionaries in 1775 modeled their newly established Continental Army not so much on their own militia tradition as on the classic example of free citizens banding together to fight foreign invaders. In this way, they could present their military establishment—to their own population, but also to the British and a larger public in the colonies and Europe—as the opposite of a rebel army. However, the farmers, craftsmen, traders, and merchants who initially rallied to defend their homes against the British at Lexington and Concord in 1775, and then fought during the Siege of Boston, soon chose to stay home rather than fight. By late 1776, Congress had begun recruiting for a regular army, basing it on existing European models while continuing to emphasize how different in outlook and character it would be.[48]

General Washington knew that if his soldiers were to become fully accepted belligerents, they would not only have to stand up against British and German regulars but also demonstrate appropriate conduct on and off the battlefield. Both during and after battle, it was essential for the revolutionaries' actions toward their enemies to bolster the justness and legitimacy of the American cause. Through their conduct as soldiers and captors, the revolutionaries must present themselves not as mere "savages fighting from behind rail fences and tree stumps," waiting only to scalp the next enemy soldier, but rather as "inheritors" of a "civilized European tradition" who were asserting "their rights by the measured application of force."[49]

~

States and armies in this period usually sought to negotiate cartels for the exchange of captives as soon as possible, sometimes even before a war started.[50] But between 1776 and 1783, the British and Congress would repeatedly find themselves unable to reach an agreement for a general prisoner exchange. As a result, tens of thousands of prisoners of war on both sides remained in enemy hands for weeks, months, and even years at a time. With few detailed standards having yet been established for how prisoners of war should be treated, and with the costs and logistics of housing and feeding such large numbers of captives creating a particular burden for the revolutionaries, it soon became necessary to seek creative solutions. The German subsidy troops who had come to North America to help the British fight a war were also to play a part in changing the basic parameters of confinement for prisoners of war.

CHAPTER 5

Capture and Surrender

German soldiers from Hessen-Kassel, Hessen-Hanau, Braunschweig-Wolfenbüttel, Ansbach-Bayreuth, Waldeck, and Anhalt-Zerbst fought all over revolutionary North America: on land and sea, in large and small numbers, during major battles and small skirmishes. They were also taken prisoner in all of these areas and struggles—and by various belligerents, American, French, and Spanish. In 1776, Hessen-Kassel soldiers, the largest German contingent in British service, took part in the Battles of Long Island and White Plains in August and October, led the decisive attack on Fort Washington on November 16, pursued the Continental Army through New Jersey during the fall, and constituted the main target for Washington's surprise attack at Trenton on December 26. In 1777 and 1778, Hessen-Kassel soldiers marched in the Philadelphia campaign and assaulted Fort Redbank. After 1778, many Hessen-Kassel regiments served as garrison units, but the Regiments von Bose and Erbprinz, as well as the *Jäger*, struggled in the southern campaigns of Lieutenant Generals Sir Henry Clinton and Charles, Earl Cornwallis, until the surrender at Yorktown in 1781.[1]

Following an eight-week trip across the Atlantic in the spring and early summer of 1777, Ansbach-Bayreuth's soldiers immediately joined Lieutenant General William Howe's Philadelphia campaign. They fought alongside British soldiers during the Battles of Brandywine and Germantown on September 11 and October 4. In 1778 and 1779, Ansbach-Bayreuth infantrymen strengthened British defenses in Newport, Rhode Island, and played a vital role during the Battle of Rhode Island on August

29, 1778. Meanwhile, Ansbach-Bayreuth *Jäger* operated on Long Island and along the Hudson River. Indeed, these soldiers proved to be so valuable that the British requested further units from Margrave Karl Alexander. After returning to New York from Rhode Island, the two Ansbach-Bayreuth regiments stayed in garrison before joining Cornwallis in Virginia by 1781. Together with some of their *Jäger*, they met the same fate as so many other British and German units at Yorktown on October 19, 1781.[2] Approximately 5,500 Braunschweig-Wolfenbüttel, Hessen-Hanau, and Anhalt-Zerbst soldiers saw service in Canada. Braunschweig-Wolfenbüttel and Hessen-Hanau units formed about half of Lieutenant General John Burgoyne's invasion force that was defeated at Saratoga on October 17, 1777.[3] Waldeck soldiers had probably the most foreign and distant area of operations among all German auxiliary units during this conflict. From 1779 to 1781, they were stationed in British West Florida. During battles and sieges at Fort Bute, Baton Rouge, Lake Pontchartrain, Fort Charlotte on Mobile Bay, and Pensacola, the Spanish took most of the Waldeck men prisoner.

Like every soldier of every rank in every conflict before and after the American Revolution, common German soldiers between 1776 and 1783 became prisoners of war by either capture (overpowered in combat) or surrender (submission to the enemy). Surrender differs from capture in that some kind of negotiation usually preceded the process, ranging from a simple exchange of words on the battlefield to elaborate day-, week-, or month-long diplomatic encounters between commanders and their envoys. The capture or surrender of one side ended violence for both sides and allowed everybody to make it through the fighting alive. If one side was unwilling to give up, even if the tactical or operational situation was hopeless, the superior force had to continue its attacks and sustain additional casualties. Such acts of unnecessary resistance, particularly during siege warfare, were considered unacceptable behavior in Western warfare and could be punished by indiscriminate killings and plundering. Soldiers on the verge of defeat who were contemplating surrender nevertheless had to be convinced that their submission would be accepted and that they would not be killed or otherwise mistreated after giving up resistance.[4]

The moment of capture or surrender was always potentially dangerous. Soldiers were at their most vulnerable when they lowered their arms and signaled capitulation to the enemy. They had to place enormous trust in the victors, relying on only a vague promise: Stop fighting and we will stop killing you.[5] Victors, on the other hand, struck such bargains only if they were convinced that the enemy also meant it. But what if something went wrong? What if one side did not keep its promise? Who or what guaranteed that the victors would not simply slaughter their now-defenseless enemies? History is full of examples where surrender or capture did not work, where a mutual understanding could not be established, resulting in atrocities. "In battle," as John Lynn puts it, "armed opponents face each other, dealing out deadly violence with a justice born of self-defense—kill or be killed." After the battle, the situation is different. Atrocities are "the province of the strong against the defenseless, of the armed against the unarmed," and their victims are usually on the "peripheries of combat": unarmed civilians, wounded fighters—or prisoners of war.[6]

In two of the most infamous massacres committed during the American War of Independence, the process of ending the fighting went horribly wrong. On May 29, 1780, 270 men from Lieutenant Colonel Banastre Tarleton's British Legion attacked about 340 Virginia Continentals under Colonel Abraham Buford in the Waxhaws, near present-day Buford, South Carolina. Buford ordered his soldiers to repulse the charging British Legion with a single volley from his entire front, but the maneuver failed. Tarleton's mounted men quickly broke into Buford's line, slashing the Continentals with their sabers. The revolutionaries' resistance ended instantly—but the killing did not. According to several accounts, the Virginians repeatedly begged for quarter, but Tarleton and his men continued the slaughter. Between 1775 and 1783, 6 or 7 percent of soldiers were normally killed in a battle. At the Waxhaws, 75 percent of Buford's men died. "Tarleton's quarter" remained notorious for the remainder of the war.[7]

A few months later, on King's Mountain, near present-day Blackburn, South Carolina, about 1,800 American partisans under command of Colonel William Campbell of Virginia surrounded a loyalist force of about 1,100 men under Major Patrick

Ferguson. Charging up the hill on October 7, 1780, shooting from the cover of trees, stumps, and rocks, revolutionary militia overpowered the loyalists after an hour-long fight, killing Ferguson, the only regular officer on the scene. Sensing that the battle was lost after their commander's death, the loyalists tried to surrender by raising white flags—only to have the flags' bearers immediately shot down by Campbell's men. When more white flags went up, their bearers again were shot.[8] The loyalists were not allowed to surrender and survive the struggle. One of the revolutionary leaders, Colonel Isaac Shelby, later admitted that it was "some time before a complete cessation of the firing on our part could be effected."[9] When the carnage finally ended, 319 loyalists lay dead and wounded on the battlefield. Campbell's force had only lost 90 men. But this was not even the final act of the drama. The surviving loyalists from King's Mountain, about 700 men, were instantly stripped of their valuables and marched to Gilbert Town, about forty miles away. During that march, the captives were badly abused; a number of them were killed. Campbell had to order that "the disorderly manner of slaughtering . . . the prisoners" be stopped.[10] In Gilbert Town, a show trial sentenced thirty-six of the captured loyalists to death. Only after nine men were already executed, hanged from the same tree, did officers finally put an end to the killings.[11]

Capture

American forces under Brigadier General John Stark and Colonel Seth Warner captured a large group of German soldiers on August 16, 1777, when they attacked a British raiding party of about 800 Braunschweig-Wolfenbüttel dragoons, Canadians, and some loyalists under command of Lieutenant Colonel Friedrich Baum, roughly five miles from Bennington, Vermont. Burgoyne had sent Baum's men to seize horses and supplies for his struggling army. A German surgeon, Julius Friedrich Wasmus, later recounted the events in his journal: "the enemy came rushing over our entrenchment and quickly took aim and fired at me." Wasmus took cover behind a tree while the bullets whistled "over and beyond" him. He stayed there, "lying on the ground," until revolutionary soldiers "urged me rather impolitely to get up." One grabbed Wasmus by the arm; another one threatened to kill him, placing "the bayonet of his gun with tightened trigger" on Wasmus's chest. Fearing for his life, Wasmus told the soldier that he was a "Braunschweig surgeon," then shook hands with his opponent and called him "friend and brother." To his relief, the American apparently understood his pleading and withdrew the gun. However, this revolutionary soldier now took an interest in Wasmus's watch: he "looked at it, held it to his ear and put it [in his pocket]." Another soldier took Wasmus's purse, while a third searched the surgeon's pockets.[12] These comments show just how perilous the moment of capture was. With a bayonet and a cocked musket pointed at Wasmus's chest, a careless word or misinterpreted gesture could have led to his immediate death. Having lost only a few valuables and some money, Wasmus was much relieved when he made it through these tense moments alive and unhurt, along with 358 common German soldiers. (See table 5 for these numbers, as well as figures from Trenton, Saratoga, the *Molly* and *Triton*, Baton Rouge, and Yorktown.)

Capture awaited common German soldiers not only on land but also on sea. In September 1779, the Regiment von Knyphausen was ordered to Canada as garrison troops. The men boarded two British transports in New York, the *Molly* and the *Triton*. Shortly after they left the harbor, a storm scattered the entire transport fleet and badly damaged the ships. The *Triton* lost its masts, anchors, and cannons and drifted helpless in the ocean. The seamen could complete only makeshift repairs, and the ship barely managed to reach Delaware Bay. There it became easy prey for two American privateers, the *Mars* and the *Comet*. Within days, the German soldiers were marched into Philadelphia's Walnut Street Jail as prisoners of war. There they met fellow soldiers from the *Molly*, who had also been captured by privateers. At least these roughly 350 men had survived.[13] Many soldiers from the Regiment von Loßberg, originally ordered to Canada together with the Regiment von Knyphausen, drowned when their transport, the *Adamant*, sank in the same storm.[14]

These German soldiers became prisoners of war through capture, not surrender. Often, however, it is difficult to draw a neat

Table 5.   Common German Soldiers Taken Prisoner of War

Battle/Siege	Numbers[a]
Trenton, 1776	848
Bennington, 1777	358
Saratoga, 1777	2,022
Molly and *Triton*, 1779	314
Baton Rouge, 1779	206
Yorktown, 1781	1,712
Total	5,460

[a] See the appendix for a detailed explanation of these numbers and their accuracy.

distinction. During the same battle or siege, some soldiers and units may have become prisoners of war after a negotiated—informal or not, written or not—surrender, while others were captured or escaped. During the Battle of Trenton on December 26, 1776, about 350 of Rall's soldiers successfully fled the battlefield while the Regiments Rall and von Loßberg rallied around Colonel Rall for two counterattacks. Only after those attempts had failed and Rall had fallen wounded did the Hessen-Kassel soldiers in these two units accept defeat. At this point, it seems, some surrender negotiations took place between General Washington's Continentals and the German units. One of Washington's aides, probably George Baylor, apparently rode over to the Hessians and spoke briefly with Lieutenant Colonel Franziskus Scheffer and Major Matthäus, now the two regiments' highest-ranking officers. While this exchange was going on, some nearby revolutionary soldiers from Nicholas Hausegger's Pennsylvania Regiment, consisting mostly of German immigrants, shouted to the Hessen-Kassel troops in both English and German, urging them to give up. We do not know the exact outcome of these negotiations, but something must have been decided, because both German units subsequently lowered their colors and grounded their weapons on the spot.[15]

The Regiment von Knyphausen, meanwhile, had been unable to join the other two regiments from Rall's brigade in their counterattacks. The unit had attempted to conduct an orderly retreat across the bridge over Assunpink Creek, only to discover that revolutionary soldiers had seized it earlier in the battle. The regiment then tried to cross the creek at a nearby ford, finding it occupied as well. They now came under heavy fire from across the creek, from behind, and even from revolutionaries rushing toward them through Trenton: they were trapped. Moreover, their commanding officer, Major von Dechow, received a fatal wound to the hip. Seeing no way to escape, the soldiers gave up and were taken prisoner—without any prior negotiations.[16] Like the men on Staten Island, at Bennington, and on the *Molly* and *Triton*, they were overpowered in battle and had to place their fate in the enemy's hands. They could only hope that they would not be massacred or attacked like the Continentals at the Waxhaws or the loyalists on King's Mountain.

We know from Johannes Reuber's account that the Trenton prisoners were not killed, but their treatment immediately after the battle was not reassuring. After being hurried across the icy Delaware River, they were thrown into a makeshift prison in Newtown before being paraded through Philadelphia. For the revolutionaries, the victory at Trenton meant more than relief from the constant British pressure. It was a manifestation of their endurance in the conflict. On December 29, 1776, General Howe reported to Lord Germain that "the Rebels will no doubt be much elated by their Success."[17]

Before Trenton, the British and their German auxiliaries had had the upper hand in the war. Over the course of the summer and fall of 1776, the revolutionaries had lost New York City and Fort Washington. In November, George Washington's remaining soldiers had barely escaped across the Hudson River into New Jersey. The weeks leading up to the Battle of Trenton had seen the Continental Army's continuous retreat through New Jersey, all the way across the Delaware River and into Pennsylvania. Fearing that the British would soon invade, Congress had fled the city, as had many citizens.[18] After the revolutionaries' surprising success at Trenton, George Clymer, a member of the Executive Committee of the Continental Congress in Philadelphia, reported triumphantly to John Hancock, the president of Congress, that the British were now "panic-struck."[19] In Hessen-Kassel, however, Friedrich II was so furious about the defeat that he immediately recalled his commander in North America, General Leopold von Heister.[20]

Washington was not yet finished. On December 30, his troops crossed the Delaware again to attack more British garrisons in New Jersey. However, the British had reacted more decisively to the Continentals' first crossing than he had anticipated. Cornwallis had been hurrying toward Trenton with a large contingent of troops, and he arrived around New Year's Day. In order to march deeper into New Jersey, Washington's men had to swing boldly behind these British forces. This daring maneuver also succeeded, and his men were able to attack the British garrison in Princeton on January 3, 1777. An enraged Cornwallis turned his men around at Trenton and tried to catch the Continentals in Princeton. But Washington's men had seen enough fighting, chasing, and maneuvering in the cold New Jersey winter. They marched toward Morristown to settle into winter quarters.[21]

With so many Hessen-Kassel prisoners in their hands after Trenton, Washington and the Continental Army had a great opportunity to showcase their resolve and determination. They realized that these captured German soldiers, who had once looked so invincible and seemingly routed the revolutionaries at will, could be used to boost morale and persuade doubters to join their cause.[22] By displaying and humiliating their captives, they could give everyone in Philadelphia a chance to see, touch, and insult the foreigners who had attacked their homes and their liberty. The troops who had ravaged New York and New Jersey during the British offensives of 1776 were now a target of derision.[23] Moreover, the prisoner parade forced opponents of the revolution to acknowledge that it was not a weak assemblage of a few rebels who were fighting the British Empire, but a strong and united force. As Christopher Marshall, a leading Pennsylvania revolutionary, reported from Philadelphia, "the Hessian prisoners, to the amount of nine hundred, arrived in this City, and made a . . . despicable appearance."[24] Even more jubilantly, the Executive Committee of Congress proclaimed their "pleasure" at having seen the "Hessian prisoners paraded in Front Street." The captured enemies had "formed a line two deep up and down Front Street from Market to Walnut Street, and most people seemed very angry they should ever think of running away from such a set of vagabonds." At the same time, however, the Executive Committee ordered that "both the officers and men" among the Hessians "should be well treated."[25]

At first glance, the Executive Committee's instructions seem contradictory to the original goal of strengthening revolutionary morale by parading and humiliating the captives. Yet in the larger context of congressional policies enacted in August 1776, when the first German auxiliaries had set foot on North American soil, it made sense. At that time, Congress had appointed a committee "to devise a plan for encouraging the Hessians, and other foreigners, employed by the king of Great Britain, and sent to America . . . to quit that iniquitous service." The idea was that such troops would gladly accept "lands, liberty, safety and a communion of good laws, and mild government, in a country where many of their friends and relations are already happily settled." Congress would provide "50 acres of unappropriated land" for each German deserter, "to be held by him and his heirs in absolute property."[26] These offers were printed on handbills in large numbers and distributed among the German soldiers. Washington was convinced that they would induce many subsidy troops to desert from the British.[27]

Humiliating and threatening the prime targets for what was essentially a propaganda campaign was risky. The parade in Philadelphia risked alienating the Hessen-Kassel captives so that they would no longer consider deserting. Washington realized this problem on December 29, 1776, one day before the scheduled prisoner parade. In a letter, he told the Pennsylvania Council of Safety that the Hessen-Kassel prisoners should be treated well after the parade and have "such principles instilled into them during their Confinement" that upon their return, "they may open the Eyes of their Countrymen."[28]

The Pennsylvania Council of Safety followed these suggestions closely. On December 31, the local citizens were told that Washington had "recommended . . . to provide suitable Quarters for [the prisoners] and it is his earnest wish that they may be well treated." Philadelphians were reminded that "these miserable creatures now justly excite our compassion—They have no Enmity with us." It was "Britain alone" that had to be fought. Echoing earlier opinions in Congress, the council stressed that these soldiers had arrived in North America only "according to the arbitrary customs of the tyrannical German princes." They had been "dragged from their native Country and sold to a foreign Monarch." Their capture, in other words, was a rescue "from the authority of the British Officers."[29] In the eyes of the American revolutionaries, captivity offered the German auxiliaries a chance to free themselves from princely tyranny and despotism.[30]

Surrender

Not every battle and siege during the American War of Independence ended with a mix of capture and surrender or led to rough treatment of new captives during prisoner parades; nor do we see frightened soldiers stripped of their valuables at gunpoint, show trials, or even massacres. Instead, we read about detailed negotiations between the two sides, followed by impressive and solemn surrender ceremonies. From Saratoga, where Burgoyne and his invading British-German army capitulated to American forces under Major General Horatio Gates on October 17, 1777, an anonymous Hessen-Hanau grenadier reported that the defeated soldiers marched out of their entrenchments "with all honors and the band playing."[31] This soldier understood that he had fallen into the hands of the enemy, but he was not subjected to moments of danger such as those experienced by Wasmus at Bennington, or by Reuber and Kappes after the Battle of Trenton. To the contrary, everyone at Saratoga moved carefully and according to well-planned steps. Nobody was belittled, threatened, or attacked.

Following the Siege of Yorktown on October 19, 1781, which marked the revolutionaries' victory in the war, the vanquished British and German soldiers were taken captive in an impressive ceremony. Johann Conrad Döhla recalled the momentous day: "all troops with all their belongings and weapons marched out of the entrenchments and the camp with cased flags but to the sound of drums and fifers." The entire army of the American and French victors stood *en parade* while the vanquished passed through. Next, the British and German soldiers arrived "at a flat place, or a large field, on which a squadron of French Hussars had formed a circle," where one defeated regiment after another grounded its arms. The men then marched "silently" back to their camp through both enemy armies. For Döhla, "all courage and determination, which usually enliven a soldier, were lost."[32] As at Saratoga, the British and German soldiers at Yorktown marched out of their camp in procession, passed their conquerors, and laid down their weapons, emerging from this ceremony as new prisoners of war. Defeated soldiers such as Döhla were emotional, but unlike Reuber and his fellow Hessen-Kassel soldiers after Trenton, they do not appear to have been terrified or even nervous.

These are common examples in a period dominated by sieges in Western warfare. Terms of capitulation regularly detailed how the defeated soldiers were to march out of their camp, garrison, or city. There are literally hundreds of examples of such ceremonies. At times, the agreements even stipulated exactly how many yards away from a particular camp the capitulating troops were to ground their arms.[33] Field battles, on the other hand, frequently resulted in relatively low numbers of enemy captives. Such fights usually ended when one side's line broke and ran away, often without being pursued by the victors.[34]

The pageantry of ceremonies such as those at Saratoga and Yorktown might be seen as exemplifying the honors of war, a code of conduct derived from knightly warfare in the Middle Ages that called on lawful belligerents to approach each other with respect before, during, and after battle.[35] These rules also accorded with the contemporary predilection for pageantry and display of courtly manners.[36] However, the few cited examples from the American War of Independence alone show that more was involved than the honors of war due a defeated army. Merely pointing to honorable surrender, for instance, does nothing to explain why the ceremonies were staged in the first place. Victors could simply have taken their captives away after the battle and successful surrender negotiations and still treated the enemy correctly. The comments by Reuber, the anonymous Hessen-Hanau soldier, and Döhla, moreover, demonstrate that we cannot focus solely on the belligerents' leadership when analyzing surrender. Common soldiers were obviously deeply involved in and affected by the events. Surrender must also be understood as more than an unfortunate end to an unsuccessful campaign. It represented the beginning of a new phase in a soldier's life: captivity. Finally, the honors of war do not explain why the revolutionaries staged complex ceremonies at Saratoga and Yorktown but a very different display of prisoners after Trenton.

Surrender rather needs to be studied as a ritual, meant to organize and make comprehensible for everybody what had happened on the battlefield.[37] For common soldiers, in particular, a surrender was ideally enacted as a rite of passage, marking their safe and respectable transition from armed soldiers to unarmed prisoners of war and reassuring them about their fate in enemy hands. At Saratoga and Yorktown, common soldiers were able to avoid the kind of dangerous and potentially deadly situations experienced by Wasmus at Bennington, the Continentals at the Waxhaws, and the loyalists on King's Mountain. If there were no such rites of passage, as was the case after Trenton, defeated soldiers became anxious. The parade in Philadelphia—also a ritual performance, but one with a very different form and meaning—left the captives fearful about their future.

Surrender ceremonies enacted as rites of passage were also a powerful tool for the winning side, turning enemy prisoners into symbolic capital and giving the victors an opportunity to demonstrate and communicate their success within their own ranks as well as to a wider public.[38] Because of their legitimizing power, rituals are especially important for revolutionary forces in society. By communicating their messages through the old order's rituals, revolutionaries assume new authority in a contested social, cultural, and political sphere.[39] In other words, enacting proper rites of passages after a victory allowed the revolutionaries to present themselves as legitimate belligerents. Moreover, in the absence of fixed, written, and enforceable laws of war, only the observance of rigidly structured rituals guaranteed a successful surrender and ended the bloodshed for both sides.

The surrender ceremony at Saratoga was held on October 17, 1777, marking the end of a British campaign that had been hampered from the outset by unexpectedly strong American resistance, forbidding terrain, and numerous strategic and tactical mistakes by British commanders.[40] The original plan was to send Burgoyne with his army south from Canada toward Albany. From New York, Howe was to march north with his troops to meet up with Burgoyne. From the west, Lieutenant Colonel Barrimore St. Leger planned a divisionary offensive through the Mohawk Valley. Thus, New England would be cut off from the other nine revolutionary colonies. All of these plans failed. St. Leger unsuccessfully besieged Fort Stanwix in August. Howe did not turn north after leaving New York but moved instead toward Philadelphia. By October, Burgoyne had lost the strong detachment at Bennington, and his logistical situation became increasingly dire. Wrecking roads as they went, revolutionary forces delayed the British for weeks and seriously threatened overstretched British supply lines. While the Battle of Freeman's Farm on September 19 could be considered a draw, the Battle of Bemis Heights on October 7 was an all-out revolutionary victory. By now it was obvious that Burgoyne's British and German soldiers could no longer fight their way to Albany. Large revolutionary militia forces flocked to the scene from all directions—Gates had about 13,000 regulars and militia under his command—and surrounded Burgoyne's troops. After several councils of war, Burgoyne decided to capitulate on October 17. With him, about 2,000 common German soldiers laid down their arms.[41] When Burgoyne's invasion from Canada was stopped, it not only foiled British plans to end the Revolutionary War that year, but also led to the important French-American Alliance of 1778. Nevertheless, the surrender at Saratoga was called a convention rather than a capitulation, and it sent Burgoyne's army on parole to Boston, as the so-called Convention Army, there to board ships bound for Europe.[42]

According to the regimental journal of Colonel Johann Friedrich von Specht of Braunschweig-Wolfenbüttel, the vanquished German troops at Saratoga left their entrenchments in the morning and "stacked their muskets together" on a nearby field around three o'clock in the afternoon.[43] Next, the British and German units marched through the Fishkill "and passed the camp of the

Americans where all . . . regiments had moved out and stood under arms." Although few of the revolutionary soldiers were "properly attired," they stood "straight and in orderly lines." Particularly impressive, "there was absolute silence in those regiments as can only be demanded from the best-disciplined troops."[44] On this occasion, the American revolutionaries were more than able to live up to the expectations of European regular officers.

The British and German soldiers at Saratoga surrendered in three precise steps: they marched out of their camp, grounded their arms on a specially designated field, and then marched past the American victors as new prisoners of war. This ceremony was clearly a rite of passage as defined by Arnold van Gennep and Victor Turner. The vanquished soldiers underwent a rite of separation in leaving behind their previous status in society as armed fighters. They then exercised a rite of transition by grounding their weapons on the field. After a brief liminal phase between their old status as armed fighters and their new status as unarmed captives, they marched past the American victors in a rite of incorporation, as they were received in society as prisoners of war.[45] These rites of passage clarified the various changes in status and command for both sides and all ranks, including the camp followers. In enacting the ritual, the British and German soldiers at Saratoga performed their defeat with their own legs, hands, eyes, and ears. This act was even more important for those among them who had not witnessed the decisive action that led to their defeat—because they had either fought away from the center of action or served in a company that was not engaged at that point.[46] Some may have heard about their defeat only from other units or by receiving orders regarding the outcome of the struggle. The rites of passage allowed them to experience and comprehend their defeat firsthand, with all their senses. On their way into captivity, as Specht also noted, the British and German soldiers even crossed a river, a classic boundary that brought the change in social position even more within their experience.[47] The emotional power of this ritual figures prominently in accounts such as that of Lieutenant William Digby, who recalled that the drums that day appeared "to have lost their former inspiring sounds." A "Grenadiers' March" was played, "seem[ing] by its last feeble effort, as if almost ashamed to be heard on such an occasion." Digby was disappointed, and "tears (though unmanly) forced their way."[48]

Some details of these rituals, however, require further comment. Johann Bense, a Braunschweig-Wolfenbüttel grenadier, wrote, "Today, we were surrendered under a convention to the Americans, stacked our muskets together on order of our own officers, and began the march toward Boston."[49] He was not the only one to describe a surrender in which it was not the American victors but rather the defeated soldiers' own officers who oversaw the grounding of their arms. An anonymous Braunschweig-Wolfenbüttel soldier wrote, "Counter to the usual practice, no enemy even came close."[50] Because of this structure, the rites of passage at Saratoga were less powerful in announcing and performing a revolutionary victory. The British and German soldiers' march past the revolutionaries after laying down their arms took precedence over the preliminary ceremony on the field, where not a single revolutionary officer or soldier was present. The process of transforming armed British and German soldiers into unarmed prisoners of war remained physically and symbolically concealed from the victors. Instead of placing the emphasis on the final acknowledgment of defeat by the vanquished (and the corresponding victory of the revolutionaries), the rites of passage performed at Saratoga gave priority to the rites of incorporation of the former British and German soldiers into society as prisoners of war.[51] It might even be said that because the German and British soldiers did not lay down their arms in the presence of the revolutionary victors, the rituals at Saratoga did not correspond to the events on the battlefield, where the revolutionaries had won a clear-cut victory and the British and Germans had suffered a complete defeat.

These rituals were the outcome of a telling exchange between Burgoyne and Gates regarding the exact way in which the defeated soldiers were to ground their arms.[52] Their negotiations constituted a striking power struggle. On October 14, Gates proposed that "the Troops under . . . Gen. Burgoyne's Command may be drawn up in their Encampment when they will be ordered to ground their Arms and may thereupon be marched to the River

Side." Burgoyne replied harshly: "this Article [was] inadmissible in an Extremity. Sooner than this Army will consent to ground their Arms in their Encampment, they will rush on the Enemy determined to take no Quarter."[53] The British commander got his way. Instead of risking a further delay—some intelligence suggested that a British relief army was approaching—Gates accepted Burgoyne's demands and allowed the British and German soldiers to march out to "the Verge of the River where . . . the Arms and Artillery are to be left, the Arms to be piled by Word of Command from their own Officers."[54]

For some historians, these negotiations show that Gates initially tried to force an unconditional surrender on Burgoyne or was overly concerned about a possible British relief army.[55] From a ritual perspective, however, it might be suggested that both commanders were very much aware that the form of the surrender would strongly affect their soldiers and carry great meaning for them. Gates attempted at first to diminish the rites of separation (the march to the field) into virtual nonexistence (the grounding of arms in camp). That would have rendered the British and German soldiers' rites of passage incomplete, which was unacceptable to Burgoyne. In turn, Burgoyne proposed rites that would be particularly advantageous for his own troops (grounding arms out of sight of the American victors). Once Gates gave in and accepted Burgoyne's suggestions, the revolutionary commander had effectively lost the struggle over the powerful meaning and performance of the rituals. The surrender at Saratoga allowed the vanquished soldiers to march away from the site of their capture without actually feeling defeated, and it denied the victors the full experience of a vital military success.[56]

At Yorktown, Washington did not repeat Gates's mistakes. The capitulation signed by Cornwallis did not offer parole to the defeated soldiers but declared that all British and German soldiers would "surrender themselves Prisoners of War to the combined forces of America and France. The Land Troops to remain prisoners to the United States. The Navy to the Naval Army of His Most Christian Majesty."[57] About 1,700 of the vanquished British troops were from German auxiliary units.[58] This siege ended a British campaign that had begun in 1778 with considerable success. Even if the northern colonies were lost, Clinton in New York and Germain in London had decided, the rich southern provinces could still be saved for the crown.[59] In February 1780, Clinton took Charleston, South Carolina, and forced roughly 5,000 Continentals and militia under Major General Benjamin Lincoln to surrender. In June 1780, after Cornwallis had taken command of the British troops, the hero of Saratoga, General Gates, met a catastrophic defeat at Camden. Fierce fighting subsequently erupted in the southern states as the new American commander of the Department of the South, Major General Nathaniel Greene, began striking back at the British. Cornwallis reasoned that only an invasion of Virginia could finally bring the revolutionaries to terms. At Petersburg in May 1781, he united with other British forces under Brigadier General Benedict Arnold and eventually moved his army to Yorktown, to set up a base of operations for campaigns in the Old Dominion.[60] There he encountered experienced American forces commanded by Major General Marie-Joseph Gilbert du Motier, Marquis de Lafayette, and new Continental recruits under Major General Friedrich Wilhelm, Baron von Steuben, which made further operations difficult.[61]

Far to the north, in Rhode Island, a French expeditionary army under General Rochambeau had landed in the summer of 1780. Initially, Washington wanted to attack the British in New York together with Rochambeau's men. He changed his plans, however, when he heard that Cornwallis had moved his army into Virginia and was occupied with Lafayette's and Steuben's Continentals. In a stunning land-sea operation, Washington and Rochambeau marched their troops onto the Virginia peninsula after August 14, 1781. On September 5, the French fleet of Rear Admiral François-Joseph, Comte de Grasse, defeated Rear Admiral Sir Thomas Graves's British ships in the Battle of the Chesapeake, which allowed the combined American and French forces to lay siege to Cornwallis in Yorktown by September 28.[62]

The investment of Yorktown was "performed by the book, by the maxims and rules that had remained standard since the days of Vauban."[63] Approximately 5,700 Continentals, 3,200 militiamen, and 7,800 French troops equipped with about 100 siege guns stood against roughly 7,000 British and German forces, who did their best to build good entrenchments around Yorktown and Gloucester Point across the York River. As Ansbach-Bayreuth lieutenant Döhlemann reported, their efforts were often hampered because they could not find a stone in this sandy soil "within a radius of two or three hundred miles."[64] The French and revolutionary troops constructed the first parallel about 600 yards away from Cornwallis's fieldworks, and on October 7, the days of open trenches began. With their drums beating and colors flying, the allies entered the first parallel and planted their banners on the parapet. On October 11, they had already completed a second parallel, about 300 yards away from Cornwallis's fieldworks. On October 14, a small allied storming party overran two important British redoubts. Cornwallis saw that his army had no chance for escape or relief. On October 17, he sent a flag of truce to Washington and asked for the cessation "of Hostilities for twenty four hours . . . to settle terms for the surrender of . . . York and Gloucester."[65]

From Döhla's account, it is obvious that the rituals enacted on the day of the British and German surrender at Yorktown also constituted rites of passage. First, the vanquished soldiers marched out of the town and passed the American and French victors lining the road. Second, they grounded their arms on a specially designated and prepared field. Third, they marched back into their camp as new prisoners of war (figure 3). Unlike the men at Saratoga, however, the defeated British and German soldiers at Yorktown had to lay down their arms under the scrutiny of the enemy's officers. Every defeated soldier understood and performed his defeat in a ritual that focused on turning armed fighters into unarmed prisoners of war and celebrating a French-American victory. Yet during this process, noted James Thacher, a physician in the Continental Corps of Light Infantry, many of the British and German soldiers did not just ground their weapons, as required, but "manifested a sullen temper, throwing their arms on the pile with violence, as if determined to render them useless."[66] This act was thus part of a power struggle within the ritual. By denying the victorious revolutionary and French soldiers the opportunity

Figure 3.   The Surrender of Yorktown, 1781

Detail of Louis Nicolas van Blarenberghe's *The Surrender of Yorktown* (1785), depicting the field on which British and German troops grounded their arms on October 19, 1781. Gianni Dagli Orti / The Art Archive at Art Resource, NY.

to use those muskets in the future, the defeated soldiers took an active role in constructing and redefining the power relationship between their military communities and their captors.[67]

The rites of passage eased the captives' transition through the precarious moments of insecurity following the battle. By performing the chess-like moves of this ritual, the defeated soldiers gained assurance that they would not be killed immediately after leaving the relative security of their camp in the city. And they did not approach the victors unarmed or humiliated: the vanquished soldiers marched out of Yorktown with their weapons in hand. Although they were surrounded by their captors, they at least felt that they could still defend themselves. In the days of the matchlock musket, it was even common for surrendering troops to march out of camp with their muskets loaded, musket balls in their mouths and matches lit, ready to fire at a moment's notice.[68]

If two belligerents could not understand each other's language of rituals, such proceedings could go horribly wrong. A prominent example is the famous "massacre" at Fort William Henry on August 9, 1757. There, according to the terms of capitulation agreed to between the French victors and the vanquished British garrison, the surrendering British regulars and provincials were allowed to march out of the fort unharmed, with safe passage to Fort Edward. The Indian allies of the French, however, did not understand these strange "European conventions of war and military professionalism" and instead wanted to take the spoils of war—prisoners and booty—that had been denied them by the agreement. Once the British had left Fort William Henry, the Indians rushed into the buildings seeking anything of value. Finding nothing—the British had been allowed "to retain their personal effects"—the Indians began to attack the seventy or so wounded and sick men left behind, acquiring some scalps and, in their understanding of proper warfare and victory in battle, thereby avenging the French betrayal in allowing the British to leave unharmed. The next morning, the British, who had spent the night in an entrenched camp away from the fort, started their escorted march toward Fort Edward. France's Indian allies were still not satisfied, and they assaulted the rear of the British column, killing and scalping as many soldiers as they could lay their hands on.[69]

The power of a successful ritual for the victors is revealed in comments by Private Joseph Plumb Martin from the Continental Corps of Miners and Sappers, who was present for the surrender at Yorktown. Rites of passage allowed Martin and his fellow soldiers to demonstrate their strength and make their success visible and tangible. On the day of the surrender, the revolutionary troops were ordered to clear the road where the British and German troops would march out. They then had to clean their uniforms and get everything "in order for this grand exhibition." They lined up beside the road, waiting for the defeated troops to leave Yorktown. After several hours, the British and Germans finally appeared, "all armed, with bayonets fixed, drums beating, and faces lengthening." It was "a noble sight" for Martin and his fellow soldiers. The defeated enemies "marched to the place appointed and stacked their arms," then "returned to the town in the same manner they had marched out, except being divested of their arms." Martin emphasized the revolutionary soldiers' preparations for the ritual, the long hours of waiting on the road, and his satisfaction upon seeing the surrendering British and German soldiers. Most importantly, he got to see the enemy march past him twice: once as defeated but armed fighters, a second time as unarmed prisoners of war. By observing these ancient rites so diligently, the revolutionaries established themselves as legitimate belligerents. By preparing and staging proper rites of passage, they showed the world that they were not an assemblage of lawless rebels but a civilized people who knew how to behave correctly in war.[70]

As the organization of the rites of passage at Yorktown shows, the American revolutionaries and their French allies used those rituals not only to guide the vanquished from one position in society to another and to celebrate their own victory, but also in subtle retaliation for the surrender of Charleston to General Clinton in 1780.[71] The British had not allowed the revolutionaries to march out of the city with colors flying and drums beating. In turn, General Washington imposed the same terms of capitulation on the British and German soldiers at Yorktown: they had to march out of that city with their colors cased and—this was particularly humiliating—with their drums beating a British or German march. Customarily, a surrendering garrison would march out with drums beating an enemy's march, meant to show respect for the opposing force. To order a garrison to march out beating one of their own marches (and with flags furled) was considered insulting.[72] Furthermore, the officer presiding over the laying down of arms at Yorktown was the same General Lincoln who had surrendered to the British at Charleston. According to one witness, the surrender at Yorktown must have been "a very interesting and gratifying transaction" for Lincoln, "having himself been obliged to surrender an army to a haughty foe last year."[73]

As at Saratoga, these acts were the result of detailed negotiations preceding the surrender. The exchanges between Washington and Cornwallis clearly show the revolutionary leader's desire to use the surrender as an explicit visualization of an all-out victory. After Cornwallis asked Washington for terms on October 17, 1781, Washington wrote that he would gladly listen to the British commander's suggestions. Cornwallis then proposed "that the Garrisons of York and Gloucester shall be Prisoners of War with the customary honours, and, for the convenience of the individuals which [he has] the honour to command, that the British shall be sent to Britain, & and the Germans to Germany" on parole. Unlike Gates in 1777, however, Washington replied that such terms were unacceptable. Instead, "the Garrisons of York and Gloucester, including the Seamen . . . shall be received prisoners of War [and] marched to such parts of the Country as can most conveniently provide for their Subsistence, and the benevolent treatment of prisoners." He stated explicitly that the "same honors will be granted to the Surrendering Army as were granted to the Garrison of Charleston." Cornwallis now grudgingly agreed "upon a treaty of Capitulation" without "annexing the condition of their [i.e., the British and German soldiers] being sent to Europe."[74]

Washington even made sure to provide Congress and the American public with a visual representation of the victory. He sent to Philadelphia the twenty-four British and German standards captured at Yorktown as a symbol of revolutionary military strength and prowess. As the *Pennsylvania Gazette* reported, the flags were "met on the Commons by the city Troops of Horse, and by them paraded through two or three streets of the city, preceded by the colours of the United States and France, to the State House, and there laid at the feet of Congress, to the great joy of a numerous concourse of spectators."[75] On December 30, 1776, this city had witnessed a very different parade when new prisoners of war, not flags, were marched through town.

~

The transition from armed soldier to unarmed prisoner of war was often perilous. Even if the vanquished made it through the initial seconds, minutes, and hours after battle, they were not necessarily safe. From a common soldier's perspective, an orderly surrender was preferable to capture. A negotiated agreement provided a certain degree of security in the absence of enforceable rules and standards. Ideally the vanquished soldiers would also be guided into captivity through a rite of passage, which offered them a safe way to give up their means of self-defense and helped them to understand and accept their new status in society. How they entered this new phase in their life, and what messages were sent to them in their moment of defeat, shaped their ideas of what to expect as prisoners of war. The American revolutionaries also benefited from such ritual performances, which enabled them to use their defeated enemies to celebrate their accomplishments and gain respect and legitimacy in the eyes of their opponents and a wider public. Once the rites had been performed, however, and the defeated soldiers' transition to prisoners of war was complete, the new captives had to be housed, fed, and guarded. The problems involved in maintaining so many prisoners of war would prove to be a challenge. At the same time, the revolutionaries would find ways to use the captive German soldiers to their benefit.

PART III

Prisoners of War

Probably around midday on January 6, 1777, Johannes Reuber and the other Hessen-Kassel prisoners of war from Trenton arrived in Lancaster, Pennsylvania, after a short but eventful stay in Philadelphia. Congress had decided that this "major city" in the American interior would be the prisoners' place of detention.[1] In Lancaster, the men were placed in the local barracks, "which were built of brick, with three wings, and surrounded by a stockade, twenty feet high and log cabins on all four corners." There Reuber and his fellow German prisoners of war met a number of British captives from various units who had already been in the building for some time. The Hessians, as Reuber noted approvingly, "were quartered in the middle wing, and everything was peaceful and quiet."[2] Regimental Quartermaster Lieutenant Matthäus Müller of the Regiment von Knyphausen, sent to Lancaster by General von Heister to supply the prisoners with pay, shirts, shoes, socks, and blankets, noted on January 20 that the men were staying in "beautiful barracks a little outside of town."[3] Such seemingly comfortable housing angered some leading members of Congress. On January 7, Congress's Executive Committee in Philadelphia had complained that British and German soldiers in revolutionary hands were "feasting on the fat of this Land" while revolutionary prisoners of war in New York lacked provisions, fresh air, and clean quarters.[4]

A few years later, in 1781 and 1782, German and British prisoners of war in turn complained about dreadful conditions in American captivity. Stephan Popp, a common soldier in the Ansbach-Bayreuth Regiment von Seybothen, taken at Yorktown on October 19, 1781, was shocked when he arrived at the barracks in Winchester, the prisoners' designated place of detention. "I still shudder when I think about [these buildings]," he wrote in his journal. Many of the huts had caved in; their walls and roofs were "rotten." Rain and snow entered the buildings, "just like wind on an open road." Worse, each hut had to accommodate "thirty-two to thirty-six men."[5] Braunschweig-Wolfenbüttel prisoner of war Johann Bense described similarly dismal conditions in Reading, Pennsylvania, where the remnants of Burgoyne's so-called Convention Army stayed after leaving Virginia. More than three hundred men were confined in the local jail, which had been built to house only sixty. Most had to stay in the open and endure the cold weather. The last year of his long captivity, Bense wrote, was the worst. He and his fellow prisoners became most "miserable and wretched men."[6]

～

The following chapters focus again on common soldiers, examining in detail the daily life of German prisoners of war during the American War of Independence. Two questions guide the analysis: How did the revolutionaries treat German auxiliaries of the British as captives, and how did the prisoners experience their time in enemy hands? The questions are simple, but the answers are rather complex. For starters, as one historian of American prisoner-of-war policies has recently emphasized, it was difficult to define who was and was not a prisoner of war during the American Revolution and what that status actually meant in practice.[7]

The account begins in 1775, when American revolutionaries were confronted with their first prisoners of war from British units. Next is a detailed study of captivity for German prisoners of war from 1776 to 1778, focusing on the Trenton prisoners. This is followed by an examination of several key changes in American prisoner-of-war treatment in 1778. A separate discussion then examines the fate of common German soldiers from the Convention Army, comparing their experiences with those of prisoners from the same army captured near Bennington in August 1777. The following chapter focuses on the period after 1779, particularly the last two years of the war, when the United States was essentially bankrupt but still had to deal with thousands of new British and

German captives. It also follows the odyssey of some Waldeck soldiers who were sent to fight the Spanish in West Florida only to be captured along the Mississippi in 1779, brought to New Orleans as prisoners of war, and ferried over to Vera Cruz, Mexico, before landing in Havana, Cuba. And finally, because this study began with a look at the social composition and recruitment of common German soldiers before they reached North America, it is only fitting to end it with a look at those soldiers who returned from captivity and also went back to their homelands once this long war was over. Thus the last chapter in this part follows the story of captivity for common German soldiers in the American War of Independence to the end of the conflict and beyond.

Overall, this part emphasizes that at the outset of the conflict, neither side knew what to do with enemy prisoners. The revolutionaries improvised and sent their first captives—British soldiers taken during the 1775 campaigns in the north—to a few inland towns in New England and Pennsylvania. Local communities and revolutionary committees then made initial decisions about prisoner-of-war treatment, based on their own wants and needs. The American War of Independence was not led by a strong central authority with sufficient power to direct and implement policies on the state, regional, and local level. The situation was often chaotic, and Congress was frequently powerless and repeatedly ignored. General Washington often disagreed with Congress, particularly over prisoner-of-war policies. His focus in 1775 was to make the British accept the revolutionaries as legitimate belligerents and treat them as such when in British hands, threatening retaliation if necessary. Once American forces took more British and German soldiers, additional revolutionary authorities and institutions began dealing with prisoner affairs. In 1777, for instance, Congress, the Board of War, Washington, and the commissary general of prisoners and his deputies attempted to manage prisoner affairs. The various states and towns where the captives were housed still pursued their own agendas. Confusion and competition rather than structure and planning often governed American prisoner-of-war treatment.[8]

One pattern, however, remained prevalent throughout the war. Revolutionaries on all levels saw prisoners of war not only as a burden—more mouths to feed, more bodies to supply, guard, and house—but also as useful enemies. British and German captives consumed resources, but they could also be utilized for purposes far beyond exchanges and cartels. Primarily that meant using the captives for labor, particularly in and around major prisoner-of-war camps such as those at Lancaster, Pennsylvania; Frederick, Maryland; and Winchester and Charlottesville, Virginia. This way, the revolutionaries lowered their expenses and benefited from their captives. Congress even hired out prisoners of war in lieu of payment for ammunition and other supplies for the war effort. For their part, the prisoners earned extra money for food and clothing and could escape their cramped and inadequate quarters. Common soldiers had little problem with being "used," as long as such usefulness also held advantages for them.

Hiring out prisoners of war, however, also meant that captivity became increasingly privatized. Local citizens, furnaces, mills, farmers, shopkeepers, and craftsmen, rather than states or Congress, kept German and British prisoners of war. It seems that Congress, the states, and the Continental Army were able to hold so many captives for such a long time only because they could hire them out and did not have to detain them closely in camps.

Revolutionaries also made other uses of prisoners of war. They pressured Great Britain into extending better treatment to captive American revolutionaries through the principle of reciprocity. In 1778, Congress attempted to hurt the British financially by changing prisoner-of-war support policies. German captives were used as a propaganda tool after their capture, in hopes that their stories of American riches and good treatment would lure other auxiliaries away from the British and disrupt the crown's war efforts. They also became a tool for expanding revolutionary authority in areas where allegiance to the cause was tenuous. They were viewed as potential recruits, settlers, even future citizens of an independent United States. The revolutionaries believed that their experiment in liberty and freedom would prove irresistible to those who had been sent to North America against their will but could now choose to join a new nation. The treatment of prisoners of war during the American War of Independence was more than just an unpleasant and costly task after a battle or siege; it became an integral part of the American war effort.

CHAPTER 6

The First Prisoners of War in Revolutionary Hands, 1775–1776

On May 10, 1775, a few weeks after the outbreak of military conflict between the thirteen North American colonies and their English motherland, revolutionary troops under Ethan Allen and Benedict Arnold captured the first large group of British soldiers at Fort Ticonderoga: about fifty officers, noncommissioned officers, and rank and file from the British 26th (Cameronians) Regiment of Foot, plus several women and children.[1] Following the raid, the two commanders sent their new captives to Massachusetts and Connecticut. The Massachusetts Provincial Congress, which had appointed Arnold, had already established a committee on April 30 that was tasked with finding out how to treat captive British soldiers. The Connecticut Assembly, which had enlisted Allen's services, also installed a committee to take "care of and provide for a number of [British] Officers and Soldiers, with their families" who were now prisoners of war in Hartford. No barracks were available there, however, and the county jail was "out of order." Not even "Pickets or any Yard" were enclosed. Towns and cities in eighteenth-century colonial America had few jails, and long-term incarceration was uncommon.[2] Forced to improvise, Connecticut quartered the captives with a number of families in and around Hartford and called upon local militia to guard them.[3] Connecticut based these measures on prior experience. During conflicts with New France, English colonies also did not keep prisoners of war in camps, barracks, or jails but assigned them to local inhabitants, primarily to save money for guards and provisions. After the Battle of La Belle Famille and the British capture of Fort Niagara in 1759, for instance, the colonists brought about six hundred

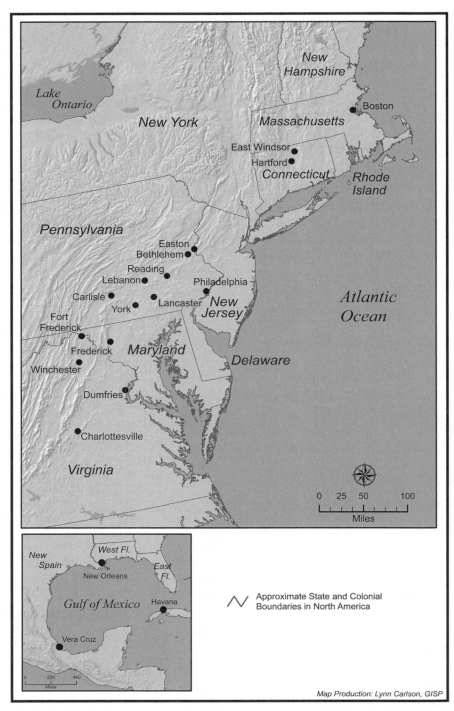

Map 2. Major Prisoner-of-War Camps for German and British Soldiers, 1776–1783

French and Canadian prisoners of war to New York and divided them into smaller groups, to be housed in various New York, New Jersey, and Connecticut towns.[4]

As fall approached in 1775, problems with prisoner-of-war support and housing began to plague Connecticut. New British captives from the revolutionary invasion of Quebec arrived, but nothing had been decided about "their confinement and support."[5] The assembly had only put a new committee in place and requested that Governor Jonathan Trumbull ask Congress how Connecticut was to pay for and supply the prisoners.[6] Neither side really understood how to treat captured enemy soldiers. This was not another eighteenth-century dynastic or imperial conflict in which it was clear who the enemy was and both sides acknowledged each other as legitimate belligerents. Particularly during the first year, the war was a muddled mix of popular unrest, freedom fight, revolt, and civil war in which the revolutionaries initially struggled for legitimacy. From the British perspective, the fighting that had broken out on April 19 constituted a rebellion, similar in character to previous uprisings by the Irish, Scots, Jacobites, and American Indians.[7] Yet Great Britain was also fighting in North America to regain control of the thirteen rebellious colonies and their population. Summarily hanging captured rebels would not support such goals.[8]

Several letters exchanged in the summer of 1775 between General Washington, commander of the newly established Continental Army, and the British military commander in Boston, Lieutenant General Thomas Gage, show how difficult it was to define standards of treatment for prisoners of war. At that point, the revolutionaries held about fifty British troops, and the British had taken about thirty revolutionaries at Bunker Hill. Lord Dunmore had sent another group of American prisoners of war to Boston. On August 11, Washington complained to Gage that revolutionary "Officers engaged in the Cause of Liberty, and their country" who had fallen into British hands "have been thrown indiscriminately, into a common Gaol appropriated for Felons," and that "no consideration" was made for "those of the most respectable Rank." The British, he said, had left the men's injuries untreated and performed amputations under the worst conditions. For

Washington, only "the Rights of Humanity," not "political Opinions," should dictate prisoner-of-war treatment. The behavior of the British since April had forced him to consider retaliation.[9] Gage admitted that the British kept all captured revolutionary soldiers in a common jail, but he defended the practice. After all, he had been willing to overlook "the Criminal in the Captive" and the fact that Washington's revolutionary soldiers were nothing but rebels "whose lives by the Law of the Land are destined to the bond" or death. Under such circumstances, Washington could not seriously expect him to observe ranks "not derived from the King."[10]

In a letter to Congress on May 11, 1776, Washington shared his thoughts on prisoner-of-war treatment. In England and France, he wrote, captured common soldiers and noncommissioned officers were sent to "some inland place, where there is an old castle, commonly surrounded with a high stone wall, and oftentimes with a moat, comprehending a pretty large place of ground." Prisoners of war were confined there under guard "as in a debtor's jail," and maintained through agents exchanged between the sides. During confinement, the victors kept an account of all expenses, to be settled "and the balance paid at the peace." Officers were not confined but were paroled to another town, "as far distant as possible from their men." Suitable places of confinement, Washington wrote, should be established in the "interior parts" of the continent. That way, it would be difficult for the prisoners to escape and "join and assist our enemies in cases of invasion." However, he also wanted Congress to act so that England would "be obliged to acknowledge us an independent State, at least so far as respects prisoners of war." If England refused, "the treatment she shows to our soldiers or seamen in her hands ought to be exactly observed upon our part to those we take prisoners from them."[11]

As Washington's threats of retaliation reflect, acceptable treatment of enemy captives at the time relied on the principle of reciprocity. Once the revolutionaries had captured a sizable number of British troops, the king and his military leadership had to treat captured revolutionaries reasonably well to protect their own soldiers and to avoid further antagonizing the colonists. For Washington, on the other hand, this also meant that British prisoners of war had to come under some kind of central control. Otherwise the British could exploit revolutionary divisions and prevent a credible threat of retaliation. Principles of humanity, although emphasized by Washington, often held little sway in a conflict that regularly pitted neighbor against neighbor. In this war, the side that held (and controlled) the most prisoners of war was in a stronger position during any negotiations, whether they concerned exchanges, provisions, pay, or supplies.

As the war escalated in 1775 and 1776, the revolutionaries indeed had an advantage in numbers, at least as far as land troops were concerned. They held about 500 British soldiers, while the British held only about 300 revolutionary soldiers. By the summer and fall of 1776, however, following General Howe's successful campaigns around New York, the British had about 4,400 American captives, while the revolutionaries had very few British and German prisoners. Because of exchanges, a rather high death rate among American prisoners of the British, and the revolutionaries' victories at Trenton and Princeton, this unfavorable ratio was markedly reduced by the summer of 1777. At that point, the British held only about 2,500 American revolutionaries. With Burgoyne's surrender at Saratoga and Congress's subsequent refusal to ratify the terms of the convention there, the revolutionaries gained the upper hand in prisoner numbers for the rest of the war. Despite heavy losses in the South after 1778, particularly in Savannah and Charleston, they usually held more British and German prisoners of war in North America than the British held revolutionary soldiers.[12]

Elias Boudinot, revolutionary commissary general of prisoners in 1777 and 1778, acknowledged that the principle of reciprocity worked in favor of American prisoners of war in New York. Before Saratoga, he wrote to General Henry Knox and Gouverneur Morris in 1782, "there was not the least attention paid either to their Food, Convenience or their Health." Their housing was so overcrowded "that they could not all lay down at a Time." Neither "Hospitals nor Medicines" were provided for the sick. "By these and other Means," said Boudinot, "one half if not three fourths of those unhappy Men perished." The "Fall of Gen[eral] Burgoyne," however, "produced a different Treatment of our Prisoners."

Thereafter he no longer worried about the mass of American prisoners of war in British hands but only about a few officers confined closely in the provost prison, New York's former new jail.[13]

These events still lay far in the future, however, when local revolutionary communities in Pennsylvania had to deal with a surprisingly large influx of captured British soldiers in the fall of 1775. At Fort Chambly on October 18 and during the Siege of Fort Saint-Jean between September and November 3, American forces under Brigadier General Richard Montgomery captured 499 British soldiers from the 7th (Royal Fusiliers) and 26th Regiments of Foot, plus 93 women and 153 children.[14] Congress decided on November 17 that these prisoners should be marched away from the main theater of the conflict. They were placed in Lancaster, Reading, York, and Carlisle. Congress again gave few instructions about how to treat these British soldiers and their families. A Pennsylvania committee, originally appointed to raise troops, was simply directed to contract for their support.[15] After receiving the captives, the Lancaster County Committee of Safety was to take "such measures with respect to the prisoners" as they thought were "most conducive to the public service." The town of Lancaster, in turn, resolved to notify the appointed contractors for supplying the prisoners of war and put the captives in the old barracks in town, built during the Seven Years' War. Lancaster then asked Congress for further instructions—for instance, whether they should keep the prisoners closely confined in the barracks under a guard or allow the officers to take private lodgings in town, and how, if needed, to pay the guard—but received no answer. The committee members had already suggested that the barracks for this purpose should be "fenced in."[16]

Reading had similar experiences with an unresponsive Congress. In a February 1776 letter, the town's Committee of Correspondence expressed surprise that about 100 British prisoners of war, including an unknown number of women and children, had suddenly arrived in town. They wanted to know exactly how these captives would be supported. In the meantime, the town appointed Henry Haller to provide the prisoners with firewood and housing. Reading also did not know how many provisions should be distributed and, more importantly, who would pay for them.

Impatient for an answer from Congress, Reading even sent a messenger to Philadelphia.[17]

Only twice in this period did Congress give towns housing British prisoners of war clear and precise instructions. In mid-January 1776, Lancaster received a response to its earlier plea for additional directions, but it was little more than agreement with measures already taken by the town. Congress approved of Lancaster's "civility" in giving British officers time to choose their own places of residence and agreed with its policy of allowing officers to muster their captive rank and file from time to time, primarily to pay them. Congress also agreed that a guard should be posted at the barracks, to preserve "the peace of the Borough," and applauded the town for supplying the captives' wives and children with meat and bread. The Committee of Inspection in Lancaster had "judged rightly in supposing that every measure . . . to render the situation of our prisoners as comfortable as possible would be agreeable to [Congress]," and Congress had promised to defray all of Lancaster's expenses. The committee was reminded that "as men, [the British prisoners of war] have a claim to all the rights of humanity; as countrymen, though enemies, they claim something more." This last statement captures the difficulty that both sides faced in this period. Congress was effectively saying that the men confined in Lancaster were not true prisoners of war, but only fellow Britons who were temporarily being detained.[18]

On January 31, 1776, the delegates prohibited the Continental Army from recruiting among British captives.[19] In the eyes of Congress, defectors could not be trusted to share the revolutionaries' values and were thus unfit for American military service.[20] However, such orders were regularly ignored on the local and state level. The first revolutionary recruitment officers had visited the British prisoners in Lancaster in January 1776. A drummer and sergeant enlisted right away, prompting immediate protests by British officers.[21] Revolutionary recruiters were still approaching British prisoners of war at Hartford and York in March and May 1776.[22]

While revolutionary leaders in Congress might have thought that they were only temporarily detaining fellow countrymen, the British officers in Lancaster felt differently. According to the

Pennsylvania Council of Safety, the humane treatment at Lancaster was met "with a very improper & indecent Return." The prisoners often "express[ed] themselves in most disrespectful & offensive Terms" and openly threatened the population with revenge. The council thereafter wanted to separate the officers from the rank and file and break up the prisoners into smaller groups so that the "opportunities of doing mischief will less correspond with their inclinations." This, they apparently believed, would allow for better and more control. Without congressional approval, on March 19, 1776, the Pennsylvania Council of Safety ordered Lancaster to remove every British officer from town. The officers from the 26th Regiment had to go to York, while the officers from the 7th Regiment were sent to Carlisle.[23]

The main concern for common soldiers in enemy hands was supplies, and British prisoners from Ticonderoga, Chambly, and Saint-Jean had ample reason to be nervous. In December 1775, Matthias Slough, a leading revolutionary and a member of the local Committee of Safety, had to pay for the prisoners' provisions out of his own pocket. Otherwise they would have received nothing at all. Only at the end of the month did Lancaster learn that British agent David Franks from Philadelphia had been appointed as agent for the prisoners and "had engaged to supply the troops [in Lancaster] with provisions."[24] However, Franks and other agents also received explicit orders from British headquarters "not to furnish any more bread and meat" to the women and children with the prisoners. Naturally this caused considerable anger. To calm the situation, William Bausman, the barracks master in Lancaster, distributed 174 blankets to the captives. The Lancaster Committee of Inspection also showed compassion by continuing to supply the captives' women and children with food.[25]

David Franks was part of the large contracting firm of Nesbitt, Drummond, & Franks. His father, Jacob Franks, was one of the wealthiest merchants in New York. Jacob had sent his two sons, Moses and David, to Philadelphia in 1740 to expand the family's business and engage in the western trade via Lancaster. Moses, however, soon went to London to oversee that end of the family's transatlantic business. The Frankses had been provisioning British soldiers in North America since the 1730s and 1740s. During the

Seven Years' War, they handled more than £750,000 in provisions for British and provincial forces. By 1776, the company had a contract to supply 12,000 British soldiers in the colonies. In 1779, Nesbitt, Drummond, & Franks alone supplied 13,700 British soldiers fighting in North America.[26]

Initially, David Franks supplied only British prisoners of war from the 7th and 26th Regiments. In early 1776, however, he was given responsibility for all British prisoners in Massachusetts.[27] As agent for British and later German prisoners of war, Franks worked under both British and revolutionary American orders. By June 1777, he even appeared in congressional records as a deputy commissary general of prisoners.[28] To organize the supply of the rising numbers of British and German prisoners in Pennsylvania, Franks subcontracted the work to an old business associate, Joseph Simon. At York, Myer Hart had a similar role. Subcontractors commonly used their own money to buy rations for the prisoners and then requested reimbursement from Franks. Between 1775 and 1778, Franks advanced funds for about 500,000 daily rations issued to prisoners of war.[29]

The system of using agents to supply the prisoners put the revolutionaries at a major disadvantage. Until 1777, they did not have an agent in New York City who could take on a role similar to David Franks's. Even then, they did not have the logistical or financial means to establish a functioning organization; nor did the British really allow them to develop one. For instance, the revolutionaries had to buy everything on British markets in New York at very high prices. As the Continental currency declined rapidly in value, this became a serious problem. The British, meanwhile, could easily buy provisions for their soldiers around revolutionary detention sites with cash or even counterfeited revolutionary bills. Moreover, they kept most of their prisoners in New York, closely confined in unhealthy quarters such as sugar houses, the provost jail, and especially prison hulks.

The British rarely occupied enough territory in North America to secure provisioning from local sources, so until 1783 they had the rations for their army in North America delivered to Cork, Ireland, and then taken by ship to North America. Rations were divided into two general categories: wet and dry provisions. Wet provisions—beef, pork, and butter—came mostly from Ireland. Dry provisions, such as flour, peas, and oatmeal, came mostly from England. Flour, rice, and fresh meat could also be obtained in the colonies. Sometimes the rations also included bacon, fish, raisins, or molasses. The major North American depots from which the bulk of the provisions were distributed to the individual armies and garrisons were Montreal, Quebec, Halifax, New York, and, for 1777 and 1778, Philadelphia. Armies or garrisons then used agents to dispense rations to the men and their units. Sometimes contractors sold their agreements with the British Treasury to subcontractors and retained only about 1 pence per ration for themselves.[30]

A full ration for one man per week might consist of seven pounds of bread or flour (biscuit for the navy), seven pounds of beef or four pounds of pork, six ounces of butter or eight ounces of cheese, three pints of peas, and half a pound of oatmeal. In addition, the soldiers received about one and a half gills of rum per day. The cost of one ration per man was calculated at 5¼ pence for the mainland colonies in 1775 and 5¾ pence in 1777. Two-thirds of a ration was considered sufficient for prisoners of war, however, because those soldiers were not engaged in campaigning and combat. This meant, as one historian has calculated, that American prisoners of war held by the British in New York actually did not receive the 2,460 calories per day that a full ration was supposed to supply, but at most 1,640 calories per day.[31]

All soldiers had to pay for their rations. Either the costs were deducted from their pay, or they received an allowance as part of their pay and then bought the food on their own or together with fellow soldiers. Rarely were full rations available. At Three Rivers in Canada, for instance, a full ration for one man per day during the Revolutionary War sometimes consisted of only one and a half pounds of bread or flour and one pound of beef or ten ounces of pork. Three pounds of bread or flour or one and a half pounds of rice per day also constituted a complete ration. The biggest problem for the British army was that the food supply from Europe was often defective. Rations reached the soldiers very late or not at all—or they arrived rotten and infested with vermin. Moreover, the British army did not distinguish between the different colonies and climates. For instance, they delivered butter to the West Indies, where it soon turned into rancid oil.[32]

In 1775 and 1776, towns often wrote to Congress requesting reimbursement for the supplies they furnished to the prisoners of war. On January 10, 1776, for instance, the Lancaster Committee of Inspection noted that the British commanding officer of the prisoners in town, Major Preston, had delivered some clothes and shoes to the soldiers of the 26th Regiment but not to the men of the 7th. By April, many of the latter were dressed in rags. The committee wanted to know whether they should provide the imprisoned soldiers with some clothing and shoes at "Continental expense."[33] In this as in many other cases, the committees in Lancaster simply resolved to "exercise [their] own Judgment" when dealing with urgent problems and needs.[34] Rarely could they wait until Congress made a decision. When Congress finally issued the first general regulations "respecting the manner of treating Prisoners" on May 21, 1776, it was merely a reiteration of earlier resolves and approved what towns such as Hartford, Lancaster, Reading, and York had already put into practice.[35] Congress stressed that common prisoners of war should receive the same rations as common soldiers in the Continental Army. If the captives were not supplied by British agents, local towns should "contract with proper persons" for provisioning the soldiers and their families. Common soldiers should receive housing, but only on condition that officers and privates not stay in the same place. Furthermore, Congress repeated that "no Prisoners [were to] be inlisted in the Continental Army" and tasked local Committees of Inspection and Observation with prisoner supervision. The new regulations also stressed that women and children with the prisoners were to be given food and firewood. Finally, in an attempt to gain some control over prisoners of war, Congress asked each colony to send a list of its captives to Philadelphia. At the same time, however, Congress relinquished control when it allowed colonies "to remove such Prisoners from place to place" as they saw fit.[36]

The Lancaster Committee of Safety made a key decision on its own early in the war, allowing British prisoners of war to leave the barracks and work for town residents. On December 27, 1775, the committee gave passes to two captives from the 26th Regiment for "employment among the inhabitants."[37] It was an inconspicuous start to a practice that would come to define the treatment of common British and German prisoners of war in revolutionary hands. On April 10, 1776, the Committee of Safety systematized its efforts and ordered a subcommittee to find out "what Tradesmen there are amongst the Prisoners in this County" and identify those "who are willing to go down & work . . . upon Wages at their respective Occupations." This subcommittee found ninety-four British soldiers among the prisoners in town who claimed to have a trade. From late July through mid-October 1776, twenty-nine of those men received permission to work in Lancaster. Seven worked as weavers, five became tailors, and others worked as wheelwrights, shoemakers, and even gunsmiths. To hire a prisoner, a prospective employer had only to appear before the county committee and present a witness.[38]

Connecticut also allowed its first British prisoners to work. A committee established for "Providing for, ordering and regulation of Prisoners" announced in early 1776 that those captured British soldiers who "were disposed to Labour as Tradesmen at their Trades . . . and pay for their own Billeting, . . . should have the benefit of their earnings for Cloathing &c and should be paid in Money 7½ d. a Day." Those who were unwilling to work still received their allowance for food at the jail, but they lost "the benefit of their Labour over and above." Most of the prisoners "very readily and thankfully accepted" the opportunity to earn additional pay. In fact, the practice became so popular that only those who were sick, disabled, or "judged too bad to be abroad, and some that were too lazy" were kept confined. Ezekiel Williams, later a deputy commissary of prisoners, was convinced that fewer prisoners had escaped under this system than would have died "in the poisonous air of the Gaol." Besides, he added, the captives performed a lot of labor around Hartford, and Congress saved approximately £1,000.[39] In other words, the system benefited both sides. The prisoners earned wages, and they did not have to stay confined in barracks, jails, or other buildings. Employers gained labor, and towns did not have to organize housing and guards for the captives.

Lancaster: A Model Site for Prisoner-of-War Detention

Founded in 1730 at the crossroads of several trading routes, Lancaster had about 3,300 inhabitants in 1775, which made it the largest urban inland settlement in the English colonies. Lancaster County benefited from rich soil and a good climate for growing wheat, rye, oats, maize, flax, and hemp. About two-thirds of the population worked on farms, one-fifth were craftsmen, and one-sixth were laborers. The vast majority of farms, 70 percent in the years between 1771 and 1780, were smaller than 300 acres. Like the rest of Pennsylvania, Lancaster County was religiously diverse but overwhelmingly Protestant. About one-third of the residents were Moravians, another third were Quakers, about one-fifth were Presbyterians, and less than one-tenth each were Lutherans or members of the Reformed Church.[40] Because of its size and location, Lancaster had been a military center during the Seven Years' War. It had served as the staging point for several expeditions, a storage depot for the British army, and a garrison for the Royal American Regiment. After 1761, the town developed into a center of manufacturing and production. By 1790, it boasted thirty carpenters, twelve bakers, three breweries, three brickyards, thirty-six shoemakers, fourteen hatters, twenty-four tailors, six dyers, and three printers. It was also widely known for its gunsmiths.[41]

The entire region was a center of German immigration during the eighteenth century. In 1740, three-quarters of all landowners in Lancaster came from German or Swiss immigrant families. By the second half of the century, between 58 and 68 percent of the county's white residents were of German origin; only 10 to 15 percent were English, and 13 to 19 percent were Scots-Irish.[42] Records of neighboring counties present a similar picture. In fact, a "German arc" stretched through Northampton, Berks, and Lancaster Counties, including the upper parts of Chester, Philadelphia, and Bucks County. By 1790, three-quarters of the population in Berks County, two-thirds in Northampton County, more than one-half in Montgomery County, and one-half in York County was German. In Greater Pennsylvania—the region stretching north and south beyond the borders of Pennsylvania proper, including the

Shenandoah Valley in Maryland and Virginia—"distinct ethnic enclaves of Germans" had developed over the course of the eighteenth century.[43] In Maryland, for instance, two-thirds of the white population was ethnically German in Frederick and Shenandoah Counties, one-half in Carroll County, and a little less than one-half in Harrison County. In total, about 110,000 German immigrants came to North America between 1683 and 1775. A large majority of them, about 81,000, went to Pennsylvania.[44]

Between the fall of 1775 and early 1777, Lancaster became the model site for prisoner-of-war detention, primarily because the barracks from the Seven Years' War could now be used for holding the revolutionaries' captives. Lancaster's barracks had been built in 1759 to relieve the population from the burden of quartering British and provincial forces assembling in the area for military expeditions into western Pennsylvania. The original U-shaped building on the corner of Duke and Walnut Streets, at the northern edge of town, was constructed under the supervision of William Henry and designed to house five hundred soldiers. It had three stories built of stone and brick, with the lower floor partially underground. Each room had a fireplace and windows, which faced the rear of the building on the lower floor and the courtyard on the upper floors. Altogether, fifty-two rooms were available when the first British prisoners of war arrived in December 1775.[45]

During the spring and summer of 1776, when Pennsylvania experienced its internal revolution, radical ideals conflicted with this housing situation and the practice of hiring out the British prisoners of war. Some revolutionaries felt that the captives should be closely confined rather than allowed out to work. On July 10, amid the turmoil surrounding the election for the constitutional convention in Pennsylvania, Lancaster ordered 150 Associators to serve as a guard in town.[46] Otherwise, as the Committee of Inspection explained to Congress on July 7, one day before the scheduled vote, the town would be "exposed to the Fury and Ravages of near Four Hundred of the prisoners taken at Chamblee & St. John's who are stationed here and cannot be confined Day or Night in the present open state of our Barracks." It had been wrong, the letter from an increasingly radicalized committee continued, to assume that by "mixing and working with the Inhabitants," the

British prisoners "would learn and be convinced of the justness of our Cause & become rather the Friends than Enemies of the rights of America." Instead, the captives had done "much mischief—they adhere with an extraordinary degree of firmness to their tyrannical Master and his Cause." The committee even found prisoners roaming through town dressed as revolutionary "Rifle Men," who they felt sure were carrying enemy intelligence between the captives and British headquarters. In short, Lancaster wanted the British prisoners of war secured and confined: "They are a dangerous set of people."[47]

After July 4, 1776, the war was no longer about "countrymen" opposing each other over taxation and other rights; it had become a war of liberation between American revolutionaries and the British. Many in the former colonies anticipated a large-scale civil war in which it would be difficult to distinguish clearly between friend and foe. Such a prospect made it inadvisable to let captured enemy soldiers live openly in the heart of a revolutionary town. As former colonists had to choose sides in mid-1776, defeated and captured enemy soldiers had to be separated from the rest of the population. Prisoners of war, particularly if they worked outside the barracks, might plot attacks against their captors. Local revolutionaries felt that they now faced two enemies: one coming from the outside, the other living in their midst.[48] Thus they not only wanted a guard in Lancaster but also hoped to "enclose" the barracks with a palisade to isolate the prisoners from the rest of the town. On July 12, Congress issued the appropriate orders, and the work was scheduled to begin only one week later.[49] However, Lancaster faced a new problem when additional prisoners arrived from Reading. Since the barracks were already full, the town had no choice but to rent space for the newcomers in private houses. The palisade around the barracks, then, would remain useless until all prisoners could be confined there.[50] Hence it was decided to expand both the barracks and the palisade. Each wing of the barracks was extended the length of four rooms, making twenty-four new rooms available.[51] The facility would now be able to house prisoners of war until 1783. In 1777, Congress's Board of War asked Lancaster's commissary of prisoners, William A. Atlee, to draw a plan of the barracks that had become the first true prisoner-of-war camp in the newly founded United States (figure 4). Congress then sent copies of this plan "to the different Places where Barracks for the reception of Prisoners are ordered to be built."[52]

Each of the 76 rooms in the barracks was roughly 263 square feet in size (17 by 15.5 feet). Assuming that the numbers from the Seven Years' War (52 rooms for 500 soldiers) were still accurate, the enlarged barracks could house about 700 prisoners of war. By today's standards, this made for very tight and crowded quarters—about 9 men per room. The palisade surrounded the building at a distance of 73 and 100 feet. It was about 15 feet high, with "a strong white oak post every ten feet." At all four corners were log houses containing quarters for the guards and a hospital. In March 1777, however, the hospital was actually used as a carpenter shop; sick prisoners had to remain in their rooms. The stockade had enough room for roll calls and vegetable gardens. Two wells with fresh water, a privy, and separate buildings for butchers and bakers were located inside the palisade. Just outside were a grave-yard and a storage area for firewood.[53]

Despite the new additions, the palisade, and all the fierce rhetoric in the summer and fall of 1776, people in Lancaster continued to hire British captives. Principles were quickly set aside when other needs and interests became more pressing. Many of the townsmen were away fighting with the militia and the Continental Army against the British and Germans in New York and New Jersey. Labor was scarce, and there were food shortages. Having additional workers available, even if they were British prisoners of war, made a difference.[54] When Washington recommended on January 1, 1777, that the Hessen-Kassel captives be sent from Trenton into Pennsylvania's "German counties," it probably had less to do with the German immigrant population in the region and more with Lancaster's reputation as a detention site, its distance from the Atlantic coast, its size and rich farmlands, its staunchly revolutionary population, and its relatively long history of housing enemy prisoners of war in this conflict. Once the captives arrived, however, the revolutionaries eagerly tried to exploit the situation. They hoped that the Hessen-Kassel prisoners might learn "from their Country Men who came here without a farthing of property and have by care and industry acquired plentiful fortunes."[55]

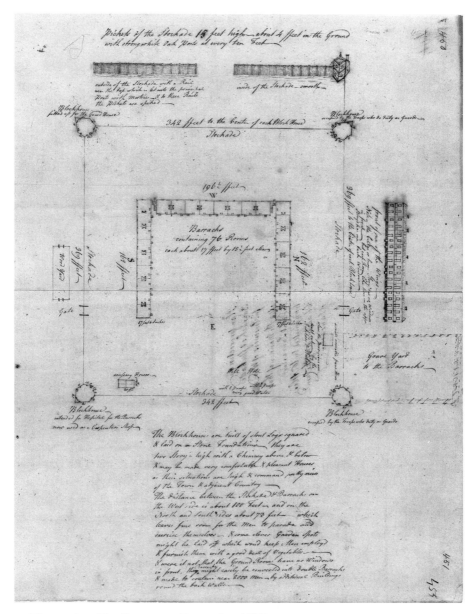

Figure 4.   The Lancaster Barracks, 1777

Plan of the Lancaster Barracks, drawn in 1777 by William A. Atlee. In the center, the U-shaped barracks are shown, surrounded by a stockade with four guardhouses. At top, the plan depicts a front view of the palisade and on the right a front view of the barracks building. Also visible are the graveyard, on the right; the wood yard, on the left; and the wells, storage house, and latrine inside the stockade. From the Papers of the Continental Congress, courtesy of the National Archives and Records Administration, Washington, D.C.

137

Revolutionary Prisoner-of-War Administration

Congress did not establish a coherent and organized system of prisoner-of-war administration once the war with Britain broke out in 1775, nor when the conflict became a war for independence in 1776. Instead, the situation remained chaotic. Local towns that housed prisoners of war made decisions based on their own immediate needs, wants, and available resources. More often than not, the role of Congress and its members was reduced to acknowledging what had already been implemented on a local level.[56] Other revolutionary authorities on the state and national level formulated prisoner-of-war policies and tried to use enemy captives for their own purposes. As a result, various institutions and officeholders competed for power and influence over captives. That prisoners of war could be used for a variety of purposes—labor, exchange, recruitment, pressure on the enemy, propaganda—might actually have contributed to the chaos. Everybody tried to make some use of them. In December 1775, for instance, Congress declared that all prisoner-of-war exchanges were to be man for man, officer for officer, and citizen for citizen. Even prisoners taken on a prize vessel could be exchanged only by Washington. Only a few months later, however, in April 1776, Congress also gave individual states the right to exchange prisoners of war taken on "private vessels."[57] And on July 22, Congress gave individual states permission to negotiate for prisoner-of-war exchanges "in the following manner: one continental officer for one of the enemy of equal rank, either in the land or sea service, soldier for soldier, sailor for sailor, and one citizen for another citizen." This way, Pennsylvania had released most captive soldiers and officers from the British 7th and 26th Regiments by November.[58]

To help with the overall war effort, Congress established a Board of War and Ordnance in June 1776. Its duties included "the care and direction of all prisoners of war, agreeable to the orders and regulations of Congress."[59] But instead of becoming the central organ and institution for running the war and managing enemy captives on American territory, the board was so overburdened by correspondence and work that it made and carried out few decisions. By October 1777, Congress established a new Board of War that included appointed, non-congressional members, able to devote all their time and efforts to conducting the war.[60] Even then, however, the workload proved too much. In addition to providing care for enemy prisoners, the Board of War had to keep accurate registers of all officers in the armed service; maintain accounts of the condition and disposition of all soldiers; keep track of arms, ammunition, artillery, and other military stores; forward all dispatches from Congress to the forces in the field; transmit all monies for public service toward the war effort; and oversee the raising, supplying, and transporting of all land forces. And this all had to be accomplished with only five appointed delegates, one secretary, and a few clerks.[61] It is no wonder that state and local authorities remained so powerful in prisoner matters. Congress and the Board of War had no choice but to rely on states and local communities for housing, guards, and supplies.

The commissary general of prisoners at Washington's headquarters should have been a central figure in the revolutionary prisoner-of-war administration. However, that position was plagued by numerous problems. First, although the call for such an officer went out in 1776, the position remained unfilled until April 1777, when Elias Boudinot finally took it. Boudinot was also made a colonel in the Continental Army.[62] Second, Washington and Congress had originally planned for this commissary general to have primary responsibility for revolutionary prisoners of war in British hands. As Boudinot knew, however, to do so, based on the principle of reciprocity, would require at least some control over the British and German prisoners of war in revolutionary hands.[63] Third, Boudinot expressed great disappointment that between all these branches and levels of revolutionary government, "no clear chain of authority was outlined." Congress, the Board of War, individual states, local committees, and Washington all issued orders to him or gave him directions. On April 29, 1777, for instance, Richard Peters from the Board of War wrote to Boudinot that "by the Constitution of the Board of War Prisoners are put under their Direction." Boudinot, Peters continued, would "no Doubt think it proper to consult [the Board of War] on Occasions of Importance."[64]

By January 1778, Boudinot had managed to appoint a number of deputies in various places where British and German prisoners of war were kept. His deputy in Massachusetts was Joshua Mersereau; in Connecticut, Ezekiel Williams; at Albany, New York, Daniel Hale; at Fishkill, New York, John Adam; at Easton, Pennsylvania, Robert E. Hooper; at Reading, Pennsylvania, Henry Haller; at Lancaster, Pennsylvania, William A. Atlee; at York, Pennsylvania, Thomas Peters; and at Winchester, Virginia, Joseph Holmes.[65] Nevertheless, Boudinot resigned from his post in frustration on March 10, 1778, in the midst of negotiating a prisoner-of-war conference. He claimed that he had to leave because Pennsylvania had called him to Congress as a delegate. His resignation letter, however, included a scathing critique of the Board of War. Because he never had enough prisoners of war under his supervision, Boudinot wrote angrily, he experienced numerous problems when negotiating exchanges with the British. The main difficulty was that the Board of War, Congress, the states, and local communities exchanged captives on their own or hired them out as prisoner-laborers.[66] Boudinot simply did not have enough leverage to press his demands with the British.

Adding to the chaos was the recruitment of enemy captives for revolutionary American forces. Although the practice was common in early modern Europe, leading revolutionaries did not approve of it. This was not just another war over imperial or dynastic goals; it had become a war of liberation, fought as much over ideology as territory. Moreover, Washington and Congress feared that the British might retaliate and recruit among revolutionary prisoners of war. On March 28, 1778, however, Congress contradicted itself by deciding to raise an independent corps under the command of the Polish count Casimir Pulaski for which German prisoners of war in and around Lancaster could be recruited. Perhaps realizing its inconsistency, Congress withdrew its permission for recruitment among the captives only two days later. Pulaski, however, was not particularly worried about Congress's directives and simply continued enlisting prisoners of war. That made the local deputy commissary of prisoners, William Atlee, uncomfortable. Atlee wrote to Congress on May 27, asking whether Pulaski's actions were acceptable. That same day, the Board of War wrote to tell Atlee that he should indeed grant an exception to Pulaski and allow his recruitment efforts. Fearful that prisoners would use this opportunity to reach British lines, however, the Board of War limited recruitment of German prisoners to those not "married in Europe, [and] who [did] not have wives in the enemy's possession." Having received the letter from the Board of War on May 29, Atlee dutifully allowed Pulaski to carry on with his recruitment campaign. He even encouraged the Hessen-Kassel prisoners to enlist and gave Pulaski's recruitment officers a "certified Copy" of the letter so that they "might meet with no opposition from the Commissaries of Prisoners in other places." However, another letter now arrived for Atlee in Lancaster, this time from the president of Congress, Henry Laurens. Written on May 29, it was a reply to Atlee's initial inquiry of May 27 and confirmed that Pulaski was forbidden to recruit among the prisoners. Laurens even characterized Atlee's opposition to Pulaski's recruitment campaign as "well founded" and his conduct as "commendable."[67]

A perplexed Atlee wrote to Congress again on June 2, asking what he was supposed to do. Should he "put a stop to . . . further inlistment of Prisoners here or not"? Only on June 5 was the issue finally resolved. Both Thomas McKean, for Congress, and Timothy Pickering, for the Board of War, wrote to Atlee, clarifying that prisoners of war should not be recruited under any circumstances. The revolutionaries, McKean wrote, currently held more British and German soldiers in their hands than the British held revolutionary soldiers. They wanted to maintain this numerical advantage to force the British into exchanging revolutionary citizens and officeholders, not just soldiers.[68]

~

When revolutionary militias and then the Continental Army took the first British prisoners of war in 1775, Congress simply sent them into various towns, leaving it to the communities to make decisions about immediate needs such as housing and food. With the revolutionaries' increasing success leading to a growing number of captured soldiers who had to be provided for, the communities where the prisoners were held were left without clear guidance about who was financially responsible for supporting them. When the town of Lancaster decided to begin allowing the tradesmen among its group of British captives to leave the barracks and work for local residents, it was a move that worked to everyone's advantage: local committees did not have to feed, guard, house, and supply the prisoners, and the captives earned much-needed extra money and provisions. Despite some controversy over the wisdom of the practice, it soon became widespread. As the revolution became radicalized in early 1776, General Washington and Congress tried to take more control of the war, including the prisoners. With the captives now seen as useful for more than just labor, it seemed that everyone, including the revolutionaries themselves, wanted to make use of the prisoners for their own purposes. It was a chaotic situation that the first German prisoners of war would soon find themselves caught up in.

CHAPTER 7

German Prisoners of War, 1776–1778

By August 1776, the American revolutionaries were fighting not only against British troops but also against thousands of German soldiers. Congress immediately made plans to induce the Germans to desert.[1] The delegates in Philadelphia considered the king's auxiliaries excellent targets for such propaganda campaigns; they did not come from Great Britain, had no real stake in the war, and surely would rather join the new nation than fight and die for despotic princes. As the war went poorly for the revolutionaries that fall, the prospect of somehow breaking those powerful troops away from George III's army in North America became increasingly attractive. The Battles of Long Island, Harlem Heights, White Plains, and Fort Washington cost the Continental Army dearly and brought the colonists to the brink of defeat. When the garrison of Fort Washington capitulated on November 16, for example, the British led 2,800 revolutionary soldiers into captivity. As Ambrose Serle, secretary to Admiral Richard Howe, stated, they had taken so many American prisoners during those months that they were "perplexed where to confine them."[2]

That was the situation on October 16, when revolutionary militiamen from Pennsylvania's Flying Camp, under command of General Hugh Mercer, captured eight soldiers from the Regiment von Trümbach along with several British soldiers near Richmond, Staten Island.[3] Mercer decided to make the most of this unexpected opportunity. In questioning one of the captives, Private Christian Geule, he heard only good news. The Hessen-Kassel soldier stated that he had been "brought from his Country by

143

force" and arrived in North America against his will. The prisoners of war, Geule continued, had "no desire to Return to their Regiments." Such statements seemed to confirm everything that revolutionary leaders had assumed about the German auxiliaries in British service. Mercer immediately ordered that the Hessians be treated with "particular civility" so that later "they may give the most favourable report of this country."[4] He wanted to show his prisoners the advantages of life in North America, then send them back to their units in hopes that their stories of America's riches would entice more German soldiers to desert. They would also be given stacks of the land offers that had been printed in August. Even General Washington expressed excitement about this plan. He proposed that the prisoners be allowed "to make their escape" after some time, to give their stories added credibility.[5]

Not surprisingly, Mercer chose Philadelphia, the revolutionary capital and one of the richest North American cities with a large German population, for his Hessen-Kassel prisoners to witness American prosperity firsthand. The captives were supervised there by Christopher Ludwick, a successful baker and staunch revolutionary who had immigrated from the principality of Hessen-Darmstadt, located close to Hessen-Kassel. Ludwick was also a co-founder of the German Society of Philadelphia. Before the war, he had regularly mediated in disputes between German immigrants and their employers over indentured servitude agreements. It would have been hard to find a better person to teach German prisoners about what other German immigrants had already achieved in North America. In a letter to John Hancock, the president of Congress, Mercer said that the Hessians should be allowed to "rest a few days" in Philadelphia to "form an acquaintance with some of their Countrymen who have experienced the advantages of free Government." What they learned, he hoped, would convince many other soldiers to "run away and come and settle in our city and be as good Whigs as any of us."[6]

Exactly one month after their capture, the eight captives were exchanged. In the eyes of Congress, these men had been "treated in such a manner during their stay in this city, that it is apprehended their going back among their countrymen will be attended with some good consequences."[7] For both contemporary observers and later commentators, such assumptions were undoubtedly accurate. One historian later claimed, without providing any actual numbers, that desertion rates among German auxiliaries rose considerably after this propaganda operation in Philadelphia.[8]

The reality, however, was more complicated. Geule and the other Hessen-Kassel prisoners may simply have told the revolutionaries what they wanted to hear in order to receive better treatment. Not one of the eight German captives taken to Philadelphia under Ludwick's care was listed as a deserter later in the war. In fact, one of them, Johannes Bornemann, advanced to the rank of corporal in 1780. American forces captured Geule and another of the Staten Island prisoners, Justus Schmidt, again in March 1781, and again they did not desert. Moreover, British, Hessen-Kassel, and American sources fail to confirm that the desertion rate among German soldiers increased after November 1776. Of the thousands of Hessen-Kassel troops in North America, only 66 deserted in 1776, and only 109 in 1777.[9] An anonymous Hessen-Kassel soldier explained in mid-September 1776 why the captives remained loyal despite all revolutionary efforts: the soldiers of the Continental Army around New York were not impressive; while British and German troops "were sufficiently supplied with provisions and rum, the Rebels lacked the latter as well as clothing."[10] Why would he and his fellow soldiers want to desert and join the losing side?

While the revolutionaries' efforts in this regard were mostly unsuccessful, German officers, ever mistrusting of their rank and file, were still alarmed.[11] Near Kingsbridge, New York, several officers announced to the revolutionaries that it was "in vain . . . to persuade the Hessians" to desert or "breed a jealousy between them and the English." According to these officers, it was "impossible to seduce [the prisoners] like those fanatics among the rebel armies, by motives of so base a nature." Hessen-Kassel soldiers would never "desert their Prince, their country, their honor, and everything else that is dear to them, (and sell their souls to the devil) for the sake of a plantation."[12] The officers countered revolutionary ideals and land offers with a traditional emphasis on loyalty and obedience.

The Trenton Prisoners in Lancaster

When the Hessen-Kassel prisoners from Trenton arrived in Lancaster after their parade through Philadelphia, the Pennsylvania Council of Safety and Lancaster's Committee of Inspection first mustered them to find any "Plate Watches & other Effects which they have plundered from the inhabitants of Jersey."[13] Continuing the propaganda efforts of Washington and Congress, however, they laid the blame on the British: "you have been taught by the British Officers to believe that it was just and right to plunder the Inhabitants of this Country." In exchange for cooperation, they offered the German soldiers better treatment in captivity. Upon reflection, the soldiers would surely realize "the injustice of . . . killing and plundering the innocent inhabitants of the Country who never offended you." Delivering up their plunder, the revolutionaries promised, would "induce us to entertain a favourable opinion of you."[14]

At the same time, the committee was uneasy about the number of prisoners in town. Considerably more German captives arrived in January 1777 than the barracks could hold. An official return listed a total of 839 Hessen-Kassel prisoners in Lancaster that month, plus 7 women and 4 children.[15] Another list from January 7, put together by Hessen-Kassel noncommissioned officers, reported 733 common soldiers, 78 noncommissioned officers, 22 drummers, 6 servants, 1 regimental drummer, and 1 provost in Lancaster—a total of 841 prisoners of war.[16] The rest of the captives taken at Trenton—Regimental Quartermaster Müller of the Regiment von Knyphausen reported 1,007, including 848 common soldiers—either had died already or remained behind sick and wounded at several places on their way from Trenton to Philadelphia and Lancaster.[17] If these men survived, they would join their fellow captives at the barracks.[18] Another concern was supplies. Within a few days of the prisoners' arrival, the entire region experienced a food shortage. On January 27, Town Major Christian Wirtz reported to the Pennsylvania Council of Safety that he was almost out of salt, which both the prisoners and their guards needed in large quantities for preserving meat.[19]

Relief was prompt for the Hessen-Kassel prisoners. On January 20, Regimental Quartermaster Müller arrived in Lancaster to deliver pay, shirts, shoes, socks, and blankets for the soldiers and find out exactly how many men Washington had taken at Trenton. Following established customs, General von Heister in New York, in command of the Hessen-Kassel troops, had sent Müller on his mission on January 3, only days after he had learned about the defeat at Trenton. As Heister wrote to Friedrich II, he was confident that Müller's deliveries would be sufficient "to help out the prisoners until they would be exchanged."[20] Müller left with 500 pairs of shoes, 500 shirts, 480 pairs of socks, and 300 blankets for tents, as well as £900 sterling.[21] On January 12, he and his "six fully-loaded wagons" arrived in Philadelphia, where he had to wait a few days until permission was granted to proceed toward Lancaster. In Lancaster, with Wirtz watching closely, Müller immediately distributed his supplies and the soldiers' pay. He stayed in town for two weeks, noting that the men were getting adequate treatment and rations. Each man received "one pound of good bread and one pound of meat" per day, and everyone had "straw for bedding, wood to keep them warm and to cook, and also the necessary cooking tools." Unfortunately, since Müller was guarded by a "member of the local committee" at all times, it was difficult for him to talk to the men and remind them "of their loyalty to their prince and fatherland." He promised that everything was being done to exchange them as soon as possible, hoping that such reassurance would keep desertion rates low. Support and control went hand in hand.[22]

However, with no exchange possible in the near future, Müller had to come back again in May. This time he delivered 600 pairs of breeches, 500 shirts, 300 pairs of shoes, and 400 pairs of socks.[23] Heister again instructed Müller to do what he could for the prisoners' relief, but also to encourage them "to serve their prince faithfully." Up to this point, he noted proudly, "almost none" of the captives had deserted, "despite promise after promise from the rebels."[24]

On his second visit, Müller noted some changes. Between Philadelphia and Lancaster, he encountered several Hessen-Kassel prisoners riding on horseback. In Lancaster, numerous prisoners were walking freely around town. Noncommissioned officers told Müller that the local revolutionaries allowed prisoners of war to work outside the barracks, and as far as fifty miles away from Lancaster. The prisoners on horseback had been laborers traveling back and forth between Lancaster and their employers. Each German prisoner who worked received food, drink, and 1 shilling in Virginia currency per day. Müller had to ask the Lancaster Town Committee to call in all the prisoner-laborers for a few days so he could distribute their goods and pay. Perhaps realizing that reporting such good living and working conditions for the soldiers in Lancaster might cause concern among his superiors about desertions, Müller added, "As well as they lived as prisoners of war with the revolutionaries, they still longed to be free and with their fellow soldiers as soon as possible."[25]

Because of the British invasion of Pennsylvania later in 1777, only one more supply transport arrived for the Trenton prisoners before their exchange in the summer and fall of 1778. General Wilhelm von Knyphausen, who took command of the Hessen-Kassel troops after Heister was recalled in 1777, sent Regimental Quartermaster Johannes Kitz from the former Regiment Rall with clothing and pay in January 1778, but Kitz never reached the captives in the Pennsylvania hinterland. Revolutionary officials revoked his permission over a dispute with British headquarters about how prisoners of war were to be supplied in the future.[26] Knyphausen was not concerned. He had heard from prisoners who had escaped and made their way back to New York that his captive rank and file still had sufficient clothing. If they received new uniforms, Knyphausen feared, they would only sell them. He also had little problem with the fact that Kitz could not pay the men "because they all worked for wages with farmers and were rather favorably situated."[27] But Knyphausen may have been too optimistic with this assessment. During his uncompleted mission, Kitz was able to talk to some common soldiers, discovering that although the men received sufficient food, the guards had confined thirty of them in the local jail "under sad circumstances." The explanation from William Atlee, the commissary of prisoners in Lancaster, was that no other rooms were available. Kitz also noted that "all prisoners" had begged him to send "uniforms and some money."[28] They were suffering from the cold, but also because the British invasion of Pennsylvania had thrown the entire state into turmoil and disrupted the already shaky supply lines.

German Prisoner-Laborers

Reports from the Hessian supply missions in and around Lancaster show that the revolutionaries had expanded the hiring out of captive German and British soldiers by 1777. Over time, private citizens, revolutionary committees, the army, states, and even Congress used and profited from the practice: captive soldiers were assets that should not be left idle. Being captured by revolutionaries during the American War of Independence thus came to mean work rather than confinement in a prison or barracks. The system worked because it also provided advantages to the prisoners: they earned extra money and escaped crowded housing. In the summer of 1777, Private Reuber was excited when authorities in Lancaster approached him and his fellow prisoners "as friends" and permitted them to "work with farmers in the country." They still received their ration—one pound of bread and one pound of meat—as a monthly payment to their noncommissioned officers. An American who wanted to hire a Hessen-Kassel soldier had only to register with the "city commander" and pay a deposit, ensuring that the prisoner would be brought back if needed.[29] If an employer did not "bring back [the prisoner], or brought him away to the English army, or let him escape, he ha[d] to pay 200 [*Thaler*] paper money to Congress."[30] Employers had to provide "food and drink, and daily . . . six *Albus* [in pay]."[31] This was as much as a day laborer earned in Dresden, Saxony, around 1764 for eleven hours of work in the summer and eight hours of work in the winter.[32] After his capture on a stormy and cold Christmas morning and a harrowing prisoner parade in Philadelphia, everything had finally turned out "all right" for Reuber.[33]

The practice of hiring out the German prisoners of war began with several roll calls at the barracks between January 6 and 10, 1777. Atlee and the Lancaster Town Committee wanted to find out how many of the prisoners had a trade and what skills they possessed. Among the captives who had arrived from Philadelphia, 315 (38 percent) claimed to have a civilian profession. Not surprisingly, considering the social composition of such units, the majority were weavers (94 men), tailors (50 men), and shoemakers (38 men). A great many other trades, however, could also be found (table 6). Even soldiers without a skill could be used as farmhands or for chopping firewood. Lancaster, a town of about 3,300 inhabitants, had a new workforce equivalent in size to a quarter of its population.[34]

On January 11, only one day after the list of tradesmen among the German prisoners of war in Lancaster was completed, the Pennsylvania Council of Safety asked one of its members, William J. Hubley, to employ all the shoemakers among the captives to make "shoes for this state." From the outset, thus, revolutionary authorities used prison labor toward the war effort. To buy the necessary leather, Hubley was advanced £2,000 in Pennsylvania currency. He had to pay his prisoner-laborers an unspecified "small allowance," for which he would later be compensated. Moreover, the Council of Safety decided that prison labor could be used for two other projects in Lancaster: building a magazine and another stone house. Captives who worked near the barracks were to return each day at noon and in the evenings for roll call. Those who worked farther out had to be at the barracks only twice a week.[35]

At this point, the Board of War intervened.[36] Its members were having misgivings about the direction in which the Council of Safety and the Lancaster Town Committee were heading. On January 31, Richard Peters, secretary of the Board of War, wrote to Lancaster that "the Prisoners of War ordered to be confined at Lancaster may be of great Disservice to our Cause if suffered to have Communication with the People of the Country." He complained that they could easily lead German immigrants in the region to fall "off from the Patriotism & commendable Zeal for the Preservation of the Liberties of their Country, for which they were distinguished in the Outset of the Dispute." To prevent such difficulties, the Board of War wanted all prisoners "strictly confined."[37]

The Council of Safety chose to ignore these directives. On February 3, Melchior Isaac was permitted to hire all the nailers

Table 6.   German Prisoners of War in Lancaster Reporting a Trade,
January 1777

Trade	Numbers of Soldiers
Weavers[a]	94
Tailors[b]	50
Shoemakers	38
Smiths[c]	17
Carpenters	15
Wagon makers	15
Masons	12
Joiners	10
Butchers	9
Plasterers	7
Bakers	6
Millers	6
Coopers	4
Locksmiths	4
Pipe makers	2
Lime burners	2
Window makers	2
Nailsmiths	2
Tanners	2
Musicians[d]	2
Bookbinders	2
Dyers	2
Barber, bomb maker,[e] distiller, gardener, hunter, knife maker, rifle maker, silversmith, slater, stonecutter, tile maker, thatcher	1 soldier each
Total	315

[a] Including linen, wool, or stocking weavers. Most were linen or wool weavers (82 soldiers).

[b] Including makers of breeches.

[c] Including blacksmiths.

[d] These may or may not have been the usual fifers and drummers in a company.

[e] Presumably from the Hessen-Kassel artillery.

Sources: "Lists of Hessian Prisoners, Lancaster, January 6–7, 1777," Peter Force Collection, Library of Congress, Washington, D.C., ser. 9, vol. 19; and "List of Tradesmen among Hessian Prisoners at Lancaster, January 10, 1777," David Library of the American Revolution, Washington Crossing, Pa., film 24, roll 11, frame 952.

among the Hessen-Kassel prisoners and take them to Philadelphia for work. The Town Committee requested clarification, asking the Board of War why the captives should not be "usefully" employed. After all, many of them were already working as shoemakers or tailors, and many more might well "be employed at the Barracks in rooms to be fitted up for them." Besides, "tanners, weavers, [and] smiths" were much "wanted in the Town." The Board of War did not stand a chance against such sentiments. On March 3, the Council of Safety even expanded the practice. Having been informed that the barracks in Lancaster were overcrowded, the council allowed prisoner-laborers to be sent out across the county. On April 17, Lancaster received permission to hire out captives to anyone whom they considered reliable and safe.[38] Only two days later, 47 local citizens hired 61 German prisoners of war in Lancaster, an average of 1.3 per employer. George Hinkle hired the largest number, 3 men. The vast majority of the men were listed as "laborers" and probably worked on surrounding farms. Only 6 had specific trades—a weaver, tailor, tile maker, miller, shoemaker, and buckle maker. Workers of all kinds were in demand, and the prisoners were ready and willing.[39]

The Lancaster barracks now housed a significant pool of manpower, and it was used to extend the local revolutionaries' reach into Pennsylvania's hinterland. Atlee declared on March 29 that only Associators should be permitted to hire the prisoners. To increase the ranks of revolutionary supporters, he also wanted to use prison labor as a reward for residents who "have shown themselves friendly to the cause of America" either by providing teams of oxen to the army and militia or through other services.[40] It is unclear, however, how strictly such regulations were observed. Some committed revolutionaries do seem to have profited handsomely. William Henry, for example, opened shoe manufactories in Lancaster, Philadelphia, and Allentown staffed primarily with prisoner-laborers.[41]

Later that year, with the Continental Army needing more supplies, Congress and the Board of War lost any misgivings they might have had about the use of prison labor. When the army lacked lead in October, the Board of War suggested that if no other workers could be found, Commissary General of Prisoners Boudinot should provide "a competent number of prisoners of war" for this task.[42] Prisoners were also hired to manufacture cannons and ammunition. Furnaces and ironworks needed many workers, primarily to cut wood for their furnaces. A number of German captives in Pennsylvania worked at the Cornwall, Berkshire, Hopewell, Elizabeth, Pine Grove, Oley, Tulpehocken, and Charming furnaces.[43] Congress even used prison labor to pay for ammunition and other war goods. In March 1783, for instance, ironworks owner John Jacob Faesch "agreed to discount" money owed to him by Congress "from a contract in 1780" in exchange for thirty-three German prisoner-laborers.[44]

Further information about German prisoner-laborers and their employers in various towns is available for the period between September and November 1777, when the British under General Howe had just invaded Pennsylvania and the prisoners of war in Lancaster had been widely dispersed in the hinterland. During those three months, 395 captives—about half of all common German soldiers in revolutionary hands at the time, most of whom were taken at Trenton—worked for 243 different employers, an average of 1.6 laborers for each employer. Only 2 employers hired 10 or more soldiers: Mark Bird from Reading hired 12 men for several of his mills and furnaces, and Curtis Grubb from Lebanon hired 10 prisoners for his furnace and other ironworks. The vast majority of employers (162) hired only 1 prisoner. The list of employers also includes Thomas Wharton, president of the Supreme Executive Committee of Pennsylvania.[45] In light of such numbers, some historians claim that German and British prison labor was indispensable in keeping the American economy afloat during the Revolutionary War.[46] Prisoners of war did not make up a significant portion of the overall labor force in the rebellious colonies, but locally they were a cheap labor force, readily available and willing to take on almost any job to earn pay and food.[47]

Even more data is available for 178 German prisoner-laborers and their employers in the Lebanon area.[48] Fifty-three soldiers are listed as having a skill or trade. Weavers (21 percent), cloth makers (13 percent), and shoemakers (7.5 percent) made up the largest groups. Others worked as wagoners, tailors, carpenters, blacksmiths, butchers, masons, barbers, leatherworkers, painters, gunsmiths, and joiners. The remaining 125 prisoner-laborers in and around Lebanon between 1777 and 1783 probably worked as farmhands or as common laborers in unspecified occupations. Only 16 men (9 percent) seem to have worked for more than one employer.

In and around Lebanon, the prisoners worked for a total of 130 employers, each of whom hired, on average, 1.3 soldiers. Only one female employer, Dorothea Preese, is recorded. Large-scale manufacturing with prisoner-laborers remained rare. In Lebanon, Curtis Grubb hired the most prisoners over the course of the war, a total of 21. Most of these men came from the Hessen-Kassel artillery and likely served as woodcutters for Grubb's furnaces. The next-largest employer, Adam Orth, hired only 5 soldiers. He also worked in the iron industry and operated the New Market Forge. Interestingly, only 41 (31.5 percent) of the 130 employers who used prison labor in the Lebanon area had also done some kind of revolutionary service—be it committee work, other official posts, or the military—or at least as having sworn the oath of allegiance to the revolutionary government in Pennsylvania. It appears that some employers hired revolutionary prisoners even though they did not actively support the cause.[49]

The possible uses for hundreds of potential laborers in and around Lancaster also interested Christopher Ludwick, the man who had guided the eight Hessen-Kassel prisoners of war from Staten Island through Philadelphia in the fall of 1776. In March 1777, he suggested to Congress that a "discreet & humane German Person" be appointed as "Guardian of the German Prisoners" in North America to muster the men in Philadelphia and Lancaster, "provide masters & Employers for them," and "be their Counsel & solemn Witness in Contracts which they may make with their Employers." In other words, Ludwick wanted to be installed as a powerful supervisor for all German prisoner-laborers. He claimed, of course, to have only the captives' wants and the public's needs in mind. After all, he wrote, "many of the Hessians & Waldeckish Prisoners of War especially single men are so well pleased with this Country and the Way of its Inhabitants that at all

Events they would rather prefer to settle here than to return to the dreary abodes of Bondage from whence they came." Allowing these soldiers and prisoners to "breath[e] in the open fragrancy of America's freedom" would be proof of "American Public Benevolence and lay them under further Obligation to a Generous & Merciful Enemy."[50]

Although this plan was never adopted, it shows how American revolutionaries tried to make use of German prisoners of war. In this case, labor would expose the prisoners to the advantages of life in America. Ludwick assumed that the German captives were waiting for a chance to leave their units and settle in North America. However, the available data again does not confirm such assertions. Among the 178 German prisoner-laborers recorded in the Pennsylvania hinterland, only 27 (15 percent) ended up deserting. This number is even lower than the expected desertion rate (18–20 percent) among all prisoners of war held by eighteenth-century European armies.[51] Moreover, most deserters around Lebanon ran away only after 1782, when conditions for prisoners of war in revolutionary hands had worsened considerably.

Given the opportunity, German prisoners usually accepted work eagerly. Hessian drummers and fifers taken captive at Trenton in 1776 willingly took part in the celebrations of the first anniversary of American independence in Philadelphia on July 4, 1777.[52] Soldiers in the Holy Roman Empire regularly worked in civilian trades; thus in some ways, captivity for the German prisoners of war resembled regular garrison life.[53] In fact, not being able to apply their trades while in captivity might have generated more fear among the soldiers: they badly needed the extra income. This confluence of interests made the prison labor system function smoothly in 1777 and 1778. American communities did not want to shoulder the burden of keeping large numbers of enemy captives and were already experiencing labor shortages. Revolutionary institutions on all levels lacked the resources, organization, and policies to adequately confine captive soldiers. Everyone realized the great potential these prisoners had to relieve such problems and even earn a profit. At the same time, however, German rank and file in revolutionary hands became decentralized and, because of the labor system, largely privatized.

Resistance

There were times in Lancaster when German prisoners of war stood up against perceived mistreatment by the revolutionaries. During the first two weeks of March 1777, for example, there was a case of orchestrated passive resistance among the Hessen-Kassel prisoners of war at the barracks. For several days, according to William Atlee, common soldiers, led by their noncommissioned officers, stopped "cleaning the filth" out of the yard. Unfortunately, no Hessen-Kassel sources mention this incident. It is clear, however, that Atlee and the revolutionaries in Lancaster viewed such behavior as a challenge to their authority and moved quickly to restore order.[54]

After the guards alerted Atlee to the prisoners' conduct, he immediately struck back where it hurt the captives most. He ordered the guard "to prevent their Women coming into Town for necessaries & also to prevent any Vegetables, Milk, & other little articles being taken in to them." Cut off from fresh food and their essential network of female companions, the prisoners gave up their protest within a day and requested shovels and spades to clean the barracks ground. To teach them a further lesson, Atlee prohibited the delivery of supplies to the barracks for another day. After this experience, he assumed, the prisoners would be "glad to do their bid" at the barracks and refrain from acting "saucy" in the future. He also interrogated the noncommissioned officers, whom he suspected to have been the real "bakers of the Frolick," and put them on bread and water for several days. Thereafter, Atlee believed, the prisoners would think twice about organizing resistance.

While Reuber did not report this incident, he gave a detailed account of a revolt staged by British prisoners at the Lancaster barracks on June 4, 1777, the birthday of King George III.[55] Regimental Quartermaster Müller from the Regiment von Knyphausen, who was in Lancaster at the time of the Hessen-Kassel resistance, also failed to report that incident but provided a comprehensive account of the events on June 4. Both Reuber and Müller emphasized that no Germans participated in the riot that day. In fact, the Hessen-Kassel prisoners of war resisted British efforts to make them join the revolt. Once the uprising was suppressed, according to Reuber, the Germans enjoyed better treatment and more freedom than their fellow British captives. However, the revolutionary guards at the barracks claimed that the Hessen-Kassel soldiers in fact "did play a very large role in the uproar." Contrary to what Reuber asserted in his journal, Lancaster's authorities temporarily forbade all prisoners of war to leave the barracks, not just the British. Müller noted angrily in his report that he was "greatly hindered . . . in distributing" shirts, shoes, socks, and blankets to the Hessen-Kassel rank and file.[56]

The revolt had begun in the evening, when roughly three hundred British prisoners of war in the barracks illuminated their windows. They gave candles to the Hessen-Kassel prisoners so that they could do the same, but the Germans declined—or so they claimed. The British prisoners then went downstairs to start several large fires in the barracks yard. As Reuber described it, much drinking and toasting went on, and the British soldiers became greatly agitated. According to Müller, British prisoners in town and the prisoners at the barracks had agreed beforehand to strike against their guards that day. Later that night, the British prisoners at the barracks overwhelmed the fifteen guards there and took away their muskets. Lancaster sent additional soldiers to the scene—Reuber even mentioned two cannons—who fired into the crowd of British prisoners in the barracks yard, killing one soldier from the British 17th Regiment and seriously wounding another. The rest of the British prisoners fled for safety. Order was restored after this attack, presumably by the Lancaster militia, but the atmosphere between the Hessen-Kassel and British prisoners was poisoned. As Reuber wrote in his journal, "Suddenly, the English turned hostile and sullen toward us because we were treated better."[57] Müller reported that the guards searched every British room and found several old bayonets as well as other weapons "made from wood." Apparently, a number of British prisoners had planned to escape from the barracks that night.[58] The Lancaster Committee of Safety concluded that the revolt was caused largely by overcrowding: there were "too many Prisoners" in the town. Guarding them had become increasingly difficult, and even basic supplies were lacking.[59]

The chance to profit from prison labor sometimes led to exploitation and abuse. One notorious case surfaced in December 1777, when George Lindenberger, a city magistrate in Baltimore, saw Richard Lemon and several other men threatening ten Hessen-Kassel prisoners of war, who were accompanied by a woman and her son, with "handcuffing, flaying, short allowances &c." When questioned by Lindenberger, Lemon claimed that the Hessians had breached a contract by refusing to go to the Sinepuxent Bay saltworks, just south of modern-day Ocean City, Maryland. As Lindenberger, who also owned shares in the saltworks, soon discovered, however, the Hessians had good reasons to resist. They originally had been hired in the Lebanon area and were told that the saltworks were in York, Pennsylvania; once there, they were informed that the saltworks were actually in Baltimore; in Baltimore, they were ordered to board a ship and "proceed still farther about 200 miles." Understandably, they no longer trusted their employers and feared being taken farther and farther away from their fellow soldiers and prisoners—with a good chance that they would never be able to return.[60] Despite Lindenberger's repeated intervention, Lemon continued to drive the soldiers before him toward the harbor "with his Sword." He told Lindenberger that the matter was "none of your Business." A few hours later, Lindenberger found out that Lemon had taken the captives to a less populous part of town and "beat them with cudgels" to make them comply and board his ship. Fearing that accounts of such violence and abuse "might have great Influence on the bad Treatment of our Brethren now in the power of the Enemy," he ordered Captain Alexander Furnival from the city guard to take the German prisoners into custody for their own protection.[61]

Expanding Authority

The British invasion of Pennsylvania began on August 25, 1777, when large British and German forces under Generals Howe and von Knyphausen landed near Head of Elk, Maryland, in the Chesapeake Bay. After an earlier attempt in the spring, Howe wanted to take control of the revolutionary capital. Washington and his Continental Army tried to block the enemy's advance but failed, first at Brandywine Creek on September 11, and again at German-town on October 4. British and German troops marched into un-defended Philadelphia at the end of September. Congress fled before the advancing enemy to York. Pennsylvania's revolutionary government found refuge in Lancaster.[62]

It was no longer safe for Lancaster to keep British and German prisoners of war in the same area. It was feared that the captives might stage a revolt, or at least try to escape. In August, when it had become clear that the invasion was coming, Lancaster's revo-lutionary authorities had collected as many prisoners of war as they could find from their employers and sent them farther into the hinterland, away from the advancing British army. In Lan-caster, Christopher Marshall witnessed the "morning bellman" walking around town, "calling upon the inhabitants that had Hessian prisoners to take them to the Barracks."[63] Considerable disagreement, however, developed between local communities, Pennsylvania, and Congress over the final destinations for the cap-tives. Reading, for instance, flatly refused to take any prisoners. Major General Thomas Mifflin and seventeen other revolutionary families had recently arrived there from Philadelphia and lobbied hard to prevent hundreds of German and British captives from coming to town.[64]

Authorities in Lancaster, thus, decided to divide the prisoners. Between 250 and 400 British prisoners of war—the numbers are not entirely clear—were marched to Bethlehem, in Pennsylvania's Moravian heartland. Most of the German captives collected in and around Lancaster were taken to Lebanon, another Moravian center. An account of firewood and straw shows that at least 840 prisoners of war were in the small town in late August 1777.[65] The arrival of so many captives severely disrupted life in these com-munities. "From then on," the Moravian journal in Bethlehem stated, "the street from the Brethren's house to the tavern became the world's playground, full of crime and filled with the roars of drums and fifes."[66]

In Lebanon, William Atlee and Curtis Grubb quartered the pris-oners in requisitioned churches, the only large buildings available in the area. They designated a single church in town as a house of worship for all denominations.[67] Records show that 200 prisoners were initially placed in the local Reformed church. Others were housed in the town's Lutheran church. The largest group, however, between 270 and 340 soldiers plus about 20 women and several children, was taken to nearby Hebron and placed in the Moravian church headed by the Reverend Christian Bader.[68]

Cramming so many soldiers into so few buildings created a difficult situation. On September 8, Atlee informed Boudinot that he had heard about cases of smallpox among the captives and wanted to move some of them from Lebanon to Reading—but Reading again refused to take them. It was thus decided that 320 German prisoners of war would be sent farther south, to Winchester, Virginia, in the Shenandoah Valley.[69] Among them was Private Reuber from the Regiment Rall. He later recalled the chaos of those days. As local revolutionaries issued one confusing order after another, many prisoners apparently took the opportunity to run away.[70]

Those who made it to Winchester, however, soon found themselves in relatively favorable circumstances. According to Reuber, the local revolutionary authorities treated the German prisoners of war better than the British prisoners because more British than German captives had tried to escape during their march south from Lebanon. While the German prisoners were quartered with citizens in town, "the English were put into a large prison and were kept there under guard." If a British prisoner "wanted to go into town and buy something, he was escorted by a guard," whereas the Hessen-Kassel men "could walk around and away as much as four hours or more and no inhabitant of this country stopped them." To Reuber, it seemed that he and his fellow prisoners from Trenton "were not kept as enemies" in Winchester "but treated as friends."[71] He also noted that the prisoners received "one pound of Bread and one pound of meat" and had to pay extra only for other supplies.[72]

The rest of the captives—about 520 men, plus several women and children—remained in Lebanon and Hebron against the Moravians' wishes. Ministers such as Bader tried everything to avoid having to house them.[73] As pacifists, the Moravians were opposed to any soldiers, particularly professional European troops, prisoners or not. Bader and his brethren believed that revolutionary committees in Lancaster and Lebanon had plotted against them and targeted their churches as detention facilities for the German prisoners.

The Moravians were probably right. Because of their pacifism and their suspected strong ties to the British—an outcome of their missionary work among American Indians—they were held in contempt by the radicals who led the revolutionary effort in Pennsylvania in 1776 and 1777. Members of the church suffered considerable persecution when they refused, for religious reasons, to take the new oath of allegiance as required by the Test Act of June 1777. Even worse, they also refused to become Associators and join the fight against Great Britain.[74] As a result, they were subjected to fines and other forms of harassment, even beatings. Some of them were also imprisoned. One of the leading Moravians in Hebron, Christopher Kucher, went to jail in June 1778, along with some coreligionists and several Mennonites, because he refused to swear the oath of allegiance. The Moravians in Hebron feared that the Reverend Bader was next in line.[75]

Sending large numbers of prisoners of war into Moravian towns such as Bethlehem, Lebanon, and Hebron was more than just a desperate move to secure housing for the captives and keep them safe and away from the British. At least indirectly, the prisoners also became a means for the revolutionaries in Pennsylvania to establish and expand their authority over a part of the population that had remained indifferent at best toward the American cause.[76] The entire revolutionary war effort came to town with the prisoners. Revolutionaries began directing almost every aspect of daily life. Militia units arrived as guards. Food supplies and other transports had to be organized. Prisoners were hired out as laborers. Private property—buildings as well as wagons—was seized for revolutionary service. Bethlehem had to quarter not only British prisoners of war but also a large Continental Army hospital.[77]

A long period of "misery" began for the Moravians in Hebron when the German prisoners of war arrived at their church.[78] Hebron consisted of only one large two-story house, with a church hall on the second floor and several outbuildings. The Reverend Bader lived with his wife and two children on the first floor. He headed a small congregation of about 140 men, women, and children. In 1777 and 1778, the German prisoners of war heavily outnumbered the Moravians. They occupied the entire church hall as well as the rest of the second floor, the stable, and several rooms on Bader's floor.[79]

With so many captives and soldiers in the region, Bethlehem and Lebanon frequently suffered from food and supply shortages, and diseases broke out. On October 27, 1777, the Bethlehem Moravians' diary reported that "the sick in the hospital die fast, we had six dead bodies last night."[80] In February 1778, Bader wrote to the Reverend Nathaniel Seidel in Bethlehem that he and his flock at Hebron were in utter despair. They were forced to live among prisoners "whose behavior was not edifying." The prisoners had damaged the church hall, and "devastation" surrounded the house. Despite his many protests, the captives remained, while Bader and his family were repeatedly told to leave. Bader felt as if they had to stay "in the midst of the Hessians, as fellow prisoners."[81] When the German prisoners of war finally left Hebron on March 1, Bader and his congregation were shocked at the sight of their church: "The hall looked like a pigsty."[82] Little did they know that the revolutionaries had a new plan for the church: the local militia wanted to use it as a powder magazine. In protest, Bader and his fellow Moravians nailed the church door shut and petitioned the Board of War. The revolutionaries, however, simply broke into the house, deposited their powder barrels, and told Bader and his family to leave. With this turn of events, the Moravians were forced to realize that a new power governed their lives.[83]

Daily Life

Despite their strong bias against the prisoners, the diaries of the Moravians at Hebron and Bethlehem provide insight into an aspect of daily life for common soldiers that is often not recorded in other sources: time off from labor and military routine. When the prisoners first arrived in Hebron in the late summer of 1777, Bader was surprised at their good behavior. On the first evening, the captives sang hymns and said "a long prayer." The following Sunday, they voluntarily cleared the hall and prepared it for Bader's service and even asked to be allowed to listen to his sermon.

Although the church hall in Hebron was "totally overcrowded" and other brethren complained about the soldiers' presence, Bader was pleased. The prisoners had "made the music" during the service and were interested in his teachings. It was probably no coincidence that he preached about the lepers healed by Jesus in Luke 17:11. Over the following weeks, he noted that several captives from Lebanon had also begun attending his service. The German prisoners even helped Bader and his family harvest their buckwheat, which had to be done earlier than usual because livestock from the neighboring Volk family had trampled a lot of grain. On September 17, the Hebron diary read: "Volk's cattle and swine cause more trouble than the Hessians." In late November and early December, Bader and his congregation learned that some of the captives wanted to join the Moravian church. The diary mentions one private and "twelve of his fellow soldiers" who "wanted to live as we do." In this, Bader believed, one could see the "workings of the holy spirit." The Moravians in Bethlehem were also surprised by the soldiers' hunger for religious services. The British prisoners there were "attentive listeners" in church. When "Mr. Webb preached to them in the courtyard," the Bethlehem journal noted, the captives told him that they had not heard "a sermon for as long as they had been imprisoned."[84] It is easy to understand how soldiers who had endured long campaigns, battles, and captivity in a distant land might have longed for the comforts of religion. Field chaplains had been sent to North America with the German auxiliaries, but they usually did not accompany the rank and file during a campaign or into captivity; if they did, they were normally housed with the officers.[85]

Most of the prisoners liked the singing and dancing as much as they liked Bader's sermons. In the evening of September 15, for instance, the men "began to fiddle near the street and became very merry." Bader was dismayed because the captives had taken the congregation's bass on this occasion. He sent a noncommissioned officer to reclaim it, but the prisoners refused to relinquish the instrument. In his nightgown, Bader went outside to talk with them. They politely "made room, doffed their hats, and begged him to leave the bass with them," but he took it back inside. Even without it, however, the prisoners continued to sing and dance.

They "formed a small circle, played the fiddle, and danced with each other." Only heavy rain finally drove them apart and back to their quarters. The next morning, Bader scolded the prisoners for their behavior and asked whether such celebrations would have been allowed in a Hessian church or vicarage. They admitted that their behavior would not have been permitted in garrison at home.[86]

Only two days later, there was another occasion for singing and dancing. A few imprisoned *Jäger* quartered in Lebanon had received permission from Daniel Oldenbruck, a captain in the Lebanon militia, to join their fellow soldiers in Hebron for a visit. Upon the *Jäger*'s arrival, their comrades "blew their horns and played the fiddle and danced in the hall." But this time the celebrations got wilder. The rank and file had apparently refused to obey their noncommissioned officers—something that happened frequently, according to the Moravian diary, because so many different prisoners from various units and principalities were confined together—and one of the German noncommissioned officers asked Bader to intervene. When Bader told the prisoners to stop, however, they ignored him as well. The militia guard that had accompanied the *Jäger* from Lebanon had joined in the revelries and "rudely" told Bader to leave. Order was restored only when the guards in Hebron finally called for Captain Oldenbruck. The *Jäger* were taken back to Lebanon and placed under arrest. The next day, the Hebron diary noted, the prisoners were again "really quiet, neat, and proper." Moreover, they "tried to make everything pretty, more than usual, because they did not want to lose their lodgings" in Hebron. The Moravians hoped that the prisoners would now see the "great power that the Reverend had."[87]

Even when the prisoners of war did not behave as Bader wanted, some always gave him hope. After a night during which the prisoners "drank a lot and made a lot of noise," several men who were "touched by the holy spirit" came to Bader, including one "already call[ed] a *Herrnhuter* [Moravian]" by his fellow captives. After some prisoners stole wood from the house and fence and burned it, even Bader had to acknowledge that they had done it not out of spite but because they needed firewood. Yet when he discovered on Christmas Eve that the prisoners had begun to "chop meat" in the rooms and church hall upstairs, he was too angry to hold a vigil as the prisoners had asked him to do.[88]

Drinking was very common among the soldiers. Not surprisingly, such behavior did not meet with Bader's approval. When a popular German noncommissioned officer who had been placed under arrest a few days earlier was released on January 1, 1778, everyone "drank heartily." For the Moravians in Hebron, it seemed as if the soldiers "did not know how to express their joy otherwise." The situation that night got out of hand. By nine o'clock, Bader's wife tried and failed to calm the prisoners. They became "so wild in the hall that we thought it was filled with stupid and mad beasts." Even the noncommissioned officers among the prisoners called for the guards and began "beating a few of the ringleaders."[89] A Hessen-Kassel sergeant blamed everything on fourteen of the seventeen women present with the captives—they all sold alcohol. "The house had fourteen taverns," he told Bader, "with thirteen of them in the church hall."[90] While these comments certainly reflected contemporary prejudices, it should be noted that eighteenth-century armies, including captives, were dependent upon a baggage train of camp followers, who supplied the men with food and other goods, including alcohol.

In January 1778, to Bader's dismay, more German prisoners of war arrived in Hebron. The captives who had been working on area farms had apparently returned for the winter.[91] Space became scarce, and Bader was forced to give up another one of his family's private rooms. Nobody knew "where else the prisoners should go." About 150 captives stayed in the house, according to the Hebron diary, with many others quartered in the surrounding buildings. In this overcrowded environment, as the diary reported on January 6, the prisoners celebrated, danced, and made a lot of noise on Epiphany. On January 7, Colonel Grubb and Captain Oldenbruck from the militia prohibited alcohol in the men's quarters.[92]

However, such measures changed little. On January 21, it seemed to the Moravians as if "all furies with Mephistopheles and Fizlipuzli" had come out to take possession of the German prisoners when they became terribly drunk.[93] Numerous fights broke out among soldiers and female sutlers. The Hebron diary blamed all these troubles on the easy availability of alcohol. More fights followed on January 22 and 23. Only on January 25, it seems, did the situation calm down a bit. "The Hessians were quiet," the diary states on that day, "they did neither have beer nor spirits." By February 2, the prisoners had apparently run out of money to buy alcohol. Perhaps they had heard about Regimental Quartermaster Kitz's planned supply transport earlier in January, and had spent their remaining money freely in the days and weeks before his expected arrival. One can only imagine the disappointment when Kitz "failed to appear with their pay and uniform parts."[94]

$\sim$

When the first large group of German prisoners of war were transported to Lancaster in 1776, the town was not prepared to deal with them. There was not enough room to house the nearly nine hundred new arrivals, and food was already in short supply. Like the British prisoners, however, the German captives were quickly seen as a source of labor for the surrounding community. Soon they were traveling freely, providing badly needed help to a large number of employers. In addition to being paid, they were housed and fed by the people they worked for, which reduced the burden of their care. The revolutionaries began to capitalize on this new source of manpower, too, controlling it to their advantage and often profiting from it financially. When the British invaded Pennsylvania, however, the German captives were split up into several smaller groups and moved farther into the state's hinterland, where they began experiencing new privations. They were about to get caught in the middle of a standoff between Congress and the British over the treatment and provisioning of prisoners of war.

CHAPTER 8

Provisions and Exchange, 1778

While Reuber and the other Hessen-Kassel captives from Trenton were living and working in and around Lebanon and Winchester, Congress changed the way in which prisoners of war received provisions, and the British followed suit. By late 1778, the two sides supplied the prisoners on their own rather than through agents, keeping accounts for later reimbursement. Numerous disputes erupted over these costs, preventing general prisoner exchanges and resulting in reduced rations for many captives for the remainder of the war. The problem started in mid-1777 when the British army in North America was temporarily struggling to repay its prisoner-of-war agents. Driven by anger over the treatment of revolutionary soldiers and seamen in British hands, particularly in New York, Congress tried to exploit the situation by altering the supply system for British prisoners of war, placing additional costs on the crown. At the same time, Congress, General Washington, and various state governments also clashed over prisoner supplies. In the end, it took until the summer of 1778 to free the Hessen-Kassel prisoners of war from Trenton through a partial exchange.

A New Provisioning System

As of August 1777, the British Treasury had not yet reimbursed Nesbitt, Drummond, & Franks for "furnishing . . . Fourteen Hundred Prisoners for which Service [British agent David Franks] has drawn upon . . . considerable Sums." Nor had the contractors been paid by December, even though they had delivered £9,600

worth of provisions to prisoners in three revolutionary states—
Virginia, Maryland, and Pennsylvania. The contractors had not
succeeded in securing the necessary certificates from the British
commanders-in-chief in North America, General Howe in 1777
and General Clinton in 1778. Without such proof that they had
delivered those provisions, the Treasury would not reimburse the
company.[1]

The revolutionary commissary general of prisoners, Elias
Boudinot, noticed that something was wrong in the fall of 1777.
By November, having yet to be repaid, British agents faced problems delivering provisions to the captives. Boudinot warned his
British counterpart in Philadelphia, Hugh Ferguson, that the prisoners would "inevitably suffer" if provisions did not arrive soon.[2]
Because Franks and his brother in London had not been reimbursed for their expenditures, they could not reimburse their subcontractors, men such as Joseph Simon in Lancaster. In May 1778,
thus, Simon notified David Franks that he would no longer act as
agent unless he was immediately paid in specie.[3] At that time, in
London, Moses Franks decided to "entirely disengage from any
further connection in this business" because the British Treasury
still had not repaid his expenses. Sarcastically, he told his brother
in Philadelphia, "If you proceed in [this business], we wish you
prosperity."[4]

Simon had demanded payment in specie because the Continental Congress had resolved on December 19, 1777, that the
British must discharge all accounts for provisioning British and
German prisoners of war in revolutionary hands either in kind
or in gold and silver. Washington had recommended such measures because they would counter British attempts to pay for the
prisoners' provisions with counterfeited bills while increasing the
amount of hard money circulating in revolutionary America. The
"means of relieving" American prisoners in British hands, Washington added, would also improve.[5] However, Congress set the exchange rate of the British pound to the Continental dollar at an
exorbitant rate, 4 shillings 6 pence to 1 dollar. This action was felt
to be justified because Howe had demanded that the revolutionaries send the provisions for their prisoners into British-occupied
Philadelphia and was not allowing congressional agents to buy any

provisions inside the city. Moreover, he had forbidden the circulation of Continental currency in British territory.[6]

In response, Boudinot announced to Hugh Ferguson in January 1778 that the British would now have to supply all of their soldiers in revolutionary hands with "every kind of Provisions" and that agents such as David Franks were no longer allowed to buy provisions in revolutionary territory. In turn, Congress would supply the American soldiers in British hands with everything they needed. Boudinot argued that the revolutionaries had the right to set up this new supply system for prisoners of war because British "agents . . . purchase every kind of Provisions at their Pleasure among us, whilst our Agent is refused the Privilege of purchasing necessary Clothing with you."[7]

Howe was truly concerned. The captives held by the revolutionaries were widely dispersed over a number of states, and without agents for the prisoners in American territory, he argued in a letter to Washington, the British would have to deliver provisions to places three or four hundred miles away from New York and Philadelphia, the two major cities under their control at the time. Boudinot's proposal would "destroy" British and German prisoners of war "by famine," he said. The soldiers' "means of existence" came "from the Nature of Things" and should be supplied "on the spot." Only clothing, pay, and other equipment could feasibly be "provided at a Distance."[8]

Washington agreed with Howe's reasoning and assured him that Boudinot's most extreme measures would not be implemented.[9] However, Congress based its ultimate decision on reports by Boudinot and the Board of War. Both concluded in early 1778 that about 1,400 revolutionary rank and file and about 350 officers were currently in British hands, mostly in and around New York. In their judgment, the British systematically mistreated these prisoners, closely confining them in unhealthy conditions on prison ships or in jails, and feeding them meager rations of only four ounces of meat and bread per day.[10] British and German prisoners of war in revolutionary hands, on the other hand, enjoyed much better conditions: "the prisoners taken from the enemy have been plentifully supplied with provisions either at the expense of these States or by Commissaries in the service of the enemy." Instead of being confined in jails, the prisoners were "permitted to work abroad and to receive the full price of their labour."[11]

In January 1778, therefore, Congress decided that British agents could no longer "negotiate bills with these United States" to purchase provisions, clothing, or anything else for their soldiers in revolutionary hands unless they first delivered accurate accounts of all their captive soldiers to the American Commissary of Purchases. Only this commissary could thereafter supply rations to the prisoners for their "weekly or monthly subsistence, as circumstances shall render necessary." In addition, receipts would be issued and had to be paid in kind or in specie by the British army within thirty days. Until these demands were met, Boudinot and his deputies were directed to "call in" all officers and privates "belonging to the enemy, and to confine them, in such places, and order them to be subsisted and treated in such manner, as shall render their situation similar . . . to that of the officers and privates, who are prisoners with the enemy." Congress, in other words, again threatened the British with retaliation. This time, with thousands of British and German soldiers in revolutionary hands after the victories at Trenton, Bennington, and Saratoga, it seemed to work. By March, Boudinot acknowledged that American prisoners of war in New York were faring better. He credited this improvement, however, primarily to the "industry and attention" of Lewis Pintard, the revolutionary agent who was finally allowed to operate inside the city.[12]

The use of agents to provision British and German prisoners of war thus ended in 1778. Congress wanted to apply continued pressure on the British through a different system. In March, a congressional committee headed by Gouverneur Morris openly admitted as much. When advising General Washington about upcoming negotiations for a general prisoner exchange, the committee stated that "no Fact can be clearer than this that Interest alone (and not Principles of Justice or Humanity) governs Men on such Occasions." The military should not be "dazzled with Misconceived or ill applied Notions of Honor." The British were having trouble obtaining enough provisions for their troops in North America; their "Supplies of Money" had begun to "run low," and they were "much affected by the Resolutions of Congress compelling them to send Provision [for prisoners] in Specie or pay for it in hard money at a par Exchange." After all, the committee continued, if both sides agreed to supply their prisoners of war through their enemy's currency, "what would be the Consequence but that our Resources must be . . . exhausted in maintaining our Enemies and this by Reason of their Knavery and our Folly." Under the new arrangement, with the exchange rate so high, the committee predicted that prisoner-of-war support would cost the British much more than the revolutionaries. The capture of Burgoyne's army at Saratoga in October 1777 had put the United States in a powerful position because "maintaining so large a Number of their Prisoners will bring in considerable Supplies of solid Coin." At the same time, the "principle of retaliation" would compel the British to grant revolutionary captives the same liberties that British and German prisoners enjoyed in revolutionary hands. The committee also advised against a general prisoner exchange; otherwise the returning American seamen, militia, and Continental soldiers would "scatter abroad thro the Country," providing "little or no Addition of Strength" to the Continental Army. From the committee's perspective, it made more sense to keep larger numbers of American prisoners in British hands than to exchange them. That way, the United States would benefit from British specie payments for prisoner support and could avoid losing exchanged American soldiers whose enlistments had expired or who belonged to state militias or were seamen from state-commissioned privateers. If an exchange were to be negotiated, the British would get their well-trained regular soldiers back and quickly add them to the strength of their army operating in North America. The committee cautioned Washington and his negotiators not to follow a "Headlong Desire of relieving the Miseries of our unhappy fellow Countrymen or a blind Attachment to Principles which the Enemy disregards." Instead, they should propose terms for the exchange that the British could not accept and intentionally let the negotiations fail. Who would "suffer most by the Accident," the committee asked rhetorically, the British or the revolutionaries? Not surprisingly, negotiations for a general cartel in the spring of 1778 went nowhere. Only a partial exchange of most of the Trenton prisoners was achieved that year.[13] Prisoners of war had become an integral part of the war effort. Their treatment and supply system were now another arena for an increasingly bitter struggle between the motherland and its former colonies.

It took the British a few more months to reach a conclusion about prisoner-of-war support. In September 1778, Joshua Loring, the British commissary of prisoners in New York, announced that the revolutionaries were thenceforth expected to supply their British captives "with Provisions, Fuel, & every other necessary of life (Clothing exempted) in like manner as we do yours." David Franks and his associates would no longer distribute any provisions or other items on the "Public accounts."[14] In November, Thomas Bradford, revolutionary commissary of prisoners in Philadelphia, instructed two of Franks's former deputies, Joseph Holmes in Winchester and William Atlee in Lancaster, to supply the German and British prisoners under their care with the same rations given to American prisoners by the British: roughly four pounds and ten ounces of bread, two pounds and ten ounces of pork, two pints of peas, four ounces of butter, and five ounces of oatmeal per man per week—significantly less than the captives had received earlier in the war.[15]

For David Franks, however, the affair was not yet over. His work as supply agent for British and German prisoners of war in revolutionary American hands, as well as his sister's marriage to New York loyalist Oliver De Lancey, made Congress suspicious of him, and he was jailed twice, in November 1778 and again in April 1779.[16] In both cases, he was accused of secretly communicating with the British enemy. Timothy Matlack, the secretary of Pennsylvania's Supreme Executive Council, published two intercepted letters from Franks to his brother Moses in London. In one letter, David reported the high costs of provisions in North America. In the other, he expressed relief about the acquittal of William Hamilton, a friend of his son, who also had been accused of treason by the revolutionaries. He wrote that too many people in revolutionary America were arrested "at the pleasure of every scoundrel." In 1780, Congress ordered David Franks to leave Pennsylvania and not to "return again to any of these United States during the continuance of the present war."[17] Franks had failed in his attempt to keep his business while also acting in the traditional role of agent for prisoners of war. In earlier wars fought without a revolutionary impetus, occupying such an intermediary position might have been possible, but no longer.

The question remains whether the Americans were justified in accusing the British of mistreating revolutionary prisoners in New York City. As Edwin Burrows notes, rumors circulated after the battles on Long Island and around New York City in 1776 that the British summarily executed captured revolutionary soldiers. Many former colonists believed such horror stories because Great Britain at the time did not yet recognize revolutionary captives as legitimate prisoners of war. Moreover, at times there were staggering numbers of revolutionary Americans in British hands. Burrows estimates that British forces in North America held 30,000 revolutionary soldiers over the course of the war. Among those, 18,000 men—about 60 percent—did not survive. Many died on the infamous prison ships in New York Harbor. The British placed prisoners of war on hulks for two main reasons: tradition—it had been done at least since 1745—and availability. Between 1775 and 1783, they occupied primarily coastal areas and cities in North America, not wider areas suitable for housing prisoners of war farther inland.[18]

Accounts of the terrible conditions under which these men were kept in New York spread throughout the revolutionary states. In January 1777, Congress appointed a commission to examine conditions for American prisoners of war in British hands. Led by the Reverend John Witherspoon, then president of the College of New Jersey, the commission concluded that the British treated their captives "with the greatest barbarity" and had even raped and assaulted women. They had also killed revolutionary soldiers who wanted to surrender. The report was printed and distributed in 4,000 English and 2,000 German copies, causing an outcry against the British enemy in revolutionary America. Whether the accusations were actually true did not matter much.[19]

Burrows concludes that the British did not set out to kill imprisoned revolutionaries intentionally. Rather, many of their captives died from a "lethal convergence . . . of obstinacy, condescension, corruption, mendacity, and indifference." After Saratoga, however, when the British first faced the uncomfortable realization that more of their own men were in enemy hands than vice versa, the treatment of revolutionary prisoners of war in New York City improved, albeit slowly. With the conclusion of the French-American alliance, the revolutionaries had also gained some legitimacy and could put added pressure on the British to treat and supply their captives adequately. By the spring of 1778, Boudinot reported that circumstances for the American prisoners in New York were "as decent as could be expected."[20]

Clinton and his later successor as commander-in-chief for North America, Sir Guy Carleton, had no intention of following Congress's 1778 regulations. When the fall of Savannah at the end of 1778 and Charleston in 1780 left thousands of revolutionary soldiers in British hands, the principle of reciprocity suddenly worked in Britain's favor again. From 1778 until the end of the war, the two sides supplied their prisoners of war on their own accounts, waiting and negotiating for later reimbursement. Great Britain could compensate such losses better than the United States. When the revolutionaries gained thousands of new British and German prisoners of war after Cornwallis's army capitulated at Yorktown in 1781, the situation became desperate. Congress did not know where to obtain the funds to purchase the provisions for these new captives, and the British steadfastly refused to issue reimbursements. During those last years of the war, Congress repeatedly pressed the British for some kind of repayment of prisoner costs, but with no success. The British were well aware that the United States was hurting financially. The plight of individual prisoners of war, on both sides, mattered little. The captives could only hope that a prisoner exchange would free them at some point.

Prisoner Exchange

A prisoner exchange, whether through an individual agreement between commanders or a general cartel between states, was traditionally the most important way in which captors made use of their captives. Exchanges freed an army's own trained soldiers and reduced the costs associated with keeping large numbers of enemy soldiers for longer periods. Such cartels had become so ubiquitous in Europe in the early modern period that some agreements were concluded before the first battles of a war were even fought.[21] During the American War of Independence, however, Congress and King George III could not reach agreement over a general cartel. Only individual agreements for partial exchanges, struck between commanders or commissaries for a specific group of captives, were negotiated and carried out, often hampered by long delays and contentious debates. Thousands of captive soldiers on both sides remained in enemy hands for years. The most persistent problem standing in the way of a general cartel was the question of the revolutionaries' legitimacy. Reaching such an accord would have meant that on some level, the British acknowledged the "rebels" as acceptable belligerents, and that was a signal they wanted to avoid sending. Partial exchanges were easier to accomplish.

Nevertheless, conflicts and competing interests made such agreements tricky for the revolutionaries. At times when they held more captives than the British, for instance, Congress was reluctant to agree to an exchange because the British would thereby gain soldiers without having to recruit and transport new troops from Europe. Washington, however, always wanted to get back as many of his Continentals through exchange as was possible. He was less concerned with soldiers whose enlistments had expired or who belonged to a state militia. Individual states repeatedly disregarded any directives coming from him or from Congress and negotiated exchanges with the British army to free their own citizens. Moreover, the British normally held many more American seamen than land forces as prisoners. They usually captured these men on privateers, outfitted by a particular state. Once exchanged, these sailors would not add to the strength of the U.S. military but would only return home or simply start privateering again.[22]

Since the outbreak of the war, there had been repeated calls from both sides for a general cartel. On March 11, 1778, Washington and Howe finally agreed to start talks. Howe instructed his commissioners to "take under their Consideration all past Transactions relative to the exchange of Prisoners, to adjust the

Differences which have so long subsisted in regard to them; to
remove all Difficulties that may arise in carrying into Execution
a General Exchange of the prisoners . . . and finally to establish
a regular and explicit Cartel for the future." But the commissioners were not to acknowledge the United States as an independent
state.[23] Washington wanted a general cartel because the usual
formula for exchange agreements in contemporary warfare—officers for officers of equal rank, soldiers for soldiers, and citizens
for citizens—was inadequate for "the diversity of Circumstances
incident to the State of Captivity" in the Revolutionary War. The
sheer variety of revolutionary soldiers and forces made this old
system unworkable. He ordered his commissioners "to adjust such
differences, to prevent others in future, so far as may be practi-
cable, and to fix the Exchange and Accommodation of Prisoners
of War, upon a more certain, liberal, and ample Foundation." At
least implicitly, Washington also hoped to make the British accept the revolutionaries' legitimacy.[24] Another major roadblock
to a general cartel was that the parties had been unable to "liqui-
date the demands" resulting from 1,821 revolutionary prisoners
of war whom the British had released from New York in the fall
of 1776. These men had been so sick, according to revolutionary
claims, that many died soon thereafter. Since then, Boudinot had
recorded these soldiers merely as "in dispute."[25] Any agreement
with the British would have to resolve this problem. Moreover,
differences existed between Washington and Boudinot on one
side and Congress on the other about the overall value of a cartel. Washington and Boudinot wanted to free as many American
prisoners of war as possible, whereas a congressional committee
adamantly opposed such an agreement because it would only help
the British. Washington was appalled by the committee's reasoning. His troops "looked up to him as their Protector," he said, and
he resented losing an opportunity to liberate "every Soldier who
was then in captivity, let the Consequence be what it might."[26]

It was thus foreseeable that a cartel could not be achieved.
When the revolutionary and British commissioners finally met on
March 31, 1778, the conference never even began in earnest. The
revolutionaries immediately broke off negotiations by rejecting
the British commissioners' credentials. Since "the establishment

of a regular and explicit cartel" concerned not only military but also civil matters, they argued, the powers for such a treaty were not "inherent in military command" and thus could not be exercised by the two commanders "merely in virtue of their military capacities."[27] The British were equally unwilling to conclude a general cartel. One of their commissioners, Brevet Colonel Charles O'Hara, even admitted after ten days of fruitless negotiations that "he was under orders to spin out the business as long as possible, and then to break off the negotiations." According to O'Hara, Howe wanted only to satisfy the demands of his army, who wanted to see an earnest attempt to free their fellow soldiers.[28]

After the failure of the cartel negotiations, both sides concentrated on achieving at least a partial exchange.[29] Congress agreed, but only because the campaign season would be so far advanced by the time the exchange was concluded that the British would not gain many troops for that year. Indeed, it was only on June 9 that Boudinot and Loring agreed in Germantown, Pennsylvania, that the American revolutionaries would release 900 prisoners of war, mostly Hessen-Kassel troops captured at Trenton, in exchange for the 1,821 American soldiers whom the British had let go in the fall of 1776.[30] Loring had initially wanted 1,200 British and German prisoners of war in the deal, but Boudinot refused, reminding Loring about the "cruel Treatment" those men had endured in New York. In fact, Boudinot believed that the British should not receive any soldiers in exchange for them. He accepted the "high number" of 900 only because Loring promised that when Clinton's force departed from Philadelphia, they would leave behind another 500 captured revolutionary soldiers.

Once an agreement was reached for the partial exchange, Boudinot organized the collection of the 900 prisoners. Revolutionary leaders predicted that it would be difficult to assemble the necessary number of German captives because they were "greatly scattered in Lancaster County" and expressed a "great aversion to an exchange." Boudinot, in particular, believed that it would be necessary to put together "a large Guard of Militia to force & guard them down" to Philadelphia. To reassure the seemingly unwilling prisoners, John Beatty, soon to be Boudinot's successor, instructed Thomas Bradford in Philadelphia to inform the

Germans that although they would have to be exchanged now, they were always welcome to return later after deserting from the British forces.[31]

A number of reports from the Hessen-Kassel headquarters seem to confirm the revolutionaries' claim that German prisoners of war wanted to stay in North America rather than return to their units. In July 1778, General von Knyphausen feared that "many [prisoners] have been enticed to remain" with the revolutionaries. On July 19, he admitted that 16 soldiers had deserted as soon as they left Lancaster for Elizabethtown, New Jersey, where the exchange was to take place. When the exchange was finally completed in November, Knyphausen lamented that 132 soldiers from the Regiments von Loßberg, von Knyphausen, and Rall were missing and would probably not return.[32]

One soldier who might have weighed heavily on Knyphausen's mind was August Wille, a *Jäger* captured at Trenton in 1776. On July 3, 1778, Wille petitioned Congress to "to allow him that particular Favour to stay in America." He claimed that he was not a "Hessian by Birth" and that he had been "forced to go into this Country with the Hessian Troops." It was "good Luck" that had led him to be captured at Trenton and taken to Lancaster, where he had found several relatives and was now "wholly determin'd to stay here."[33] Cases such as Wille's fired the revolutionaries' determination. Did not his petition alone prove that these men had come to North America against their will and would fare much better in the newly founded United States than back in the Holy Roman Empire? Many historians later followed such anecdotal evidence and wrote at length about German prisoners of war who "decided to settle down here and become coworkers in the structure of . . . modern American life."[34]

Reuber first heard about the pending exchange in August. Over the following weeks, he noted, numerous prisoners who worked as hired labor in the area around Winchester were brought back to town. Those employers "who did not deliver their Hessians" had to pay heavy fines. However, some of the prisoner-laborers "went away again at night, back to their old masters in the country and stayed there." But Reuber was excited about the exchange and wanted to return to the British lines quickly. On October 30, he wrote from Elizabethtown that the former prisoners "were ferried across the harbor . . . onto Staten Island." There they finally met their Hessian "brothers" again. "What joy and happiness this was. We were . . . free."[35]

Indeed, the revolutionaries' hopes and Knyphausen's fears notwithstanding, most of the German prisoners of war who were exchanged in 1778 seem to have felt like Reuber. Even when given ample opportunity to run away or remain behind on their marches from Lancaster, Lebanon, and Winchester to Elizabethtown for their exchange, fewer captives deserted than Beatty and Boudinot expected. William Atlee in Lancaster wondered openly how Bradford in Philadelphia had lost only "about a dozen" prisoners en route to Elizabethtown when the men supposedly had called the area around Lancaster "New Germany" and guards had been in short supply during the march. Colonel Thomas Hartley's regiment, which originally had been ordered to guard the prisoners, had been ordered to Washington's headquarters. With only local militia at hand, there had been "much less certainty of securing the prisoners."[36]

Such loyalty among the Trenton prisoners is consistent with other reports that the Hessen-Kassel headquarters received during the men's captivity. In October 1777, Knyphausen had proudly reported to Friedrich II that twenty-six prisoners of war had managed to flee American captivity and make their way back to New York. Three months later, in January 1778, he proudly reported to Kassel that a number of prisoners captured at Trenton in December 1776 had come back from captivity "on their own." In March, just weeks before the exchange negotiated in Germantown, he wrote Friedrich II that two captured noncommissioned officers from his own regiment had escaped and arrived in New York after secretly traveling more than 120 miles.[37]

Regimental Quartermaster Müller had counted 910 noncommissioned officers, musicians, and privates from the Regiments Rall, von Knyphausen, and von Loßberg in revolutionary hands in January and February 1777. In May 1778, Knyphausen calculated only 869.[38] A total of 741 men from these three regiments were accounted for during the Germantown exchange. That means that at most, 169 men (18.6 percent), based on Müller's figures, or 128 men (14.7 percent), based on Knyphausen's, stayed behind and might have been deserters.[39] Knyphausen reported 132 missing soldiers (15.2 percent out of 869 soldiers) on November 7, 1778.[40] This group, however, must have included a number of soldiers who had died during captivity, were sick or unfit at the time of the exchange, or later returned to British lines on their own. Some may not have been exchanged because that would have exceeded the total of 900 men for whom the agreement between Boudinot and Loring was negotiated. The actual desertion rate among the three Hessen-Kassel regiments captured at Trenton, thus, was probably considerably lower.[41]

British records still listed 39 men from the Regiment von Knyphausen and 32 from the Regiment von Loßberg as prisoners of war at the end of 1778, long after the Germantown exchange. Not including the Regiment Rall, for which separate numbers are not available, the maximum number of possible deserters from Hessen-Kassel records, 169, thus would have to be reduced by 71. As a result, no more than 98 Hessen-Kassel prisoners (10.8 percent out of 910 men) might have stayed behind, become deserters, and tried to make a life, at least temporarily, in North America rather than return as soldiers for George III. Taking Knyphausen's lower numbers from May 1778 as the basis for such calculations, only 57 Hessen-Kassel prisoners of war (6.6 percent of 869 men) might have stayed behind in revolutionary territory after the exchange.[42]

British numbers were often unreliable. Yet even American records indicate that at least 28 German prisoners of war from Trenton were not included in the exchange and officially remained behind in Winchester as prisoners of war in September 1778. American authorities failed to account for only 13 German captives in this region.[43] Moreover, in December 1780, 14 prisoners of war from the Regiments Rall, von Knyphausen, and von Loßberg were still listed as prisoners of war by the revolutionaries in Philadelphia.[44] Subtracting these figures for listed prisoners of war in Winchester and Philadelphia from the available totals of missing soldiers, either 169 or 128 men, would result in maximum possible desertion rates of between 9.9 and 14 percent, not even counting that some prisoners might have died, returned later, or become sick over the summer of 1778 and could not march toward Elizabethtown for the exchange in the fall. These possible desertion rates, whether from German, British, or American sources, are certainly high, but nowhere near as high as some of the anecdotal evidence suggests, and certainly lower than the revolutionaries had hoped.[45] They are also lower than the average expected desertion rate of 18 to 20 percent among eighteenth-century European armies.[46]

During the march from Lancaster to Philadelphia and onward to Elizabethtown, only a few Hessen-Kassel prisoners decided to desert. From the Regiments von Knyphausen and von Loßberg, a total of 16 soldiers ran away. Atlee in Lancaster wrote about a dozen German prisoners who had escaped on their march to Philadelphia. Further lists of those prisoners sent out from Lancaster to Philadelphia include 14 soldiers whose names were crossed out, presumably because they were no longer available for exchange.[47] Either the prisoners had no real chance to desert on their march to Elizabethtown—Atlee's and Boudinot's complaints about a lack of guards make such a conclusion unlikely—or the vast majority of them simply wanted to return to British lines.[48]

An episode involving two higher-ranking deserters from the Hessen-Kassel army, Ensigns Karl Friedrich Führer from the Regiment von Knyphausen and Karl Wilhelm Kleinschmidt from the Regiment Rall, confirms the overall picture emerging from these admittedly limited and often muddled numbers. Both men had been captured at Trenton. On March 28, 1778, the revolutionaries released them on parole, together with the rest of the captured Hessian officers, and they soon arrived in Philadelphia, which at this point was still under British occupation. There, Knyphausen discovered that both officers had accumulated enormous debts that needed to be repaid. He threatened both with detention, but instead of going to jail, Führer and Kleinschmidt defected to the American revolutionaries on August 7.[49]

When the British left Philadelphia, Führer and Kleinschmidt made Congress an offer to raise a corps of German deserters among the Trenton prisoners. They claimed to be driven by a "zeal . . . to Shew our gratitude for the Friendship we Received of the Americans during our Imprisonment of fifteen Months." The reason so few German soldiers switched sides, according to the officers, was that the revolutionaries did not have enough "non-commissioned officers with whom [the men] [could] speak" in their native tongue. Thus, they wanted to focus their recruitment efforts on this group of captives. For themselves, the two ensigns boldly requested commissions as majors in the Continental Army.[50]

Congress and the Board of War were intrigued, as were Washington and General von Steuben, and they decided on September 2 to support the plan. However, they did not make the two deserters officers in the new unit, to be called the German Volunteers, but gave each of them only a captain's pay. To receive a full commission, Führer and Kleinschmidt would have to recruit at least thirty men within the next three months. Lieutenant Colonel Wilhelm Klein, a German immigrant, would lead the overall recruitment effort for the new unit.[51]

However, not as many German prisoners decided to enlist with the German Volunteers as Führer and Kleinschmidt had promised. They recruited only twenty-four men among the prisoners, and five of those recruits soon deserted again, presumably making their way back to their old units.[52] As Knyphausen reported to Friedrich II, the two officers had failed to persuade Hessen-Kassel prisoners of war to switch sides when the men marched through Philadelphia toward Elizabethtown for the exchange in 1778.[53] On October 20 of that year, the Board of War asked Congress to lay aside "the Plan for recruiting the Corps, to be called the German Volunteers." Klein, a "worthy Man" and a "good Officer," was to be transferred to Brigadier General Casimir Pulaski's corps. Führer and Kleinschmidt, however, could not be trusted and were to be dismissed with just one month's pay. Another high-ranking German deserter, Lieutenant Gustav Juliat, had been offered a commission in Pulaski's corps but then returned to British lines. It was believed that Juliat had told Major Ferguson about Pulaski's lax defenses around Little Egg Harbor. Ferguson's subsequent raid there caused a number of casualties. Concerned with his own reputation, Pulaski blamed the disaster entirely on Juliat, discrediting him and other potential defectors.[54]

On November 19, 1778, Führer and Kleinschmidt petitioned Congress to let them continue with their efforts, although the

Germantown exchange had already been completed. Maybe, they suggested, those German prisoners who had left unwillingly could now be persuaded to return. But this plan also failed. Several leaflets were distributed among German troops stationed in and around New York, but very few soldiers came over from the British in the following weeks. Führer and Kleinschmidt were persistent. They claimed that a "Number of the Germans in the Enemy's Army would have come if an Opportunity had offered" and complained that Congress had halted their efforts at the very moment when they "had the greatest prospect of getting Recruits fast." They even begged Congress to allow them to remain in the service of the American revolutionaries and offered securities from a merchant in Philadelphia. However, they also wanted Congress to pay them $50 for each recruit—how much of that money was meant for their own pockets, they did not state.[55] Congress had had enough of such plans and rejected all of Führer's and Kleinschmidt's pleas.[56] The revolutionaries seemingly accepted at this point that not as many German soldiers and prisoners as they had hoped would switch sides. In October and November 1778, in fact, Hessen-Kassel desertion rates fell. Charles Ingrao counted 422 Hessen-Kassel deserters for 1778 and only 362 men for 1779. For 1780, he listed only 288 deserters among all Hessen-Kassel troops.[57]

Angered by the poor treatment of revolutionary prisoners being held by the British, Congress had decided to retaliate by changing the system through which provisions were supplied to the British and German captives in revolutionary hands. The move had the hoped-for effect of placing greater financial pressure on the crown and made it difficult for the British army to obtain and deliver adequate provisions. Moreover, until there was compliance with Congress's new demands, the prisoners being held by the revolutionaries were no longer to be treated any better than the British were treating the revolutionary captives. The result was reduced rations and deteriorating conditions for the British and German prisoners of war. With the two sides at a standoff, and also refusing to hold a general prisoner exchange, and with Congress in desperate financial straits as the number of new prisoners increased, the captives' circumstances only worsened. Until a partial prisoner exchange was finally negotiated for most of the Trenton captives, the German soldiers remained caught in the middle of a bad situation. They had become the unwitting pawns in a new power struggle between Congress and King George III.

CHAPTER 9

The Convention Army, 1777–1781

The fate of the Convention Army in revolutionary hands merits special attention. These men (and their camp followers) occupied a rather strange position as British and German "captives." When General Burgoyne and his army laid down their weapons at Saratoga on October 17, 1777, the agreement with General Gates made the troops not prisoners but parolees, to be held temporarily until they could be sent back to Europe, to take no further part in the war.[1] To that end, the British and German soldiers, about 3,300 and 2,300 men respectively, marched to Boston, where they were supposed to board ships for transport across the Atlantic. They certainly had been vanquished and had come under enemy control—they were supervised in Boston by Major General William Heath—but they had not become prisoners of war, and they continued to think of themselves as a functioning, intact force. British, Braunschweig-Wolfenbüttel, and Hessen-Hanau military hierarchies, rules, and regulations remained in place. The prisoners' own officers still commanded the rank and file, and the men's regiments and companies were in charge of their day-to-day activities, guards, supplies, and provisioning.

However, Congress never let the Convention Army go to Europe. Revolutionary leaders repeatedly delayed the men's departure under various pretexts while quartering them in old revolutionary barracks outside Boston on Winter Hill (the German units) and Prospect Hill (the British units). In January 1778, Congress prevented the embarkation of Burgoyne's men, claiming that the United States had not yet received notice that the British had ratified the Convention of Saratoga. Because doing so would have

185

implied that Great Britain acknowledged the United States as a sovereign state, Parliament was unlikely to pass it. In turn, Congress refused to ratify the convention and in fact voided the entire agreement. Again, revolutionary leaders had tried to use defeated and captured enemy soldiers to force the British into recognizing the United States as a legitimate belligerent in the conflict.

After 1778, Congress effectively turned the Convention Army into de facto prisoners of war. In the winter of 1778/79, the captives were ordered away from Boston, all the way south to Charlottesville, Virginia.[2] Once there, they knew that they would probably never be allowed to leave for Europe on parole. It took another two years before Congress ended the charade and officially declared Burgoyne's men prisoners of war on April 5, 1781.[3] By that time, they had been moved from Charlottesville to Winchester, Virginia; officers were no longer permitted to remain with their rank and file, but instead were on parole in East Windsor, Connecticut.[4] Soon the men were marched north again, to Reading, Pennsylvania. Cornwallis's campaign in Virginia had made it too dangerous to keep such a large contingent of enemy soldiers nearby. In April 1781, the history of the Convention Army merged with that of the other British and German prisoners of war in revolutionary hands.

From the revolutionaries' perspective, Congress had good reasons for not allowing the Convention Army to leave for Europe on parole. Letting these men go would have freed thousands of British troops in European garrisons to join the fight in North America. In addition, these de facto captives gave the revolutionaries significant leverage when negotiating prisoner treatment with the British. The victory at Saratoga handed them an advantage in prisoner numbers that lasted for the remainder of the war, except for a short period after the fall of Charleston. Moreover, because the Convention Army was under Congress's command, it would be more difficult for state governments to interfere or, as they had done in other cases, negotiate their own exchange agreements with the British.

By early modern European standards, Burgoyne had to be commended for the Convention of Saratoga. In defeat, he managed to preserve his entire army for potential use in the future.[5]

The revolutionaries achieved a full victory over Burgoyne's men only when they refused the parole and marched the vanquished to various places of confinement in Massachusetts, Virginia, and Pennsylvania. Over the course of the war, Congress broke up the Convention Army into smaller and smaller groups of captives. By 1783, the army had completely lost its coherence and structure. At the same time, farmers and city dwellers could make greater use of Burgoyne's former soldiers as laborers and recruits. Officers became valuable bargaining chips during exchange negotiations.

Winter Hill

The German contingents of the Convention Army on Winter Hill tried to keep up regular everyday military life as if they were just another garrisoned army. Revolutionary troops had built the barracks as temporary housing two years earlier, during the Siege of Boston, but had not repaired or maintained the buildings since.[6] To prevent the spread of disease among so many soldiers crowded together in decrepit spaces, General von Riedesel, commander of the German contingents of the Convention Army, ordered his men to dispose of trash at marked locations rather than throw it into water ditches. Soldiers also had to sweep their buildings twice a day. In the summer of 1778, Riedesel ordered everyone to bathe. Furthermore, soldiers could relieve themselves only at specially built latrines. Diseases spread nevertheless, and numerous soldiers fell ill and died. Between July and October 1778, typhus spread through the camp and killed forty-eight men. This epidemic, and the fear that it might spread to Boston, may have played a role in Congress's decision to march the Convention Army to Charlottesville later that year.[7]

Because of the special status of Burgoyne's men, German officers still commanded their own rank and file on Winter Hill. Among the Bennington prisoners, by comparison, this was no longer the case. There, American guards, local revolutionary authorities, and commissaries replaced the prisoners' previous military structures. Johann Bense, a Braunschweig-Wolfenbüttel common soldier, emphasized in his journal how much on Winter Hill was actually organized by the vanquished troops, not their captors.

Every Thursday, for instance, the men paraded "with hautboy players" before Riedesel and Major General William Phillips, the commander of the British Convention Army contingents. All regiments kept their own guards, consisting of one captain, two company officers, and sixty soldiers. If any soldier wanted to leave the barracks, he had to obtain a pass from the American town major in Cambridge. However, it then had to be signed "by our own officers."[8]

Bense's journal is the only surviving firsthand account from a German common soldier who lived in the barracks on Winter Hill.[9] Various orders from the Hessen-Hanau regiment, however, tell of experiences similar to Bense's. On December 3, 1777, this unit's commander, Colonel von Gall, ordered all soldiers to parade in front of their barracks so that he could check whether they kept themselves clean and combed their hair. Gall also arranged for a number of officers to stay with the men in the barracks to keep up military discipline and prevent desertion. To that end, he allowed his common soldiers to buy food only in small groups, not individually. They were also forbidden to speak or interact in any way with American citizens and soldiers.[10]

After several desertions, Riedesel set up a chain of secret guards on Winter Hill. Every officer's prime concern before, during, and after a campaign—victorious or not, in enemy hands or not—was desertion. At night, several noncommissioned officers guarded the roads running through the encampment. During the day, two or three noncommissioned officers from each regiment watched the barracks but stood away from the revolutionary posts. They had to stop any soldier who wanted to leave the barracks without a pass. To be more effective, these guards had to act inconspicuously. They should not "stand tall," as soldiers on guard would regularly do, but "sit down, lie down, as they wish, so that nobody notices that they are on guard." They also had to report, in secret, those soldiers whom they saw talking to locals. Riedesel explicitly directed that the rank and file not be informed about these measures.[11] He also prohibited gambling in the barracks, believing that debt contributed significantly to desertion. In principle, running away from camp in early 1778 could even be punished by hanging. In practice, returning or captured deserters were usually pardoned.[12] In May 1778, Phillips called on each soldier on Winter and Prospect Hills to endure captivity as a "service to his country," showing the changing view of military service in this period.[13]

During the Convention Army's stay at Boston, Heath acknowledged that the revolutionaries had little real power over the British or German soldiers inside the barracks because he lacked enough guards. On July 11, 1778, he wrote to the Massachusetts Council that he had only 271 guards left in and around Boston, including Cambridge, Bunker Hill, and Medford. As a result, he noted angrily, the Convention Army essentially guarded itself.[14] Not surprisingly, given these circumstances, German soldiers sometimes viewed their time on Winter Hill positively. In March 1778, Gall noticed how well the American revolutionaries behaved toward him, that fresh provisions were forthcoming, and that his common soldiers, with the proper passes, were free to walk around town. They would have fared even better, he noted, if Burgoyne had "given in" to revolutionary requests more often. During those weeks, Gall's men recovered from the arduous campaign of 1777. Their appearance improved by the day, and he was impressed with the "fresh colors" of their faces.[15]

Initially, revolutionary commissaries made food available to the Convention prisoners. The soldiers received their ration as a monetary payment, 2½ Stüber (3 d.) per day. Direct trade with local citizens was forbidden, but Bense reported that it was common. Orders against direct trade with locals were renewed frequently, indicating that they were broken just as often. Female camp followers on Winter Hill, married or not, received rations only if they worked for a unit. Although, as Gall noted, enough food was usually available, very little of it was fresh. Therefore, Riedesel sometimes bought fresh food for his troops, especially for the sick.[16]

With the area suddenly having to feed more than 5,000 men plus their camp followers, food became scarce and expensive over time. In March 1778, the inhabitants of Boston sent a petition to the Massachusetts Council and House of Representatives asking that the Convention Army be removed because of the "exorbitant price of every necessary of life." Unscrupulous middlemen, it said, bought food elsewhere and then sold it in the city at grossly inflated prices, adding "insult to extortion."[17] To understand the

scale of the problem, consider how much those captives consumed. A provisioning account prepared by Joshua Mersereau,
commissary of prisoners in the region, indicates that the German
soldiers on Winter Hill, three British regiments (the 53rd, 71st,
and 4th), and some other prisoners from several "broken" units
used 52,417 pounds of flour, 40,516 pounds of beef, 6,433 pounds
of pork, 6,982 pounds of rice, 542 pounds of soap, 3,634 quarts
of molasses, 844 quarts of salt, 321 pints of peas, and 344 gills of
vinegar between January 1, 1778, and February 28, 1779.[18] On
April 21, 1778, the inhabitants of Charlestown, near Winter and
Prospect Hills, also asked the Massachusetts Council and House
of Representatives to remove the enemy army from the area. Back
in 1775, they said, the Continental Army had been stationed in
town and had caused "great destruction." After the Siege of Boston, the inhabitants had hoped to repair the extensive damage
to their houses and again make use of their land, but the arrival
of the Convention Army in 1777 had brought new calamities and
deprivations.[19]

But the captives suffered just as much. In June 1778, most soldiers on Winter Hill had only torn uniforms to wear. Their baggage had not been brought to them from the north, and they
lacked provisions as well. The soldiers could buy additional supplies only with specie, at a high price.[20] Only briefly, in September,
did the situation improve. That month, provisions arrived, and
the men suddenly received meat, bread, and good rice. Unfortunately, they still had not heard anything about their departure to
Europe and continued to live in a state of limbo. For Gall, it was
almost too much: "We are the living dead; nobody hears or knows
anything from the fatherland."[21] In October 1778, Gall again complained of hardships for his men near Boston. He believed that
the revolutionaries were preventing the Convention Army from
going to Europe primarily because of the hard money with which
he and his soldiers paid for food, lodging, clothing, and other ne-
cessities. "They have already received thousands of guineas from
us," he lamented, "and will receive many more in the future."[22]
One of the ways in which local residents profited from the Convention Army, as Sergeant Cole from the guard noted, was by exchanging paper money for the soldiers' hard cash. They were also

eager to sell the captured soldiers goods that were not distributed by commissaries, especially liquor.[23]

Complaints about prisoners of war came from communities that were unable to make use of the Convention prisoners. To them the captives were a burden, consuming supplies, inflating prices, and bringing disease and unruliness. Because of their special status, for instance, the soldiers could not be hired out legally or utilized like regular prisoners of war. The Bennington prisoners, on the contrary, who were also transported to Boston, were placed on "one or more ships" in the harbor, fitted out "for the purpose of confining the prisoners."[24] Both citizens and Massachusetts's revolutionary authorities subsequently could hire them out as laborers. On September 9, Boston's Committee for Fortifying the Harbor asked the Massachusetts Council for the use of 100 German prisoners, admitting that it could not find other laborers for this task. Only desperate German captives on prison ships, it seems, were willing to accept such offers.[25] The inhabitants of West Springfield also petitioned for German prisoner-laborers. They claimed that twenty Braunschweig-Wolfenbüttel prisoners from Bennington had stopped in town earlier and done some work for the citizens. The town needed these men because most other laborers had "gone into the public service." On a prison ship, West Springfield pointed out, prisoners of war were costing the state money, whereas when they worked, employers could provide clothing and other necessaries at "reasonable prices." In other words, not only would "the distresses of [the] prisoners be relieved but those who are now a burden may become a real service to the state."[26]

Convention soldiers, however, were of use to the locals only if they deserted. Only then could they be hired as cheap laborers or enlisted as recruits. Gall reported in September 1778 that the inhabitants of Cambridge and Boston repeatedly tempted his men to run away because they were such good craftsmen and had skills that "could not be found often here [in North America]."[27] In July he had reported that Hessen-Hanau soldiers who worked for local residents after running away from the barracks received good pay "and additional food and drink, as much as they wanted." Moreover, in his opinion at least, they did not have to work very hard.[28]

The revolutionary guards were just as dismayed about such activities as the German officers. Sergeant Thomas Cole, from the American guards of Colonel Jacob Gerrish's militia regiment, repeatedly received orders to prevent Convention soldiers from working for American inhabitants. On July 13, he noted in his orderly book that General Heath was greatly angered that Convention Army soldiers regularly walked away from the barracks without proper passes, essentially becoming deserters. Already, "a great number of soldiers" had found work in the vicinity and were "scattered for many miles."[29] Indeed, the lack of revolutionary guards on Winter and Prospect Hills and the seemingly uninspired performance of those few who were present suggest that local residents very much wanted to increase the men's chances of running away.[30] Two German deserters who later returned to their units reported to their officers about a house in Charlestown that was designated for collecting deserters from Winter and Prospect Hills and recruiting them into American forces.[31]

By May 1778, a congressional propaganda campaign was targeting German soldiers on Winter Hill, resembling earlier efforts at other detention sites. A pamphlet reminded officers and soldiers alike that the revolutionaries were fighting a just war for "the rights of mankind" and wanted only to "establish total freedom in the new world." Since the German soldiers had been brought to North America "against their will," they should refuse any further service to George III. In addition, Congress offered 800 acres of land to any captain who deserted together with forty of his men. Any other officer or noncommissioned officer who came over with some rank and file would receive 20 acres per soldier. Common soldiers who deserted could expect 50 acres. If they brought their equipment along, they could receive an extra $20 in cash.[32]

Twenty-six Braunschweig-Wolfenbüttel soldiers deserted from Winter Hill in May 1778, and thirty-eight in June. It is unknown whether such relatively high numbers had anything to do with the American efforts to lure away the men. During those two months, besides trying to guard the soldiers even more closely, German officers and noncommissioned officers appealed to the common soldiers' feeling of camaraderie, urging them not to leave their fellow soldiers to suffer in captivity. Familiar with the North

American plantation system and labor relations, they warned their men that locals, although ostensibly offering wages, really wanted to turn them into "slaves."[33]

It is impossible to determine the success of such appeals and warnings. However, the number of desertions declined notice-ably in the fall of 1778—contrary to what Congress had hoped. Of course, this could also have resulted from the news, which started as a rumor, that the Convention Army would soon leave Boston. It seems that individual soldiers, rather than face a foreign society and country on their own, decided instead to stay with their fellow soldiers, at least for the moment. That way, they would not be alone and would have the chance to return to Europe eventually. As Stephan Huck points out, the initial British success in nearby Rhode Island that summer may have renewed the Convention Army's hope that the fortunes of war were turning in their favor. Desertion in such a situation would be the wrong choice.[34]

Charlottesville

In January 1779, after a long and arduous march from Boston, the Convention Army arrived at the Albemarle Barracks in Charlottesville. The men were now farther away from freedom and parole than ever. Precise numbers for the German troops while in Charlottesville, and in fact for the rest of the war, do not exist. Huck assumes that about 1,250 Braunschweig-Wolfenbüttel soldiers arrived in Virginia from Boston.[35] A British return lists 1,099 German rank and file from Braunschweig-Wolfenbüttel and Hessen-Hanau present in the Albemarle Barracks in October 1779. Including officers, staff, musicians, servants, and common soldiers, 1,533 German military personnel appear in this overview.[36]

The huts in which the common soldiers of the Convention Army were supposed to stay in Charlottesville were unfinished when the columns arrived from Massachusetts. Bense describes the buildings as made out of "trees put on top of each other in a square" (figure 5). The walls were cold and drafty; "there were no fireplaces, bunks, doors," and only a "miserable roof," which exposed the men to "rain, snow, and cold weather."[37] Braunschweig-Wolfenbüttel clerk Johann Christoph Dehn wrote that the men started fires in their huts for some warmth but were soon "smoked" when the fumes could not escape. At night, wind and cold air crept in from all sides, and cases of frostbite were reported. Complaints were futile because "everybody was suffering the same fate." Moreover, it was difficult to obtain food during those first weeks. The supplies that had been gathered for the Convention Army's arrival were largely rotten and unusable once the men had finished their long trek from Massachusetts.[38]

The men themselves finished building their quarters. Once the barracks were completed, accommodations improved markedly in the spring and summer of 1779 and even seem to have been more hospitable than the men's previous quarters in Boston. In his orders for the buildings at Charlottesville, Riedesel arranged for each hut to house no more than twelve people. Walkways had to be kept clean and leveled, and separate ditches for sewage had to be dug.[39] Hence, the barracks looked comparatively comfortable in 1779 and seemingly even included four buildings with pool tables, presumably for the officers on duty.[40]

The captives, still nominally parolees waiting to be shipped back to Europe, could go no farther than a radius of about one mile from their huts. To control their movements, they were ordered to build a palisade around the barracks. According to Bense, however, they mounted a successful resistance against such orders after their arrival in Charlottesville in January 1779: "Our people did not want to do this . . . and the entrances and exits [to the barracks] remained open."[41]

The officers, although still present in Charlottesville, lodged with local residents in the area but soon had little control of the men's daily life in the barracks. Gall admitted as much in September 1779 when he reported that with Phillips and Riedesel having been exchanged, Colonel von Specht of Braunschweig-Wolfenbüttel was now in command of the Convention Army. This change in leadership did not matter much, said Gall, because Specht "did not have real command of the army"; Congress made the key decisions. The soldiers in Charlottesville "did not lose anything" by the departure of their commanding officers "because everybody had to look out for himself as much as was possible."[42]

Figure 5.   The Albemarle Barracks in Charlottesville

German and British soldiers from the Convention Army were brought to
these barracks near Charlottesville, Virginia, during the winter of 1778/79.
They stayed there until early 1781. Engraving by William Lane, 1789. Courtesy of the John Carter Brown Library, Brown University, Providence, R.I.

Over time, daily life for the Convention Army soldiers at Charlottesville became similar to that for regular prisoners of war. One
problem was the constant ebb and flow of rations and supplies,
which often forced the soldiers to search elsewhere for food or
run away altogether, at least temporarily, to work. In 1779, Gall
claimed that the Convention troops were suffering mainly because
of politics in London, New York, and Philadelphia. His men were
not receiving their pay because British headquarters did not want
to send hard cash into American territory. With Congress having
agreed to deliver rations to the Convention Army only if the British immediately reimbursed them at an exorbitant exchange rate,
British headquarters delayed such reimbursements or refused
them altogether, to hurt the revolutionaries financially. As a result, Gall wrote angrily, his soldiers "were innocently sacrificed."[43]

However, Gall could also have directed his anger at Riedesel,
who believed that the more pay the men were owed, the less
likely they were to desert.[44] Official reports listed only thirty-seven
deserters among the Braunschweig-Wolfenbüttel troops for the

entire time between their arrival in Virginia in early 1779 until the end of the war. After 1781, when the soldiers of the Convention Army lost their special status and were declared regular prisoners of war, not a single deserter is listed. Such extremely low desertion rates do not reflect a particularly high degree of loyalty or unit cohesion but rather the simple fact that the rank and file continued to slip out of the control of their superiors, making it impossible to maintain an accurate list.[45] As individuals or in small groups, Convention soldiers did their best to survive and make a living as laborers or recruits with American or French forces.

Only when rumors spread that an exchange might finally happen or that the Convention Army might indeed be sent to Europe on parole did men who had run away to work in the countryside return to the barracks. Yet even those numbers diminished as time wore on. When the soldiers were moved to Winchester in February 1781 and then to Reading four months later, with the accompanying change in their status, all units were in disarray. From the Hessen-Hanau regiment in Winchester, for instance, we know that Colonel James Wood, who supervised the Convention Army in Virginia, ordered Colonel Johann Christoph Lenz, who took command when Gall was exchanged, to separate the officers from the noncommissioned officers and common soldiers. Once the Convention soldiers became regular prisoners of war, Lenz no longer saw his rank and file. In fact, he and the other remaining captive officers from Burgoyne's former army had to leave for East Windsor, Connecticut, on parole.[46]

Also exchanged by 1782, Lenz heard about his men only occasionally, when escaped Hessen-Hanau or other German soldiers came into New York. In June, he heard that his soldiers were working on their own "somewhere in the country" and met only once a month in the barracks near Reading to certify the rolls. Lenz doubted that such meetings even took place, because he had heard that the revolutionaries kept most noncommissioned officers confined in jail.[47] In June 1781, Riedesel complained to the duke of Braunschweig-Wolfenbüttel that he could not exchange even 100 dragoons because he was able to find only 81 men from the unit. This did not surprise him, for the Convention Army was

"scattered all across America." He did not even know whether regimental units such as the dragoons still existed.[48]

Some desertion seems to have happened with the consent of
the officers, at least implicitly. Gall and Lenz certainly saw how
much their men suffered in revolutionary hands, particularly after
1779, and now understood running away from camp as a mere
attempt to survive. When Lenz lamented the increased "depar-
tures" among his regiment after 1780, he also stressed that these
soldiers did not "act with evil intent" but only because they lacked
sufficient provisions.[49] It seems that desertion, under such circumstances at least, took on an entirely new meaning among the ranks
of the Convention Army. If it meant running away in order to
reach British lines, it became a laudable attempt to escape from
American captivity; Burgoyne reportedly called such acts "honorable desertion[s]," according to Deputy Commissary Mersereau.
In 1779, Mersereau complained that more than 700 soldiers from
the Convention Army had run away and rejoined British or German units.[50] In 1781, Major Päusch from the Hessen-Hanau artillery wrote proudly about some of his men who had run away from
Charlottesville and reached New York after marching through
"woods and swamps where there were no paths" to avoid "being
captured."[51] Washington had noted in May 1778 that illegally recruited soldiers from the Convention Army had become a problem because they ran away again, back to British lines, at the next
opportunity. He assumed that British headquarters actually encouraged them.[52] In 1779, the *Virginia Gazette* called on the population around Charlottesville to capture runaway soldiers from the
Convention Army who were trying to make their way to New York
with false papers or by claiming to be defectors. These soldiers,
usually wearing "short coarse linen coats" or "linen overalls," carried "their regimental coats in knapsacks," which they would need
later to cross into British lines.[53]

⁓

When the more than 5,000 soldiers of the Convention Army laid
down their arms at Saratoga, the terms of surrender gave them
special status as an intact force, temporarily detained on enemy

territory and awaiting return to Europe. However, Burgoyne's troops soon found themselves caught in the middle of another standoff between the U.S. Congress and Great Britain. The British were hesitant to ratify the capitulation agreement and thereby recognize the United States as a legitimate belligerent; Congress was in no hurry to relinquish such a large group of captives because it viewed them as useful for its own goals. Over the next four years, the soldiers were moved from place to place and broken up into smaller and smaller bands, so that by 1782, the Convention Army had ceased to exist as a coherent unit. When the war ended, its remnants were scattered across areas and towns in Massachusetts, Connecticut, New York, Pennsylvania, Maryland, and Virginia. Despite the initial agreement, Burgoyne's men had lost their special status and become regular prisoners of war, with all the attendant hardship and deprivation. In the end, the revolutionaries defeated them twice: first on the battlefield, and then in captivity.

CHAPTER 10

Continuity and Change,
1779–1783

In the fall of 1779, hundreds of German prisoners of war from the *Molly* and *Triton*, mostly from the Hessen-Kassel Regiment von Knyphausen, worked in and around Philadelphia in various iron- and saltworks and as carpenters, smiths, woodcutters, day laborers, and farmhands.[1] On October 11, only sixteen days after the capture of the *Triton* in Delaware Bay, 116 soldiers from the Regiment von Knyphausen, out of a total of 314 captives, had already been hired out as prisoner-laborers.[2] A return from February 1780 shows 356 soldiers from the regiment working for numerous employers in the area, obviously including some remaining captives from Trenton and other battles. Many probably worked for the same employers who had hired them back in 1777 and 1778, when this unit had been imprisoned the first time.[3] In many ways, thus, the experience of captivity for German prisoners of war after 1779 was similar to that for captured soldiers in revolutionary hands earlier in the conflict. Prisoners of war worked in various trades and lived either in barracks or outside among the local population. Captivity often resembled regular garrison life in the Holy Roman Empire. However, those conditions did not apply to all German prisoners in North America, and they changed significantly as the war progressed.

The first change came when the new provisioning system of 1778 resulted in fewer supplies for prisoners of war, and the United States' severe financial crisis began to impede the war effort. A decisive change occurred after the Siege of Yorktown in 1781, when thousands of new prisoners left Congress and the Continental Army searching desperately for ways to cut the costs of prisoner upkeep. This resulted in a fundamentally different approach to handling enemy captives by 1782. Congress now recruited German prisoners of war for the Continental Army and, to make money, released them upon payment of a ransom or sold them into indentured servitude. The new policies also turned German captives into a political tool for establishing a more centralized federal government. Control over prisoners became a means to control the war effort and the United States. Captivity for German troops after Yorktown, thus, was very different from Johannes Reuber's stays in Lancaster and Winchester in 1777 and 1778, and from what the captives around Lebanon experienced in the same period.

Everyday Life, Work, and Struggles

When two Ansbach-Bayreuth and two Hessen-Kassel regiments marched into American captivity after the surrender of Yorktown on October 19, 1781, the captives feared retribution for the extensive damage they had done to the region during Cornwallis's campaign. British troops, including their German auxiliaries, had "ruined many plantations in Carolina and Virginia, burned an entire magazine of cavalry uniforms and leather goods, thousands of hundredweights of cotton, . . . a lot of tobacco [and] took many cattle," wrote Justus Eggertt, who served with Johann Conrad Döhla in Company von Quesnoy. Moreover, "more than 3,000 blacks" had fled their masters and gone over to the British and German troops under Cornwallis.[4] Thus the enemy's courteous approach came as a surprise. "We remained unharmed," noted Stephan Popp in his journal, "and nothing was taken from us by force—neither parts of our uniforms nor the baggage."[5]

It is hard to imagine the sense of isolation that these captives must have felt in North America. Colonel von Gall from the Hessen-Hanau regiment experienced great self-doubt in 1780 and constantly pondered whether he had done enough to ensure the well-being of his men. He was sick and felt weak most of the time and even feared that he would die soon. For three years, he had not heard anything from Hanau.[6] However, families and friends at home had not forgotten about their loved ones. In fact, they were distressed about the troops' fate. An announcement published in Ansbach on December 21, 1781, declared that all complaints about the capture of the principality's soldiers in North America were henceforth forbidden. There were to be no more discussions of the subject, under penalty of fines, lashes, or even jail.[7]

Some of the soldiers' female partners and wives were present during the campaign and also in captivity, and they, too, regularly worked. Hannah Morman, a female captive from the British 17th Regiment, applied on August 18, 1779, for permission to work in Philadelphia. She explained that she had been very sick during her confinement but now wanted to "walk out" of the New Gaol "once or twice a week" so that she could "be more capable of procuring some nourishment which at this time I am not able to provide."[8] Döhla reported on July 13, 1782, that three wives of fellow soldiers in the Regiment von Seybothen had come to Frederick from New York and were staying with their husbands and other prisoners in the barracks.[9] As members of a "military community," staff, camp followers, and other personnel were understood to be as much prisoners of war as were the soldiers. In December 1778, William A. Atlee, chairman of the Lancaster Committee of Observation and Correspondence and responsible for the prisoners of war in town, asked Thomas Bradford, the commissary of prisoners in Philadelphia, how many rations he should distribute to the "wives & children of Prisoners of war." He believed that half a ration would be sufficient.[10] Toward the end of the war, in the spring of 1782, Congress became concerned about three hundred British prisoners of war in York, Pennsylvania, who had "the same Number of Women and Children" with them.[11] The women and children had apparently proved to be such a burden that Congress decided to stop delivering rations to them. Those who could not "support themselves" were to receive passports and be allowed to return to New York.[12]

As at home, conflicts sometimes erupted between the men in captivity. Ansbach-Bayreuth prisoners after 1781 at least partly blamed their officers for the difficult conditions in Winchester, where they stayed initially after the surrender at Yorktown, and Frederick. Captivity appears to have eroded the usually strict discipline among the rank and file and emboldened a number of common soldiers to resist what they considered unjust treatment at the hands of their own superiors. On October 29, 1781, for instance, while still on the march from Yorktown to Winchester, Fourier Adam Knoll from Döhla's Company von Quesnoy was arrested and "handed over to the American guards." He apparently had argued with Second Lieutenant Andreas Gottlieb von Ciriacy and even took away the officer's sword when he was threatened with punishment.[13]

The Ansbach-Bayreuth officers who remained with the prisoners worked together with American guards to discipline unruly soldiers.[14] Lieutenant Prechtel noted on November 5, 1781, that "the soldiers have been visited at least two or three times per week by their officers. To prevent mischief, one subaltern from the Ansbach-Bayreuth regiments had to be on guard at the barracks daily."[15] American guards in Frederick also killed at least one Ansbach-Bayreuth soldier, Private Johann Gärtner from Company von Quesnoy. He was shot by a revolutionary patrol on July 1, 1782, after he had escaped from the barracks and was discovered in town.[16] In August 1782, Major Friedrich Ernst von Beust, commanding officer of the Ansbach-Bayreuth prisoners, and Major Mountjoy Baily from the American guard in Frederick agreed that all Ansbach-Bayreuth prisoners of war detained in the town's jail should receive only two-thirds of a ration to "deter the men from walking away."[17]

In March 1782, Döhla reported a conflict between a group of soldiers from Company von Quesnoy—including himself—and some noncommissioned officers. He and some of his fellow common soldiers blamed Sergeants Wolfgang Stölzel and Georg Kniewaßer for giving false reports about one of their fellow common soldiers. As a result of those reports, six soldiers were sentenced to close confinement. However, "the entire Company von Quesnoy resisted" the orders and prevented the imprisonment of their comrades. On March 22, the troublemakers had to appear before Beust, at which time they negotiated an agreement with him and his adjutant, First Lieutenant Herrman Lindemeyer. Six of the men would go to jail voluntarily in order "to satisfy" the company's commanding officers, Captain Georg Heinrich von Quesnoy and Lieutenant von Ciriacy. Lindemeyer promised the men "with hand and mouth" that they would stay in jail for only two days. However, he did not keep his word. Döhla and the others had to stay in jail for two weeks among "vermin, lice, fleas, rats, and mice."[18]

Marches were commonly an exhausting experience for German prisoners of war in revolutionary hands. The captives were almost constantly on the move, partly because of the ever-shifting theaters of war, but also because of concerns about their housing, supplies, and security. The revolutionaries generally brought their prisoners to areas that were secure from British raids and offered sufficient food supplies, preferably including large buildings, barracks, jails, or churches for housing the captives. In the North American landscape, the distances between such places could be vast. After being captured at Yorktown, the Ansbach-Bayreuth and Hessen-Kassel prisoners of war were first ordered to march to Winchester in the Shenandoah Valley, a distance of about 250 miles.[19] Having been ordered to leave their tents behind, the men had to sleep in the open, in near-constant rain. When they finally reached the Shenandoah River on November 4, they had to wade through chest-deep water. Once on the other side, they thought they "would freeze to death because everything was so cold."[20] According to Döhla, the British and German captives increasingly became "exhausted and sick."[21] The British prisoners apparently staged a revolt against such treatment. To quell the resistance, American guards fired into the prisoner column, killing one British soldier and wounding three others.[22] On November 5, about 2,100 British and German prisoners arrived in Winchester. They were placed in barracks vacated only a few months earlier by the prisoners from the Convention Army.[23]

The Yorktown prisoners' stay in the Shenandoah Valley lasted only a few weeks. At the end of January 1782, Congress ordered the Ansbach-Bayreuth and Hessen-Kassel regiments to Frederick, with only the sick and wounded to remain in Virginia.[24] Although it was not very far from Winchester to Frederick, the cold weather and deep snow in the Blue Ridge Mountains caused the soldiers much misery. Their baggage had not yet been brought to them in Winchester, and according to Popp, "nobody had good stockings or shoes [and] Breeches and shirts were worn out." Many soldiers

resorted to wrapping rags around their feet, which were nevertheless "torn open in short time and they got frostbite all over."[25] In
late January, the conditions grew even worse. The extreme cold
prevented the prisoners from lying down to sleep, so they walked
around at night to prevent freezing. Döhla was furious. He felt
that the revolutionaries treated them like dogs, not fellow hu-
mans.[26] On the Maryland shore, the situation finally improved.
The prisoners were quartered with local residents while resting
during the march. They could stay in "warm rooms" and received
good provisions. Not surprisingly, Popp was excited about the "inhabitants of Maryland," who "seemed to be better people than
the Virginians." He noted one day, "I have spent the first night
peacefully on the floor of a room and have slept all through the
night."[27]

Burgoyne's Convention Army troops were subjected to the longest, most arduous and exhausting marches among all the German and British captives. Their removal to Charlottesville, a trip
of about seven hundred miles, was undertaken in the middle of
winter without adequate clothing and supplies. Congress had re-
routed the de facto prisoners' baggage straight from Canada to
Virginia. Thus the men had only a little relief when the British
crown gave them 4,000 blankets, which they remade into long
pants and gloves. When the first of six columns—three German
and three British—left on November 5, 1778, everyone, officers
and men alike, was angry at Congress.[28] As Colonel von Gall from
Hessen-Hanau wrote back home, it was a "bad thing" to send soldiers "in such season on this long march." He felt sure that many
of the captives would become sick and die.[29] He could not hide his
anger from his men. "A common soldier," he wrote, "does not feel
differently from an officer."[30]

The Braunschweig-Wolfenbüttel clerk Johann Christoph Dehn
related in a letter how the men had to cross countless rivers and
mountain ranges in the worst possible weather, had to march
through "wastelands and wilderness" while facing constant harassment from the population, and were forced to pay premium
prices for food. At night they had to camp in snow three or four
feet deep.[31] Desertion rates soared during this ordeal. The official Braunschweig-Wolfenbüttel account noted 30 deserters by

November 24 and another 20 by the end of the month. In December, 114 men took off from the Convention Army, and in January, just before their arrival at Charlottesville, another 15. Despite Gall's prediction, however, the death toll remained rather low. Returns listed only two Braunschweig-Wolfenbüttel soldiers who died during the long march to Virginia.[32]

Two years later, when the Convention Army was moved to Pennsylvania after a brief stay in Winchester, they found that nothing had been prepared for their reception. According to Johann Bense, for more than eight weeks they lived "in the open" on the banks of the Schuylkill River, "tortured by great heat [during the day] and at night by cold and rain." Their final destination was Reading—but again no housing was available. The common soldiers were ordered to build some barracks, but in a show of defiance they refused, constructing straw huts instead. In response, the revolutionaries treated them "very harshly." Only when the soldiers were given a second order to build the barracks did they finally comply—and luckily so. On October 21, a fire destroyed all the straw huts, making everyone have to work much harder to construct sufficient shelter before the onset of winter.[33]

With the war entering its fifth year, the revolutionaries wanted more than ever to use the prisoners of war as laborers. Silas Condit from Trenton hired two Hessian prisoners in March 1780, although one of them was severely ill and stayed so "for a long while." The other was "entirely destitute of Cloaths" when he arrived in New Jersey. When Thomas Bradford, the commissary for prisoners in Philadelphia, recalled the two men in July, Condit asked to keep "them a while longer," on the grounds that "almost every person that used to be hired are engaged in the Military Duty or Service."[34] A sick laborer was better than no laborer at all.

Employers who wanted to hire prisoner-laborers often left pre-printed security deposit forms and promissory notes at coffee houses around Philadelphia. Those reveal another reason why these men were so much in demand: they usually worked cheap.[35] In January 1779, three German captives in Philadelphia were released to Michael Shubart, Adam Foult, and James Butland for a security deposit of $300 each, equivalent to 37.7 silver dollars at the time.[36] However, on September 30, after the *Molly* and *Triton* were captured and hundreds of new prisoners of war arrived in Philadelphia, Heinrich Lange required a security deposit of only 21 silver dollars. A British prisoner-laborer's security deposit was only 26.3 silver dollars. The deposits for four German captives hired out between October 1779 and March 1780 were between 25 and 28 silver dollars.[37] Strikingly, rates for blacks—often seamen and runaway slaves captured on British ships—remained much higher, presumably reflecting a greater likelihood of escape. In May 1779, for instance, a promissory note shows that a William Williams required a deposit of 78.7 silver dollars. An Adam (no last name was given) cost 83.3 silver dollars in September, and another black prisoner-laborer, Will, captured on the Sloop *Elizabeth*, was released only for a deposit of 218 silver dollars. The black girl Hetty/Nelly, also captured on a ship, cost roughly 150 silver dollars in March 1780. Slaveholders who learned that their escaped slaves had reappeared as prisoners of war tried to reclaim them. When Archibald Ritchie from Virginia heard from Major John Webb of the Virginia Line that his runaway slave Abraham had been captured on a British ship and was "now a prisoner of war in Philadelphia," he promptly wrote to Thomas Bradford to have him returned.[38]

The German soldiers captured on the *Molly* and the *Triton* and at Bennington and Yorktown wanted to work to earn additional money. As weavers or woodcutters, they could "fend off hunger" or even earn "a shirt to wear."[39] Private Haßfurther from Company von Quesnoy "went to work as an apprentice for a German shoemaker" on November 1, 1781, only a few days after the surrender at Yorktown.[40] During the march from Winchester to Frederick in early 1782, Popp remarked that not only sick and wounded prisoners had remained behind in Virginia, but also "those who worked in the area."[41] Later that spring, many of the Ansbach-Bayreuth and Hessen-Kassel prisoners in Frederick left the barracks to "search for work" in the region.[42] Justus Eggertt was hired as a teacher "by a German settlement." Although he received little cash, he "had a good time" because he lived "very well" and received plenty of food and new clothing.[43] Weavers, tailors, shoemakers, masons, carpenters, wagon makers, millers, and butchers were constantly in demand at Winchester and Frederick.[44]

Unlike their fellow soldiers earlier in the war, however, these captives also felt more pressure to find work. They wanted to escape an increasingly desperate situation. When the men from the *Molly* and the *Triton* were taken to Philadelphia, they were initially placed in the New Gaol. A three-story building on Walnut Street that had been erected in 1773–74 as a county jail, it had been used by the British in 1777 and 1778 to detain revolutionary American prisoners of war. The U-shaped building, consisting of two stories plus a basement, had walls about three feet thick and was surrounded by an external wall twenty feet high. Two wings extended from the main building. Each floor of the main building contained eight rooms, twenty by fifteen feet, with two windows and a fireplace. Each floor of the wings contained five rooms, ten by fifteen feet.[45] A detailed return of German prisoners of war in Philadelphia shows that 162 soldiers were held captive there between 1780 and 1782.[46] Most of them, 86 men (53.1 percent), worked at some point as prisoner-laborers. Twenty-six prisoners (16 percent) died during that period.[47] Including British prisoners of war, 20 captives died in the prison in April 1781 alone.[48] Not surprisingly, the prisoners sought hard to escape such an unhealthy environment.

By this point in the war, there was little supervision of the captives by any revolutionary authority. They could freely leave the barracks and search for work. In November 1781, the Board of War noted that the Yorktown prisoners in Frederick had received considerable help to escape "by Whigs for the sake of their labour and by the disaffected from a desire to serve the Enemy."[49] In 1776 and 1777, by contrast, prisoner-laborers had received their rations via British agents, American revolutionaries had put together lists of the tradesmen among the prisoners before hiring them out, and guards and committees had held regular roll calls. After 1779, it seems, only the captives' noncommissioned officers and those officers still present tried to exert some control over the rank and file.

Unable to stop their soldiers from leaving camp for work, noncommissioned officers at least tried to lead their men on labor "missions." In 1780, for instance, Sergeant Philipp Rauthe supervised several Hessen-Kassel prisoners from the New Gaol in

Philadelphia who had agreed to work as woodcutters for Colonel John Mitchell, the adjutant quartermaster general of the Continental Army. When the men felt cheated out of their pay, amounting to $1,433, it was Rauthe who complained to Mitchell, in a letter written in broken English. The men badly needed the money, he said, because they were in an "unhappy Situation, being Closely Confined on prisoners allowances and no appearances of a Releasement," but the "Work was by us honestly performed." Having been accused by the desperate soldiers of embezzling their pay, Rauthe continued: "I hope you will pay us as Soon as Posable as the men . . . really bleame me and thinks I Drew the money from you and Cheated them." If Mitchell did not intend to pay the men, Rauthe asked to be sent a certificate that he "did not Recive" anything before. At the same time, he reminded Mitchell that "surly Congress doas not intend to . . . make Slaves of their prisoners of War." The men had performed honest work, and "it was Genourous of Congress to give us the priviledge of working for pay but as ungenorous to let us work and not pay us."[50]

Some noncommissioned officers were ordered by their commissioned officers to spend extra time in captivity to control the rank and file and attempt to prevent desertion. For example, Sergeant Wolff from the Regiment von Loßberg was not exchanged with the other Trenton captives in 1778 and remained around Lancaster as a prisoner. In 1780, he marched a group of German prisoners from Lancaster to Philadelphia for exchange. He must have performed well, for William Atlee, the commissary of prisoners in Lancaster, praised him in a letter to Bradford as "a very good kind of man," adding that Wolff had been "of great use to me here & always had his liberty to walk about, without being confined" and would be "useful to you also in managing the others."[51] Wolff indeed stayed in revolutionary hands until the end of the war. General Friedrich Wilhem von Loßberg, commander of all Hessen-Kassel forces in 1782 and 1783, praised Sergeant Wolff in a letter to Friedrich II on August 10, 1782. Loßberg at that point had heard that the Hessen-Kassel prisoners of war in Philadelphia had loyally resisted American efforts to recruit them for the Continental Army.[52] He attributed such commendable conduct to "Sergeant Wolf[f] from the Regiment Alt-Loßberg and Fourier

Wiegand from the Regiment von Knyphausen . . . whose care and attention to the [captured soldiers] had earned them much trust. Through their own, honest determination and persuasion, [Wolff and Wiegand] were able to encourage [the captured soldiers] to be steadfast and loyal and to keep that resolve."[53]

During the first days after their surrender, Popp and Döhla expressed satisfaction with their fate and had little reason to complain, let alone desert. They had to bake their own bread, but they were given one pound of meat per day.[54] On the march toward Winchester, which ended on October 22, 1781, Popp even reported that their guards had allowed them to search for water and firewood on their own. Moreover, local farmers and shopkeepers eagerly served prisoners who paid in specie. "Silver money was quite rare in Virginia," Popp noted. When the prisoners of war reached the town of Fredericksburg, however, the situation changed. Many soldiers ran out of hard money. Popp admitted that "those were hard times for us." The prisoners also received meager provisions. After their arrival in Winchester, the conditions became even worse. Summarizing his experiences in captivity after Yorktown, Popp noted: "Because of bad provisions, we were forced to sell everything we owned; often, it took a long time until we received something. Daily, we had hunger and cold in abundance."[55]

Popp and his fellow soldiers suffered in Winchester primarily because the local authorities could not provide enough food for their prisoners. After Yorktown, Congress mandated that prisoners of war receive only two-thirds of a regular ration, the same as the British distributed to their captives. However, there was no established procedure for procuring even those smaller rations. Without fixed contracts with agents or commissaries, provisions for Continental soldiers and prisoners of war often had to be requisitioned from local residents. This created unrest among the population and never produced an adequate amount of supplies.[56] Having suffered from "impressments," the citizens of Winchester reportedly wanted to destroy the barracks after the Yorktown prisoners left for Frederick at the end of January 1782. They wanted to ensure that no more troops or prisoners would be quartered in or near town.[57] The new secretary at war, General

Benjamin Lincoln, also specified that "no provision is to be drawn for any prisoners who are out at work."[58] The more the captives worked as prisoner-laborers, in other words, the less food had to be provided.

By December 7, 1781, according to Döhla, the prisoners had missed their daily ration of flour for twenty days.[59] James Wood, whose department was responsible for delivering provisions to the army and the prisoners, blamed the supply problems on the fact that "there has been no regular mode adopted for procuring Provisions." No contracts had been negotiated, and the states had "repealed all the laws for empressing."[60] On December 23, Major Richard Claiborne, the deputy quartermaster general in Virginia, wrote to Timothy Pickering, the quartermaster general, that the prisoners in Winchester were enduring a "calamitous situation." He readily admitted that his department was in disarray. They could obtain neither money nor credit, and his staff came and went from their jobs as they pleased.[61]

In fact, most of the provisions that the Ansbach-Bayreuth and Hessen-Kassel captives received at Winchester and Frederick during the last two years of the war were insufficient.[62] Döhla complained frequently that they were given only rotten bread or flour. Only prisoners who had access to hard money could buy additional food. In such cases, local citizens offered anything a soldier might possibly want or need: "Bread, cheese, butter, eggs and all kinds of other food such as beets, potatoes, cabbage, spirits, whiskey, punch, and cider." In Winchester, several marketeers had conveniently built huts near those of the prisoners.[63] At the end of October 1781, however, some prisoners had to sell parts of their uniforms and equipment to obtain food from such marketeers. Döhla, for instance, sold a glass bottle on October 30, and he said that many British prisoners had sold their entire uniforms in order to buy rum, brandy, or whiskey. Entirely destitute of any clothing, they had to wrap themselves in blankets. At the same time, the prisoners in Frederick almost revolted on November 22, 1782, after receiving 100 head of cattle from the revolutionaries instead of the whiskey they had been promised.[64]

In February 1782, now at Frederick, the Ansbach-Bayreuth prisoners received flour only because their own officers bought it for them from local farmers.[65] The men later had to reimburse their superiors at a cost of 2 pence per pound. By mid-April, Döhla fell sick with "fever and severe headaches." He was not the only one who was suffering, as he noted in his journal: "Many soldiers in our regiments were sick, half of Company von Quesnoy was sick. Most of them had hot, cold, and putrid fever." The reason for these problems was simple: "We were receiving bad food, rough bread and . . . almost rotten . . . salt meat, sometimes also stinking herring." In addition, "many prisoners went barefoot and half-naked, most did no longer have a shirt to wear, and if they still had clothing, it was filled with lice and vermin."[66]

Only in June did the situation in Frederick improve a little. The men finally received some pay from New York and could afford to buy additional provisions. One pound of butter cost them 8 pence, and twelve eggs could be had for 6 pence. Even salad was available. Overall, Döhla noted in his journal, six soldiers at that time could eat well for 3 or 4 pence a week. By July, however, the money had apparently run out again, and the prisoners were being offered "rotten herring" instead of meat.[67]

As before, the prisoners' own units were responsible for delivering pay, blankets, and small items of clothing such as shirts and stockings to their men in enemy hands. After Yorktown, the Ansbach-Bayreuth soldiers marched toward Winchester with only the uniforms they had worn during the siege and the pay they had received under Cornwallis's command. By the end of October, they seem to have spent all their remaining money. To provide some relief, according to Döhla, Beust advanced each prisoner 1 Spanish dollar.[68] In Winchester, the prisoners again received no new clothing.[69] Margrave Karl Alexander was upset by the situation. In a letter, he described how disturbed he was upon learning that "the poor prisoners have not been supplied with money or uniforms." He repeatedly called on Colonel Voit von Salzburg to see that the prisoners "did not suffer" until their exchange or liberation.[70]

By mid-December 1781, Beust had to borrow money from a local merchant so that he could again advance some pay to the prisoners. This time, however, he could give them only half a Spanish dollar each.[71] Upon arrival in Frederick in February 1782, the

prisoners still had not received pay from New York or any clothing. On March 14, Beust again could distribute only an interim
payment.[72] In New York, Voit von Salzburg was finally prepared to
provide them with supplies. On March 31, he dispatched his regimental quartermaster, Carl Wilhelm Meyer, with pay and clothing.[73] As he explained to Adjutant General von Schlammersdorf
in Ansbach, the British had caused this long delay; Voit von Salzburg had to negotiate with them to receive permission for Meyer's
transport. General Clinton, Voit von Salzburg found out, had no
interest in supplying the prisoners because he wanted to avoid
sending large sums of hard money into the American interior,
helping thereby to stabilize a collapsing revolutionary economy.
In May, with the new British commander, General Carleton, arriving in New York, Voit von Salzburg feared that Meyer's transport
would be both the first and last such delivery to the prisoners.[74]

In April 1782, while Meyer was on his way to Frederick, Voit
von Salzburg received the first detailed information about his soldiers in captivity. Two common soldiers, Musketeer Dörner and
Carpenter Pelz, had escaped and reached New York safely. They
did not bring good news. The prisoners "had not received pay for
six months," they were in need of clothing, and "the provisions
distributed to them were extremely bad."[75] Tellingly, Popp did not
find anything worth reporting in his journal between February 26,
when he wrote about the dire conditions in the barracks at Frederick, and April 30, when the prisoners finally received new clothing
and pay from Regimental Quartermaster Meyer.[76] Döhla reported
the details in his account: each soldier received two shirts, one
pair of shoes, stockings, a coat, a pigtail ribbon, a neckerchief, one
pair of cloth breeches, and two pairs of linen breeches. For the
last five months without regular pay, the soldiers received a total
of 10 Spanish dollars.[77] Without the new clothing and uniform
pieces, Popp stated, the captives could not have "covered themselves" for much longer.[78]

As Voit von Salzburg had predicted, the prisoners had to wait
a long time until additional clothes and pay arrived in Frederick.
In August and October, he blamed both the British headquarters and George Washington for the supply problems. The British
were attempting to limit the amount of money he could send to

the prisoners, and Washington "tries to prevent correspondence [with the prisoners] and intends to allow a flag of truce only every six months."[79] As a result, only one year later, in February 1783, the prisoners again received supplies, but no pay. Regimental Quartermaster Ludwig Flachshaar from the Hessen-Kassel Regiment von Bose gave each man one pair of stockings, soles for shoes, shirts, and blankets.[80] Regimental Quartermaster Johann Georg Daig, who had been dispatched with supplies and pay on December 11, 1782, had not yet reached the prisoners in Frederick.[81] Militiamen in Chester County, Pennsylvania, had seized his twenty-three wagons, ignoring the pass he had been given by Washington, Congress, and the British headquarters.[82] It took the county committee several weeks to release some of the wagons. Daig finally arrived in Frederick on March 28, 1783, but with only four wagons. Each Ansbach Bayreuth prisoner of war now received five months' pay (about 9 Spanish dollars).[83] The last time the Yorktown prisoners received pay in captivity was April 30. At that point, peace had already been announced.[84] Overall, the Ansbach-Bayreuth and Hessen-Kassel prisoners of war after Yorktown had much less support from their commanders than the prisoners of war captured at Trenton in 1776. It took almost six months after the surrender for Döhla, Popp, and their comrades to receive their first delivery of clothing and pay. In early 1777, Reuber and the prisoners from Trenton had had to wait only about two weeks before Regimental Quartermaster Müller arrived in Lancaster with supplies and pay.

While common soldiers eagerly welcomed the chance to work for additional food, pay, and clothing, their officers were much less enthusiastic. In late July 1782, Colonel Voit von Salzburg reported to Ansbach that the prisoners' condition was truly desperate. While delivering supplies and pay in Frederick, Regimental Quartermaster Meyer had encountered soldiers walking around half-naked and hungry. Voit von Salzburg realized that many of the captives had to go "into the country to work with farmers," even though "not all of [them] . . . will return to the regiments." He was especially worried that German immigrants in the region might persuade the men to stay in North America. The barracks in Frederick "were bad and each company did not have more than one floor." Moreover, "permissions to send flags [i.e., transports of pay and clothing] were hard to get."[85] After Yorktown, it was also clear that the British had lost the war in North America. German soldiers now had very good reasons to desert.

The Captors' View

It would have been difficult for the revolutionaries to guard prisoners more closely even if they had wanted to. The number of available guards was usually inadequate. This was not a new problem. On January 6, 1778, the Massachusetts Council in Boston had had to forbid the recruitment of guards among deserters from the Convention Army on the prison ships. After all, "the public" was placed "much in danger" when these former soldiers from Burgoyne's army guarded current prisoners of war from the same units, blurring the boundary between friend and foe.[86] In 1780, while the Convention Army was at Charlottesville, Colonel Francis Taylor's regiment of guards and the local militia at the barracks had only 124 rank and file fit for duty, and Colonel Joseph Crockett's Western Battalion had only 74 privates fit for duty—of whom 28 reportedly lacked clothes.[87]

In February 1782, when hundreds of German captives from Yorktown arrived at the barracks in Frederick, the Maryland Council ordered fifty militiamen from Montgomery County to guard the prisoners, but "not a Man . . . joined Major [Baily]," who was put in charge of the guards. The council angrily demanded the "strictest Compliance" with its orders, but to no avail. In April, Baily reported from Frederick that he had only "29 Men to guard the Prisoners." Complaining of the "great Aversion of our People to this Kind of Duty," the Maryland Council then asked Major General William Smallwood to leave some of his troops behind as guards: "the Prisoners are Continental prisoners and ought to be guarded by the Continent." Meanwhile, Baily had to be "very mild with the Prisoners" in Frederick because he did not have enough guards. Only when he reported in July that he was "almost destitute of a Guard" did Smallwood agree to order some "Invalids of the Regular Troops for this Service."[88] However, it was November before a company of Continentals arrived in town.[89]

In Winchester, Popp reported that he "could not complain about the guards." After all, there were only a few, and they allowed the German captives "to walk into town unimpeded."[90]

So much freedom for prisoners of war inevitably led to problems, particularly in New England, where the population was more hostile toward British and German soldiers than elsewhere. In January 1778, for instance, after a trip to Boston, Asa Douglas from Barrington complained to the Massachusetts Council about his encounter with a number of Bennington captives who were walking around freely and talking "sasey" to local inhabitants. He regarded the prisoners as a disgrace to "our young men that fought and bled at Bennington," and asked the authorities to "hang or banish" them from the community before there was "burning and blood" in town.[91]

Congress continued to struggle for greater control of prisoners of war. Since 1778, it had prohibited all prisoner exchanges that did not include reimbursement for prisoner upkeep. The British, however, were aware of the United States' difficult financial situation and repeatedly rejected such talks. States increasingly began negotiating their own exchanges, disregarding Congress. In January 1780, to avoid losing oversight of the captives altogether, Congress finally allowed Washington and his commissary general of prisoners to negotiate again with the British over prisoner exchanges without first requesting repayment for the costs of upkeep. To that end, all prisoners of war "by whomsoever captivated" were to be considered prisoners of the United States, and all captured enemies had to be delivered into the care of the commissary general of prisoners. Individual states remained responsible only for the "safe keeping" of the prisoners, at Continental expense. To keep track of the captives, Congress also resolved that commissaries of prisoners in towns and states were to send monthly returns to the Board of War.[92] However, these rules were frequently ignored. In March 1780, New Hampshire was reprimanded by Congress for the many "inconveniences" it had created with its prisoner exchanges and was required to agree publicly that all future exchanges would be made only through congressional agencies and institutions such as the Board of War and the commissary general of prisoners.[93]

These Continental institutions, however, remained just as inconsistent, even contradictory, in their handling of foreign captives after 1778.[94] In 1779, the Board of War voiced new concerns over the practice of hiring out prisoners, worrying openly about the numerous captives from the *Molly* and *Triton* who walked around freely in Philadelphia and worked for wages. By the end of October, Bradford was ordered to "take back, & confine" all prisoner-laborers, "whoever has them."[95] At the same time, however, on October 6 the Board of War allowed a small group of German noncommissioned officers, "the Hessian Prisoners of War Gleim, Schwartz, Meinguth & Rubenkonig, Serjeant Majors," to walk freely "in the city during the day time, to procure any little conveniences for their countrymen" in the New Gaol.[96] Moreover, the board repeatedly called on Bradford that year to find prisoners of war who were willing to work for various persons.[97] In November 1779, Continental Commissary General of Prisoners John Beatty asked Bradford "by whose authority so many of the Prisoners are admitted to go at large in the City and Country & labor for hire among the Inhabitants," while inquiring in the same letter whether Bradford could "get me a good Servant lad who will serve for a Waiter from among the Prisoners."[98]

As in the early years of the war, Congress, the Board of War, and the commissary general of prisoners had few resources with which to manage prisoner affairs after 1778. When the Chester County militia seized German supplies for the prisoners in Frederick at the end of 1782 and later released only four of the wagons, Congress and the Continental Army were powerless to stop them. If Congress tried to act, it usually encountered stiff opposition. In Winchester, many of the local residents were disappointed when the Yorktown prisoners were removed in June 1782. Although they had previously complained repeatedly about the burden that the prisoners placed on them, particularly through requisitioning and other means of procuring food supplies, the prisoners' removal meant the loss of a much-needed labor force and hundreds of consumers with hard money. When the deputy commissary general of prisoners in Virginia, Joseph Holmes, tried to assemble a guard from the local militia for the prisoners' march from Winchester, he had trouble finding any men for the mission.[99] Colonel John Smith, county lieutenant from Frederick County in Virginia, flatly "refuse[d] to comply," claiming that he could not send the militia out of state without authorization from the governor or the Council of Safety because "the inhabitants of this place & in its Vicinity are backward in parting with the pris[oners]." They had recently found out that "a considerable sum of money is coming from New York for both Officers & Soldiers." In other words, Winchester was eagerly awaiting the arrival of pay for the prisoners, expecting that this money would be "put into the hands of the Contractors" for supplying them. The citizens of Winchester did not want to lose an opportunity to profit from their captives.[100]

In the residents' petition to Congress, however, they did not base their appeal on self-interest. Instead, they argued that moving the prisoners was "unnecessary." The prisoners could be supplied at a low cost in Winchester, and a new guard, 437 militiamen and 15 light dragoons, had been ordered to be "constantly on that duty." Moreover, Congress could easily contract "with proper persons" for the supply of the prisoners. Conditions for the captives would improve, and fewer would run away or wander the region searching for work. The petition did mention that the town desired the promised pay for the prisoners, which would provide a "plentiful circulation of Specie" in the region.[101] As Colonel North told Benjamin Lincoln on January 6, 1782, "It is shocking to see the dispositions of the Inhabitants of this Town. Nine-tenths of them are turned sutlers."[102] Even the captives noted that Winchester was trying to keep them in town. "The inhabitants of Virginia have let go us German troops very reluctantly," Popp wrote in his journal. "Quite a few of them went to Philadelphia and petitioned Congress, but to no avail."[103] Döhla reported on January 27 that the "inhabitants of Virginia did not like that we left them." But this came as no surprise to him; the citizens had "always received good hard money and pay" from the prisoners.[104]

The secretary at war did not agree with the residents of Winchester, and neither did Congress. After all, as Lincoln pointed out, Congress would save considerably with this move.[105] Even Virginia's governor, Benjamin Harrison, was angry when he heard about Winchester's attempts to profit from the prisoners:

I am sorry the inhabitants of Winchester & the Counties in its neighborhood should be displeased at the removal of the prisoners. If they are the losers by it, it is their own doings. Every Letter to the Executive from that part of the Country since their being placed in that town has been filled with complaints that they were riotous, were starving and that the people would not suffer provisions to be taken to support them, tho' they were assured that that mode wouldn't be used longer than 1st of January. I was also informed that even the guards were so negligent of their duty that great numbers of them have escaped, nay even assisted by the Country people in doing it and furnished with hunting shirts to disguise them; similar representations I dare say have been made to [General] Washington and Congress and therefore it is that they are removed.[106]

In the end, Congress and Governor Harrison prevailed: the prisoners were moved. In April, Meyer delivered their pay, shirts, shoes, and other items in Frederick, not in Winchester.

Waldeck Soldiers in Spanish Hands

After Saratoga, the American War of Independence became an imperial struggle when France and Spain entered into the conflict on the revolutionaries' side.[107] To protect West Florida, which had become an English colony after Spanish Florida was taken from France in 1763 and divided, British headquarters in New York sent a body of troops under Brigadier General John Campbell to Pensacola in late 1778, including the entire Waldeck regiment with 707 men.[108] They had arrived in North America in October 1776, fought at Fort Washington in November 1776, and then stayed in garrison on Staten Island until October 1778. Of all the German auxiliaries used by the British in North America, this unit served in the most distant, exotic, and foreign area of operations.[109]

The regiment's campaign on the Gulf Coast and along the Mississippi proved disastrous. Between 1779 and 1781, the entire unit fell into Spanish hands. A small group of 55 soldiers from Company Alberti was captured near New Orleans on the

Amite River on September 4, 1779.[110] A second, larger group of 210 soldiers from the grenadiers, Company von Hanxleden, and Company von Horn then became prisoners in Baton Rouge and several surrounding posts on September 21.[111] The remainder of the regiment surrendered with other British and loyalist forces at Pensacola in May 1781. While Pensacola's captured garrison was sent on parole to New York, the first two prisoner groups, a total of 265 men, had to endure a long stay in Spanish captivity. Before their exchange in 1782, the Waldeck prisoners of war spent ten months in New Orleans, a month in Vera Cruz, and more than a year in Havana, Cuba.[112] German evidence reveals that the Spanish used these captives only as a recruitment pool, not in the many other ways that the American revolutionaries utilized them. Since the British in West Florida and Louisiana had had no success in fighting the Spanish, there was also little incentive for the Spanish governor of New Orleans, Bernardo de Gálvez, to use the captives for prisoner exchanges.

Whether on campaign or as prisoners of war, the main problem for the Waldeck men was the climate. On March 19, 1779, the regiment's commander, Colonel Johann Ludwig Wilhelm von Hanxleden, reported that because of the intense heat, "many soldiers got sick and died." Twelve men had already died since their departure on December 14, 1778, from Kingston, Jamaica, a way station on the trip south from New York. In total, Hanxleden had only 609 infantrymen and 10 soldiers from the artillery available for duty in Pensacola.[113] From 1776 to the end of the war, 358 Waldeck soldiers died from sickness, and only 37 from wounds received in combat.[114]

The soldiers in West Florida and Spanish Louisiana felt cut off from the rest of the world. Underscoring their feelings of distance and foreignness, their letters and memoirs repeatedly mention encounters with American Indians, as both allies and enemies.[115] The regimental chaplain, Philip Waldeck, wrote from Pensacola in March 1779:

> We live now at the far end of the Gulf of Mexico, in West Florida, a dreary, unfarmed, desolate, and . . . barren country. Isolated from the world, we learn nothing about events in Europe [or]

North America. In front of us is the Gulf of Mexico, behind us are wastelands, which are only crossed sometimes by roaming hordes of wild Indians on the hunt. For twelve miles around Pensacola, one cannot find a place to grow a head of lettuce but only white sand.[116]

In May, Hanxleden expressed anger over the "rotten salted provisions" and the hard work his men had to perform on the forts, which had been in disrepair for a long time. Knowing that the regiment, or at least some parts of it, would soon have to leave for the Mississippi River, he feared the "unhealthy" weather in an area where the air was full of mosquitoes from which "one could not hide by day or night."[117] Not surprisingly, Waldeck's ruler, Prince Friedrich Karl August, upon hearing where and how his soldiers lived and fought, complained to Lord Germain in London that because his unit "has suffered so much from the Climate of West Florida," the principality could not recruit new soldiers fast enough to replace those who died. Politely but unequivocally, he requested that "whenever a proper opportunity offers, such a Station might be allowed to these Troops as would be more suitable to the nature of their Constitution."[118]

In August 1779, 276 Waldeck soldiers from the grenadiers and Companies von Hanxleden and von Horn were sent to various British garrisons on the Mississippi, including Fort Bute, Baton Rouge, and Fort Panmure (modern-day Natchez). The British wanted to strengthen the defenses in this region to avoid another disaster like the quick capture of Vincennes by George Rogers Clark back in February. However, the British garrisons and their German reinforcements did not know at the time that King Charles III of Spain had declared war on May 8, and that Governor Gálvez had known about it since July 21. Hoping to surprise the British and prevent an assault on New Orleans, Gálvez wanted to strike directly at Pensacola, the heart of British West Florida, but a hurricane severely damaged his fleet before it could set sail. The governor then set out on land to destroy at least the surrounding smaller British garrisons before they could learn about the Spanish declaration of war. However, the Spanish movements had not remained completely hidden. Fearing a Spanish attack and judging Fort Bute to be indefensible, the British commander in the region, Lieutenant Colonel Alexander Dickinson, had moved the bulk of his forces to Baton Rouge. Only a small garrison of about twenty Waldeck men under Captain Georg von Haacke remained behind, and they were promptly overwhelmed on September 7. Gálvez's large force then advanced toward Baton Rouge and took it on September 21 after a short fight.[119]

Hanxleden reported that his men had fought bravely, even when faced with a force that included four hundred American Indian "savages" whose behavior was more "animal-like" than human. After the surprise attacks by the Spanish, only about five hundred British and German soldiers remained in Pensacola, not enough to defend the place adequately. Hanxleden felt abandoned at what seemed to him the end of the world. Not even British ships made it to Pensacola anymore. The garrison was so desperate to receive any news that they hired some locals to make an overland trip to Georgia to establish communications with New York.[120]

As for the prisoners in Spanish hands, Hanxleden knew only that the men were paid until December 24, 1779. He soon learned about supply problems. The British ration of 3⅓ pence for a common soldier was insufficient in Florida. To his dismay, Hanxleden also discovered that a hundred of the captives had already fallen ill. He fully expected that more than half of them would die soon. To relieve the situation and supply the men, the British commander at Pensacola sent two agents, Captain Christian Friedrich Pentzel and Commissary Philip Marc, to the prisoners quartered in New Orleans, but they never reached the men. They were placed under arrest at St. Jones for nine weeks and could not enter the city or even talk to any of the captured officers. Hanxleden assumed that this had to do with Gálvez's second attempt to seize Pensacola in early 1780, which also failed because of a hurricane.[121]

Hanxleden did not hear from his captured soldiers in Louisiana again until July 21, 1780. That day, several captive officers arrived in Pensacola on parole, but they did not bring good news. Between September 1779 and the spring of 1780, they reported, the prisoners had been treated well. Once the Spanish had taken Mobile, however, the situation worsened. With the conquest of West Florida all but secured, the Spanish tried to enlist as many

Waldeck captives as possible into their army. Owing to a lack of food, those efforts met with considerable success. According to German sources, out of 206 captured Waldeck rank and file, only 166 men remained in captivity as summer approached in 1780. The rest, presumably, had entered military service with the enemy or had died.[122] From other lists, it appears that of the 265 Waldeck soldiers of all ranks taken prisoner in 1779, 80 (30.2 percent) died of sickness by 1782. In the same period, a total of 117 soldiers (40.1 percent) seem to have deserted, presumably to join the Spanish army.[123]

Such stunningly high death and desertion rates can be explained only by taking a closer look at the men's treatment in Spanish hands. As Hanxleden and the other officers knew, when the Spanish decided to take their men away from New Orleans, first to Vera Cruz and then to Havana, they lost all control over them. As was customary, captured officers could no longer visit their rank and file to counteract the Spanish overtures. Hanxleden knew as well about the added pressures his men faced in Vera Cruz and Havana, two infamously "unhealthy places." Furthermore, the Spanish refused to enter into a prisoner cartel with the British. It seemed to Hanxleden that the prisoners had been "abandoned in this remote corner of the world."[124]

Hanxleden did not live to see his dire predictions come true. On January 3, 1781, the British commander in Pensacola placed a force of several hundred Waldeck, British, and loyalist soldiers, as well as some American Indians, under Hanxleden's command and dispatched them to retake Mobile. Arriving before the Spanish defenses on January 6, Hanxleden prepared for an attack the next morning. During that attack, however, the Spanish stayed in their works and calmly fired upon the approaching British force, killing Hanxleden and stopping the assault.[125] Lieutenant Colonel Albrecht von Horn took over the remaining Waldeck forces in Pensacola. He also commanded the unit when the long-awaited Spanish army under Gálvez finally appeared before the town and its defenses in March. The siege began at the end of April and was over within days. After "a bomb fell into a powder magazine," Horn reported to his prince, "further resistance was impossible." The surrender was agreed for May 8. That day, "We marched out of our works to a designated spot with all military honors, flags flying, and music playing," Horn wrote. "There, we laid down our muskets, and had to hand over our flags and cannons." Unlike the Waldeck men taken prisoner in 1779, however, Horn and the remainder of the regiment were able to avoid long-term captivity. They went to New York on parole.[126]

Several letters from two captured field officers, Lieutenants Andreas Brumhard and Karl Heinrich Strubberg, reveal more about the fate of the captured Waldeck rank and file. Both officers stayed with or near their men until early 1781, when they were exchanged to Kingston, Jamaica. Even then, they continued to report on their own experiences in Spanish hands and what they heard from others about the rank and file. Like Hanxleden, Strubberg and Brumhard stressed the sickness and death caused by the hot Caribbean climate. Brumhard's unit at the time numbered only 135 men, yet during July and August 1779, while they were still on campaign around Baton Rouge, he reported that about 23 soldiers had died of various fevers, and that 70, "including all officers and noncommissioned officers," were sick. At any given moment, he himself expected "to suffocate" from the great heat. On the march to New Orleans after their capture, Lieutenant Leonardi had "died of a fever," and the "sickness got worse by the day" among other Waldeck prisoners.[127] In a return from December 1779, 23 Waldeck soldiers were listed as "dead since prison"—a full 10 percent of the 233 soldiers recorded as prisoners of war in this list.[128]

Strubberg also had little positive to say about their time in Spanish captivity. "We were sent to and fro," he wrote in May 1781 after his exchange. They had spent ten months, until July 1780, in New Orleans and then about a month in Vera Cruz. Afterward, they had gone to Cuba. Two officers, fourteen noncommissioned officers, four drummers, one surgeon, and ninety common soldiers still remained there after Strubberg's and Brumhard's exchange. Desertion had become rampant. Out of a total of 195 prisoners listed by Strubberg for May 20, 1780, only 3 were allowed to leave on parole, 6 were exchanged, and 13 died, but 62 (31.8 percent) deserted. All of them probably entered Spanish military service.[129]

Brumhard, who was sick most of the time in New Orleans, healed quickly in the sea air on their travels to Vera Cruz and Havana. Once in Cuba, however, he and his fellow soldiers suffered markedly because they did not have enough money for adequate provisions and had no chance to obtain any in the near future. The common soldiers, in particular, were "almost naked" because their uniforms were worn and could not be replaced. The officers wanted to help, but they too had neither money nor credit.[130]

Strubberg reported on the prisoners in Cuba again in September 1781. Waiting in Kingston for a possible exchange of the remaining prisoners in Spanish hands, he learned that the situation there was deteriorating by the day. The prisoners were receiving provisions only every two or three days. Most of them no longer had anything to wear. The Spanish may well have created these conditions to make their prisoners defect. Strubberg, however, also faulted the British commissary in Jamaica, which was responsible for both British and German prisoners of war but did little to supply the Waldeck men. But there was little that he could do. As an auxiliary, he and the other officers could not act on their own and had to rely on the British for all negotiations. "Oh, how much has West Florida ruined our beautiful Regiment," he wrote in summarizing his experiences since 1779. "I want to cry, thinking about the beautiful and strong company of grenadiers that had to bury half of their best soldiers, not counting deserters, in the span of three months at the Mississippi."[131]

In October 1781, Strubberg, Brumhard, and their small party of exchanged officers and soldiers decided to leave Kingston for New York, mainly because Haacke, who had stayed behind in Cuba with the remaining captives, had written that if the prisoners were to be exchanged at all, they would be sent directly to New York. However, Strubberg's and Brumhard's trip took a very long time: they did not arrive in New York until December 31. After leaving Jamaica, their merchantman was stuck in a calm for weeks between Cuba and Hispaniola. They even had to return to Jamaica for new provisions before finally making it around Florida and up north.[132] Only in January 1782, it seems, were the remaining Waldeck prisoners in Cuba exchanged and sent on their way to New York.[133] A Spanish officer relayed the good news to Strubberg and Brumhard in June.[134] Two returns compiled by Haacke on January 5 and 6, 1782, reveal that only eighty-five common soldiers came back from Cuba.[135]

Indentured Prisoners

The Siege of Yorktown in October 1781 secured victory for the American revolutionaries in North America, but it left them with roughly 5,300 new prisoners of war. During captivity, these British and German soldiers faced frequent hardships. One of the main reasons for their problems was that Congress and the United States, finally working under the newly ratified Articles of Confederation, were essentially bankrupt. Because both sides had been supplying captives on their own, without agents, since 1778, and the British refused to reimburse the revolutionaries for these expenses during the war, Congress ran out of money for adequate prisoner supply at the end of 1781. After searching for ways to reduce the costs of keeping so many enemy soldiers in American hands, by June 1782 the new congressional leaders had come up with a plan: they would make use of the German prisoners of war by recruiting them for the Continental Army, releasing them after payment of a ransom, or selling them into indentured servitude. The captives had become human capital, a means of gaining manpower or cash for the revolutionary cause.

The origins of these new prisoner-of-war policies go back to 1779 and 1780, when inflation became rampant and the Continental currency was in free fall. A serious financial crisis was now hampering the revolutionary war effort. As one historian stated, there was considerable "evidence of national bankruptcy" at the end of 1781.[136] To overcome this crisis, a group of powerful nationalists in Congress and the Continental Army, led by the new superintendent of finance, Robert Morris, sought to strengthen central authority in the Continental government vis-à-vis the states.[137] Only through such a realignment of power, they thought, could finances be reorganized and the war finally be won. Morris stressed a particularly "aggressive, nationally oriented program," including a number of new taxes meant to provide "independent revenue for the Confederation government and federal responsibility for funding the war debt."[138] Regarding prisoner support, he and Secretary at War Lincoln met with General Washington on December 5, 1781, to discuss "the safe keeping and cheap feeding" of these enemies in their hands.[139]

A major problem was that Congress could not deliver the food the prisoners needed because it no longer had credit with local merchants, many of whom refused to sell their products for worthless paper money. The revolutionaries' policy of agreeing to prisoner exchanges only if they were reimbursed for their costs had backfired; the British were able to cope much better with the financial strain of keeping prisoners of war for a long time. Requisitioning also failed to bring in enough supplies and only antagonized the local population.[140] States such as Maryland and Virginia did not feel responsible for feeding captives on their own accounts. After all, on January 13, 1780, Congress had declared that "all prisoners of war, whether captivated by the army or navy of the United States, or by the subjects, troops, or ships of any particular State . . . be deemed and treated, in all respects, as prisoners of war to the United States."[141]

On March 15, 1782, the British and the American revolutionaries met again for another prisoner-of-war conference in Elizabethtown, New Jersey. From the start, both sides had very different goals in mind, virtually ensuring that the negotiations would ultimately break down. The revolutionaries—represented by Major General Henry Knox and Robert Morris's assistant, Gouverneur Morris—primarily wanted a settlement of subsistence accounts for prisoners of war. They did not want a general exchange of captives because that would hand fully trained soldiers back to the British and give them an opportunity to plan another major campaign. The British were also uninterested in a general prisoner exchange. They knew about the United States' financial crisis and did not want to aid their enemies by reducing the number of captive soldiers Congress had to feed. Not surprisingly, the conference ended on April 20 without any result.[142]

A few days later, on May 1, Robert Morris called some of the revolutionaries' principal decision makers into his office to address future prisoner supplies and policies. After some discussion, the assembled leaders agreed that "the Hessian . . . Prisoners should be Sold, the British close Confined and put to short allowance."[143] This way, the revolutionaries hoped both to save funds and to retaliate against the British for the failed prisoner conference. But what did Morris and his collaborators mean when they proposed to sell German prisoners of war? And why was this plan limited only to German captives?

Morris and other leading revolutionaries in Congress and the army considered the German prisoners of war, who were widely dispersed in the backcountry, "less of a security risk" and, as auxiliaries, "less attractive" to the British during exchange negotiations.[144] On May 6, 1782, thus, they agreed that German captives could now be recruited for the Continental Army.[145] Those who refused to join could ransom themselves by paying 80 Spanish dollars, an amount considered adequate to cover each man's expenses for food in captivity. Prisoners who wanted to be liberated but who had no desire to defect to the revolutionaries and no funds to pay the ransom could sell themselves into indentured servitude for three years. German prisoners who chose one of these three options would over time become "free Citizens of these States."[146] The Germans would be eager for this opportunity, a congressional subcommittee concluded on May 15, because a considerable number of them, "from a dislike to the service into which they have been involuntarily hired and from a prospect of amending their conditions, have expressed a desire of entering some of them into the military service of the U.S. and others into a reasonable period of common service, with a view of eventually becoming Citizens & Settlers within the said States."[147]

British prisoners of war, on the other hand, had their work permits canceled on June 7 and were recalled from their employers. Congress believed that its new policy offered the prisoners too many opportunities for escape.[148] In fact, Congress would soon demand repayment of prisoner expenses from the British again, and even allow the secretary at war to reduce their rations.[149] On June 21, 1782, however, in another of the many policy reversals by Congress between 1776 and 1783, the delegates decided that British captives could be hired out again as long as employers paid a deposit of twenty French guineas into the new Bank of North America for each prisoner-laborer. Moreover, British prisoners of war could also swear the oath of allegiance and become citizens of a state of their choice after six months.[150]

The plan was clearly meant to reduce the costs of prisoner up-keep and place the burden of guarding captives on employers, but it failed from the start. Virtually no employer would pay such high deposits for British prisoner-laborers. The secretary at war even had the local prisoner-of-war commissaries in York, Reading, and Lancaster arrested and court-martialed for "disobedience of orders & neglect of duty" after Brigadier General Moses Hazen, whose regiment was stationed in the region as guards, informed Congress that they and their assistants were allowing British prison-ers to leave camp and work for the local population "without bail" and without the proper passes.[151] Congress reversed itself again on July 3, deciding that the new policy had resulted in more escapes and even fewer available funds than the previous approach. Brit-ish prisoners of war were again recalled and ordered to be put in close confinement.[152] By the summer of 1782, the new policy al-lowing prisoners of war to be recruited into the Continental Army, to pay a ransom, or to be sold into indentured servitude applied only to German captives.

Two underlying considerations contributed to these decisions. First, Robert Morris, Benjamin Lincoln, and other revolutionary leaders believed that German soldiers—unlike British soldiers— were eagerly waiting for an opportunity to switch sides and stay in the newly founded United States, even as indentured servants. As auxiliaries, so these revolutionaries thought, the men had been brutally impressed into British service by petty princes in the Holy Roman Empire and would readily accept any offer that allowed them to escape from their oppressive armies and instead follow the lead of the many other Germans who had immigrated to North America earlier in the century. German prisoners of war, in other words, had nothing to lose from these offers. The British, not the German auxiliaries, were the true enemy.

Second, while Morris, Lincoln, and other congressional nation-alists had failed with most of their ambitious financial plans in 1781 and 1782—nearly all "fell on a deaf ear" on the floor of Con-gress or were simply "swallowed up by ad hoc committees"—they at least seemed to have succeeded in prisoner matters.[153] By June

1782, the Continental Army began recruiting German prisoners of war.[154] The new recruits came not from the states but rather from a Continental reservoir of manpower. That the German captives were foreign to North America, paradoxically, would work to the advantage of such plans. The Continental government, rather than individual states, demanded and laid claim to the former enemies' allegiance. The United States had made them prisoners of war, and the United States would employ them as soldiers. General Washington had even suggested to Lincoln on April 27 that these men "be recruited for the Continent & not carried to the credit of the States' quotas, with whose Lines they are to serve."[155] If German captives did not join the Continental Army but paid the ransom in cash, they would at least pay for their own subsistence and swear the oath of allegiance to the United States. Those who could not pay the ransom would show up in Morris's account books as indentured servants (figure 6). The ransom paid for these men by their employers constituted an independent source of income for the United States. In the end, Morris and his collaborators hoped, former German prisoners, whether they joined the revolutionary military, paid the ransom, or became indentured servants, would become citizens of the nation, not of an individual state.[156]

Of course, ransom payments and recruitment of prisoners of war had a long tradition in Western warfare.[157] What made the German troops' captivity in 1782 and 1783 different was the linking of ransom payments to indentured servitude—something that did not exist in contemporary Europe. In fact, these German captives came to resemble the so-called Redemptioners of earlier decades, immigrants who, upon landing in North America, were given time to repay the fare for their transatlantic passage either on their own or by finding another citizen who would cover the cost in exchange for labor. Such treatment of prisoners of war had North American precedents. During imperial wars and conflicts between New France and the English colonies, many captive soldiers from New England were sold into servitude in order to pay for their upkeep in Canada and remedy labor shortages. Servitude was also used to reimburse governments or individuals who had bought back white prisoners from American Indians. There was a regular trade in captives, especially in the Northeast.[158] Redeemed

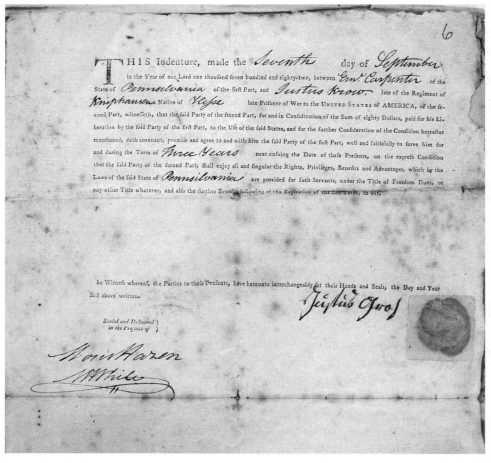

Figure 6.   Indenture for Justus Groh from the Regiment von Knyphausen, 1782

A preprinted indenture signed September 7, 1782, in which Justus Groh, a Hessen-Kassel prisoner of war from the Regiment von Knyphausen, agreed to serve Emanuel Carpenter from Lancaster for a total of three years. Carpenter had paid $80 for Groh's "liberation" and "the use of these states." Witnessed by General Moses Hazen. Courtesy of LancasterHistory.org, Lancaster, Pa.

captives then had to work off the expenses—just as the arrangement was explained to the German soldiers in 1782.[159]

The emissaries whom Morris and Lincoln sent to inform the German prisoners of war about the new plans reflected these broader
ideas. To Frederick and Winchester, Morris sent Colonel Wood,
who had previously supervised the captives from the Convention
Army and was already responsible for prisoners of war in Virginia
and Maryland. For the captives around Lancaster, Lincoln relied
on Hazen, whose regiment not only stood guard in town but was
also one of the few truly Continental bodies of troops in the army.
Hazen's regiment had originally been recruited from refugees in
Canada after the American invasion of 1775. Later, Congress gave
Hazen permission to enlist soldiers all over the eastern seaboard.
By 1782, the regiment was still the largest unit in the army that
was not part of a state line. Hazen looked eagerly to the German
prisoners as possible recruits.[160] Entering this unit would make the
former prisoners of war soldiers of the United States, not troops
from Pennsylvania, Virginia, or New York.[161]

So that all the captives could hear their offers, revolutionary
authorities across the eastern seaboard recalled German prisoner-
laborers from their employers in the spring and summer of 1782.[162]
The response, however, was unexpected. A July 1782 letter from
prisoners of war in the Regiment von Knyphausen to their regimental commander in New York, Colonel von Borck, reveals that
the men were actually frightened by the American plans. They
complained in "extreme despair" that the revolutionaries now
viewed them not as prisoners of war but "as members of the Turkish nation."[163] American emissaries had visited them twice over the
preceding few days with a "barbarous proposition." Since a prisoner exchange was impossible and the British refused to pay for
their upkeep, the captives were offered the chance to pay 80 Spanish dollars and swear the oath of allegiance to be discharged from
their confinement. Those who could not pay this amount could
serve with "safe people" for three years and work off the ransom.
These plans, the men stressed in their letter, "completely stunned
us and were cruel." They refused to accept such terms because
they had come "into this land as free soldiers," not as servants.[164]

This letter may or may not have expressed the general sentiments among the prisoners, and the expressions of utmost loyalty may or may not have been sincere. However, other cases
present a similar picture. In fact, wherever German prisoners of
war were held in 1782 and 1783, men resisted the new American
prisoner policies, which resulted in added pressure, even threats.
Private Bense from the former Convention Army, for instance,
noted in his journal that several revolutionaries in the summer of
1782 offered the prisoners in Reading the possibility of entering
"serfdom" in order to be released from captivity. Because most
prisoners did not agree to such propositions, they were "treated
harshly." According to Bense, more than 300 men were brought
into a jail in Reading that was designed for only 60 convicts, where
many of them had to live in the open and endure rain and cold
weather. Another 200 prisoners, mostly craftsmen, were marched
away to Lancaster. When 42 noncommissioned officers ran away
from Reading, they all were placed in the jail's dungeon. It was
only under such harsh conditions, wrote Bense, that a number
of prisoners agreed to serve in the Continental Army or become
indentured servants.[165] A noncommissioned officer from Hessen-
Hanau, Sergeant Samuel Vaupel, who had escaped from Reading,
reported later that the German prisoners of war received only ten
ounces of meat and bread per day during the summer of 1782.
The revolutionaries also forbade noncommissioned officers from
speaking to their men, presumably to have more influence over
their decision making. Vaupel assumed correctly that "the prisoners were mistreated in order to make them enlist." As the soldiers
hinted in a letter to him on September 22, they would be forced to
agree to the American proposals if they did not receive help from
their superiors very soon.[166]

One small group of German prisoners received a lot of attention and support from General von Loßberg. In April 1782, thirty-
five German captives had begun working as woodcutters for John
Jacob Faesch, a Swiss immigrant who operated a furnace in Mount
Hope, New Jersey.[167] Thirty men came from the Regiment von
Knyphausen, all taken captive on the *Molly* and *Triton* in 1779; two
came from the Hessen-Kassel Regiment Erbprinz and were taken
at Paulus Hook in 1779; two others were from the Hessen-Hanau

artillery, captured at Bennington in 1777; and one, Jacob Peter, was from the Hessen-Kassel artillery and had been a prisoner since Trenton in 1776.[168] According to available American and Hessen-Kassel accounts, several officers from General Hazen's regiment, including Captain Anthony Selin, a Swiss or German immigrant, visited the prisoner-laborers at Mount Hope in November 1782 to explain their choices: enlistment, ransom payment, indentured servitude, or close confinement at the New Gaol in Philadelphia. Faesch believed that his workers would either pay the ransom or go back to Philadelphia. He did not think they would enlist with the revolutionaries.[169] The men did in fact refuse to serve as soldiers, but they asked Selin for more time to consider the other proposals.[170]

In February 1783, with the war winding down, some of the German prisoner-laborers in Mount Hope tried to escape to New York. They made it as far as Newark, New Jersey, before being caught.[171] In early March, Selin and some other officers from Hazen's regiment returned to Mount Hope and asked the Germans again about their intentions. The prisoners now refused to enlist or ransom themselves, so Selin began marching them back to Philadelphia. One day into the march, however, the prisoners suddenly changed their minds, or so Faesch claimed. They "entered into a voluntary agreement with him, who advanced and paid . . . Thirty Pounds Pennsylvania Currency a Head."[172] On March 13, however, Faesch certified that he had received the discharges from Secretary at War Lincoln only after deducting 80 Spanish dollars per prisoner from the amount Congress owed him from a contract in 1780. Congress in this case used German prisoners of war as payment for manufactured goods, particularly arms and ammunition. The men had little choice, for Continental soldiers were marching them to the prison in Philadelphia. Of course, the revolutionaries understood such arrangements differently. In his report about the incident at Mount Hope, General Hazen stated that the prisoners should be thankful for this opportunity and think about how advantageous it was for "a mercenary Soldier and a Prisoner of War to become, at his own Election, a free Citizen in the State."[173] However, not all of the thirty-five prisoners heeded such recommendations and signed indentures with

Faesch. On March 11, he returned two of them for detention with Hazen.[174]

In a letter to Loßberg dated March 20, 1783, the remaining German prisoners from Mount Hope, now indentured servants, told a very different story. Captain Selin had announced to them on his second trip to Mount Hope that they were completely at his mercy "because they were Continental Servants," to which they replied that they were not servants but "the King's Soldiers." Angered by this response, Selin drew his sword and threatened to kill them, even striking two of them, Leopold Zindel and Valentin Landau, with the blade. He then marched them off under guard and placed them under arrest, without food or water.[175] Before that, the soldiers had "consulted with each other" at length and decided to decline the American offers. Only because of Selin's pressure and a lack of food, Jacob Peter from the Hessen-Kassel artillery stressed, did they give up and agree to the indenture with Faesch. Peter also claimed that they did not understand that they were signing an oath of allegiance and an indenture for three years; nobody had explained the English documents or translated them into German.[176] It is difficult to determine who told the truth in this case. Undeniably, the American revolutionaries exerted considerable pressure to make as many German captives as possible sign up with the Continental Army, pay the ransom, or become indentured servants. However, the prisoners of war at Mount Hope almost certainly talked to Selin, a German immigrant, in their native tongue. Their later claim that they did not understand what they heard and signed is unconvincing.

Once the Continental Congress ratified the preliminary peace treaty with Great Britain on April 15, 1783, both sides agreed to release all prisoners of war.[177] As Loßberg reported to Friedrich II of Hessen-Kassel on May 16, however, this release did not extend to the captives from Mount Hope.[178] Although the men had heard of the peace agreement and wanted to return to their units, Faesch did not let them go. American authorities no longer considered them prisoners of war but treated them as indentured servants who had to work off their debts accrued in captivity.[179] Understandably, Faesch feared that his new servants would try to run away. As a precautionary measure, he posted an announcement around Mount Hope.[180] Dated April 28, it offered a reward of $10 to anyone who captured one of Faesch's German servants more than three miles away from the ironworks. After all, Faesch stated there, he had employed the Germans "agreeably to a Resolution of Congress," on a valid contract with the Board of War.[181]

That, at least, was the information that Loßberg received in July 1783 after he had sent Major Carl von Bauermeister to ask American authorities about the fate of the soldiers at Mount Hope.[182] The Continental Congress and Lincoln let Loßberg know that he would have to negotiate directly with Faesch about their release.[183] Bauermeister also learned that "the War Council has no jurisdiction over the Hessian, Brunswick, and Hessen-Hanau soldiers who have been sold out of imprisonment," and only "the owners of these men" could decide their fate, based "upon the desires and intentions of the foreign soldiers." Finally, Congress told Bauermeister that no "German soldiers may return to the British army unless the owners are reimbursed in cash for their outlay."[184] At this point, five men from Mount Hope had been able to buy their freedom with their wages and were back in New York. But the other twenty-eight soldiers were still with Faesch and complained in another letter that they had "suffered much, and will suffer more." They begged their officers "not to abandon Your Country men, Your comrades, the Children entrusted to Your care," and even offered "to defray the costs for their liberation from arrears of their pay and paternal fortunes."[185]

When Friedrich II heard how his captive soldiers were being treated in North America, he was furious. Condemning "American arbitrariness," he ordered Loßberg to do everything in his power to bring home every Hessen-Kassel "subject" (*Landeskind*). He even offered to pay for the liberation of all the soldiers from Mount Hope as a reward to the men for their "exceptional loyalty."[186] In the end, Loßberg did in fact pay Faesch £296 for twenty-four of his indentured German prisoners.[187] By August 1783, however, shortly before the Hessen-Kassel troops left North America for their homeland in the Holy Roman Empire, only twenty-two men had returned from Mount Hope.[188] Some of the remaining soldiers, it seems, had played both sides and used their newly bought liberty to stay behind in the United States.[189]

Other German captives reacted as strongly to these new prisoner policies. In Frederick, Döhla described great confusion in the spring and summer of 1782. Something was going on, he noted on June 1, but the prisoners did not know what. Suddenly, every Ansbach-Bayreuth and Hessen-Kassel captive held at the jail in Frederick was released, and a roll call was held. Moreover, Döhla heard that all prisoner-laborers working outside of Frederick were recalled.[190] As of June 4, Lieutenant Prechtel reported, American citizens were forbidden to keep a prisoner at home. Anyone who disobeyed this rule faced a heavy fine, had to serve three years as a sailor on a ship, or was given thirty lashes.[191]

Between August 27 and September 1, 1782, the revolutionaries finally announced their new propositions to the men in Frederick. Döhla wrote:

> We . . . received permission from Congress to swear the oath of allegiance to the country; those who wanted this, could ransom themselves [by paying] . . . 80 Spanish dollars, or could be bought out of captivity by a citizen and then work off the money. . . . Also, recruiters from the American Continentals, or republican troops, arrived in Frederick and were allowed to enter our barracks. They promised 30 Spanish dollars in bounty money; 8 dollars at once and the rest once the recruit arrived at his regiment. The permission to enlist only extended to German troops; the English could not be enlisted or engaged.[192]

Noting several important details of Morris's larger plan, Döhla stressed that the recruiters came from the Continental Army, not from state militias or other units, and that the plan was limited to German troops. Moreover, these troops would swear the oath of allegiance to the United States, not to a particular state.

According to Döhla, a number of Ansbach-Bayreuth and Hessen-Kassel prisoners signed up with the Continental Army over the next three weeks. The first transport left Frederick on September 24 with more than fifty recruits. Döhla was not surprised: the recruiters had come into the barracks every day and "brought . . . music and also women."[193] In the same period, by contrast, only three Ansbach-Bayreuth prisoners in Frederick agreed to become indentured servants—one of whom was bought "by his cousin, who lived in Baltimore"—and Döhla did not mention a single soldier who had paid the ransom in cash.[194] On October 17, Döhla reported that a Private Schmidt had run away in November 1781 after stealing money from one of his comrades but was caught and imprisoned in Philadelphia. Schmidt, who had a wife and children in New York, apparently had been bought out of jail by an American and worked as an indentured servant. His wife and children had supposedly joined him from New York.[195]

Prechtel's journal confirms that many more soldiers enlisted in the Continental Army than ransomed themselves or agreed to serve as indentured servants. On October 22, 1782, Prechtel reported that a second transport of recruits had left Frederick with about twenty men from the four German regiments in captivity. On December 21, Döhla noted roughly forty Ansbach-Bayreuth deserters among Charles Armand Tuffin's corps marching through Frederick while guarding British prisoners of war.[196] Overall, until April 30, 1783, after peace was announced and shortly before the Ansbach-Bayreuth troops left Frederick for New York, Döhla provided details about thirty Ansbach-Bayreuth and fifteen Hessen-Kassel soldiers who joined American forces, but he mentioned only four, possibly five, fellow soldiers who became indentured servants. This evidence is only anecdotal, and the numbers cannot be taken at face value. However, they do reveal a trend. Soldiers preferred to join the Continental Army or other revolutionary units rather than become indentured servants. Most of them had had several years of military service before coming to North America and, even if they had learned other trades, probably considered themselves professional soldiers at this point. Still, the numbers are not overwhelming. Desertion or even defection remained a difficult decision. In North America, in contrast to Europe, it became virtually impossible to reverse such choices later and return to their homelands or units after the war.

Lieutenant Colonel Friedrich von Scheer from the Hessen-Kassel Regiment von Bose, who accompanied his men into captivity after Yorktown, as Major von Beust had done for the Ansbach-Bayreuth troops, later explained to Loßberg why the number of deserters among the two regiments in captivity had risen sharply in 1782. The problem began in November 1781, shortly after the surrender at Yorktown, when it became possible for local citizens to hire his men. As prisoner-laborers, the men received "good pay and food," and also "got to know women." In September 1782, those prisoner-laborers were recalled, but they were immediately allowed to ransom themselves, become indentured servants, or enlist in the Continental Army. Scheer attempted to report these practices to Loßberg, but "the Commissary of Prisoners forbade it." At the end of the war, once Scheer had given orders to leave Frederick on May 13, 1783, Maryland announced "at the barracks" and in "all public places" that the prisoners could stay and become citizens with all rights and liberties.[197]

It is probably impossible to definitively resolve these conflicting accounts, some of which say that numerous German prisoners joined the Continental Army, while others say that the captives loyally tried to resist all American efforts to recruit or sell them. Sufficient sources are simply not available, and local circumstances had a great influence, too. American numbers, unfortunately, cannot fill in the gaps. According to the War Department, at least 295 German soldiers were discharged from captivity by paying the ransom of 80 Spanish dollars; the superintendent of finance reported a profit of $23,617.45 from January 1782 until June 1783.[198] When the Department of the Treasury published the accounts of Robert Morris in 1791, it listed $27,873 in profit from "the discharge of German prisoners." This would mean that a maximum of 348 German soldiers had bought their freedom between August 1782 and the end of the war.[199] Both numbers are too low and most likely reflect the fact that many citizens who hired German soldiers in this period neglected to report it to avoid having to pay the required sum to the superintendent of finance. This might account for why Congress and other revolutionary authorities so often ordered that prisoners of war be closely confined. It was an effort to gain greater control of the captives.

A list of casualties among the Braunschweig-Wolfenbüttel troops provides more insight. About 5,000 men from this principality served in North America between 1776 and 1783. Near Bennington and at Saratoga, American revolutionaries captured roughly 2,000 soldiers from Braunschweig-Wolfenbüttel. Among those, 44

Table 7.   Casualties among Braunschweig-Wolfenbüttel Troops, 1776–1783

Casualties	Foreigners	Subjects
Shot on the battlefield	59	57
Drowned	24	21
Frozen to death	21	—
Suicide	3	3
Accidents	10	4
Died (wounded)	14	20
Died (sickness)	404	406
Sentenced to death	3	—
Deserters	359	290
Discharged	509	106
Missing (prisoners)	131	169
Indentured (prisoners)	44	155
Defectors (prisoners)	30	58
Chased away	10	—
Total	1,621	1,289

Source: "Namentliches Verzeichnis aller vom Herzogl. Braunschweigischen Corps in America vor dem Feind gebliebenen, an Wunden oder Krankheit gestorbenen, desertirten, oder auf sonstige Art abgegangenen Officiers, Unterofficiers, Gemeine und Knechte," Niedersächsisches Staatsarchiv Wolfenbüttel, 38B Alt Nr. 260.

foreigners (*Ausländer*) and 155 subjects (*Einländer*), a total of 199 men (10 percent), agreed to become indentured servants (table 7).[200] The same return listed 30 foreigners and 58 subjects who enlisted in the Continental Army (4.4 percent). Most deserters (259 men)—5.2 percent out of 5,000—and most discharges at the end of the war (509 men)—10.2 percent out of 5,000—were recorded among foreigners. Although these numbers are probably too low and reflect how difficult it was for the Convention Army to keep accurate records during the last two years of the war, they still reveal that fewer German soldiers than the American revolutionaries expected accepted the offer to join the United States via the Continental Army, ransom payments, or indentured servitude.

The example of fifty Braunschweig-Wolfenbüttel and Hessen-Hanau prisoners of war, captured in 1777, who suddenly arrived in New York Harbor on British ships in late December 1782 is probably more telling than many lists and numbers. In contrast to the prisoners at Mount Hope, these men had enlisted with American forces in the fall of 1782 and had agreed to serve as marines on the frigate *South Carolina*. Unfortunately for the prisoners, the British navy captured the ship on December 21, only a few days after it had left its harbor in Philadelphia.[201] Brought to New York by the British navy, the fifty German defectors and new revolutionary marines were interrogated by their former officers.[202] To the last man, they denied the charge of defection, claiming that their service on the revolutionary ship was part of a clever scheme to escape from captivity. After five years in revolutionary hands, suffering from meager provisions and crowded quarters, they had learned from loyalists around Philadelphia that British ships were lingering in Delaware Bay, waiting for the *South Carolina* to leave its harbor. They decided to enlist on this ship only because they knew that it would soon be captured by the British, and they would thus be brought back to New York and finally freed from captivity.[203]

The officers accepted this tale, reinstated the former prisoners, and quickly accused the American revolutionaries of prisoner mistreatment.[204] Within days, the men were again receiving their regular pay.[205] What the officers did not know, and what their soldiers wisely concealed, was that they had actually fought very hard on the *South Carolina*, together with American seamen, to avoid British capture—behavior that one would not expect from prisoners of war who were using the ship as a vehicle for escape.[206] Like the prisoners in Mount Hope, these seemingly powerless captives manipulated the revolutionaries, the British navy, and German officers, playing them off against each other to their own advantage.

~

After Yorktown, the conditions for common German soldiers in revolutionary hands deteriorated steadily. While the revolutionaries had essentially won the war militarily at this point, their growing financial crisis meant that they could provide fewer and fewer provisions to their increasing numbers of prisoners. In addition, there was no reliable system of supply. In 1782, in a major shift in prisoner-of-war policy, a desperate Congress devised a way to use the prisoners themselves to help replenish the American coffers and gain recruits: a captive could now buy his freedom and become a citizen by serving in the Continental Army, paying a ransom, or becoming an indentured servant. The prisoners of war thus became a human resource for the new nation and its army. Captivity for these German soldiers had become a personal debt— a sum to be repaid with cash, labor, or military service. Nevertheless, some prisoners of war, as the men from Mount Hope and the *South Carolina* show, still found a way to exploit this situation by playing their captors and officers off against each other.

CHAPTER 11

Release and Return

On May 13, 1783, captivity ended for Johann Conrad Döhla and Stephan Popp. The good news had been announced to the prisoners in Frederick on April 22. Just one day before, General Washington had written the British commander in North America, General Carleton, announcing cessation of hostilities "by sea and by land." As was customary, Washington suggested, "arrangements" should be made for the "liberation of all prisoners." He invited Carleton to send a "number of Officers, to attend the march of the prisoners though the Country, and to prevent any irregularities."[1] By April 29, according to Lieutenant Prechtel, the prisoners had complete freedom to go wherever they pleased in Frederick, as long as they came back to the barracks at night. On May 9, they were officially liberated from their status as prisoners of war. Retaking control of their troops, Prechtel and the other officers who had accompanied their men into captivity ordered a new Ansbach-Bayreuth guard at the barracks. One officer, one sergeant, and twenty-four common soldiers were charged with maintaining discipline and making sure no one deserted.[2]

Four days later, around noon on their "day of deliverance," the Ansbach-Bayreuth regiments who had surrendered with Cornwallis at Yorktown on October 19, 1781, marched out of Frederick, where they had "spent a miserable year and four and a half months in captivity . . . [and] had been hungry and poor very often."[3] They were on their way to New York, where they would have some free time before being "given back into the service of the army" and boarding ships bound for Europe.[4] The march was relatively short and posed no major difficulties for these battle- and

242

campaign-hardened veterans. However, as at Ochsenfurt in 1777, several resisted what they considered unjust treatment at the hands of their own superiors. According to Döhla, on May 14, only one day after leaving Frederick for New York, Sergeant Nikolaus Scholl "falsely" accused Private Andreas Rettenberger of "grumbling" against Major von Beust, the commanding officer from the Regiment von Seybothen. Beust then arrested Rettenberger. In response, a "great revolt" erupted among the former prisoners. The camaraderie among the rank and file had obviously not weakened in captivity. Two companies refused to continue marching and demanded that Rettenberger be released. Some soldiers, according to Döhla, even took off their uniforms and "threw them at the feet of Major Beust," complaining that the officers had treated one of their own "not as a soldier but as a criminal and wrongdoer." Every man in Döhla's Company von Quesnoy went to their captain and testified to Rettenberger's innocence. As a result of such remarkable support from his fellow soldiers, the officers questioned Rettenberger again and now found him innocent. Sergeant Scholl, because he had given a false report, was "strongly reprimanded."[5]

Desertion and Defection

Release and exchange were not the only ways common German prisoners of war left American captivity between 1776 and 1783. Since 1782, prisoners had been able to defect by enlisting in the Continental Army, secure their freedom by paying a ransom, or agree to become indentured servants. Numerous prisoners over the years had simply run away, sometimes returning later, sometimes not. Among them was Christoph Öste from Fürstenhagen in Hessen-Kassel. Like Reuber, he was a common soldier in the Regiment Rall and had been taken prisoner at Trenton on Christmas Day of 1776. In January 1777, as a prisoner at Lancaster, Öste was recorded as a linen weaver. Soon he was probably hired out, like so many other Trenton captives. At some point he must have decided to stay in North America, because he did not appear on the exchange lists for the Trenton prisoners in 1778. He resurfaced in the records only in 1783, when he was listed in Hessen-Kassel as one of the "scoundrels" who had deserted during captivity and remained behind in the newly founded United States. By the mid-1790s, Öste apparently lived near Carlisle, Pennsylvania, was married, and had baptized a daughter. By the 1800s, he had moved farther west into Ohio, anglicized his name to John Christopher East, and become a successful farmer.[6]

When the former Ansbach-Bayreuth prisoners of war stopped in Lancaster on their march back to New York from captivity in 1783, Döhla met a number of soldiers from the Regiments Voit von Salzburg and von Seybothen who "had taken service" with the Continental Army since their capture in 1781.[7] In Philadelphia, officers placed the Ansbach-Bayreuth soldiers in the New Gaol as a precaution against further desertion because so many of them "were well known" in the city, having been part of the British occupation in 1777–78. Once again, such harsh action prompted considerable "unrest" among the soldiers.[8] Perhaps not surprisingly, desertion became more frequent when the units left Philadelphia on May 22. That day, two men from Company von Quesnoy ran away and "took with them the new uniform and all baggage of Lieutenant von Ciriacy and the equipment of Fourier Knoll and other fellow soldiers from a wagon they had to guard."[9]

Yet broad statements must be made with care. Once the former prisoners of war from Ansbach-Bayreuth were back in New York and in garrison in Springfield on Long Island, they met four of their fellow soldiers who had previously been counted as deserters but had now voluntarily returned. One of them had escaped from captivity in March 1781 and served for twenty-one months with revolutionary forces under General Greene. Another returned to Long Island after serving on an American privateer. The third returnee had enlisted with a French unit after the surrender of Yorktown. The fourth had originally been listed as a deserter from captivity but had in fact ransomed himself following the American prisoner-of-war policy changes of 1782.[10] It is difficult, of course, to assess these men's motives for returning to their old units. They may well have heard that peace was announced and that the troops would soon return to Europe. The commanding officer of all Ansbach-Bayreuth troops, Colonel Voit von Salzburg, announced a general pardon for deserters and defectors in several newspapers, which undoubtedly made the decision to come back easier.[11] Individual examples require a careful examination of the circumstances. Not every soldier who ran away during captivity intended to stay in North America. Desertion or defection, like military service in general, was often only a temporary measure, a stopgap to overcome a crisis, especially in captivity. Despite stern regulations and orders, as Voit von Salzburg's general pardon shows, officers and German princes generally accepted such realities.

Throughout captivity, Döhla regularly recorded what happened to his fellow soldiers in Company von Quesnoy, including those who deserted, defected, or ran away only temporarily. His numbers are relatively reliable because he was often employed by his officers to write company and regimental rosters.[12] On October 24, 1781, for instance, during the march of the new Ansbach-Bayreuth prisoners from Yorktown to Winchester, he noted, "Private Hof, from Company von Quesnoy, remained behind and was listed as missing." Beyond making it clear that this soldier had left the unit, this statement does not indicate whether he ran away temporarily, joined American forces as a defector, was trying to reach British lines, or simply stayed behind to work. In this particular case, Döhla does provide some further clues, which point toward desertion. Hof apparently left camp at night, under the pretense of fetching water from a nearby well. The next day, his comrades discovered that he had also stolen a kettle and two glass bottles from the company store.[13] Family connections, on the other hand, explain drummer Johann Schindelbauer's desertion in December 1781. He was one of the four soldiers from Company von Quesnoy whom Döhla met again in Springfield after returning from captivity in Frederick. According to Döhla, Johann had followed his brother Georg, also an Ansbach-Bayreuth soldier, who ran away on October 13, before the capitulation of Yorktown, and signed up with a Virginia militia unit.[14]

The main reason for desertion or defection in captivity was bad or inadequate provisions. On December 7, 1781, the same day that Döhla reported that the prisoners had received very little flour over several weeks, two of his comrades, Christian Taubald and Nikolaus Schwab, ran away from the barracks. These two prisoners, however, did not want to stay in North America or enlist with revolutionary troops; they wanted to make their way back to New York.[15] Neither man made it. Taubald fell ill and had to return to the prisoner camp in Frederick on February 15, 1782. Revolutionary patrols brought back Schwab. He tried to escape a second time in July, again unsuccessfully.[16]

Pay was another reason for soldiers to run away from captivity—but not just the lack of pay. On May 2, 1782, Döhla reported that one of his comrades, Michael Meyer, had deserted from the barracks right after the prisoners received a payment of 10 Spanish dollars for their last five months of service. Meyer apparently took his money and ran away, leaving "behind considerable debts." He was not the only soldier to do so. According to Döhla, more than twenty prisoners from both Ansbach-Bayreuth regiments ran away at least temporarily shortly after pay and new clothing had been distributed. The Maryland militia, however, caught thirteen of them.[17]

Over the entire span of Döhla's captivity—including the time after the August 1782 policy changes—only 15 out of 102 men in Company von Quesnoy (14.7 percent) definitely defected to revolutionary American or French troops.[18] Another 16 ran away, but it is not clear whether they defected, deserted—even just temporarily—or escaped to return to British lines. Thus the maximum possible desertion rate for this unit during captivity was 30.4 percent. At home in Ansbach-Bayreuth, such deserters had considerable time to return voluntarily before their property was confiscated. For the troops in North America, this period of forbearance lasted two or more years. Only in August 1786, for instance, did Ansbach confiscate the property of five soldiers "who had deserted during captivity in North America" and did not return.[19] If the high desertion rates Döhla reported were accurate, they could certainly have also resulted from an announcement by the American revolutionaries in Frederick. On May 11, 1783, after peace had been declared and German officers and noncommissioned officers had regained control of their men, the revolutionaries offered every German soldier "the liberty to remain in the country, wherever he wanted, and work unrestricted, engage in trade, or be a farmer." Each man "would also be considered and kept as a native citizen of America and enjoy all customary liberty."[20]

Ansbach-Bayreuth muster lists provide a detailed record of desertions and other developments among the troops between 1781 and 1783, at least as far as the official records were concerned.[21] Considering only the returns for the 102 common soldiers in Döhla's Company von Quesnoy, the overall desertion rate in captivity—the period from the surrender at Yorktown on October 19, 1781, until the official release of the prisoners on May 9, 1783—was rather low. In fact, only five common soldiers from the company were officially listed as deserters (4.9 percent). However, between May 10, when Döhla and his comrades were officially released by the revolutionaries and again stood under command of their own superiors, and June 24, eleven men deserted (10.8 percent). Ten of those soldiers ran away between May 10 and May 25, when the former prisoners were marching from Frederick to New York. For this muster period, surprisingly, a new category appears in the returns, "Absent in the United States" (table 8). The ten soldiers who were recorded under this vague rubric had not returned from captivity—for whatever reason—but were not (yet) listed as deserters. Perhaps the Ansbach-Bayreuth headquarters hoped they would come back eventually. Including these men in the calculations, assuming from the circumstances and the dates of their disappearance that they probably wanted to stay in the United States, the official total of desertions from this unit between Yorktown and the return to New York is twenty-six (25.5 percent). This new category in the returns may have been added so that the British would still have to pay subsidies for these men. After all, they had not deserted, been transferred, or died.

A general return dated November 19, 1783, and signed by Adjutant General von Schlammersdorf, provides the most complete overview of the official casualty count and desertion rates in Ansbach-Bayreuth.[22] It lists 1,293 soldiers who left for North America in March 1777. Over the years of the conflict, an additional 1,068 men were sent across the Atlantic as reinforcements. Thus, a total of 2,361 Ansbach-Bayreuth soldiers served in North America.[23] The recorded deaths, desertions, discharges, and cases of missing soldiers are shown in table 9.

According to these figures, the maximum number of possible deserters among the Ansbach-Bayreuth troops—including missing

Table 8. Common Soldiers in Company von Quesnoy, 1781–1783

Period	Prisoners	New York[a]	Total	Died[b]	Deserted	Transferred
10/19/1781	89	13	102	5	—	—
10/20/1781–12/24/1781	84	13	97	5	—	—
12/25/1781–6/24/1782	80	11	91[c]	6[d]	—[e]	—
6/25/1782–12/24/1782	73	12	85	1	5	—

Period	Present	Absent (United States)	Absent (Guard, sick, etc.)	Total	Died	Deserted	Transferred
12/25/1782–6/24/1783	30	10[f]	25	65	—	11	9

[a] Soldiers who had stayed in New York—sick, wounded, or in other functions—when the company embarked in early 1781 to join the campaign of Lord Cornwallis and soldiers who accompanied officers on their parole after October 19, 1781.

[b] Killed in action, died of wounds and/or sickness.

[c] There is a discrepancy of one soldier in the sources. The total for the first half of 1782 should be 92, not 91 as listed here.

[d] In the overall returns, 7 soldiers were listed in this category. In this particular roster, only 6 men were marked as dead.

[e] One fifer, Johann Semmelmann, was listed as a deserter for this period, but he was not counted as a common soldier.

[f] In the returns, 11 men were listed in this category. In this particular roster, only 10 men were marked as "Absent in the United States."

Source: National Archives/Public Record Office, Kew, England, T38/812, no. 2.

248

Table 9. Ansbach-Bayreuth Casualties, 1777–1783

	Regiment von Eyb/ Voit von Salzburg	Regiment Voit von Salzburg/ von Seybothen	*Jäger*	Artillery	Total
Recalled	10	3	21	—	34 (1.4%)
Invalids	37	48	41	5	131 (5.5%)
Died	163	195	49	9	416 (17.6%)
Killed in Action	10	7	18	—	35 (1.5%)
Discharged	9	18	208	2	237 (10%)
Deserters	113	69	88	9	279 (11.8%)
Missing	114	74	—	—	188 (8%)
Total	456 (19.3%)	414 (17.5%)	425 (18%)	25 (1%)	1,320 (56%)

Source: "Liste der im Month Martii 1777 nach America abmarchirten Hochfürstl. Brandenburgischen Trouppen, und der bis 1782 incl. nachgesandten Rercouten, ingleichen der inzwischen abgegangenen Mannschaften, dann wie solche mit den 19ten Nov: effective bestanden," New York Public Library, Bancroft Collection, no. 75.

soldiers, and counting all units as well as every year on campaign and in captivity between 1777 and 1783—was 467 (19.8 percent). At the end of the war, almost as many soldiers were discharged as had previously deserted, primarily *Jäger*. The maximum number of soldiers who may have remained behind in North America between 1777 and 1783 was 704 (29.8 percent), counting everyone who was discharged, deserted, or went missing. Such numbers, if accurate, are actually relatively low in light of the fact that the average expected desertion rate in eighteenth-century European armies was already 18 to 20 percent. The numbers from Ansbach-Bayreuth also include discharged soldiers and men who ran away during captivity, traditionally a time when desertion rates increased.[24]

These numbers from the end of the conflict were certainly higher than desertion rates among prisoners earlier in the war.

In 1778, the exchange of the Trenton captives resulted in a maximum desertion rate of 14.7 to 18.6 percent. Even this range does not take into account that some soldiers may have died in captivity, become sick or unfit for transport or exchange, run away and later returned, or not been exchanged that year.[25]

Additional numbers from Braunschweig-Wolfenbüttel prisoners among the Convention Army confirm such findings. Overall, this duchy sent about 5,000 men into British service between 1776 and 1783. Of those, 2,902 (58 percent) did not return to Europe after the war because they had died, deserted, gone missing, or been discharged. Based on a report from General von Riedesel, 1,327 common Braunschweig-Wolfenbüttel soldiers surrendered at Saratoga on October 17, 1777. Including officers, musicians, drummers, staff, and servants, a total of 1,795 Braunschweig-Wolfenbüttel military personnel laid down their arms that day and joined the rest of the Convention Army for long years in revolutionary hands.[26] According to the available official lists, 407 soldiers among these troops (22.7 percent) deserted by 1783.[27] Particularly after 1779, however, it is almost impossible to ascertain even the most rudimentary numbers. For months in 1781, 1782, and 1783, for example, only one or two soldiers were recorded as deserters. Such low numbers do not reflect reality but rather indicate the difficulty of establishing figures for an entire unit when the individual soldiers were dispersed widely in various larger and smaller groups for which no reliable records exist.

Some anecdotal evidence suggests that the situation was desperate for the Convention Army in the last months of the war. From Reading in March 1783, Captain Heinrich von Cleve wrote that he could confirm a total of only 400 Braunschweig-Wolfenbüttel soldiers in town or in Lancaster, Frederick, and Philadelphia from the entire Convention Army, including musicians, surgeons, noncommissioned officers, and common soldiers. Overall, this accounts for only about one-third of the roughly 1,250 Braunschweig-Wolfenbüttel soldiers who had originally arrived in Charlottesville in 1779. In particular, Cleve blamed the terrible living conditions around Reading for the high number of soldiers who simply disappeared and melted away into the countryside. As before, however, it is unclear how many of those deserters were gone for good.[28]

The official Braunschweig-Wolfenbüttel casualty list for the Revolutionary War names 587 captives—11.7 percent, assuming a total of about 5,000 troops—who did not return because they deserted, defected, went missing, or became indentured servants. Not surprisingly, almost five times as many foreigners (509) as subjects (106) received discharges at the end of the war. This was a clear sign that those men were not wanted back in Europe or had already been promised such a discharge when they enlisted.

When the desertion rates for Braunschweig-Wolfenbüttel troops during captivity are compared with those recorded during a campaign, stark differences appear. For 1776/77, only 10 soldiers were listed as deserters, 5 of whom had run away while the corps was still in Europe. Throughout the war, taking the required strength of the Braunschweig-Wolfenbüttel troops—4,300 soldiers—as the basis for further calculations, this yielded a desertion rate of less than 1 percent. However, desertion seems to have increased not only in captivity but also in garrison. For 1778 and 1779 in Canada, for instance, there were at least 27 attempted desertions (no more than 1 percent of the Braunschweig-Wolfenbüttel corps' required strength).[29] Contemporary armies expected about 1 to 3 percent of their men to desert each year, and even more during wartime.[30]

For Hessen-Kassel, Charles Ingrao counted a total of 2,949 deserters both on campaign and in captivity.[31] With about 25,688 soldiers from this principality having served for the British between 1776 and 1783, this would make for an overall desertion rate of 11.5 percent. The most desertions happened at the end of the war, in 1783, when 734 men ran away. The pending departure for Europe must have forced many of the common soldiers to make a final decision—stay in North America or go back to Hessen-Kassel. Even if the number of all missing soldiers among the Hessen-Kassel troops is added to the number of deserters, the maximum possible desertion rate climbs only to 15.5 percent. Among those, foreigners accounted for 47 percent.[32] Rodney Atwood, however, based on an estimated 18,970 Hessen-Kassel soldiers who served in North America, accounted for 15,956 killed, dead, settlers in Nova Scotia, returnees during the war, or returnees in 1783 and 1784. That leaves 3,014, or 15.9 percent, who stayed behind in the United States.[33]

These numbers indicate that desertion rates for German auxiliaries while on campaign were lower than contemporaries expected at the time and rose above average expectations only while
the men were prisoners of war after 1781. The Regiment von
Bose, for instance, went into captivity on October 19, 1781, with
a total of 365 soldiers. By May 28, 1783, 104 men (28.5 percent)
had deserted from this unit.[34] Of the 284 common soldiers, 91 (32
percent) deserted in the same period.[35] These returns, however,
do not factor in the time and place of desertion. As the Ansbach-
Bayreuth numbers show clearly, it made a difference whether a
soldier ran away from his unit before or after April 29, 1783, when
peace was announced in Frederick and the former prisoners prepared to march back to New York. A return from the Regiment
Erbprinz for the same period also fails to provide this important
detail.[36] In this unit, 125 common soldiers (25.5 percent) deserted
between surrender on October 19, 1781, and the end of the war.[37]
Still, even when these numbers are compared to numbers from
other contemporary European armies, they do not seem particularly high. The French army in the first half of the eighteenth century expected an average desertion rate of about 20 percent in any
given unit. The corresponding figure for the Prussian army was 18
percent. Only during the French Revolutionary and Napoleonic
Wars, when military service became service to one's nation, did
average desertion rates drop to about 10 percent. At that point,
desertion was no longer "just" a crime of perjury; it had become
an act of treason.[38]

A few sources provide at least some information about individual soldiers who deserted and stayed in North America. Information on nineteen former German auxiliaries who deserted from
captivity, served in either the Continental Army, Charles Armand
Tuffin's Legion, or Casimir Pulaski's Legion, and later settled in
York, Pennsylvania, survived in the sketchbook of Lewis Miller, a
prominent local carpenter, the son of a German immigrant from
Schwäbisch Hall, and a keen chronicler of daily life in his hometown. Leonhard Baumgardner from the Regiment von Seybothen,
for instance, deserted from the barracks in Winchester on October 2, 1782, and joined Charles Armand Tuffin's Legion (figure 7). He was discharged in 1783 and married a Margaret Dinkel

Figure 7.   Leonhard Baumgardner

Lewis Miller's watercolor drawing of Leonhard Baumgardner, an Ansbach-Bayreuth
prisoner of war who defected to Armand's
Legion in October 1782 and was discharged
at York, Pennsylvania, in 1783. Courtesy of
the York County Heritage Trust, York, Pa.

in 1785. Together they had six children. Margaret also brought two illegitimate children into the marriage, one of whom took Baumgardner's name. Baumgardner appears in the Pennsylvania censuses of 1790, 1800, and 1810 as a resident of York, where he also served in the militia from 1786 to 1788. He became a successful blue dyer in town and bought several plots of land after 1796. In 1828, he was rewarded for his military service with a land warrant for 100 acres.[39]

Peter Engelmohr, a friend of Baumgardner's in York, deserted from captivity after the Battle of Trenton and never returned to the Regiment von Knyphausen. He had been hired as a prisoner-laborer by Charles Canary from Lancaster in 1777, probably as a tailor. In 1780, he appeared on a list of taxables in York and married Gertrude Dinkel, who was from the same family as Baumgardner's wife. Peter lived a long and successful life. He attended the First Reformed Church in town and died in 1844, at the age of eighty-seven.[40]

Not all of Miller's nineteen identified German deserters and defectors fared so well. Conrad Budin, from the Ansbach-Bayreuth Regiment Voit von Salzburg, for instance, received a pension of $8 by 1818 for veterans living in "reduced circumstances." He had originally been taken captive at Yorktown with the other Ansbach-Bayreuth troops and then defected in October 1782 to serve in Charles Armand Tuffin's Legion. This unit was disbanded in York in 1783, and Budin obviously decided to remain there. He married an Elizabeth Sechrist, whose family was probably connected to the brewery in town, where Budin himself may have worked, at least initially.[41]

More is known about a number of German captives who deserted and remained in the United States around Frederick. Local researchers there have compiled a list of 182 German soldiers who came through the area as prisoners of war at various times between 1776 and 1783 and then deserted, never to return to their units.[42] Not surprisingly, most of them came from the Hessen-Kassel Regiments Erbprinz and von Bose, as well as the Ansbach-Bayreuth Regiments Voit von Salzburg and von Seybothen, whose men were held in Frederick from early 1782 until the end of the war.[43] Some of them stayed only briefly in Maryland before moving on to Pennsylvania, Virginia, or Ohio. Others lived long lives in the region. Johann Peter Rückert, for instance, was still alive in 1850 at the age of ninety-two. He had deserted from the Regiment Voit von Salzburg during the Siege of Yorktown and left behind a wife in Ansbach when he decided not to go back.[44]

A number of soldiers from Döhla's company were among these men. Johann Georg Adam and Johannes Schindler, who deserted on May 22, 1783—taking with them Lieutenant von Ciriacy's new uniform, as well as other items belonging to fellow soldiers—apparently established themselves in Frederick.[45] Adam got married and had two children with his wife, Maria Magdalena, in 1786 and 1789. He later owned a sizable lot in Frederick. Schindler married an Eleanora Lahe in July 1787 and also stayed in town.[46] Another soldier from Company von Quesnoy, Peter Meyerhofer, had even more success. He married a Catharina Hardt in February 1783, several months before his desertion date was officially recorded as May 13. His first son, Christian, was born in October of the same year. Records from 1792 show him as a mason and the part owner of three lots in Frederick. He died in 1831 at the age of seventy-five. Two more soldiers from Company von Quesnoy, Johann Adam Seyfert and Johann Adam Strickstroh, also remained in Frederick for some time after their desertions in May 1782 and 1783 respectively. Both married, had several children, and appear to have owned property.[47]

One other Ansbach-Bayreuth deserter who remained in Frederick, Johannes Kolb, is apparently the same man who tried to desert during the infamous mutiny in Ochsenfurt on March 10, 1777.[48] Back then, he was caught after a few days and brought back to the troops; but in June 1782, he got away for good. He went on to become very successful in western Maryland. In 1792 he bought twenty-six acres of land, twenty-three of which he patented in 1793. After adding another forty-seven acres, he patented ninety-four acres in 1796 before selling all of it in May of that year. In 1812, he patented yet another sixty acres. All that time, he was married to Anna Barbara Engel. This marriage, however, could not be established without some objections being voiced by some of Kolb's former comrades, who made it known that he still had "a wife living in Baren Thissen [Bayreuth]."[49] Indeed, on April 2,

1777, two Bayreuth city officials had questioned Kunigunda Kolb, his wife back home, about her husband's whereabouts after the Ochsenfurt mutiny. They even put together a list of the couple's belongings, in case they would have to be confiscated.[50]

Discharge

In the winter of 1782/83, faced with the prospect that the war in North America would end soon and that the subsidy soldiers would be coming back to their homelands, German principalities began planning ahead. Knowing that they would have to support the returned troops on their own, without British subsidies. Hessen-Kassel, Hessen-Hanau, Ansbach-Bayreuth, and the other states with auxiliaries in North America decided to slash the number of soldiers their units would bring home. After hearing the first "rumors about a pending peace agreement between the British crown and the United States," Margrave Karl Alexander gave secret orders to Colonel Voit von Salzburg on January 4, 1783, to discharge "everybody, be it officers, noncommissioned officers, or common soldiers," who wanted "to stay in America" after peace was officially announced. Foreigners among his troops who were shorter than five feet would not even be allowed to return to Ansbach-Bayreuth; they had to be discharged in North America, England, or Holland before reaching the borders of the Holy Roman Empire. Schlammersdorf made it clear that this order must be kept from the rank and file, lest they leave their units too early.[51] In fact, he ordered Voit von Salzburg to wait with the announcement until the final muster of the troops before they left North America.[52] Similarly, Friedrich II of Hessen-Kassel told General von Loßberg to discharge all foreigners among the troops who had a *Kapitulation* (contract) before their arrival in Europe.

The British happily accommodated such plans. They were eager to get the auxiliaries off their books and find settlers for their territories in Canada, particularly Nova Scotia, New Brunswick, and Upper Canada (Ontario). To that end, they offered land grants, exemptions from tax payments and quit rents, and other government support. Those areas were also the destination for some 40,000 loyalists after the war.[53] Rumors and news about

Canada spread quickly among the German soldiers. Döhla noted that a number of Ansbach-Bayreuth *Jäger* who had heard about the opportunities offered by the British in Nova Scotia requested a discharge before embarkation. Soldiers who wanted to settle in Canada received free transportation and provisions en route to their destination as well as about 150 acres of land and exemptions from all taxes for twelve years.[54] Even officers and priests such as Field Chaplain Johann Christoph Wagner sought discharges to settle in this part of the British Empire.[55]

One of the discharged Ansbach-Bayreuth common soldiers was Johann Conrad Hetterich from the Regiment von Seybothen. Born December 12, 1752, in Laubersreuth, in the principality of Brandenburg-Kulmbach, he had joined the military just before Karl Alexander sent his two infantry regiments into British service in North America. Hetterich served with Regimental Quartermaster Daig between 1777 and 1783 and most likely took part in Daig's supply mission to the Ansbach-Bayreuth and Hessen-Kassel prisoners of war in March 1783. Overall, he must have done fairly well during the war. In 1778, he was able to lend 20 *Gulden* (£3) to a fellow soldier, Adam Lauwaldt from Günthersdorf.[56]

After his discharge in July 1782, Hetterich decided to go to Bear River, Nova Scotia, a settlement area of about 11,000 acres that had been divided between former Waldeck soldiers in the north, Hessen-Kassel and Braunschweig-Wolfenbüttel men in the south, and an assembly of former auxiliaries from other principalities, including Ansbach-Bayreuth, in the center. In total, about one hundred individuals came. Hetterich again fared rather well. He did not have to wait until land was allotted to him but rather bought land that had previously been given to another former soldier, Caspar Schaefer. Either he did not go to Nova Scotia alone or he married soon after his arrival, because in 1784 he was recorded in the community with a wife, Eleanor, and one child. Over the years, Hetterich acquired more land. In 1787 he bought a total of 280 acres, and in 1811 another 166 acres. In 1825 he was able to sell 100 bushels of potatoes to local merchants Betts and Turnbull and began "herding of winter cattle." Before his death, Hetterich became one of the most prominent citizens and farmers in the region and was a founding member and church warden of the

Anglican Church of St. John in Bear River. In his will, probated in Annapolis, Nova Scotia, on March 4, 1839, he left 300 acres to one of his two daughters, Christina, who had married into the local Harris family.[57]

These details come to us through some remarkable correspondence between Hetterich and his family back in Laubersreuth, during the war and after.[58] In a touching letter from April 26, 1784, his father shared his disappointment upon learning that his son had not returned from North America with the other Ansbach-Bayreuth soldiers:

> When your comrades arrived, I went to Bayreuth and looked forward to seeing you again. When I came home and your mother learned you were not with them, she cried bitterly and so did your brothers and sisters. They all hope that you and your sweetheart[59] would come and see the new buildings[60] and after that, Erhard, your dear brother, wants you to spend two days with them and your little sister, too. She thought when you would come you would bring her something nice. But her hopes did not come true. . . . We wish you dear son, health, happiness, and a long life. We will stay your faithful parents, brothers, and sisters as long as we live.[61]

Hetterich's success was something of an exception. From the original fifty or more families of discharged German auxiliaries in Bear River, only thirty-five were still there in 1788 when government assistance for new settlers ended. By 1791, only twenty-one remained. It seems that the harsh life in Nova Scotia, and perhaps also the lack of knowledge about farming among men who had been soldiers most of their lives, made them seek opportunities elsewhere. Many went to cities such as Halifax or even back to New York.[62]

Hetterich initially went to Nova Scotia with a group led by Captain Christian von Molitor. This Ansbach-Bayreuth officer had been removed from his post in March 1782, after he married an American woman without princely consent.[63] At the end of the war, in August 1783, Molitor successfully petitioned the British to grant him and a number of his comrades land in Nova

Scotia. Eleven men, two women, and seven servants went north.[64] The members of this group possessed a wide variety of skills and trades. Among them were Chaplain Wagner; Quartermaster Jacob Kalneck; Field Surgeon Friedrich Arnold; Johann Ronn, a silversmith; Lorenz Will, a blacksmith; Friedrich Ensenberg, a shoemaker; Georg Astmann, a carpenter; and Carl Honeffer, a farmer and miller. Molitor and this group so impressed General Carleton that he recommended that land be given to them "free of quit rents, fees, or expenses of any kind" and praised Molitor as a "Gentleman much respected by his late Corps."[65] Upon the men's arrival in Nova Scotia, however, Governor Parr complained that despite their skills, they had brought no tools.[66] Molitor seems to have received about 700 acres of land in Clements Township/Bear River and soon brought north another, larger group of Ansbach-Bayreuth soldiers: forty-five men, fifteen women, fourteen children, and eleven servants. He went on to serve as a local justice of the peace and had six children with his wife. After 1788, however, he was gone from the area. He returned at least temporarily to New York. From there, he invited Hetterich to join him in the city, where he now knew twelve other former Ansbach-Bayreuth soldiers with a "good income."[67] By 1807, Molitor had obviously returned to Nova Scotia, because he died in Halifax that year.[68]

Men from other German contingents had the same experiences as the former captives from Ansbach-Bayreuth. On August 25, 1783, Captain Andreas Wiederholdt submitted a list of eight lieutenants from the Hessen-Kassel regiments Jung von Loßberg, Platte, Donop, Knoblauch, and du Corps who wanted to leave for Nova Scotia along with four women, nine children, twenty-five servants, and Field Chaplain Rudolph Vernau. Two other officers, Carl and Ferdinand von Freyenhagen, asked to be permitted to return to Hessen-Kassel for their families and then come back to Nova Scotia.[69] Hessians also went into Upper Canada, particularly to Cataraqui, today North Marysburgh in Prince Edward County. Various returns from 1784 listed about thirty former German soldiers with eight women, about ten children, and several servants in this settlement.[70]

In total, 109 Hessen-Kassel soldiers went to Nova Scotia in 1783. Local historians have identified at least 233 German soldiers and their families from various auxiliary units and principalities.[71] Of course, compared to the approximately 40,000 loyalists who went to Canada at the end of the war, this was a very small group. One of Nova Scotia's attractions was the vast amount of available land after the expulsion of Acadians following the Seven Years' War. Another may have been the fact that many German soldiers were already familiar with the area—either because they had been stationed there or because they had traveled through the port of Halifax at some point during the war. We know, for instance, that about 80 Braunschweig-Wolfenbüttel soldiers were stationed at Lunenburg in 1778 and 1779. The Hessen-Kassel Garrison Regiment von Stein was stationed in Nova Scotia for five years after 1778. Out of the 537 men in this unit, 48 (8.4 percent) settled in the region.[72]

Return

Most German auxiliaries returned to their homelands after the war. The thoughts that Döhla expressed in his journal may well be representative. Scholars simply do not have sufficient information about what common soldiers said or felt at the end of the war to draw general conclusions. On August 30, 1783, Döhla arrived in England with his fellow Ansbach-Bayreuth soldiers. The trip across the Atlantic from New York had taken just twenty-seven days. On September 20, the men landed in Bremerlehe, where they were mustered one last time by Commissary Fawcett, who had negotiated the original subsidy treaties. That day, Döhla noted, they also received their last British rations. At Bremerlehe, more of the foreigners among the Ansbach-Bayreuth troops were discharged. At least in some cases, this seems to have happened against their will. Döhla reported "great grumbling" among soldiers who were angry that they "were not allowed to enter the prince's lands" and were sent away on foreign territory.[73]

On November 16, the Regiment von Seybothen arrived in Schwarzach, the first town in Bayreuth-Kulmbach territory. They were greeted, Döhla noted, by "many fellow countrymen." When they reached Kulmbach, the returning troops were swept up into a parade. There were "thousands of people" in attendance—so many that the men could hardly march into town. Despite a persistent cold rain, everyone was festive, and numerous speeches were given. Family members joyfully took their brothers, sons, and husbands into their arms. Others were heartbroken upon learning that their loved ones had "died or remained behind" in North America. The returned men were quartered with the local population. Döhla was particularly lucky; he got to stay with a butcher's widow, enjoying "food and drink and everything in abundance." In a poem recited in honor of the returning soldiers, Friedrich Wilhelm, Baron of Reizenstein, did not dwell on the unsuccessful war but rather welcomed the troops' return from the New World. "You are back," he exclaimed with relief, "you are brought back."[74]

Four days later, the regiment left Kulmbach in the morning. By one o'clock in the afternoon, again on a very rainy day, they had reached the principality's capital, Bayreuth. As before, fellow countrymen and family members met the soldiers outside the city. Again they marched into town in a parade. It obviously mattered little that these men had returned from a war they had lost. Upon reaching the city's barracks, Döhla was overcome with happiness when he was greeted at the gates by his father. After six long years, they "hugged and kissed and thanked God."[75] A poem recited that day reflects the joyful mood:

Aus dem fernen Schlachtfeld kommt	From the battlefield far away,
Ihr heut glücklich wieder!	You happily returned today!
Seht! Entgegen schallen Euch	Look! Toward you sound
Unsere frohen Lieder.	Our happy songs.
Lange schon erflehten wir	For a long time we begged for
Diese Freuden-Scene—	This joyous scene—
O! Der Himmel hört Gebet,	Oh! Heaven listens to our prayer,
Sieht die frommen Thräume.	Sees our devout dreams.
. . .	. . .
Seht! Dort wirft ins Kriegers Arm	Look! There, into the warrior's arm
Sich die Gattin wieder;	The wife throws herself again;
Freudenthränen hemmen ihr	Tears of joy still prevent
Noch die Jubellieder—	Her songs of jubilation—

Sie sinkt an die Narben-Brust	She sinks onto the scarred chest
Liebetaumelnd nieder.	Lovingly.
Ruft mit Herzenfreude laut:	Calls out with joy in her heart:
"Gott!—Ich hab' ihn wieder!"	"Lord!—I got him back!"[76]

After his experiences in North America, Döhla decided to request a discharge, effective December 1, 1783. After "fifteen years, minus four months," during which he had served his prince "honorably and loyally, on land and on water," he left the army. Still very much the professional soldier, he stayed on three extra days to help with several regimental rosters. On December 4, the entry in his journal simply stated, "Left Bayreuth and went home and ceased to be a soldier."[77] He was obviously not penniless after serving in the military for so many years. At home in Zell, he donated a richly decorated tablecloth for the pulpit to the local church. In a personal prayer at the end of his journal, he wrote, "Great and almighty God! . . . I thank you for your protection and help and that you saved me from ruin and captivity and . . . from a people in distant lands with a foreign language."[78]

Particularly touching in its expression of joy and gratitude for the troops' return is a letter from Margaretha Meyer in Gerabronn to her son, Regimental Quartermaster Meyer in the Regiment von Seybothen, dated November 23, 1783. Upon hearing of his return from North America, she wrote:

> [I] thank the highest, triune Lord a thousand, thousand, and one million times. [I] praise Him and thank Him forever. Through His grace, you have returned to our country. . . . My tears of joy will not stop running until I see you again. . . . But if you don't come soon, my dear, we won't see each other again in this world. . . . I have been sick all year and I am nothing but a bag of bones. Every day I feel as if I am suffocating. . . . I have asked my Dear Lord to stay alive only long enough to see you.[79]

After the war, men such as Meyer often left the army because their princes awarded them sought-after positions as administrators, which offered a steady income and considerable prestige. Meyer, for instance, became the *Kastenamtmann* in Mainbernheim (a senior administrator who supervises various legal and financial matters in a local district).[80] Johann Christoph Döhlemann, who advanced from corporal to lieutenant during the war, became the *Klosteramtmann* (the senior administrator for landholdings and the property of monasteries dissolved during the Reformation Era) in Münchaurach and *Kammeramtmann* (the head of local tax collection and public finances) in Ernskirchen.

Common soldiers who lacked such means and skills often stayed in the army for as long as they could endure the hard life. It was forty-eight years before a few surviving Hessen-Kassel soldiers who had fought in North America during the American War of Independence began receiving a pension. In 1831, the Electorate of Hesse resolved that each surviving "old American"—only common soldiers or noncommissioned officers—would be given a pension.[81] Depending on their rank and length of service, as well as on whether they had been wounded, each veteran was entitled to 2 to 3 *Thaler* (9–13 s.) per month.[82] Widows were eligible for between 0.5 and 1 *Thaler* (2 s. 3 d.–4 s. 6 d.).[83] By June 1831, authorities had located 396 surviving veterans of the American War of Independence and approved their claims. They later examined additional petitions.[84] It was estimated that pensions for these veterans and their widows would cost 21,540 *Thaler* (about £4,840) in 1831.[85] By 1833, claims for 658 veterans and 1,217 widows were approved.

That, of course, was only a very small percentage of the tens of thousands of Hessen-Kassel soldiers who had served for the British between 1776 and 1783.[86] To prove the claims in their petitions, soldiers described battles such as Red Bank, Long Island, and Trenton and listed, as best as they could, their officers.[87] Most applicants also stressed age, poverty, and sickness. They begged to receive their pensions as soon as possible, because they might not live much longer. Since only veterans still living in the electorate could receive pensions, several veterans who had moved away came back. Conrad Schröder, for instance, had moved to Hanoverian Göttingen but now returned to Hessian Witzenhausen.[88]

Out of hundreds of petitions, the successful request of Johannes Adler, who was seventy-nine years old in 1831, stands out. He described himself as an "American warrior" who had grown old and infirm. Respectfully, he reported that he "did not have any bowel movement for twenty-one days" and thus was "swollen from the chest down to his legs." He was lying in a room "as cold as a dog kennel" and lacked "money, bread, firewood, or any other support." Despite being sick, Adler did not forget to ask for pensions for his comrades Conrad Meyer, Daniel Lodenhose, Hermann Finkeldey, Hermann Schneider, Jacob Schuch, and Johannes Pfeiffer.[89] Another such petition came from Johannes Battenberg from Schorbach near Ziegenhain. He stated that at seventy-six he was too old to continue playing the barrel organ for money. He had been in the Regiment von Knyphausen and fought on Long Island and at Fort Washington in 1776. He was captured at Trenton and "remained in captivity for one and a half years" before being exchanged with the rest of his unit in 1778.[90]

The petition of the widow Lippold, who had gone to North America at the age of nine with her father, Sergeant Hornickel from the Regiment Landgraf, provides some insight into the lives of soldiers' families. In 1782, at the age of fifteen and still in North America, she married Gottlieb Lippold, a gunsmith in the Regiment von Angelelly. Lippold had returned to Hessen-Kassel "after two years, completely in tatters," having "lost all his tools" in captivity. He stayed in the army and served throughout the French Revolutionary Wars. He died in 1809, leaving behind his wife and five children. As of September 1831, his widow was receiving a pension of 1 *Thaler*.[91]

In 1855, the daughter of a Sergeant Kramer in Wolfsanger wrote one of the last petitions. She asked for a pension because she was "poor, sick, and bedridden." She thought she had a good chance to receive payments because in 1849 she had already been granted 8 *Thaler* (£1 16 s.) as a one-time "extraordinary pension." This time, however, because she was the daughter of a veteran but not a widow, Hessian authorities denied the request. The very last recorded petition came from the ninety-year-old widow of Gottfried Alliand. On February 1, 1861, she asked for an increase in her current pension. The request was approved, and thereafter she received 1 *Thaler* 15 *Groschen* (7 s. 4 d.).[92]

The situation in Ansbach-Bayreuth after 1783 was no different from that in Hesse. Veteran common soldiers and noncommissioned officers received almost no support later in life. A

Wohltätigkeit- oder Invaliden-Cassa (charitable and disability fund) established in Brandenburg-Kulmbach in 1771 was meant to distribute payments to invalid, poor, or sick soldiers and their widows, but not veterans. It was initially funded with a deposit of 3,000 *Gulden* (£450) from the *Landschaft.*[93] In Brandenburg-Ansbach, the *Fränkische Invaliden-Cassa* (Franconian disability fund) was founded in 1779 and was financed through fees paid for furloughed soldiers and by property confiscated from deserters. Indeed, this *Cassa* was initially established from property confiscated from a Musketeer Baumann, who had defected to the American revolutionaries.[94] In 1796, both *Cassa* owned about 51,750 *Gulden* (£7,762). However, only the Bayreuth *Cassa* had begun paying out money. In 1794, sixteen invalid soldiers and their widows received support. Moreover, a school for forty children of Bayreuth veterans was built. The Franconian *Cassa* could not pay out money until its assets exceeded 40,000 *Gulden* (£6,000). In 1798, it still had only 27,212 *Gulden* (£4,081).[95]

In 1806, a rumor that generous pensions were to be paid from the estate of the late Karl Alexander spread like wildfire among the former Ansbach-Bayreuth soldiers. Soon after his death in January, a number of veterans approached Ansbach's chief of police, Carl Christoph Schnitzlein, about a "special disposition" in the margrave's will that supposedly granted all surviving soldiers of the wars in North America and Holland "a lifelong pension." Because Schnitzlein did not know how to handle such inquiries, he asked for instructions from Berlin (Ansbach-Bayreuth had been under Prussian rule since 1791).[96] Over the next days and weeks, he even received the petitions for these alleged pensions. On April 24, several former Ansbach soldiers asked Schnitzlein whether it was true that Bayreuth veterans had already been called in to collect their pensions.[97] Ansbach veterans also became angry upon hearing that a public notice in Bayreuth had allegedly announced these pensions to veterans of the American War of Independence. They promptly pointed out to the administration that their regiment "had served loyally" at Ochsenfurt in March 1777 when Bayreuth troops had mutinied first.[98]

With the situation in Ansbach-Bayreuth getting out of hand, *Kriegs- und Domänenrath* Culemann, the Prussian official who oversaw tax collection and administered royal domains, made it clear in a letter of April 29, 1806, that the margrave's will contained no disposition about pensions for veteran soldiers. To end the rumors, he ordered that this information be made public throughout Ansbach-Bayreuth.[99] An investigation suggested that the rumors had started when the Prussian administration directed local authorities in Ansbach-Bayreuth to record every "unsupported invalid soldier" who had served in North America between 1777 and 1783. This announcement was coincidentally published on the same day that Karl Alexander died.[100] Somehow the two events had become linked, leading to the rumor about pending pensions. Despite Culemann's efforts, such rumors continued to float among the population, and another special announcement was published that again stressed their inaccuracy.[101] Nevertheless, on May 21, eighteen more veterans from towns and villages such as Crailsheim, Lautenbach, Wiesenbach, and Gerabronn applied for the rumored pensions. It is sad to read this petition, which expresses the men's gratitude for what they thought were going to be rewards demonstrating how much the prince had cared about his soldiers' "loyalty and fearlessness" in faraway North America.[102]

~

Captivity officially ended for the German prisoners of war in May 1783. Many of them, however, had been free since before the conclusion of peace. A certain number of them had been exchanged over the course of the war, and since 1782 it had been possible for German captives to buy their freedom through military service, ransom payments, or indentured servitude. Numerous prisoners, although certainly not as many as the revolutionaries had hoped, had deserted and defected, whether to escape the difficult living conditions or because they had met and married local women. Some who had run away in captivity returned to their units later and went back home with their comrades. Others settled in North America, in response to tempting offers both from the revolutionaries, who offered them American citizenship and all the attendant liberties, and from the British, who offered them free land in their Canadian territories. In some cases the German principalities even encouraged their subsidy soldiers to stay in the United States, particularly those who had been recruited as foreigners, out of concern for the cost of having to resume support for such a large number of returning troops. Most of the former prisoners went home, however, where they received a hero's welcome but little, if any, financial support. The Holy Roman Empire to which Reuber, Döhla, and Popp returned would soon be engulfed in another war, larger and more devastating than anything Europe had seen since the Thirty Years' War. The new wars of the nineteenth century would be fought not with subsidy troops but with conscripts. The number of men on the battlefields of Europe and the world would increase dramatically, and so would the number of soldiers who became prisoners of war.

Epilogue

A little-known treaty, negotiated and concluded soon after the American War of Independence, points toward the future of prisoner-of-war treatment and its challenges in the nineteenth and twentieth centuries. In 1785, the United States and Prussia agreed on a Treaty of Amity and Commerce that also, for the first time in international law, defined precisely how captors were to treat enemy soldiers in their hands. Although it was only a bilateral agreement, this treaty was the precursor to later definitions of the laws of land warfare in the U.S. Army's General Order No. 100 (the Lieber Code) of 1863, the Hague Conventions of 1899 and 1907, and the Geneva Conventions of 1929 and 1949.

Following the peace agreement with the British crown in 1783, the newly independent United States eagerly sought to conclude treaties of amity and commerce with various European nations in order to offset its severed trade relations with Great Britain. In mid-1784, Congress instructed its three distinguished commissioners in Europe, Thomas Jefferson, Benjamin Franklin, and John Adams, to negotiate with small states such as Tuscany and Portugal, as well as powerful states such as Prussia.[1] The initiative came at the right time. The Prussian envoy in Paris, Count Wilhelm Bernhard von der Goltz, had already suggested the possibility of a trade agreement with the United States in December 1783.[2] In February 1784, the Prussian envoy at The Hague, Baron Friedrich Wilhelm von Thulemeier, reported to Berlin about his initial conversations on the subject with John Adams. Prussia was particularly interested in tobacco imports, while the United States sought Prussian cloth.[3] The following month, King Frederick II of

268

Prussia ordered that official negotiations be conducted in Paris between Goltz and Franklin and at The Hague between Thulemeier and Adams. The basis for these talks was the United States' pact with Sweden, concluded in April 1783.[4]

Thomas Jefferson, however, had more on his mind than trade agreements. In the fall of 1784, in preparation for future negotiations, he drafted an agreement outline addressing situations that might arise under four different conditions: (1) when both contracting parties were at peace; (2) when one party was at war with another power; (3) when both parties were at war with a common enemy; and (4) when both parties were at war with each other.[5] With respect to the fourth category, he added two new articles: Article 23 was needed to protect trade and other commerce during wartime; Article 24 was titled "Prisoners of war to be well used."[6]

In the full draft of a model treaty, probably written in September 1784 for negotiations with Denmark, Jefferson fleshed out his ideas for both new articles. When both contracting parties were at war with each other, Article 23 would protect noncombatants such as merchants, women, children, scholars, farmers, artisans, manufacturers, and fishermen from molestation, plundering, or burning of property because their occupations were "for the common subsistence and benefit of mankind."[7] Article 24, which became one of the longest clauses in the treaty, would regulate prisoner-of-war treatment:

And to prevent the destruction of prisoners of war by sending them into distant and inclement countries, or by crowding them into close and noxious places, the two contracting parties solemnly pledge themselves to each other and to the world that they will not adopt any such practice; that neither will send the prisoners whom they may take in war from the other into the East Indies or any other parts of Asia, or Africa, but that they shall be placed in some parts of their dominions in Europe or America in wholesome situations; that they shall not be confined in dungeons, prison-ships, nor prisons, nor be put into irons, nor bound, nor otherwise restrained in the use of their limbs; that the officers shall be enlarged on their paroles within convenient districts and have comfortable quarters, and the common men be disposed in cantonments open and extensive enough for air and exercise, and lodged in barracks as roomy and good as are provided by the party in whose power they are for their own troops; . . . [and all common soldiers] shall be daily furnished by them with such ration as they allow to a common soldier in their own service; the value whereof shall be paid by the other party on a mutual adjustment of accounts for the subsistence of prisoners at the close of the war; . . . that each party shall be allowed to keep a commissary of prisoners of their own appointment with every separate cantonment of prisoners in possession of the other, which commissary shall see the prisoners as often as he pleases, shall be allowed to receive and distribute whatever necessaries may be sent to them by their friends and shall be free to make his reports in open letters to those who employ him. . . . And it is declared that neither the pretence that war dissolved all treaties, nor any other whatever shall be considered as annulling or suspending this and the next preceding article; but on the contrary that the state of war is precisely that for which they are provided, and during which they are to be as sacredly observed as the most acknowledged articles in the law of nature or nations.[8]

If adopted, this treaty would indeed become the first international agreement to explicitly protect civilian noncombatants and captives in war. Moreover, these stipulations were to remain in force even if one side was tempted to dissolve the treaty unilaterally.

Unfortunately, Article 24 did not appear in the final version of the United States' treaty with Denmark.[9] However, together with Article 23, it was introduced into the negotiations between Thulemeier and Adams at The Hague by all three American commissioners on November 10, 1784.[10] By including both articles in the discussions with Prussia, the commissioners and Congress hoped to "[diminish] the calamities of war." Frederick II, in turn, would set a shining example by adopting the proposals.[11] Congress declared in a letter to Berlin that "by the original Law of Nations, war and extirpation was the punishment of injury." As such conflicts became more humanized, "slavery instead of death" was a common fate for prisoners of war. "A farther step" was the exchange of prisoners instead of enslavement. "Why," Congress asked, "should not this Law of Nations go on improving?" Much time had passed "between its several Steps," but why should not "those steps be quickened?"[12] The United States clearly wanted the Treaty of Amity and Commerce with Prussia to be much more than a trade agreement. It was meant to reach beyond the unlikely case of a war between Prussia and the United States, to set new standards of prisoner-of-war treatment in future wars.[13] Concluding this treaty with the powerful king of Prussia would ensure that its stipulations would be met with respect and attention. As Jefferson wrote later to Elbridge Gerry, "We are glad to close this treaty on account of the respect paid to whatever the King of Prussia does. Of all the powers not holding American territory, a connexion with him will give us the most credit."[14]

Prussia accepted the American suggestions and signed the treaty on September 10, 1785.[15] Jefferson, Franklin, and Adams had already signed for the United States in July and August. In December 1784, Frederick II's state minister and main advisor, Gebhard Werner Graf von der Schulenburg, had expressed some surprise at the far-reaching American proposals, but he agreed with the stipulations. Articles 23 and 24, he wrote to Frederick II, merely reflected what Prussia's own policies had been for some time.[16]

This treaty thus needs to be included in the history of well-known agreements and international treaties regulating the treatment of noncombatants and captives in war, which usually begins with the Lieber Code and then leads from the Hague Conventions to the Geneva Conventions.[17] The American War of Independence, which was simultaneously a war of liberation, a revolutionary struggle, and a civil war, and which began at a time when only customary rules governed the conduct of war and the treatment of prisoners of war, had led to the formulation of written treaty law in peacetime. At the end of the eighteenth century, unwritten rules and traditions, or cartels concluded after a war had broken out, were no longer considered sufficient to regulate how belligerents approached captured enemies.

In 1786, Jean Nicolas Démeunier was preparing an essay on the United States for his *Encyclopédie méthodique*, and he had sent

Jefferson a draft, asking for comments. In response, Jefferson explained his reasons for including both Article 23 and Article 24 in the proposed Treaty of Amity and Commerce. It was British "cruelty" toward American prisoners of war between 1776 and 1783, he stated, that had created a "sense of . . . necessity" for such regulations. After all, "upwards of 11,000 American prisoners [had died] in one prison ship (the *Jersey*) and in the space of three years." Moreover, the British had not fed their American prisoners while they occupied Philadelphia in 1777 and 1778; they had taken American prisoners to the East Indies; and they had impressed countless American seamen into their navy.[18] As a result, American patriots were forced to fight "against their country," an assault not only on their bodies but also on their minds.[19] Thus Article 24 was the American revolutionaries' reaction to their treatment as captives during the war. But what about their role as captors?

In order to include this perspective in the treaty with Prussia, the revolutionaries would have had to address other issues, such as the dangerous moments of capture and surrender when the vanquished were most vulnerable. Article 24 was also silent on the fact that the revolutionaries had worked hard to disrupt the British war machine between 1776 and 1783 by inducing German prisoners of war to desert. Furthermore, Jefferson's treaty did not include any stipulations regarding how to obtain prisoner housing. In 1777 and 1778, Moravians in Lebanon, Pennsylvania, had learned a painful lesson about what it meant when hundreds of German prisoners of war, quartered in their town and church, also brought the revolutionary state to town, including militia guards, committees and their resolutions, the Continental Army, and requisitions of property or supplies. The stipulation in Article 24 regarding prisoner-of-war supplies, moreover, did not reflect the fact that American revolutionaries had effectively ended the traditional system for supplying captives through agents in 1778. This had subsequently led to severe food shortages for German and British prisoners. Understandably, from his nationalist perspective in 1785, Jefferson did not want to hear about measures that showed American revolutionaries not as victims of British tyranny but rather as exploiting every opportunity to attack their enemies, including through their treatment of prisoners of war.

Most importantly, however, Article 24 said nothing about the use of prison labor. In December 1775, American revolutionaries in Lancaster hired out prisoner-laborers from the first large group of British captives who arrived in town. By 1777, this practice had developed into a full-fledged labor system involving local citizens and committees, state governments, and Congress. In fact, the revolutionaries were able to keep thousands of British and German prisoners of war detained for months and years only because they hired so many out. Employers and the prisoners' own units, not Congress and the states, had to keep the prisoners paid, fed, clothed, and secured. Until 1781, captivity for common German (and British) soldiers was essentially privatized. For long periods of the war, it was not clear who actually supervised and controlled enemy captives. Indeed, the practice of hiring out prisoners of war harked back to earlier times, when captivity was more of an individual contractual agreement between captor and captive. Moreover, prisoner-laborers between 1775 and 1783 often were not paid, lacked food, or had to work under harsh conditions— but Article 24 of the U.S.-Prussian treaty of 1785 did not speak to such cases. Only the 1863 Lieber Code attempted for the first time to regulate labor services performed by prisoners of war, asserting that they could work "for the benefit of the captor's government, according to their rank and condition," but not for private citizens or enterprises.[20]

In 1782, following the victory at Yorktown and experiencing a serious financial crisis, Congress decisively revised its prisoner-of-war policies. German, but not British, captives could now enlist in the Continental Army, pay a ransom for their freedom, or sell themselves into indentured servitude. Jefferson's draft did not touch on these issues, nor on the considerable pressure placed on common German prisoners to accept one of the proposals. Surviving records detail reduced rations, overcrowded quarters, even physical violence. Article 24 of the United States' treaty with Prussia was an enormous step toward increased protection of prisoners of war and the codification of their rights into international law, but the revolutionaries' actions of 1782 and 1783 also set a dangerous precedent for captivity in war during the nineteenth and twentieth centuries.

APPENDIX

Common German Soldiers Taken Prisoner

From available German, British, and American sources, it is difficult, and in most cases impossible, to establish precise numbers of common German soldiers taken captive between 1776 and 1783. Prisoner returns and rosters were notoriously inaccurate. However, to provide some numbers and to gain a general sense of how many common German soldiers became prisoners of war during the American War of Independence, a few key battles and other clashes were examined in more detail for this study. As best as can be determined from available sources, numbers will be provided for common German soldiers who were taken prisoner by the revolutionaries at Trenton (1776), near Bennington (1777), at Saratoga (1777), on the British transports *Molly* and *Triton* (1779), around New Orleans and Baton Rouge (1779), and at Yorktown (1781). The analysis frequently discusses one or another of these groups of prisoners. The numbers presented here are also the basis for table 5.

Trenton

Lieutenant Colonel George Osborn, British commissary of muster for the foreign troops, obviously did not want to admit that a large number of soldiers had been taken prisoner at Trenton on Christmas Day 1776. He claimed that only about 700 men had become captives that morning, while "300 Rank & File" had managed to escape. On March 12, 1777, the *London Gazette* reported, on the basis of Osborn's numbers, " that the prisoners and missing amounted to about 700."[1]

Of course, George Washington's letter to the Executive Committee of Congress on the day after the battle and Colonel Stephen Moylan's report to Congress and the American public referenced a larger number of prisoners taken at Trenton. According to the commander of the Continental Army, 918 German soldiers, including 740 common soldiers, had fallen into revolutionary hands on December 26, 1776.[2] If nothing else, a high number of prisoners taken in battle was the best evidence of a particularly important victory.

Ironically, the most detailed, and in all likelihood most accurate, count of Hessen-Kassel prisoners of war taken at Trenton was conducted by the defeated troops themselves. Immediately upon hearing about the defeat in New Jersey, General von Heister, commander of all Hessen-Kassel forces in North America, sent Lieutenant Müller, regimental quartermaster of the Regiment von Knyphausen, on a mission to determine their numbers as precisely as possible so that they could be supplied with pay, clothing, shoes, and blankets. On January 3, 1777, only a few days after the battle, Müller departed from New York.[3] When he returned in March, he gave a detailed account of all the Hessian prisoners of war he had been able to locate. While following the prisoners' travel route from Trenton, New Jersey, to Lancaster, Pennsylvania, where they would spend much of their captivity, Müller also counted the wounded and sick prisoners who had to stay behind. He even recorded the names of the prisoners he met on his mission and the places where he met them.

In total, Müller listed 1,046 Hessen-Kassel prisoners of war in revolutionary hands in early 1777, including officers, noncommissioned soldiers, drummers, fifers, and rank and file. Only 1,007 of those men had been taken captive at Trenton. The Regiment von Loßberg was listed with 322 prisoners, the Regiment von Knyphausen with 322, the Regiment Rall with 318, and the Hessen-Kassel artillery with 45. To these numbers, Müller added 20 grenadiers and 19 *Jäger* who had been captured on other occasions, most likely at Princeton, New Jersey, on January 3, 1777. From these lists, it appears that a total of 848 common soldiers from Hessen-Kassel were taken prisoner at Trenton. But it also seems that only

831 of these men were still alive when Müller was on his mission between January and March 1777.[4]

Bennington

In a letter to the Massachusetts Council, Benjamin Lincoln reported on August 18, 1777, that 26 enemy officers, 3 surgeons, 37 common British soldiers, 38 Canadians, 155 loyalists, and 398 German soldiers had been taken prisoner near Bennington, Vermont. From this list, however, it is not clear whether he also included noncommissioned officers in his figures. If so, about 40 noncommissioned officers can probably be deducted from the group, which would result in about 358 common German soldiers who marched into revolutionary hands that day.[5]

Saratoga

Determining how many British and German soldiers surrendered at Saratoga on October 17, 1777, is challenging, not because of a lack of sources but because we cannot tell which of the various available returns for that day is most accurate.[6] A report signed by General Burgoyne, later also presented to Congress, listed a total of 3,379 British soldiers. For the German troops, under command of General von Riedesel, it recorded 2,382 men, including 1,792 common soldiers, 188 servants, 75 drummers, 19 surgeons, 167 noncommissioned officers, 47 staff members, and 94 officers.[7] These men came from the Braunschweig-Wolfenbüttel Regiments von Rhetz, von Specht, and von Riedesel as well as the Braunschweig-Wolfenbüttel Battalion von Barner, the dragoons, and the grenadiers. From Hessen-Hanau, the Regiment Erbprinz and the artillery fell into revolutionary hands.

On the American side, James Wilkinson, General Gates's adjutant general, reported a total of 5,863 British and German troops in revolutionary hands on October 31, including officers, noncommissioned officers, musicians, and all other staff members. Among those, 4,991 were common British and German soldiers. For the Germans from Braunschweig-Wolfenbüttel and Hessen-Hanau,

2,022 common soldiers, 217 sergeants, 83 drummers and fifers, and 122 officers and staff members were listed. These two reports obviously differ by 230 men with respect to the common German soldiers alone.[8]

At British headquarters, yet another number was reported. The deputy adjutant general, Lieutenant Colonel Robert Kingston, listed 2,442 British and 2,198 German soldiers who surrendered at Saratoga. Additionally, he noted that Burgoyne's army suffered 1,933 casualties before October 17 and had to deal with 400 captured soldiers and 300 deserters over the course of the campaign. Moreover, Burgoyne's army at Saratoga, according to Kingston, included 598 sick and wounded.[9] Taken together, these numbers present us with a minimum of 1,792 and a maximum of 2,022 common German soldiers who surrendered at Saratoga. Since Wilkinson's American and Specht's German numbers correspond to some extent, their figure of 2,022 is favored in this study.

The *Molly* and *Triton*

A Philadelphia prisoner return compiled for October 11, 1779, listed 340 prisoners from the Regiment von Knyphausen, including soldiers captured earlier than September 22 and 26, when the *Molly* and *Triton* were taken by privateers.[10] A Hessen-Kassel return for the Regiment von Knyphausen for September 1779, however, listed 380 prisoners of war from this unit, including 314 common soldiers.[11] The British mentioned only 205 prisoners of war at this time and also include captives taken as far back as Trenton in 1776.[12] It can be assumed that the October 1779 prisoner return from Philadelphia, which was taken on-site, was relatively accurate, but it did not distinguish precisely between ranks and places or skirmishes where the prisoners were taken. Thus, it is likely that a number of soldiers were included in this list who did not fall into revolutionary hands on the two British transports. For that reason, this study uses the lower number of common prisoners of war given in the monthly returns of the Regiment von Knyphausen.

New Orleans and Baton Rouge

In late 1778, the British headquarters in New York sent the entire Waldeck regiment to Pensacola, Florida, at which point it numbered 707 men.[13] A small group of 55 soldiers from Company Alberti were captured near New Orleans on the Amite River on September 4, 1779, 49 of whom seem to have been common soldiers.[14] A second, larger group of 210 soldiers from the grenadiers and Companies von Hanxleden and von Horn became prisoners in Baton Rouge and several surrounding posts on September 21, but it is unclear how many of them were common soldiers. The remainder of the regiment surrendered with other British and loyalist forces at Pensacola in May 1781. Colonel von Hanxleden reported a total of 206 common soldiers as captives for 1779, which is the number used for table 5.[15]

Yorktown

As at Saratoga, the number of prisoners taken at Yorktown and Gloucester Point on October 19, 1781, cannot be ascertained exactly.[16] According to a British return for October 18, the day before the surrender of the city and the post at Gloucester, Cornwallis's army numbered 6,995 soldiers, including officers, staff members, noncommissioned officers, and rank and file. There were 1,920 men from German units, including 1,597 common soldiers.[17] An American return compiled for the surrender, by contrast, counted 7,050 soldiers in Cornwallis's army. Among them were 1,951 Germans, with 1,625 common soldiers. In yet another American return, which included all British and German troops captured during the entire campaign and siege, the total was 7,073 men, with 1,712 German common soldiers.[18]

The German captives taken on that day served in four major contingents: two Ansbach-Bayreuth infantry regiments and the Hessen-Kassel Regiments Erbprinz and von Bose. In addition, several Ansbach-Bayreuth and Hessen-Kassel *Jäger* were stationed at Gloucester Point.[19] The commander of the Ansbach-Bayreuth regiments, Colonel Voit von Salzburg, reported to Margrave Karl

Alexander that 1,077 of his soldiers—including all ranks—were captured at Yorktown. The number of common Ansbach-Bayreuth prisoners ranges between 909 and 948 men in various returns.[20] The monthly return of the Regiment Erbprinz listed 463 men in American captivity for October 1781. Among those, between 367 and 425 men were rank and file, depending on the return.[21] For the Regiment von Bose, the monthly return for October 1781 listed 274 common soldiers as prisoners of war. Other returns for this unit give numbers after Yorktown ranging between 271 and 281.[22]

British numbers for prisoners of war always seem low; therefore, this study relies on German and American numbers. At Yorktown on October 19, 1781, at least 1,712 common German soldiers fell into revolutionary hands. This number includes 948 Ansbach-Bayreuth common soldiers, 425 from the Hessen-Kassel Regiment Erbprinz, 271 from the Hessen-Kassel Regiment von Bose, and 68 *Jäger.*

Notes

Abbreviations Used in the Notes

Bense, "Marschroute"	Marschroute von Braunschweig bis America Nebst den Vorschehnissen & Gegebenheiten der Herzoglich Braunschweigschen Troppen die 1. Division [von Johann Bense], Niedersächsisches Staatsarchiv Wolfenbüttel, VI Hs 18, Nr. 7
Bethlehem Diary	Bethlehem Diary, Moravian Archives, Bethlehem, Pa., vol. 31
BHQ	British Headquarters (Sir Guy Carleton, Lord Dorchester) Papers, David Library of the American Revolution, Washington Crossing, Pa., film 57
Boudinot Papers	Elias Boudinot Papers, Library of Congress, Washington, D.C.
Bradford Papers	Bradford Family Papers, Historical Society of Pennsylvania, Philadelphia, Collection 1676
CVSP	William Pitt Palmer et al., eds., *Calendar of Virginia State Papers and Other Manuscripts, 1652–1781*, 11 vols. (Richmond: R. F. Walker, 1875–1893)
DLAR	David Library of the American Revolution, Washington Crossing, Pa.
Döhla, "Marschroute"	Marschroute und Beschreibung der merkwürdigsten Begebenheiten nach, in und aus Amerika von Johann Conrad Döhla in Zell, für Johann Adam Holper in Münchberg, 1811, New York Public Library, Bancroft Collection, no. 47
Döhlemann, "Tagebuch"	Tagebuch und Briefe [von Johann Christoph Döhlemann], Private Collection of Dr. Adolf Lang, Ahnatal
GStA PK	Geheimes Staatsarchiv Preußischer Kulturbesitz, Berlin
HAV	Acta, die ad Serenissimum . . . erstattete unterthänigst Rapports, höchst Ihroselben in Königl:

Großbrittani: Subsidien überlaßenen Infanterie
Regiments hierauf ertheilte gnädigst Ordres
und Resolutiones, de Anno 1777 usque 1783,
Bayerisches Hauptstaatsarchiv, Munich, Abt. IV:
Kriegsarchiv, HS 1053

Hebron Diary — Hebron Diary, Moravian Archives, Bethlehem, Pa., box 2, Bd. 1

HETRINA — Inge Auerbach and Otto Fröhlich, *Hessische Truppen im amerikanischen Unabhängigkeitskrieg (HETRINA): Index nach Familiennamen*, 6 vols. (Marburg: Archivschule Marburg, 1972–87)

HSP — Historical Society of Pennsylvania, Philadelphia

JCC — Worthington C. Ford et al., eds., *Journals of the Continental Congress, 1774–1789*, 34 vols. (Washington, D.C.: U.S. Government Printing Office, 1904–37)

Kappes, "Notizbuch" — Notizbuch des Captain d'Armes Jeremias Kappes aus dem Amerikanischen Feldzug, 1776–1778, Landes- und Murhardsche Bibliothek der Stadt Kassel, Tgb. Nr. 77/76

LB Ks — Landes- und Murhardsche Bibliothek der Stadt Kassel

LC — Library of Congress, Washington, D.C.

LDC — Paul H. Smith et al., eds., *Letters of Delegates to Congress, 1774–1789*, 25 vols. (Washington, D.C.: Library of Congress, 1976–2000)

LMCC — Edmund C. Burnett, ed., *Letters of Members of the Continental Congress*, 8 vols. (Washington, D.C.: Carnegie Institution of Washington, 1921–36)

Meyer, "Tagebucheinträge" — Tagebucheinträge und Briefe, sowie Briefe der Familie und anderer Bekannter [von Carl Wilhelm Friedrich Meyer], Private Collection of the Meyer Family, Rügland

MNR — RG 93: War Department Collection of Revolutionary War Records, Miscellaneous Numbered Records, National Archives and Records Administration, Washington, D.C.

NdsStA Wf — Niedersächsisches Staatsarchiv Wolfenbüttel

NYPL — New York Public Library, New York, N.Y.

Papers RM — James E. Ferguson et al., eds., *The Papers of Robert Morris, 1781–1784*, 8 vols. (Pittsburgh: University of Pittsburgh Press, 1973–84)

PCC — RG 360: Papers of the Continental Congress, National Archives and Records Administration, Washington, D.C.

PFC — Peter Force Collection, Library of Congress, Washington, D.C.

Popp, "Geschichte" — Geschichte des Nordamerikanischen Krieges besonders was die beiden Bayreuthisch und

	Ansbachischen Regimenter anbelangt: Von einem bei dem Bayreuthischen Regiment von Seyboth gestandenen Soldaten aufgezeichnet namens Stephan Popp von 1777 bis 1783, Private Collection of Dr. Robert Arnholdt, Würzburg
Prechtel, "Beschreibung"	Johann Ernst Prechtel, "Beschreibung derer vom 7. Mart: 1777 bis 9. December: 1783 in Nord-America mitgemachten Feld-Züge," Bayerisches Hauptstaatsarchiv, Munich, Abteilung IV: Kriegsarchiv, HS 580/1
PRO	Public Record Office/The National Archives, Kew, England
Relationes Gall	Relationes aus Amerika vom Hessen-Hanauischen Infanterie Regiment unter Oberst Wilhelm Rudolf von Gall, Staatsarchiv Marburg, Best. 10e, Nr. I/19
Relationes Heister	Relationes vom Nord-Amerikanischen Krieg unter General von Heister, Staatsarchiv Marburg, Best. 4h, Nr. 3098
Relationes Knyphausen	Relationes vom Nord-Amerikanischen Krieg unter General von Knyphausen, Staatsarchiv Marburg, Best. 4h, Nr. 3099
Relationes Loßberg	Relationes vom Nord-Amerikanischen Krieg unter General von Loßberg, Staatsarchiv Marburg, Best. 4h, Nr. 3102
Reuber, "Tagebuch"	Tagebuch des Grenadiers Johannes Reuber. Eingefügt Bericht eines Anderen über die Belagerung Gibraltars 1782 und die Eroberung von Mannheim 1795, von Reubers Hand geschrieben, Landes- und Murhardsche Bibliothek der Stadt Kassel, 8° Ms. Hass. Nr. 46/1
StA	Staatsarchiv
StadtA	Stadtarchiv
TJP	Julian P. Boyd et al., eds., *The Papers of Thomas Jefferson*, 30 vols. (Princeton: Princeton University Press, 1950–2000)
UB	Universitätsbibliothek

Introduction

1. Schwoerer, *"No Standing Armies!"*; Wilson, "German 'Soldiertrade.'"

2. On traditional and more recent approaches to military history, see Citino, "Military Histories"; Black, *Rethinking Military History*. On the American context, see Higginbotham, "Early American Way of War"; Carp, "Early American Military History"; Lee, "Early American Ways of War." On Germany, see Nowosadtko, *Krieg, Gewalt und Ordnung*; Messerschmidt et al., *Militärgeschichte*.

3. Krammer, *Prisoners of War*, 1; Kroener, "Der Soldat als Ware," 271–72.

4. See, for instance, Speer, *Portals to Hell*; Bischof and Overmans, *Kriegsgefangenschaft*; Krammer, *Nazi Prisoners of War*; Oltmer, *Kriegsgefangene*; Franklin,

"POW/MIA Myth." A recent German collection of essays examining prisoners of war in all ages, from antiquity to modern times, remains a rare exception to this trend: Overmans, *In der Hand des Feindes.*

5. E.g., Colley, *Captives*; Demos, *Unredeemed Captive.*

6. Best, *Humanity in Warfare*; Best, *War and Law*; Flory, *Prisoners of War*; Howard, Andreopoulos, and Shulman, *Laws of War*; Karsten, *Law, Soldiers*; Rosas, *Legal Status*; Ziegler, "Die Bedeutung von Hugo Grotius."

7. Abell, *Prisoners*; Anderson, "Treatment of Prisoners"; Bowman, *Captive Americans*; Burrows, *Forgotten Patriots*; Cohen, *Yankee Sailors*; Dandridge, *American Prisoners*; Lemisch, "Listening"; Lindsey, "Treatment of American Prisoners"; Lloyd, *History*; Metzger, *Prisoner*; Ranlet, "In the Hands of the British"; Turner, "American Prisoners."

8. Dixon, "Divided Authority"; Haffner, "Treatment of Prisoners"; Miller, "Dangerous Guests"; Doyle, *Voices.* The *Journal of the Johannes Schwalm Historical Association* focuses entirely on German subsidy troops and their experiences, including captivity, in North America during the American Revolution.

9. Springer, *America's Captives*; Doyle, *Enemy.*

10. Atwood, *Hessians*, 257.

11. Andrews, "'Myrmidons'"; Atwood, *Hessians*; Bezzel, *Die Haustruppen*; Eelking, *Die deutschen Hülfstruppen*; Elster, *Geschichte der stehenden Truppen*; Fischer, *Washington's Crossing*; Huck, "Soldaten gegen Nordamerika"; Kipping, *Truppen*; Lowell, *Hessians*; Städtler, *Die Ansbach-Bayreuther Truppen*; Stephens, "'In Deepest Submission'"; Wilhelmy, *Les mercenaires allemands.*

12. Kapp, *Der Soldatenhandel*, is one of the earliest studies on this topic, condemning the practice from a nationalist perspective. See also Preser, *Der Soldatenhandel in Hessen*; Losch, *Soldatenhandel.* For a revision, see Wilson, "German 'Soldiertrade'"; Mauch, "Images of America." Because of the size of its contingent in British service, Hessen-Kassel has always received the most attention. See Ingrao, *Hessian Mercenary State*; Taylor, *Indentured to Liberty.*

13. For instance, Auerbach, "Die hessischen Soldaten"; Dippel, *Germany and the American Revolution*; Kipping, *Hessian View*; Gräf et al., *Krieg in Amerika*; Gräf et al., *Adliges Leben.*

14. See, for instance, George Bancroft's epic ten-volume *History of the United States of America.*

15. Andrews, "'Myrmidons,'" 220–25. Andrews argues convincingly that it was the "Hessians" whom Jefferson described as "foreign mercenaries" in the Declaration of Independence. An earlier draft accused George III of hiring "Scotch and foreign mercenaries." For a different interpretation, see Fetter, "Who Were the Foreign Mercenaries?"

16. Armitage and Braddick, *British Atlantic World*; Games, *Migration*; Greene and Morgan, *Atlantic History.*

17. Hohrath, "'In Cartellen,'" 142–47.

18. Wette, *Der Krieg des kleinen Mannes.*

19. Following the lead of Pierre Bourdieu, "capital" is defined very broadly here. Capital can encompass material things, including those with symbolic value, as well as intangible goods such as prestige, status, and authority. Various types of capital can be converted into other types of capital in the effort to accumulate power. Bourdieu, *Outline*, 178. See also Bourdieu, *Distinction*; Bourdieu, "Forms"; Bourdieu, "Social Space."

20. Eltis, *Coerced and Free Migration.*

21. Overmans, "'In der Hand des Feindes,'" 29.

22. At Yorktown in 1781, the German Regiment Deux-Ponts (Zweibrücken) fought in the French army. Schmitt, "'Hessians and Who?'"; Selig, "George Washington's German Allies."

23. Maza, "Stories in History"; Davies, *Fiction in the Archives*; Bonnell and Hunt, *Beyond the Cultural Turn.*

24. Schulze, "Ego-Dokumente," 28; Peters, "Zur Auskunftsfähigkeit"; Peters, "Wegweiser zum Innenleben?"; Peters, *Ein Söldnerleben.*

Introduction to Part I

1. Rehm, "Niedervellmar."

2. Reuber, "Tagebuch," fols. 51–52. Reuber made two copies of the original journal for his sons. One of these copies can be found at the Stadtarchiv Frankfurt am Main; the other was sold to the United States in a 1961 auction at Sotheby's. Two more copies (by different transcribers) are at the New York Public Library. See also Auerbach, *Die Hessen*, 304–16; Junghans, "Der amerikanische Feldzug," 155–57, 167–68, 183–86. A short summary of Reuber's experiences can be found in Breiter, "Auf den Spuren."

3. Ansbach-Bayreuth was not a united principality but consisted of two separate territories, Brandenburg-Ansbach and Brandenburg-Kulmbach (often also referred to as Brandenburg-Bayreuth or Kulmbach-Bayreuth), governed jointly by Margrave Karl Alexander since 1769. He had been margrave of Brandenburg-Ansbach since 1757. Prussia took control of Ansbach-Bayreuth in 1791 when Karl Alexander relinquished the throne, sold his dominium, and retired to a country estate in England. In 1806, during the Napoleonic Wars, the newly established Kingdom of Bavaria took over Ansbach-Bayreuth. Endres, "Ansbach-Bayreuth"; Holle, "Die politische Verfassung"; Müssel, "Bayreuth 1769." Two Ansbach-Bayreuth infantry regiments were sent into British service in 1777. The Regiment von Eyb was from Brandenburg-Ansbach. Originally commanded by and named after Colonel Friedrich Ludwig von Eyb, it was commanded by Colonel August Voit von Salzburg after 1778 and renamed accordingly. The Regiment von Seybothen was from Brandenburg-Kulmbach. It was originally commanded by Voit von Salzburg but was subsequently renamed after its new commander, Johann Heinrich von Seybothen.

4. Popp, "Geschichte," 4–5. Popp probably only kept notes during the war, then edited them into a journal later. From the last entries, it is clear that he edited his work at least until 1797 and also exchanged drafts with Johann Conrad Döhla, another Ansbach-Bayreuth common soldier who wrote a detailed journal of the war in North America. An undated remark in "Urkunden und Acta des Historischen Vereins von Oberfranken zu Bayreuth die amerikanische Expedition der brandenburger Truppen betr." (StadtA Bayreuth, Hist. 15) states that Döhla, a teacher, owned a diary from the War of Independence that Popp, also a teacher, was supposed to have as well. From several marginal notes in Popp's journal, it becomes apparent that he distributed his journal widely among his fellow American veterans. A notation next to Popp's entry about the *Sybilla*, the British ship on which he returned to Europe in 1783, reads: "I was on this ship, too. Koernich." This was probably Wolf Koernich, a corporal in Company von Seybothen in the Regiment von Seybothen (Popp, "Geschichte," 262–63). Döhla and Popp also copied newspaper articles into their journals. The two journals

almost seem to have been a communal effort to write a history of the war in North America from the perspective of Brandenburg-Kulmbach. Döhla, Popp, and Koernich were all members of the Regiment Voit von Salzburg. Popp's journal has been published in English and German—albeit with varying degrees of editorial skill and accuracy. See Popp, "Popp's Journal"; Kestler, "Geschichte des Nordamerikanischen Krieges," 317–54.

5. *Onolzbachische Wöchentliche Frag- und Anzeigungs-Nachrichten*, March 12, 1777.

6. Ochsenfurt was part of the Prince-Bishopric of Bamberg and Würzburg. Ansbach-Bayreuth's harbor on the River Main, Markt Stefft, was too small for embarking so many troops, but later reinforcements left from there. Lochner and Retzer, "Ansbach-Bayreuther Truppen."

7. Some sources mention between thirty and fifty wounded soldiers, others only six or seven. One source even claims that a soldier was killed in the skirmish. Most evidence points toward a smaller number of wounded soldiers. StA Würzburg, Militärsachen Nr. 95, fols. 35–57; ibid., Domkapitel Protokolle, 1777; ibid., Lichtbildsammlung 337. See also Döhlemann, "Tagebuch," 2–5; Prechtel, "Beschreibung," Bemerkungen; William Fawcett to Lord Suffolk, April 17, 1777, PRO CO 5/140, fols. 137–38v; Henry Laurens to John Gervais, August 5, 1777, *LDC*, 7:418–25.

8. Meyer, "Tagebucheinträge," 2. Eintragung.

9. StA Würzburg, Militärsachen Nr. 95, fols. 50–56. The embarkation returns list twenty-five deserters. "Embarkation Muster, Nijmegen," March 25, 1783, PRO SP 81/187.

10. Charles Rainsford to Lord Suffolk, March 28, 1777, ibid.

11. George Osborn to Lord George Germain, May 15, 1777, PRO CO 5/94, fol. 428.

12. Ibid., fol. 426.

13. Rainsford to Lord Suffolk, March 28, 1777.

14. To date, only Stephan Huck has produced a detailed study of social composition among German auxiliaries between 1776 and 1783. Huck, "Soldaten gegen Nordamerika." Atwood, *Hessians*; Auerbach, *Die Hessen*; Ingrao, *Hessian Mercenary State*; and Taylor, *Indentured to Liberty,* provide only partial insight into this topic.

1. Subsidy Treaties

1. Among the vast literature on this topic, see, for instance, Schwoerer, *"No Standing Armies!"*

2. Wilson, *German Armies*, 259, 268.

3. Hessen-Kassel had sent its first subsidy troops—1,600 infantry soldiers and four cavalry companies— into Danish service in 1677. Böhm, *Hessisches Militär*, 3; Losch, *Soldatenhandel*, 7. Some historians argue that Hessen-Kassel's 1684 agreement with Spain was the principality's first true subsidy treaty. Eckhardt, "Hessische Truppen," 108.

4. Selig, "George Washington's German Allies."

5. Köster, *Die Neuesten Staatsbegebenheiten*, 2:167, 388.

6. Auerbach, *Die Hessen*, 27–45; Köster, *Die neuesten Staatsbegebenheiten*, 2:167–68. Clinton was knighted and promoted to lieutenant general in 1777.

7. Auerbach, *Die Hessen*, 46–65.

8. Fawcett's name is often spelled "Faucitt" in primary sources and secondary literature.

9. Ingrao, *Hessian Mercenary State*, 136.

10. Huck, "Soldaten gegen Nordamerika," 1. This is a fairly conservative estimate. It does not include, for instance, the number of reinforcements for 1780, for which no records could be found.

11. Atwood, *Hessians*, 25–29, 254; Ingrao, *Hessian Mercenary State*, 136–38.

12. Seehase, "Die hessischen Truppen," 145, 167. This number is lower than the number of Hessen-Kassel soldiers, 25,688, who served at some point during the war in a Hessen-Kassel unit under contract with the British. Seehase's calculations are based on the *HETRINA* database.

13. After 1736, Hessen-Hanau was nominally part of Hessen-Kassel. It was ruled, customarily, by the prince hereditary of Hessen-Kassel. The two principalities were kept separate after Friedrich II's secret conversion to Catholicism in 1749 had become public.

14. "Return of the Hessen-Hanau Regiment," March 25, 1776, PRO SP 81/183.

15. "Berichte des Major Päusch aus America," StA Marburg, Best. 4h, Nr. 3106.

16. Kapp, *Der Soldatenhandel*, 118, 124.

17. Katcher, *Encyclopedia*, 113; *HETRINA*, 6:6.

18. Kapp, *Der Soldatenhandel*, 876, 269.

19. Burgoyne, *Third English-Waldeck Regiment*, v–vi.

20. HETRINA, 5:8–9; George Osborn to Lord George Germain, May 15, 1777, PRO CO 5/94, fol. 426.

21. Ibid., 5:21–71. However, ninety-two men did not leave for North America, because they received a discharge, went on furlough, died, or deserted.

22. Burgoyne, *Third English-Waldeck Regiment*, 242. On the Waldeck troops, see also Canstein, *Der waldeckisch-englische Subsidienvertrag*; Reid, "Waldeckische Truppen."

23. StA Nürnberg, Rep. 105, Nrn. 1–3.

24. Städtler, *Die Ansbach-Bayreuther Truppen*, 21.

25. "Embarkation Muster," March 25, 1777, PRO SP 81/187.

26. Städtler, *Die Ansbach-Bayreuther Truppen*, 21.

27. William Fraser to Evan Nepean, August 21, 1782, PRO HO 32/1. The Anhalt-Zerbst troops served mostly as garrison troops in Canada, particularly in and around Quebec.

28. Wilson, "German 'Soldiertrade,'" 758–86.

29. Huck, "Soldaten gegen Nordamerika," 28.

30. Schumann, *Die Markgrafen*, 262.

31. Ingrao, *Hessian Mercenary State*, 122.

32. Geisler, *Geschichte und Zustand*, 567.

33. On military migration, see recently Asche et al., *Krieg, Militär und Migration*.

34. Schiller, *Kabale und Liebe*, 2. Akt, 2. Szene.

35. Krauseneck, *Die Werbung für England*, 3. Auftritt, 12 and 4. Auftritt, 18.

36. Ibid., 12. Auftritt, 47.

37. Auerbach, *Die Hessen*, 290–92.

38. Ibid., 292–99; Auerbach, "Marburger." On Seume's service in the Regiment Erbprinz, see Seehase, "Die hessischen Truppen," 155.

39. Auerbach, *Die Hessen*, 301–303.

40. Huck, "Soldaten gegen Nordamerika," 9–10.

41. Karl Wilhelm Ferdinand to General von Riedesel, September 14, 1776, ibid., 50.

42. For a thorough analysis of such criticism, see Wilson, "German 'Soldier-trade'"; Wilson, *German Armies*, 242–97.

43. Suck and Hamecher, *Mirabeau, Schlieffen*, 55–76.

44. Ibid., 106. Ludwig Wekhrlin asked in 1781, "Will [writers] ever grow tired of accusing the Germans of [concluding] subsidy treaties?" Wekhrlin, *Chronologen*, 12:36. Ingrao, *Hessian Mercenary State*, 139, cautions us not to think that there was widespread criticism of the soldier trade, even among Enlightenment thinkers.

45. "Gesang bei dem Abmarsch," UB Bayreuth, Hist. Verein Oberfranken, B150. See also "Gesang bey dem Abmarsch," Staatliche Bibliothek (Schlossbibliothek) Ansbach, Ms. Hist. 485a.

46. On similar songs for Hessen-Kassel, see Kipping, *Hessian View*, 12–13.

47. *Bayreuther Neuer Zeitungs-Calender*, 1778; StA Bamberg, C 18/I. It is worth noting that there were close blood ties between Brandenburg-Ansbach and George III. George II of Hanover had been married to Wilhelmina Carolina, sister of Wilhelm Friedrich, Margrave Karl Alexander's grandfather.

48. Scott, "Foreign Mercenaries."

49. Quoted in Atwood, *Hessians*, 31.

50. Quoted in ibid., 59.

51. Warren, *History*, 1:278, 283. See also Ingrao, "'Barbarous Strangers,'" 954.

52. On this topic, see also Neimeyer, *America Goes to War*, 44–64.

53. For the following argument and quotes, see Sikora, "Söldner."

54. On republicanism, see in particular Wood, *Radicalism*; Rodgers, "Republicanism." For the German context, see Frevert, *Militär und Gesellschaft*; Nowosadtko, "Ordnungselement," 5; Pröve, *Militär, Staat*.

55. Bradburn, *Citizenship Revolution*, 11–12; Dederer, *War in America*, 113–22.

56. To be part of the nation, at least in Prussia, it was necessary to serve in the army. For that reason, conscription was established in the 1810s. Since women were not conscripted and thus could not serve in the army, they were essentially excluded from the nation. Frevert, *Militär und Gesellschaft*, 13.

57. For instance, only by eradicating their previous identity—and thus nationality—could the soldiers of the French Legion become legitimate fighters for this nation. Sikora, "Söldner," 233.

58. Royster, *Revolutionary People*, 25–53; Martin and Lender, *Respectable Army*, 66–69, 171–79.

59. Royster, *Revolutionary People*, 333, 351.

2. Recruitment Patterns

1. Kroener, "Vom 'Extraordinari Kriegsvolck.'"

2. Even when not engaged in fighting, these newly enlarged armies lost massive numbers of soldiers to disease. In a striking example, the Russian army lost 44 percent of its soldiers in the Seven Years' War to typhus, dysentery, or the plague. Luh, *Kriegskunst*, 57–61.

3. Sikora, *Disziplin und Desertion*, 213–15. For developments in Great Britain, see Brewer, *Sinews*. In general, see Anderson, *War and Society*, 83; Hale, *War and Society*, 46; Tallett, *War and Society*, 5–7.

4. Wilson, *German Armies*, 283.

5. Sikora, *Disziplin und Desertion*, 216.

6. Ingrao, *Hessian Mercenary State*, 122; Böhm, *Hessisches Militär*, 3.

7. Bezzel, "Ansbach-Bayreuther Miettruppen," 191–93.

8. Dallhammer, *Ansbach*, 118–19.

9. Black, *Military Revolution?*, 40; Parker, *Military Revolution*, 48; Tallett, *War and Society*, 69.

10. One foot in Bayreuth equaled 11.7 inches by current U.S. standards. Fikkert, *Geldwesen*, 90.

11. Rainsford, "Transactions," 445.

12. "Kopie der Verordung vom 11. April 1777," StadtA Ansbach, AM 994, fol. 181; Seehase, "Die Hessischen Truppen," 145, 147.

13. Hell, "Von der Aushebung entbehrlicher"; Pröve, "Zum Verhältnis."

14. "Regelungen für Anwerbungen, 1739," StA Nürnberg, Rep. 116, Tit. XXIX, Bd. III,1 Nr. 62aaa, Art. 5.

15. Ibid., Art. 1–3.

16. "Anwerbung von Vagranten, 1747," ibid., Nr. 68.

17. Kroener, "Soldat oder Soldateska?"

18. Sikora, *Disziplin und Desertion*, 235.

19. Ibid., 222–23.

20. "Verordnung zum Einfangen von Vagranten, 29. März 1769," StadtA Ansbach, AM 994, fol. 148.

21. Ingrao, *Hessian Mercenary State*, 117–20. However, Taylor claims that the *Hufen-Edikt* was intended not to save poor farmers but to create a pool of marginalized men available for military service; *Indentured to Liberty*, 5–7, 51–73.

22. Städtler, *Die Ansbach-Bayreuther Truppen*, 97. In a March 1777 letter, Döhlemann described his journal as a communal effort with Captain von Erckert. For a long time, Döhlemann's journal and the letters were considered lost. The author would like to thank Horst Lochner (Bayreuth) and Adolf Lang (Ahnatal) for access to this material.

23. Johann Christoph Döhlemann to Joachim Döhlemann, January 29, February 2, and February 6, 1777, in Döhlemann, "Tagebuch."

24. Joachim Döhlemann to Johann Christoph Döhlemann, February 9, 1777, ibid.

25. Ibid.

26. Johann Christoph Döhlemann to Joachim Döhlemann, February 23, 1777, ibid.

27. Johann Christoph Döhlemann to Joachim Döhlemann, November 24, 1777, ibid.

28. The others were Waldeck and Anhalt-Zerbst.

29. Huck, "Soldaten gegen Nordamerika," 46.

30. Ibid., 55–57.

31. Huck, "Verkauft und Verraten?"; Elster, *Geschichte der stehenden Truppen*, 376.

32. Quoted in Huck, "Soldaten gegen Nordamerika," 57.

33. After 1776, Friedrich II of Hessen-Kassel sent recruitment requests to the principalities and duchies of Brandenburg-Ansbach, Solms-Braunfels, Wied-Neuwied, Wied-Runkel, Wied-Hachenburg, Neu-Isenburg, Wittgenstein, Erbach, Lippe-Detmold, and Kirchberg; the imperial cities of Wetzlar, Frankfurt a. M., Worms, Speyer, Cologne, Friedberg, Heilbronn, Wimpfen, and Mühlhausen; and the imperial and *Hanse* cities of Bremen, Hamburg, and Lübeck. All of these territories and cities were either neighbors of Hessen-Kassel or located nearby. Requests were denied by cities from the Hanseatic League; Brandenburg-Ansbach, where Margrave Karl Alexander would soon begin recruiting for his own subsidy troops; Erbach; and Cologne. Main centers for Hessen-Kassel recruitment efforts in foreign territory were Wetzlar, Frankfurt a. M., Offenbach, and Lippe-Detmold. Kipping, *Truppen*, 39–41.

34. Huck, "Soldaten gegen Nordamerika," 73–76.

35. Baron von Eichbegg, for instance, had to leave several cities of the Hanseatic League after it was discovered that he engaged in clandestine recruitment for Hessen-Kassel. Kipping, *Truppen*, 39–40.

36. Huck, "Soldaten gegen Nordamerika," 76–80.

37. Ibid., 81.

38. Ibid., 83–86.

39. Ibid., 75, 86–89.

40. Nowosadtko, "Ordnungselement"; Sikora, *Disziplin und Desertion*, 218–20.

41. Huck, "Soldaten gegen Nordamerika," 93.

42. Ibid., 94–95.

43. See chap. 3 for additional data.

44. Huck, "Soldaten gegen Nordamerika," 90, 92–93.

45. Tallett, *War and Society*, 93–104.

46. Quoted in Huck, "Soldaten gegen Nordamerika," 91.

47. Ibid., 93.

48. See recently Pohlmann, *Auswanderung*; Strathmann, *Herzogtum Braunschweig*.

49. Huck, "Verkauft und Verraten?," 95–96.

50. See, for instance, Brinck, *Auswanderungswelle*.

51. Huck, "Soldaten gegen Nordamerika," 96–97.

52. Landgraf Friedrich II to General von Loßberg, September 5, 1783, Relationes Loßberg, fol. 167.

53. Huck, "Soldaten gegen Nordamerika," 95.

54. Quoted in Atwood, *Hessians*, 52.

55. "Hochzeitsbuch," Pfarramt St. Georgen (Bayreuth), fols. 120–34.

56. Ibid.

57. Sikora, *Disziplin und Desertion*, 236–39. For examples from other European states, see Parker, *Army of Flanders*, 47.

58. Heinritz, "Versuch einer Geschichte," 1: 98–100, 103–107.

59. Ibid., 1:107, 112, 114.

60. Ibid., 2:72.

61. "Verordnung vom 16. Juli 1762 zur Listenführung," StadtA Ansbach, AM 994, fol. 120.

62. "Die Anwerbung und Desertiones diesiger Soldaten betr.," ibid., fols. 120, 152, 162, 187, 200, gives the regulations for recordkeeping in Ansbach in 1762,

1769, 1772, 1778, 1779, and 1781. To keep the lists updated, churches had to provide information about births, deaths, and communions in their parishes. People also had to notify their district before moving to another part of the principality.

63. "Über die Kanton-Verfassung," GStA PK, II. HA, Nr. 23, Nr. 6.

64. StadtA Bayreuth, Nr. 28197.

65. Stadt-Syndicus Tröger, Bayreuth, to the cities of Kulmbach, Hof, Wunsiedel, Neustadt a. d. Aisch, Münchberg, and Kreuth, February 6, 1777, StadtA Bayreuth, Nr. 23285.

66. Friedrich Jacob Kirchmeyer, Kulmbach, to Stadt-Syndicus Tröger, Bayreuth, February 8, 1777, ibid.

67. Johann Salomo Walz, Neustadt a. d. Aisch, to Stadt-Syndicus Tröger, Bayreuth, February 8, 1777, ibid.

68. Stadt-Syndicus Tröger, Bayreuth, to the cities of Kulmbach, Hof, Wunsiedel, Neustadt a. d. Aisch, Münchberg, and Kreuth, February 14, 1777, ibid.

69. Bürgermeister und Rath, Hof, to Stadt-Syndicus Tröger, Bayreuth, February 16, 1777, ibid.

70. Johann Conrad Döhla was not released from military service in 1777. He kept a detailed journal about his military service and captivity in North America, which he edited after the war and gave to his friend and comrade Adam Holper, who in turn gave it to his son, Johann Adam Holper, in 1811. The original has unfortunately been lost. For a widely used edition of Döhla's journal, based on a copy deposited in the Universitätsbibliothek Bayreuth, see Waldenfels, *Tagebuch eines Bayreuther Soldaten.* The copy of Döhla's journal in Bayreuth, complete with Waldenfels's notes and markings in the text, is available at UB Bayreuth, Hist. Verein Oberfranken, Ms. 112. For an English translation of the Döhla journal, see Burgoyne, *Hessian Diary*; Tilden, "Doehla Journal." Another edition in the United States is based on a copy of the journal in the New York Public Library: Döhla, "Amerikanische Feldzüge." The latter copy seems to be closest to the original, and all quotes in this study are taken from it.

71. Bürgermeister und Rath, Wunsiedel, to Stadt-Syndicus Tröger, Bayreuth, February 8, 1777, StadtA Bayreuth, Nr. 23285; Bürgermeister und Rath, Münchberg, to Stadt-Syndicus Tröger, Bayreuth, February 10, 1777, ibid.

72. Out of twenty-eight names listed ibid., Johan Erhard Müller (Wunsiedel), Johann Conrad Döhla (Wunsiedel), Johann Conrad Haßfurther (Münchberg), Adam Holper (Münchberg), Georg Samuel Hofmann (Münchberg) and Matthäus Neumüller (Kreuth) also appear in "Embarkation Muster, Nijmegen," March 25, 1783, PRO SP 81/187.

73. Döhla, "Marschroute," 1.

74. "Verordnung vom 16. Juli 1762 zur Listenführung," StadtA Ansbach, AM 994, fol. 120.

75. Enrollirungs-Geschäfte, StadtA Bayreuth, Nr. 28197.

76. "Regelungen zu Enrollierung und Militärdiensten vom 12. Januar 1778," StadtA Ansbach, AM 994, fols. 187–87v. A *Hintersasse* was a foreigner who resided within the principality but did not have the same rights as *Bürger* or *Unterthanen.* A *Schutzverwandter* was someone who had moved into a territory and, for certain service or payments, enjoyed protection there. *Hirten-Söhne*, the sons of herdsmen or shepherds, also did not possess the full rights of subjects.

77. "Regelungen des Enrollierungsprozesses vom 2. November 1779," ibid., fol. 200.

78. Sikora, *Disziplin und Desertion*, 242. See Ingrao, *Hessian Mercenary State*, 125, on Prussia as the defining model for the Hessen-Kassel *Kantonsystem.*

79. Atwood, *Hessians*, 39–40. In peacetime, each Hessen-Kassel infantry company, including furloughed men, ideally numbered four officers, eight noncommissioned officers, three tambours, and ninety common soldiers. "Journal des Regiments von Knyphausen," LB Ks, 4° Ms. Hass. Nr. 163, 3.

80. Eckhardt, "Hessische Truppen," 100–10.

81. "Aktenstücke, Correspondenzen und Aufzeichnungen," LB Ks, 2° Ms. Hass. Nr. 247, fols. 73–74v.

82. Quoted in Eckhardt, "Hessische Truppen," 110–11.

83. Ingrao, *Hessian Mercenary State*, 134. See also Ingrao, "Kameralismus und Militarismus."

84. Quoted in Auerbach, "Marburger," 330–31.

85. Atwood, *Hessians*, 133; Auerbach, "Marburger," 327–28; Böhme, *Die Wehrverfassung*, 26–27; Ingrao, *Hessian Mercenary State*, 132.

86. Böhme, *Die Wehrverfassung*, 27; Fuchs, "Idee und Wirklichkeit," 34; Hollenberg, "Landstände und Militär," 107.

87. Eckhardt, "Hessische Truppen," 111–12; Atwood, *Hessians*, 44.

88. Seehase, "Die hessischen Truppen," 156.

89. Those units included Colonel Rall's grenadiers, Johannes Reuber's unit, and the Garrison Regiments von Wissenbach, Huyn, Stein, and Bünau. Böhm, *Hessisches Militär*, 43–50; Seehase, "Die hessischen Truppen," 141, 153–59.

90. Ingrao, *Hessian Mercenary State*, 148–50.

91. Auerbach, "Marburger," 323–25.

92. Quoted in Auerbach, "Die Festung Ziegenhain," 221.

93. Auerbach, "Marburger," 327.

94. See, for instance, German interpretations written during the Third Reich that lament the "sale" of "German blood" to Great Britain and ascribe the mutiny to the soldiers' intense "longing for freedom." Berbig, *Revolte*, 154.

95. Popp, "Geschichte," 9.

96. Ochsenfurt is located in a rich wine-growing region.

97. Popp, "Geschichte," 10–15. Popp had a point. On their march to Ansbach, the Bayreuth soldiers had been closely guarded by *Jäger*. The entire village of Ketteldorf, where some 400 Bayreuth soldiers stopped for the night on March 3, 1777, was surrounded by *Jäger* and Hussars. "Abmarsch," StA Nürnberg, Rep. 165a Nr. 1551, fols. 25v–26.

98. Döhla, "Marschroute," 3–6.

99. StA Würzburg, Lichtbildsammlung 337. See also ibid., Domkapitel Protokolle, 1777.

100. "Aussage von Herrn Olnieger (Fischbach)," StA Würzburg, Militärsachen Nr. 95, fol. 57. See also Franz Willhelm Freyherr von und zu Gutenberg, Major-Domo, to the Prince-Bishop of Würzburg and Bamberg, March 11, 1777, ibid., fols. 39–40.

101. See also Möller, *Das Regiment der Landsknechte*, 71–76; Wilson, "Violence."

102. Christian von Molitor, "Journal," NYPL, Bancroft Collection, no. 66, vol. 1, pt. 3, item 154, entries of March 10 and March 11, 1777.

103. See chap. 3 for more on these gifts.

3. Social Composition

1. Kappes, "Notizbuch"; *HETRINA*. Company rosters generally provide information on soldiers such as age, marital status, height, hometown, prior service, and entry date. Muster lists often give only rank and name. Jeremias Kappes was born in 1734 in Merzhausen near Ziegenhain. He entered military service in 1753, at the age of nineteen. In 1776, after his company and regiment had left for North America, he became captain d'armes, a noncommissioned officer responsible for supplies. During or shortly after the war, he became a sergeant. "Common soldiers" in this chapter refers to all soldiers listed in the records as *Gemeiner* (private), *Gefreiter* (private first class), *Füsilier* (fusilier), or *Musketier* (musketeer). An embarkation return for the Regiment von Knyphausen, compiled March 27, 1776, lists 132 men for the entire Company von Dechow, among them 4 officers, 12 noncommissioned officers, 3 drummers, 1 orderly, 8 sutlers and servants, and 104 common soldiers. "Etat du régiment de Knyphausen à Bremerlehe le 27me Mars de l'Année 1776," PRO SP 81/183.

2. German units were named after their owners, so companies changed names and commanders frequently, but the companies themselves did not change. For the sake of clarity, the original name, Company von Dechow, is used throughout this study.

3. "Grundliste der löbl. Hauptmann von Tritschlerischen Compagnie," StA Nürnberg, Rep 107/III, Nr. 118. Next to the common soldiers, we find twenty-four officers, twenty-four noncommissioned officers, five fifers, fifteen tambours, one hautboy player, and one carpenter in this company between 1783 and 1793. Seven common soldiers were promoted to corporal, and three corporals became second lieutenants in the same period.

4. The only other surviving company rosters from Ansbach-Bayreuth troops in the eighteenth-century are "Grundliste der hochfürstl. brandenburg-ansbachischen Hauptmann von Güß'schen Compagnie," StA Nürnberg, Rep. 107/III, Nr. 120; "Grundliste des hochfürstl. Husaren-Corps," UB Bayreuth, Hist. Verein Oberfranken, Ms. 115. All other available lists from Ansbach-Bayreuth give only ranks and names.

5. Städtler, *Die Ansbach-Bayreuther Truppen*, 95. See also Prechtel, "Beschreibung," 598; and Adjutant General von Schlammersdorf to Jägerhauptmann von Waldenfels, March 18, 1782, HAV, 403–10, for information on Tritschler's company in North America and his promotion to the rank of captain in 1783. The original Prechtel journal can be found at the Huntington Library, San Marino, Calif. Two more copies are at the Staatsarchiv Nürnberg (Rep 12/2, Nr. 485) and the UB Bayreuth (Hist. Verein Oberfranken, Ms. 188). See also Burgoyne, *Ansbach-Bayreuth/Prechtel Diaries*; Burgoyne, *Hessian Officer's Diary*.

6. Elster, *Geschichte der stehenden Truppen*, 377–78. Dragoons were infantry soldiers who traveled on horseback but fought dismounted. The same usually applied to mounted *Jäger* units.

7. Atwood, *Hessians*, 39; Bezzel, "Ansbach-Bayreuther Miettruppen," 193.

8. For firsthand accounts of *Jäger* troops in North America, see Tustin, *Diary*; and Johann von Ewald's famous thoughts about partisan warfare, translated in Selig and Skaggs, *Treatise*. See also Hanger, *Life, Adventures*.

9. Atwood, *Hessians*, 45–46. See HAV, 403–10, for detailed plans to enlarge the Ansbach-Bayreuth *Jäger* battalion into a *Jäger* regiment with six companies.

10. Luh, *Kriegskunst*, 129–75.

11. Atwood, *Hessians*, 44.

12. "Pay for Ansbach-Bayreuth Soldiers," NYPL, Bancroft Collection, no. 65, item 136. For Hessen-Kassel, the British Treasury actually calculated 1 pound at 5 ⅚ *Thaler*. Atwood, *Hessians*, xi. We have to keep in mind that soldiers commonly had to pay for their provisions, uniforms, medical care, and even future recruitment campaigns. Pröve, *Stehendes Heer*, 135. As noted earlier, this study uses the early eighteenth-century conversion rate of 1 *Thaler* for 4 shillings 6 pence.

13. "Hinterlassenschaften einiger Soldaten aus dem Voit'schem Regiment," December 6, 1782, HAV, 471.

14. Böhm et al., *Uniformen*, 23.

15. Auerbach, "Marburger," 321–23; Fischer, "Eiserngespartes aus America"; Fischer, "Wer alles hat."

16. "General-Kontobuch," StA Marburg, Best. 118a, Nr. 951, 70, 73, 77.

17. Quoted in Auerbach, *Die Hessen*, 170.

18. Ingrao, *Hessian Mercenary State*, 160–61.

19. "Acta, die verschiedene Gnaden Ertheilungen," StA Nürnberg, Rep. D 12/2, Nr. 487. The Ansbach-Bayreuth infantry headquarters and the Cammer und Landschafts-Raths Collegium (Treasury Department) investigated each claim and decided whether it was justified.

20. Margrave Karl Alexander gave orders for the *Gnaden-Ertheilungen* on October 13, 1777.

21. One *Simra* was measured at about 318 liters in Nuremberg (about 220 kilograms or 485 pounds of grain). Usually, cash for the purchase rather than the grain or wood itself was handed out. One *Klafter* at the time measured between 3.1 and 3.5 cubic meters, or 109–23 cubic feet. Fickert, *Geldwesen*, 91; StA Nürnberg, Rep. D 12/2, Nr. 487, no. 182: Johann Mittermeyer.

22. StA Nürnberg, Rep. D 12/2, Nr. 487, no. 84: Margaretha Winter.

23. Zottl, "Die Hungrigen," 79.

24. StA Nürnberg, Rep. D 12/2, Nr. 487, no. 27: Eva Maria Schmidt, and nos. 244–45: Schauer.

25. Ibid., nos. 210 and 219: Anna Margaretha Mayer.

26. For his journal, see Prechtel, "Beschreibung."

27. Kappes does not provide exact dates for six soldiers. Three of these men came from the guard and thus can be counted as veteran soldiers. Two came to the company from other units in the same regiment.

28. Huck, "Soldaten gegen Nordamerika," 113–16.

29. Ibid., 115–17.

30. On regional origins of soldiers, see also ibid., 98–99.

31. For one soldier, Heinrich Jäger, Kappes's list is not exactly clear, but evidence from the *HETRINA* points in that direction.

32. For the following, see Seehase, "Die hessischen Truppen," 135–72.

33. Altogether, seven different recruitment transports brought Hessen-Kassel recruits to North America. The first left Hessen-Kassel on May 11, 1777, another one on November 9–10, 1777. Next were February 28, 1778; March 3, 1779; March 21, 1780; February 24, 1781; and finally March 23, 1782. Over the course of the war, between 6,300 and 7,000 additional soldiers were added to the units sent initially in 1776. Ibid., 167.

34. "Über die Kanton-Verfassung," GStA PK, II. HA, Nr. 23, Nr. 4.

35. For the following numbers and data, see Huck, "Soldaten gegen Nordamerika," 101, 103, 106, 303.

36. The imperial earldom came under the rule of Brandenburg-Ansbach when Duke Wilhelm Heinrich von Sachsen-Eisenach died in 1741 without an heir. Schumann, *Die Markgrafen*, 328.

37. Huck, "Soldaten gegen Nordamerika," 106–10.

38. Margrave Karl Alexander to Prince-Bishop Adam von Seinsheim, February 19, 1777, StA Würzburg, Militärsachen Nr. 97, fol. 195. According to the brief diary of Johann Gerhard Theiss, a (Catholic) Ansbach-Bayreuth soldier in the Ansbach regiment, Piret—or Pieret/Pirett—died from a fever in New York on October 14, 1777. Schmitt, "J. G. Theis."

39. Huck, "Soldaten gegen Nordamerika," 110–11.

40. Ibid., 132–33.

41. Winter, *Untertanengeist*, 449–52.

42. Huck, "Soldaten gegen Nordamerika," 132–33.

43. Wehler, *Feudalismus*, 1:91–92.

44. See also Pröve, *Stehendes Heer*, 141.

45. Huck, "Soldaten gegen Nordamerika," 137–38; Schlenkrich and Bräuer, "Armut, Verarmung," 99.

46. Pröve, *Stehendes Heer*, 135–36, 139, 141, 252–58.

47. Four of those eleven noncommissioned officers advanced from the ranks during the war. Several soldiers in Company von Dechow, while they might have not been married, apparently had their brothers with them in the same unit. It is difficult to determine such relationships exactly, but there seem to have been at least sixteen brothers in Company von Dechow.

48. Maß- und Rangierbücher: Füsilier-Rgt. v. Loßberg, StA Marburg, Best. 10c, Nr. 205. For many other Hessen-Kassel regiments, the surviving lists do not give such details.

49. Hagemann, "Militär, Krieg," 63.

50. Huck, "Soldaten gegen Nordamerika," 118.

51. Ibid., 118.

52. Ibid., 122–23; Hagist, "Women of the British Army"; Mayer, *Belonging to the Army*; Rees, "'Multitude of Women'"; Blumenthal, *Women Camp Followers*.

53. Huck, "Soldaten gegen Nordamerika," 119, 121, 124.

54. LB Ks, 2° Ms. Hass. Nr. 247, fols. 24v, 95, 97v–98v.

55. "Etat du Regiment de Son Altese Serenissime le Prince Heréditaire de Hesse Cassel, á son Embarquement á Wilhelmstadt le 25ᵉ Mars 1776," PRO SP 81/183.

56. "Etat du Regiment de Knyphausen à Bremerlehe le 27ᵐᵉ Mars de l'Anneé 1776," ibid.

57. "Embarkation Muster, Nijmegen," March 25, 1783, PRO SP 81/187; "Return of Ships Carrying Hessian and Ansbach Troops from Holland under Direction of William Cumming, [April 2, 1777]," BHQ, no. 473.

58. "Rations for Foreign Troops, 1782–1783," PRO WO 60/18, 98.

Introduction to Part II

1. On the Battle of Trenton, see Fischer, *Washington's Crossing*, 206–62. For German research and discussions, particularly on the question of who was

ultimately responsible for the Hessen-Kassel defeat, see Hildebrand, "Trenton 1776."

2. Fischer, *Washington's Crossing*, 234. For the numbers given here, see Fischer's appendixes F and H.

3. There is no evidence for the assumption, expressed by many historians since, that the German soldiers in Trenton were drunk that morning because of a raucous Christmas celebration. Ibid., 240.

4. Ibid., appendix N.

5. See table 5 and the appendix in this study for further information on this number.

6. Ibid., 251–59, 551. Fischer lists a total of 368 German soldiers who escaped (that number includes musicians, drummers, women, children, and other camp followers).

7. Reuber, "Tagebuch," fols. 97–97v; Slagle, "Von Loßberg Regiment," 112.

8. Reuber, "Tagebuch," fol. 97v.

9. Ibid., fol. 99. However, Reuber also wrote about other citizens who brought bread and alcohol for the captives.

10. Kappes, "Notizbuch," 64.

11. Wiederholdt, "Tagebuch," LB Ks, 4° Ms. Hass. Nr. 216, 46. This is a copy of Wiederholdt's original journal. It is often stated that the original—with several colored maps—can be found in the J. G. Rosengarten Collection in the Van Pelt Library at the University of Pennsylvania as "Tagebuch des Andreas Wiederholdt." However, notes within this bound volume (e.g., p. 76) and a note at the end of the journal in Kassel (p. 215) show that both are copies. Wiederholdt's grandson apparently emigrated to the Unites States in 1880. He may have taken the original journal with him, but there is no further trace of it. One copy remained in Kassel, and another copy was made from that one for Joseph G. Rosengarten. In another bound volume that Rosengarten received from Germany, several colored maps and drawings of key events and places were found. Those maps were originally created by Wiederholdt. General von Knyphausen to Friedrich II, October 10, 1777, Relationes Knyphausen, fol. 68, mentions several maps that Knyphausen received from Wiederholdt, via Regimental Quartermaster Müller. See also Gräf et al., *Krieg in Amerika*, 421.

12. Reuber, "Tagebuch," fol. 99. The old jail in Philadelphia, on the corner of Third and Market Streets, was used as a barracks during the Revolutionary War.

4. Prisoners of War in Western Warfare

1. Karsten, *Law, Soldiers*, 10; Rosas, *Legal Status*, 43.

2. Karsten, *Law, Soldiers*, xiv.

3. Ibid., 25–26.

4. Ducrey, "Kriegsgefangene," 65–66.

5. Karsten, *Law, Soldiers*, 5–8.

6. Ducrey, "Kriegsgefangene," 65–78; Flory, *Prisoners of War*, 11; Ober, "Classical Greek Times," 18.

7. Grady, "Evolution," 19.

8. Rüpke, "Kriegsgefangene," 83, 89, 98.

9. Nöding, "'Min Sicherheit si Din,'" 100–103, 111.

10. Parker, "Early Modern Europe," 43–44; Rosas, *Legal Status*, 48; Strickland, *War and Chivalry*, 34–39, 53, 183–87, 194–97.

11. Oeter, "Die Entwicklung des Kriegsgefangenenrechts," 43.

12. Friedman, *Encounter*, 56, 70, 76; Rosas, *Legal Status*, 47–48; Stacey, "Age of Chivalry," 36.

13. France, *Western Warfare*, 107–27; Strickland, *War and Chivalry*, 204–24.

14. Rosas, *Legal Status*, 46–47.

15. Keen, *Laws of War*, 2.

16. Ibid., 4; Strickland, *War and Chivalry*, 31–34.

17. Strickland, *War and Chivalry*, 32.

18. Oeter, "Die Entwicklung des Kriegsgefangenenrechts," 43–44.

19. Parker, "Early Modern Europe," 42.

20. Oeter, "Die Entwicklung des Kriegsgefangenenrechts," 44.

21. Howard, "Constraints on Warfare," 3.

22. Ziegler, "Die Bedeutung von Hugo Grotius."

23. Grotius, *The Laws of War and Peace (Chapter VII, I.2, III.1, and V.1)*, in Friedman, *Law of War*, 1:66–67. See also Grady, "Evolution," 44–49; Kroener, "Der Soldat als Ware," 278.

24. Nöding, "'Min Sicherheit si Din,'" 106–11.

25. On such issues, see Kroener, "Soldat oder Soldateska?"; Kroener, "Kriegsgurgeln"; Rosas, *Legal Status*, 49.

26. Oeter, "Die Entwicklung des Kriegsgefangenenrechts," 44.

27. Kroener, "Der Soldat als Ware," 272–77.

28. Oeter, "Die Entwicklung des Kriegsgefangenenrechts," 51–53.

29. Ibid., 47.

30. Kroener, "Der Soldat als Ware," 272, 275, 277, 279, 292–94; Parker, "Early Modern Europe," 44–49; Rosas, *Legal Status*, 52.

31. Hohrath, "'In Cartellen,'" 152–63; Kroener, "Der Soldat als Ware," 277, 295.

32. Kroener, "Der Soldat als Ware," 286–87.

33. Ibid., 282–83.

34. Oeter, "Die Entwicklung des Kriegsgefangenenrechts," 15–16. Geoffrey Parker stresses the importance of "deconfessionalization" of warfare after the Thirty Years' War when examining such developments. Parker, "Early Modern Europe," 54.

35. Vattel, *Law of Nations*, 421.

36. Ibid., 421.

37. Rosas, *Legal Status*, 65.

38. Ibid., 60. See the epilogue in this study on the 1785 treaty between the United States and Prussia that contained detailed standards for prisoner-of-war treatment.

39. Oeter, "Die Entwicklung des Kriegsgefangenenrechts," 52.

40. Starkey, *European and Native American Warfare*, 38. The Seven Years' War is often referred to as the French and Indian War in the United States.

41. Dederer, *War in America*, 84, 127–30.

42. Kroener, "Der Soldat als Ware," 281.

43. Dederer, *War in America*, 123.

44. Haudenosaunee (Iroquois) warriors were shocked that the revolutionaries regularly killed their American Indian opponents. Venables, "'Faithful Allies,'" 147–50.

45. Parker, "Early Modern Europe," 56; Selesky, "Colonial America," 67–70, 85.

46. Colley, *Captives*, pt. 2; Foster, *Captors' Narrative*, 14; Steele, "Surrendering Rites," 142–43, 150; Starkey, *European and Native American Warfare*, 28–29.

47. Starkey, *War in the Age of Enlightenment*, 163–66. See also Dederer, *War in America*, 172.

48. Dederer, *War in America*, 208–13.

49. Selesky, "Colonial America," 75; Starkey, *European and Native American Warfare*, 135.

50. Consider, for instance, the cartel between France and Great Britain for 1777; see *Treaty and Convention, for the Sick, Wounded and Prisoners of War*.

5. Capture and Surrender

1. Atwood, *Hessians*, 58–143.

2. Städtler, *Die Ansbach-Bayreuther Truppen*, 23–25.

3. Burgoyne's commission to lieutenant general in 1776 pertained only to the American colonies. He was promoted to major general in the British army in 1772.

4. Strickland, *War and Chivalry*, 222–24.

5. On such asymmetrical trust, see Frevert, *Vertrauen*, 7–66.

6. Lynn, *Battle*, 231, 245. See also Lee, "Restraint and Retaliation."

7. Ferling, *Almost a Miracle*, 436–37; Pancake, *This Destructive War*, 70–71.

8. Pancake, *This Destructive War*, 84.

9. Quoted in ibid., 120.

10. Quoted in Ferling, *Almost a Miracle*, 436.

11. Ibid., 459–63; Pancake, *This Destructive War*, 85.

12. Quoted in Doblin and Lynn, *Eyewitness Account*, 72. For the original German, see NdsStA Wf, VI Hs 11, Nr. 248, Bd. 2.

13. See the appendix for an explanation of these numbers.

14. Wiederholdt, "Tagebuch," LB Ks, 4° Ms. Hass. Nr. 216, 150–51, 162–91; "Liste von dem . . . Fusilier Regiment . . . von Knyphausen," Bradford Papers, box 26, folder 6; "State of the Prisoners of War at Philadelphia," October 11, 1779, ibid.; "Return of the German Prisoners of War in the New Gaol at Philadelphia," December 11, 1780, ibid., folder 8; Slagle, "Von Loßberg Regiment," 157–58.

15. Fischer, *Washington's Crossing*, 251–52.

16. Ibid., 252.

17. General Howe to Lord George Germain, December 29, 1776, PRO CO 5/94, fol. 29v.

18. Bodle, *Valley Forge Winter*, 16–17.

19. George Clymer to John Hancock, December 28, 1776, PCC, item 137, vol. 3, 44.

20. Friedrich II of Hessen-Kassel to General von Heister, April 7, 1777 (draft), Relationes Heister, fol. 494.

21. Fischer, *Washington's Crossing*, 324–62.

22. See also Atwood, *Hessians*, 98.

23. A bilingual pamphlet published in Bucks County, Pennsylvania, described in detail how Hessian troops in New Jersey had allegedly raped young girls and women, pillaged and burned houses, driven away cattle and sheep, stolen clothing and other valuables, and destroyed everything else that they could not carry away. *Bucks County*; Force, *American Archives*, 5th ser., 3:1188.

24. Duane, *Extracts*, 109–10.

25. Executive Committee to John Hancock, December 30 and 31, 1776, PCC, item 137, vol. 3, appendix, 49; Force, *American Archives*, 5th ser., 3:1484.

26. *JCC*, 5:640, 654–55. Another version of this pamphlet was also printed and distributed in 1776, translated by Lieutenant Colonel Hermann von Zedtwitz on orders of General Washington. A third version of the leaflet, reemphasizing the injustice of the so-called soldier trade, was distributed after November 1777. Auerbach, *Die Hessen*, 265, 268. In a letter to Thomas McKean on August 28, 1776, Benjamin Franklin even mentioned a particularly smart plan for distributing the handbill among the German soldiers: the handbills, with "Tobacco Marks on the Back," should be taken to Staten Island in drift canoes; the smoking soldiers would then read the text "before the officers could know the Contents of the Paper and prevent it." *JCC*, 5:707–708; *LMCC*, 2:59–60. Christopher Ludwick, an immigrant from Hessen-Darmstadt and a committed revolutionary, claimed to have rowed to Staten Island, on orders of Washington, to distribute the leaflets. Condit, "Christopher Ludwick," 375.

27. "Flugblatt," August 14, 1776, Relationes Heister, fol. 370. See also Auerbach, "Die hessischen Soldaten," 147; Auerbach, *Die Hessen*, 162, 264–73; Butterfield, "Psychological Warfare," 237.

28. Fitzpatrick and Matteson, *Writings of George Washington*, 6:453.

29. "Draft of an Address of the Pennsylvania Council of Safety, Philadelphia," December 31, 1776, DLAR, film 24, roll 11, frames 665–67. See also "Address of Council of Safety, 1776," in Linn et al., *Pennsylvania Archives*, 1st ser., 5:146; Force, *American Archives*, 5th ser., 3:1512.

30. Philadelphia's German newspaper published parts of this announcement and other related items: "Die letzten Nachrichten aus den Jerseys," *Heinrich Miller's Pennsylvanisher Staatsbote*, January 2, 1777; "An das Publicum," ibid., January 8, 1777.

31. "Tagebuch eines Grenadiers," StA Marburg, Best. 10e, Nr. I/23, 160–61.

32. Döhla, "Marschroute," 435–40.

33. PRO CO 5/597, fols. 310–74, provides details on the British surrenders to the Spanish at Pensacola and Natchez in 1781. Descriptions of similar ceremonies date back as far as 321 B.C.E., when the Roman army had to pass under the legendary yoke made of spears after being defeated by the Samnites. T. Livius, *History of Rome*, 9.4–9.6. For the late twentieth century, we could study the surrender of Argentinean troops to the British on June 14, 1982, during the Falklands War, when, in a long line at Port Stanley, the Argentineans marched to a specially designated place and grounded their arms. *Das Parlament*, June 14, 2002, no. 24.

34. See, in general, Duffy, *Siege Warfare*, 100. For the North American context, see Ian K. Steele's discussions of the surrenders at Canso (1744), Louisbourg (1745), and Fort Massachusetts (1746), as well as his analysis of the interplay

between European, colonial American, and native American customs of war, in "Surrendering Rites," 151–54. It is also worth noting that the British War Office put together and collected copies and summaries of no fewer than twenty-six different conventions and capitulations signed between 1775 and 1783. PRO WO 36/1–4.

35. Parker, "Early Modern Europe," 48–49.

36. See, in general, Elias, *Über den Prozess.*

37. On studying warfare and the military in such terms borrowed from cultural history, see Lipp, "Diskurs und Praxis."

38. Bourdieu, *Outline*, 178. See also Bourdieu, "Forms"; Bourdieu, "Social Space."

39. Kertzer, *Ritual*, 15–16.

40. Higginbotham, *War of American Independence*, 175–203. See also Phifer, "Campaign to Saratoga."

41. See the appendix for a discussion of these numbers.

42. Higginbotham, *War of American Independence*, 175–203. See chap. 9 on the fate of these men in revolutionary hands.

43. Specht was commander of the Braunschweig-Wolfenbüttel regiment named after him. It seems that the journal was actually written not by Specht himself, but by his adjutant, Lieutenant Anton Du Roi. Specht, *Specht Journal*, xiii–xix. A copy of the original German journal can be found in the New York Public Library as "Auszug aus dem Journal von der Braunschweig'schen Brigade des Obersten Specht," Bancroft Collection, no. 77.

44. Specht, *Specht Journal*, 101–102.

45. Bell, *Ritual*, 39–40; Gennep, *Rites of Passage*, 2–3, 11–20; Turner, "Liminalität und Communitas," 251–53, 260.

46. See the classic description of the radically different "personal angle of vision" on the battlefield in Keegan, *Face of Battle*, 128–33.

47. Gennep, *Rites of Passage*, 22, 192; Bellinger and Krieger, *Ritualtheorien*, 13.

48. Baxter, *British Invasion*, 319–20.

49. Bense, "Marschroute," fol. 9. For an English translation of parts of Bense's journal, see Doblin and Lynn, "Brunswick Grenadier." Bense served in the grenadier regiment of Lieutenant Colonel Breymann.

50. "Fragment eines Tagebuchs," NdsStA Wf, VI Hs 5, Nr. 23, fols. 119–20.

51. Arnold van Gennep stresses the "length and intricacy" of each stage in a rite of passage. *Rites of Passage*, 28.

52. For a full text of the eventual convention, see Dabney, *After Saratoga*, appendix, 81–82.

53. General Gates to General Burgoyne, and replies, October 14, 1777, PFC, ser. 7E, item 13.

54. "Articles of Convention," October 17, 1777, ibid.

55. Ketchum, *Saratoga*, 420; Mintz, *Generals of Saratoga*, 221.

56. James Wilkinson, Gates's adjutant, defended the convention before Congress by stating that Gates had "no Time to contest the capitulation" with General Burgoyne because the British still had enough provisions and another British column was making "progress up the Hudson River." James Wilkinson to Congress, October 30, 1777, PCC, item 57, 23–24; James Wilkinson to General Gates, November 4, 1777, PFC, ser. 7E, item 14.

57. "Articles of Capitulation," PRO 30/11/74, fol. 128.

58. See the appendix for an explanation of these numbers.

59. Higginbotham, *War of American Independence*, 352–88; Conway, *War of American Independence*, 122–29.

60. Higginbotham, *War of American Independence*, 367–68.

61. Royster, *Revolutionary People*, 190–254; Martin and Lender, *Respectable Army*, 99–103.

62. Higginbotham, *War of American Independence*, 380–82.

63. Ibid., 382.

64. Johann Christoph Döhlemann to Joachim Döhlemann, November 29, 1781, in Döhlemann, "Tagebuch."

65. "Yorktown Surrender," October 19, 1781, PRO 30/11/1, fol. 118. Gloucester was a small post on the other side of the York River. The British and German forces there surrendered to American and French troops under the Duc de Lauzun and M. de Choisy.

66. Thacher, "Diary," 282–84.

67. Following Marshall Sahlins and Pierre Bourdieu, a ritual can be understood as a tool for "social and cultural jockeying" and a "performative medium for the negotiation of power in relationships." Bell, *Ritual*, 79.

68. Wright, "Sieges," 643.

69. Anderson, *Crucible of War*, 195–201. For a detailed analysis of these events, see Steele, *Betrayals*.

70. Scheer, *Private Yankee Doodle*, 240–41.

71. This multivocality or ambiguity of a ritual is one of its great sources of strength. Gennep, *Rites of Passage*, 28.

72. Wright, "Sieges," 641.

73. Thacher, "Diary," 282–84.

74. George Washington to Lord Cornwallis, October 17, 1781, PRO 30/11/74, fol. 120; Lord Cornwallis to George Washington, October 17, 1781, ibid., fol. 122; George Washington to Lord Cornwallis, October 18, 1781, ibid., fol. 124; Lord Cornwallis to George Washington, October 18, 1781, ibid., fol. 126.

75. "Yorktown Flags Arriving in City," *Pennsylvania Gazette*, November 7, 1781.

Introduction to Part III

1. Reuber, "Tagebuch," fol. 100. Reuber gives January 12, 1777, as his arrival date in Lancaster. However, the first prisoner lists from Lancaster are dated January 6, 1777. On December 31, 1776, the Pennsylvania Council of Safety informed the Lancaster Committee that the Hessen-Kassel prisoners of war would leave Philadelphia on January 2, 1777. Pennsylvania Council of Safety to the Lancaster Committee, December 31, 1776, PFC, ser. 9, vol. 18; Lists of Hessian Prisoners, Lancaster, January 6–7, 1777, ibid., vol. 19.

2. Reuber, "Tagebuch," fol. 100.

3. "Ausführliche Relation," Relationes Heister, fols. 530–31v.

4. Executive Committee to Congress, January 7, 1777, PCC, item 133, 35–37.

5. Popp, "Geschichte," 226–29. The revolutionaries knew that Winchester was not prepared to receive a large number of prisoners of war. Colonel Joseph Holmes to Governor Nelson, October 26, 1781, in *CVSP*, 2:569. On November

6, 1781, Holmes admitted that roughly 1,000 prisoners had to camp out in the open. He had little hope of providing quarters for these men any time soon. Joseph Holmes to William Davies, November 6, 1781, ibid., 2:578–79.

6. Bense, "Marschroute," fols. 15v–16.

7. Springer, *America's Captives*, 21.

8. Ibid., 3.

6. The First Prisoners of War in Revolutionary Hands, 1775–1776

1. Allen, *Narrative*.

2. See, in general, Meranze, *Laboratories of Virtue*.

3. Force, *American Archives*, 4th ser., 2:776, 3:1022–23; Ezekiel Williams to Elias Boudinot, September 13 and 15, 1777, Boudinot Papers. Williams wrote Boudinot on the occasion of the latter's appointment as commissary general of prisoners. In the same letter, he reported on prisoners taken at Fort Saint-Jean in May 1775. Those men were "put out in like manner," mostly in Litchfield County, Connecticut.

4. Steele, "When Worlds Collide," 14–16.

5. This most likely refers to either Governor Skene from Ticonderoga and Crown Point or Lieutenant Moncrieff, who were ordered to Hartford as prisoners of war on July 5, 1775. It might also refer to several soldiers from Forts Saint-Jean and Chambly captured in mid-September 1775. *JCC*, 2:126–27; "List of Resolves of Congress Regarding Prisoners of War, 1775–1780," PCC, item 183, 2–6.

6. Force, *American Archives*, 4th ser., 3:1023, 4:124.

7. Dederer, *War in America*, 172.

8. Starkey, *War in the Age of Enlightenment*, 149, 163–66.

9. George Washington to Thomas Gage, August 11, 1775, PRO CO 5/92, fol. 256; Fitzpatrick and Matteson, *Writings of George Washington*, 3:416–17. See also Bowman, *Captive Americans*, 15–16, 29; Metzger, *Prisoner*, 152.

10. Thomas Gage to George Washington, August 13, 1775, PRO CO 5/92, fol. 256.

11. George Washington to Congress, May 11, 1776, Force, *American Archives*, 4th ser., 6:423–25.

12. Bowman, *Captive Americans*, 29–31.

13. Elias Boudinot to Henry Knox and Gouverneur Morris, March 14, 1782, *LDC*, 18:395–98. This report was written in preparation for an upcoming prisoner conference in Elizabethtown.

14. Lancaster Committee of Safety to the Continental Congress (draft), December 9, 1775, HSP, AM 6093, 6; "Return of the Prisoners of the 26th Regim[t] taken at S[t] Johns & in the River of S[t] Lawrence who arrived in Lancaster," ibid., 32.

15. John Hancock to Walter Livingston, Dept. Commissary General, November 17, 1775, PCC, item 12A, vol. 1, 19; *JCC*, 3:358–59.

16. "Minutes of the Lancaster County Committee of Safety," December 9, 1775, PFC, ser. 8D, item 86.

17. *JCC*, 4:113; Reading Committee of Correspondence to Congress, February 4, 1776, PCC, item 69, vol. 1, 91.

18. *JCC*, 4:66–67.

19. "List of Resolves," PCC, item 183, 2–16. The congressional resolve of January 31, 1776, was largely repeated in the resolves of May 21, 1776.

20. On February 5, 1781, despite the Continental Army's manpower shortage, Washington ordered American recruitment officers not "to Inlist any Deserter from the enemy, nor any person of Disaffected or Suspicious character, with Respect of the Government of these States." "Washington's Orders, New Windsor, December 1780–February 1781," National Archives and Records Administration, Washington, D.C., RG 93, ser. 5: Washington's Orders, vol. 48, 232.

21. Arthur St. Clair, Lancaster, to Congress, January 27, 1776, PCC, item 161, 485.

22. British Prisoners, Hartford, to Congress, March 21, 1776, PCC, item 78, vol. 18 (P), 55; Daniel Robertson, Royal Regt. of Emigrants, York, to Congress, May 9, 1776, ibid., vol. 19 (R), 25.

23. Pennsylvania Council of Safety to Congress, February 20, 1776, PCC, item 69, vol. 1, 95; "Minutes of the Lancaster County Committee of Safety," March 19, 1776, PFC, ser. 8D, item 86.

24. For more on provisioning of prisoners and David Franks, see chap. 8.

25. "Minutes of the Lancaster County Committee of Safety," December 12 and 27, 1775, PFC, ser. 8D, item 86; Lancaster Committee of Inspection to Congress, January 10, 1776, PCC, item 69, vol. 1, 51.

26. "Treaties with Nesbitt & Co. and Atkinson for Victualling Troops with Provisions and Rum," PRO T 64/106, no. 1; John Robinson to William Knox, July 6, 1779, PRO CO 5/151, fol. 219. See also Wolf and Whiteman, *History of the Jews of Philadelphia*, 27–33, 38.

27. Lancaster Committee of Correspondence to Congress, December 21, 1775, PCC, item 69, vol. 1, 45; Lancaster Committee of Correspondence to Congress, January 10, 1776, ibid., 51.

28. Wolf and Whiteman, *History of the Jews of Philadelphia*, 86–87; *JCC*, 8:422; Daniel Chamier to David Franks, February 25, 1777, Records of Colebrooke, Nesbitt, Colebrooke & Franks, LC.

29. Pencak, *Jews and Gentiles*, 204.

30. Curtis, *Organization of the British Army*, 81–89, 106–107, 113–14; Baker, *Government and Contractors*, 26, 50.

31. Burrows, *Forgotten Patriots*, 19–20.

32. Curtis, *Organization of the British Army*, 90–98, 158; Baker, *Government and Contractors*, 25–35, 50.

33. Lancaster Committee of Inspection to Congress, December 21, 1775, PCC, item 69, vol. 1, 45; Lancaster Committee of Inspection to Congress, April 11, 1776, ibid., 125.

34. Lancaster County Committee of Correspondence to Congress, December 21, 1775, ibid., 45.

35. Some historians claim that these resolves set standards instead of merely reiterating what local committees had already enacted. Haffner, "Treatment of Prisoners of War," 80, 89–92; Dixon, "Divided Authority," 118.

36. Force, *American Archives*, 4th ser., 6:1675–77; *JCC*, 4:369–74. See also Springer, *America's Captives*, 20.

37. "Minutes of the Lancaster County Committee of Safety," December 27, 1775, PFC, ser. 8D, item 86.

38. "Minutes of the Lancaster County Committee of Safety," April 10 and July 23–October 12, 1776, ibid.

39. Ezekiel Williams, Wethersfield, to Elias Boudinot, September 13 and September 15, 1777, Boudinot Papers.

40. Wood, *Conestoga Crossroads*, 5–7, 47, 58; Henderson, *Community Development*, 11, 13–14, 43, 201.

41. Wood, *Conestoga Crossroads*, 74–77; Evans, "Lancaster Borough," 147.

42. Wood, *Conestoga Crossroads*, 7; Henderson, *Community Development*, 45.

43. Fogleman, *Hopeful Journeys*, 74, 81–85.

44. Wokeck, *Trade in Strangers*, 46.

45. Evans, "Lancaster Borough," 151; Gordon, "Barracks in Lancaster," 80–92; Wood, *Conestoga Crossroads*, 77–80.

46. "Minutes of the Lancaster County Committee of Safety," July 10, 1776, PFC, ser. 8D, item 86. Pennsylvania's colonial assembly was dissolved on May 20, 1776. By June 8, several county committees had chosen delegates to attend a provincial convention, to begin on June 18. This convention called for statewide elections on July 8. Ousterhout, *State Divided*, 137–38; Ryerson, *Revolution*, 207–46.

47. Lancaster Committee of Inspection to Congress, July 7, 1776, PCC, item 69, vol. 1, 165.

48. See, in particular, Miller, "Dangerous Guests."

49. Congress to the Lancaster County Committee, July 12, 1776, PFC, ser. 9, vols. 15–17; Lancaster Committee of Inspection to Congress, July 7 and July 13, 1776, PCC, item 69, vol. 1, 165, 181.

50. Lancaster Committee of Inspection to Congress, July 23, 1776, PCC, item 69, vol. 1, 197.

51. "Minutes of the Lancaster County Committee of Safety," September 17, 1776, PFC, ser. 8D, item 86.

52. William A. Atlee to George Ross, March 12, 1777, PCC, item 60, 445–50. See also Overton and Loose, "Prisoner-of-War Barracks"; Sener, *Lancaster Barracks*. "Board of War," March 20, 1777, PCC, item 147, vol. 1, 111. For orders to send the plan to Virginia and Connecticut, see "Board of War," March 12/13, 1777, ibid., 95–96; and "Board of War," n.d. [Summer?], 1777, ibid., 353–54.

53. William A. Atlee to George Ross, March 12, 1777, PCC, item 60, 445–50.

54. Kennedy, "Home Front," 332–38.

55. Executive Committee to General Washington, December 28, 1776, PCC, item 133, 10–11; General Washington to Robert Morris, January 1, 1777, PCC, item 152, vol. 3, 426.

56. See also Dixon, "Divided Authority," 316.

57. "Resolves of Congress Regarding Prisoners of War," April 3, 9, and 12, 1776, PCC, item 183, 2–16.

58. *JCC*, 5:599; "Minutes of the Lancaster County Committee of Safety," November 30, 1776, PFC, ser. 8D, item 86.

59. *JCC*, 5:435.

60. Schaffel, "American Board of War"; Dixon, "Divided Authority," 80.

61. *JCC*, 5:434–35; Schaffel, "American Board of War."

62. "Board of War," June 4, 1777, PCC, item 147, vol. 1, 201; Boyd, *Elias Boudinot*, 33–34.

63. Haffner, "Treatment of Prisoners of War," 14–15; Metzger, *Prisoner*, 71–76.

64. Richard Peters to Elias Boudinot, April 29, 1777, Boudinot Papers.

65. Elias Boudinot to William A. Atlee, January 7, 1778, PFC, ser. 9, vol. 23.

66. Elias Boudinot to General Heath, Board of War, March 10, 1778, PCC, item 78, vol. 2 (B), 341.

67. Henry Laurens to William A. Atlee, May 29, 1778, *LDC*, 9:767–68, and the notes to this letter.

68. William A. Atlee to Congress, June 2, 1778, PCC, item 78, vol. 1 (A), 173; Thomas McKean and Timothy Pickering to William A. Atlee, June 5, 1778, PFC, ser. 9, vol. 24.

7. German Prisoners of War, 1776–1778

1. For more details, see chap. 5.

2. Quoted in Burrows, *Forgotten Patriots*, 9.

3. Hugh Mercer to John Hancock, October 17, 1776, in Force, *American Archives*, 5th ser., 2:1093–94; "List of Prisoners Taken at Richmond on Staten Island and Sent to Philadelphia," n.d., PCC, item 159, 202. On this affair, see also Retzer, "Hessian Prisoners." Those Hessen-Kassel men were among the first German soldiers taken prisoner by the American revolutionaries. Before that, we know only about several Waldeck prisoners of war taken in late September. "Waldeck Prisoners and Their Employers, September 23 to November 11, 1776," PFC, ser. 9, vol. 18.

4. Hugh Mercer to George Washington, October 16, 1776, George Washington Papers, ser. 4: General Correspondence, LC; Hugh Mercer to John Hancock, October 17, 1776, in Force, *American Archives*, 5th ser., 2:1093–94.

5. Hugh Mercer to John Hancock, October 19, 1776, PCC, item 159, 198–99.

6. Quoted in Condit, "Christopher Ludwick," 375; Hugh Mercer to John Hancock, October 19, 1776, PCC, item 159, 198–99. See also Butterfield, "Psychological Warfare," 236–40; Berger, *Broadsides and Bayonets*, 106.

7. John Hancock to George Washington, November 16, 1776, in Force, *American Archives*, 5th ser., 4:705–706.

8. Condit, "Christopher Ludwick," 376. See also Fischer, *Washington's Crossing*, 375–79.

9. Ingrao, *Hessian Mercenary State*, 158. See also Auerbach, *Die Hessen*, 162, 264–70, on what she calls "wishful thinking" by the revolutionaries.

10. Quoted in Auerbach, "Die hessischen Soldaten," 147.

11. Copies of the leaflets from August 18 and August 27, 1776, were promptly sent back to Kassel. Relationes Heister, fols. 370, 397.

12. Quoted in Auerbach, *Die Hessen*, 270.

13. Pennsylvania Council of Safety to the Lancaster Committee of Inspection, January 5, 1777, PFC, ser. 9, vol. 19.

14. "Address to Hessian Prisoners," January 10, 1777, ibid.

15. "Return of Prisoners in Lancaster," January 1777, ibid. This number includes noncommissioned officers. The officers and their servants had been sent to Dumfries, Virginia.

16. "Lists of Hessian Prisoners, Lancaster," January 7, 1777, ibid. Fifteen sick and wounded soldiers appear in these lists, plus a wounded officer and one common soldier who had died.

17. See the appendix for a discussion of these numbers.

18. A list of trades for the German prisoners of war in Lancaster also included a count, showing a total of 830 prisoners. "List of Tradesmen among Hessian Prisoners at Lancaster," January 10, 1777, DLAR, film 24, roll 11, frame 952. A revolutionary return from February 10, 1777, listed 913 prisoners of war in Lancaster, of whom 843 were "in good health," 61 were sick, 1 worked with a carpenter, and 1 was absent with "permission of Committee." Interestingly, this count also included five Waldeck soldiers who had been "inlisted into our service," seemingly against Congress's and Washington's explicit orders. "Return of Prisoners in Barracks at Lancaster," February 10, 1777, PFC, ser. 9, vol. 19.

19. Christian Wirtz to Thomas Wharton, January 27, 1777, DLAR, film 24, roll 11, frame 1113.

20. General von Heister to Friedrich II, December 5, 1777, Relationes Heister, fol. 471.

21. For the following, see in general "Ausführliche Relation," ibid., fols. 530–51. Soldiers usually did not receive special winter clothing. In cold months, when they lived in huts or houses, they had to remake their tents into blankets to keep warm.

22. See also Lt. Colonel George Osborn to Lord Germain, December 30, 1776, PRO CO 5/94, fols. 390–93v, where Osborn observed that "Gen[l]. de Heister is preparing an intelligence Officer, to carry every Comfort and Relief he is able to give to the . . . Prisoners with the Enemy, and will take every Method in his power to prevent their entering into the Rebel Service."

23. "Journal des hessischen Corps," LB Ks, 2° Ms. Hass. Nr. 185, fol. 249v.

24. General von Heister to Friedrich II, June 5, 1777, Relationes Heister, fol. 563.

25. "Relation von der zu denen in Gefangenschaft sich befindenden drey Regtern gethanen 2ten Reise," Relationes Knyphausen, fols. 97–98.

26. For details, see chap. 8.

27. General von Knyphausen to Friedrich II, January 21, 1778, Relationes Knyphausen, fols. 160–61v.

28. "Abschrift der Relationen des Regimentsquartirmeister Kitz über seine Reise zu den gefangenen Offizieren," ibid., fols. 188–88v.

29. It is unclear exactly what kind of authority Reuber meant by "city commander." He seems to be describing the town major or chief of police. At the time, that was Christian Wirtz. Kessler, *Lancaster in the Revolution*, 79.

30. Auerbach, *Die Hessen*, 313, transcribes the sign that Reuber gives after "200" as R or *Reichsthaler* (*Thaler*), a common currency in the Holy Roman Empire. At the time, 1 *Thaler* was worth about 4 shillings 4 pence. Thus 200 *Thaler* were worth about 44 pounds.

31. The *Albus* was a Hessian currency. There were 32 *Albus* in 1 *Thaler*. In northern parts of the Holy Roman Empire, 1 *Thaler* was worth 24 *Groschen*. Thus, 6 *Albus* were about 4½ *Groschen* or about 7 pence.

32. Sprenger, *Das Geld der Deutschen*, 105, 130, 132, 150.

33. Reuber, "Tagebuch," fols. 100–101v.

34. "Lists of Hessian Prisoners, Lancaster," January 6–7, 1777, PFC, ser. 9, vol. 19; "List of Tradesmen among Hessian Prisoners at Lancaster," January 10, 1777, DLAR, film 24, roll 11, frame 952. See also "List of Tradesmen among Hessian Prisoners," in Linn et al., *Pennsylvania Archives*, 2nd ser., 1:435.

35. "Pennsylvania Council of Safety—Employing Prisoners," January 11, 1777, PFC, ser. 9, vol. 19.

36. Members at the time were John Adams (president), Richard Peters (secretary), Roger Sherman, Benjamin Harrison, James Wilson, and Edward Routledge. Schaffel, "American Board of War," 185.

37. Richard Peters to the Lancaster Town Committee, January 31, 1777, PFC, ser. 9, vol. 19.

38. Melchior Isaac to the Lancaster Town Committee, February 3, 1777, ibid.; Lancaster Town Committee to the Board of War (draft), February 1777, ibid.; Council of Safety to the Lancaster Town Committee, March 3, 1777, ibid.; Pennsylvania War Office to the Lancaster Town Committee, April 17, 1777, PFC, ser. 9, vol. 20.

39. "List of Hessian Prisoners and Their Employers," April 19, 1777, ibid. Three of these prisoner-laborers came from the Waldeck regiment.

40. "Minutes of the Lancaster County Committee of Safety," March 29, 1777, PFC, ser. 8D, item 86.

41. William Henry Papers, HSP; Salay, "Arming for War," 151–53. See also Kessler, *Lancaster in the Revolution*, 9.

42. "Board of War," October 28, 1777, PCC, item 147, vol. 1, 375.

43. Salay, "Arming for War," 181–83. On prisoner-laborers at ironworks, see Cramer, "From Hessian Drummer to Maryland Ironmaker"; Montgomery, "Early Furnaces."

44. "Certificate," March 13, 1783, MNR, no. 31713. See chap. 10 for more details on this case.

45. "List of Hessian Grenadiers and Jäger and Their Employers," September–November 1777, PFC, ser. 9, vol. 21; "List of the Hessian Artillery Corps and Their Employers," September–November 1777, ibid.; "List of Hessian Soldiers from the Regiments von Loßberg, Rall, and von Knyphausen," September–November, 1777, ibid. The lists were apparently put together on order of the Board of War. The board had written to Boudinot on November 7, 1777, that it wanted to see a full return of all British and German prisoners of war and for whom they worked. Richard Peters to Elias Boudinot, November 7, 1777, Boudinot Papers.

46. Auerbach, *Die Hessen*, 168.

47. See also Kennedy, "Home Front," 334.

48. Information for the data presented here was taken from Sowers, "Hessian Prisoners."

49. Ousterhout, *State Divided*, 162, states that many in Pennsylvania did not swear the oath of allegiance or otherwise declare their loyalty to the state, even after passage of the Test Act in June 1777. A large number of revolutionaries were opposed to the constitution as adopted in September 1777 and feared that their oath might prohibit future reform. In York, for instance, only about one-quarter of the population took the oath.

50. Christopher Ludwick, Philadelphia, to Congress, March 8, 1777, PCC, item 41, vol. 5, 175, 178.

51. Sikora, "Das 18. Jahrhundert." Desertion did not necessarily result in a permanent absence from a unit. Soldiers who ran away from their unit in captivity often came back again later or tried to make their way back to British lines. For instance, Heinrich Lange and Heinrich Mardorf were recorded as deserters

in Sowers's list of prisoner-laborers around Lebanon but later returned to their unit. Sowers, "Hessian Prisoners," 16.

52. Thomas Burke to Richard Caswell, Governor of North Carolina, July 5, 1777, *LMCC*, 2:399.

53. See chaps. 2 and 3 for more details on trades among eighteenth-century soldiers.

54. For these and the following events, see William A. Atlee to George Ross, March 12, 1777, PCC, item 60, 445.

55. Reuber, "Tagebuch," fols. 101–102.

56. "Relation," Relationen Knyhausen, fols. 97v–98.

57. Reuber, "Tagebuch," fols. 101v–102.

58. "Relation," Relationes Knyphausen, fol. 98.

59. "Minutes of the Lancaster County Committee of Safety," June 5, 1777, PFC, ser. 8D, item 86.

60. George Lindenberger, Baltimore, to Richard Peters, Board of War, December 13, 1777, Boudinot Papers.

61. Ibid. In the lists of prisoner-laborers for September–November 1777 discussed above, nine soldiers appeared as prisoner-laborers with Lemon: Corporal Stock, Conrad Richter, Conrad Nisel, Heinrich Zimmermann, Matthias Glotzbach, Christian Meyer, Franz Heinrich Homuth, Cilias Melchior, and Johannes Herold. Lindenberger also wrote a letter about this case to Governor Johnson in Maryland. George Lindenberger to Gov. Th. Johnson, December 13, 1777, Maryland State Papers, Rainbow Series, Maryland State Archives, Annapolis, Red Books, XVI:171. Another report to Governor Johnson came from Charles Frederick Wiesenthal, who stated that such treatment made "thinking people uneasy." Charles Frederick Wiesenthal to Gov. Th. Johnson, December 12, 1777, ibid., 170.

62. Taaffe, *Philadelphia Campaign*; Conway, *War of American Independence*, 91–93.

63. Marshall, "Remembrancer," Papers of Christopher Marshall, HSP, vol. D.

64. Thomas Mifflin, Reading, to Richard Peters, Board of War, August 23, 1777, Boudinot Papers.

65. "Firewood and Straw Furnished to Prisoners at Lebanon from August to October 1777," MNR, no. 35045. See also "Return of Hessian Prisoners Sent to Lebanon," August 25, 1777, PFC, ser. 9, vol. 21; "List of the Hessian Regiment von Loßberg Marching to Lebanon," August 27, 1777, ibid.; "List of the Hessian Regiment Rall Marching to Lebanon," August 27, 1777, ibid.

66. Henry Haller, Reading, to William A. Atlee, August 29 and September 6, 1777, ibid.; Bethlehem Diary, "Memorabilia," 241.

67. Sowers, "Hessian Prisoners," 58–59.

68. "Return of Hessian Prisoners Sent to Lebanon," August 25, 1777, PFC, ser. 9, vol. 21. This return is badly damaged and difficult to read.

69. William A. Atlee to Elias Boudinot, September 9, 1777 (copy), ibid. For the period September 22 to October 5, 1777, 520 prisoners of war were listed for Lebanon. That means that about 320 men must have left around September 22. "Firewood and Straw," MNR, no. 35045.

70. Reuber, "Tagebuch," fols. 102–102v. See also "List of Hessian Prisoners Sent to Winchester," September 20, 1777, PFC, ser. 9, vol. 21.

71. Reuber, "Tagebuch," fols. 105v–106.

72. "Report on Treatment in Captivity," February 24, 1783, BHQ, no. 7000.

73. Hebron Diary, December 19, 1777.

74. Ousterhout, *State Divided*, 138, 162.

75. Hebron Diary, April 25 and June 10, 1778.

76. On state-building during the War of Independence, see Higginbotham, "War and State-Formation."

77. Slaski, "Lehigh Valley," 53, 61–65; Neisser, "Items of History," 315.

78. Hebron Diary, "Memorabilia 1777." The church's diary, three volumes running from 1774 to 1835, is written in German. Only a few select parts of it have been published in English. See Bader, "Extracts"; Heisey, "Extracts."

79. Hebron Diary, December 19, 1777.

80. Bethlehem Diary, October 26–27, 1777, 209.

81. Rev. P. C. Bader, Lebanon, to Rev. Br. Nathanael Seidel, Bethlehem, February 14, 1778, Lebanon (Quitopehiu, Hebron), Moravian Archives, Bethlehem, Pa., LeA.

82. Hebron Diary, March 1, 1778; William A. Atlee to Melchior Isaac and M. Stone, February 10, 1778, PFC, ser. 9, vol. 23.

83. Hebron Diary, April 29–May 6, 1778.

84. Ibid., August 29–31, September 17–28, November 18, and September 14, 1777; Bethlehem Diary, September 14, 1777, 191.

85. See, for instance, Burgoyne, *Diaries of a Hessian Chaplain*; Burgoyne et al., *Diary of Lieutenant von Bardeleben*; Burgoyne et al., *Hessian Chaplains*; Retzer, "Philipp Theobald."

86. Hebron Diary, September 15–16, 1777.

87. Ibid., August 30 and September 18–19, 1777.

88. Ibid., December 1, 24, and 29, 1777.

89. Ibid., October 28, 1777, and January 1, 1778.

90. Ibid., January 1, 1778.

91. Between December 17, 1777, and December 18, 1778, about ninety-three German prisoners came back to the Lebanon/Hebron area according to bread returns in "Various Accounts, David Krause, Lebanon," September 1777–February 1778, MNR, nos. 035106–109.

92. Hebron Diary, January 6–7, 1778.

93. "Fizlipuzli" is a reference to the Aztec god of war, Huitzilopochtli.

94. Hebron Diary, January 21–25 and February 13, 1778.

8. Provisions and Exchange, 1778

1. Nesbitt, Drummond, & Franks to the Treasury, via John Robinson, August 8, 1777, PRO T 1/534, fols. 183–83v; "Memorial of Arnold Nesbitt, Adam Drummond, Moses Franks," December 18, 1777, ibid., fol. 181.

2. Elias Boudinot to the British Commissary of Prisoners, November 12, 1777, BHQ, no. 743.

3. Wolf and Whiteman, *History of the Jews of Philadelphia*, 87.

4. Quoted in Pencak, *Jews and Gentiles*, 204.

5. George Washington to Congress, November 1–3, 1777, PCC, item 153, vol. 5, 168.

6. Elias Boudinot to the British Commissary of Prisoners, Hugh Ferguson, January 10, 1778, PCC, item 78, vol. 2 (B), roll 91, 337. See also *JCC*, 9:1036–37.

7. Elias Boudinot to Hugh Ferguson, January 10, 1778, PRO CO 5/95, fol. 147. The dispute over provisioning prisoners of war had begun in the spring of 1777, when the revolutionaries complained that they were not allowed to keep a commissary with their prisoners in New York. Thomas Warton, jun., to Elias Boudinot, May 28, 1777, Boudinot Papers; Elias Boudinot to General Washington, June 26, 1777, ibid. In November 1777, Ferguson called on Boudinot to send supplies for American prisoners into Philadelphia. The men there were suffering from "want of cloathing," and many were without pants, shirts, shoes, and stockings. Yet the British still provisioned them with the "allowance the King is pleased to afford" prisoners. As Ferguson stressed, "The pay and cloathing of prisoners of war . . . are ever it seems furnished by the army to whom they . . . belong." Hugh Ferguson to Elias Boudinot, November 28, 1777, ibid.

8. General Howe to General Washington, January 19, 1778, PRO CO 5/95, fols. 145–45v.

9. General Washington to General Howe, January 30, 1778, ibid., fol. 149.

10. "Report by Elias Boudinot," 1777, PFC, ser. 7E, item 12.

11. *JCC*, 9:1036–37.

12. "State of the American Prisoners in New York," March 10, 1778, PCC, item 78, vol. 2 (B), 345–49.

13. Committee at Camp to George Washington, March 9–10?, 1778, *LDC*, 9:244–49.

14. Joshua Loring to Col. John Beatty, October 28, 1778, PCC, item 78, vol. 14 (L), 247–49.

15. Thomas Bradford to Joseph Holmes at Winchester (in copy to Fort Frederick and to Atlee in Lancaster), November 14, 1778, HSP, AM 639.

16. "Board of War," November 7, 1778, PCC, item 147, vol. 2, 359–60; David Franks to Congress, November 7, 1778, PCC, item 78, vol. 9 (F), roll 95, 197.

17. Quoted in Wolf and Whiteman, *History of the Jews of Philadelphia*, 91.

18. Burrows, *Forgotten Patriots*, xi, 9, 11–12, 44, 180.

19. Ibid., 63, 72, 82–83.

20. Ibid., xi, 117–18, 122, 130, 144.

21. Hohrath, "'In Cartellen,'" 141–70.

22. On such problems, see Springer, *America's Captives*, 16, 18, 25.

23. "General Howe's Instructions," March 5, 1778, PRO CO 5/95, fol. 230.

24. "General Washington's Instructions for Col. William Grayson, Lt. Cols. Robert H. Harrison and Alexander Hamilton," March 28, 1778, ibid., fol. 246. See also Knight, "Prisoner Exchange," 206.

25. Elias Boudinot to General Henry Knox, March 14, 1782, Boudinot Papers.

26. Quoted in Knight, "Prisoner Exchange," 204. See also Bowman, "New Jersey Prisoner Exchange Conferences," 149–50.

27. American Commissioners to British Commissioners, April 10, 1778, PRO CO 5/95, fol. 250.

28. Quoted in Boyd, *Elias Boudinot*, 61.

29. William Knox to William Fraser, November 17, 1778, PRO CO 5/141, fols. 172–73v.

30. "Exchange Agreement, Germantown, Pennsylvania," June 9, 1778, PFC, ser. 7E, item 12.

31. Elias Boudinot to General Washington, June 28, 1778, ibid.; John Beatty to Thomas Bradford, June 30, 1778, Bradford Papers, box 21, folder 5.

32. General von Knyphausen to Friedrich II, July 6, July 19, and November 7, 1778, Relationes Knyphausen, fols. 386–86v, 398v–99, 474–75.

33. August Wille, Lancaster, to Henry Laurens, July 3, 1778, PCC, item 42, vol. 8, 175. His petition was read and tabled on July 10, 1778. A list of Hessen-Kassel prisoners of war compiled by Regimental Quartermaster Müller in February 1777 shows Wille, a soldier in Captain von Ewald's Company, as sick in the Philadelphia hospital. "Ausführliche Relation," Relationes Heister, fol. 531.

34. Volm, *Hessian Prisoners*, 25.

35. Reuber, "Tagebuch," fols. 106v, 110v.

36. William A. Atlee to Thomas Bradford, August 14, 1778, Bradford Papers, box 21, folder 6; "Board of War," June 16, 1778, PCC, item 147, vol. 2, 97.

37. General von Knyphausen to Friedrich II, October 17, 1777, January 21 and March 23, 1778, Relationes Knyphausen, fols. 60v, 160v, 204.

38. "Liste der hess. zu Philadelphia sich befindenden Truppen," May 1778, ibid., fol. 356v. On Müller's lists, see the appendix. It is not entirely clear how many deserters, sick, wounded, or dead soldiers, and prisoners of war from all units were included in Knyphausen's numbers. "Soldiers" and "prisoners of war" here refer to noncommissioned officers, musicians, and privates. The musicians also include regimental hautboists. To achieve some kind of comparability, the numbers include only soldiers from the Regiments Rall, von Knyphausen, and von Loßberg, as far as they were listed separately. Men from the artillery or captives from other German contingents were excluded.

39. "Journal des hochlöblichen," LB Ks, 4° Ms. Hass. Nr. 169, 164–66.

40. General von Knyphausen to Friedrich II, November 7, 1778, Relationes Knyphausen, fols. 474–75.

41. The Trenton prisoners were exchanged on four different dates in 1778: July 19, August 6, August 10, and October 27. To illustrate the problems surrounding these numbers, consider, for instance, that two common prisoners, Kube and Wolf, died on February 5 and February 8, 1777, in Lancaster, after Regimental Quartermaster Müller had already left for New York, but were still included in his count of present soldiers.

42. "State of the Hessian Troops at New York, June–December 1778," PRO CO 5/182, fol. 97.

43. Miles, "Winchester Hessian Barracks," 29. He states for Winchester: "Clearly a very small number of Hessians from Trenton had stayed behind in Virginia."

44. "Return of the German Prisoners of War in the New Gaol at Philadelphia," December 11, 1780, Bradford Papers, box 26, folder 8; on November 6, 1779, and February 12, 1780, Lancaster recorded twelve men from the three regiments still in captivity. "List of Hessian Soldiers Sent to Philadelphia from Lancaster for Exchange, June 17–June 21, 1778," and July 29, 1778, PFC, ser. 9, vols. 24–25; "Return of Prisoners of War at Lancaster," February 12, 1780, ibid., vol. 27; "List of German Prisoners at Lancaster," November 6 and November 20, 1779, ibid.

45. See also Barth, Doernemann, and Schwalm, "Trenton Prisoner List," 2. The authors here state that "contrary to popular belief, only a small number of those soldiers captured at Trenton deserted. Rather, a large percentage were exchanged during the period of June through August 1778."

46. Sikora, "Das 18. Jahrhundert."

47. General von Knyphausen to Friedrich II, July 19, 1778, Relationes Knyphausen, fols. 398v–99; "British Prisoners of War, 1776–1779," HSP, AM 620; "List of Hessian Soldiers Sent to Philadelphia from Lancaster for Exchange, June 17–21 and July 29, 1778," PFC, ser. 9, vols. 24–25.

48. In a list of deserters for the period between June 1 and July 4, 1778, Knyphausen recorded a total of 236 soldiers for all Hessen-Kassel forces in North America. The Regiments Rall, von Knyphausen, and von Loßberg were listed with 73 deserters; 47 men (64 percent) were subjects, while 26 (36 percent) were foreigners. General von Knyphausen to Friedrich II, July 6, 1778, Relationes Knyphausen, fol. 386.

49. "Journal des Regiments von Knyphausen," LB Ks, 4° Ms. Hass. Nr. 163, 92. See also General von Knyphausen to Friedrich II, April 20 and August 23, 1778, Relationes Knyphausen, fols. 257, 260–60v, 210; Jones, "Karl Friedrich Führer."

50. Ensigns Führer and Kleinschmidt to Congress, August 26, 1778, PCC, item 78, vol. 13 (I–K), 479.

51. "Board of War," August 29, 1778, PCC, item 147, vol. 2, 241–42; Ensigns Führer and Kleinschmidt to Congress, October 9, 1778, PCC, item 78, vol. 13 (I–K), 489.

52. "Board of War," October 25, 1778, PCC, item 147, vol. 2, 339–40. See also Miles, "Winchester Hessian Barracks," 28; *JCC*, 14:754.

53. General von Knyphausen to Friedrich II, November 7, 1778, Relationes Knyphausen, fols. 474v–75.

54. Neimeyer, *America Goes to War*, 57–58.

55. "Führer, Kleinschmidt, Lüdemann, and [F]reylinghausen to Congress," November 19, 1778, PCC, item 43, 88–89.

56. In 1780, Kleinschmidt wrote Knyphausen and unsuccessfully asked for a pardon. On October 6, 1781, he was captured at Yorktown by the Regiment von Bose while spying for the revolutionaries. He was placed under arrest on a prison ship. Miles, "Winchester Hessian Barracks," 56–57, n. 35. In 1781, Führer applied for a pension from Congress. After the failed recruitment campaign for the German Volunteers, he had apparently served with Virginia troops in 1779 and 1780 and now felt that he was entitled to a pension because he had given up so much for the American cause. After all, as he stressed, the British had hanged and burned him in effigy. Karl Friedrich Führer, Philadelphia, to Congress, November 15, 1781, PCC, item 42, vol. 3:F, 75.

57. Ingrao, *Hessian Mercenary State*, 158.

9. The Convention Army, 1777–1781

1. For a full text of the agreement, see Dabney, *After Saratoga*, 81–82.

2. For this congressional resolve on January 8, 1778, see PCC, item 57, 129.

3. General von Riedesel to Lord Germain, May 10, 1781, PRO CO 5/183–84, fol. 148; "Extracts of Colonel Wood's Orders," April 5 and 12, 1781, ibid., fol. 150. Colonel James Wood supervised the Convention Army in Charlottesville and Winchester, Virginia.

4. Colonel Lenz to Wilhelm IX, April 13, 1781, StA Marburg, Best. 4h, Nr. 3111, fols. 4–5v; Colonel Lenz to Wilhelm IX, August 28, 1781, ibid., fols. 6–6v.

5. Huck, "Soldaten gegen Nordamerika," 206.

6. Ibid., 211.

7. Ibid., 212–13.

8. Bense, "Marschroute," fols. 10–10v.

9. Other letters, memoirs, and journals come from officers, who usually stayed in private houses in surrounding communities such as Cambridge.

10. "Ordrebuch," StA Marburg, Best. 4h, Nr. 3152, fols. 66, 68v–69, 71.

11. Ibid., fols. 81v–82v.

12. Huck, "Soldaten gegen Nordamerika," 215.

13. Quoted in ibid., 217.

14. General Heath to the Council of the State of Massachusetts, July 11, 1778, PFC, ser. 7E, item 85, ser. I.

15. Colonel von Gall to Wilhelm IX, March 16, 1778, Relationes Gall, fols. 68–74v.

16. Huck, "Soldaten gegen Nordamerika," 214.

17. "Memorial of the Inhabitants of Boston," March 23, 1778, PFC, ser. 7E, item 83, boxes 31–34.

18. "Provisioning Account," Joshua Mersereau Papers, LC. The 4th and 71st Regiments of Foot were not part of the Convention Army.

19. "Memorial of the Inhabitants of Charlestown," April 21, 1778, PFC, ser. 7E, item 83, boxes 31–34.

20. Colonel von Gall to Wilhelm IX, June 5, 1778, ibid., fols. 79–80v.

21. Colonel von Gall to Wilhelm IX, September 26, 1778, ibid., fols. 85–86v.

22. Colonel von Gall to Wilhelm IX, October 10, 1778, ibid., fols. 87–90v.

23. "July 11, 1778 and August 8, 1778," Thomas Cole, Orderly Book, LC.

24. "Massachusetts Council, Resolve," August 25, 1777, PFC, ser. 7E, item 82, 182–83; General Heath to Elias Boudinot, August 30, 1777, Boudinot Papers.

25. "Memorial of the Committee for Fortifying the Harbor of Boston to the Council of the State of Massachusetts," September 9, 1777, PFC, ser. 7E, item 82, 210.

26. Justin Ely, West Springfield, to the Council of the State of Massachusetts, September 18, 1777, ibid., 238. Between September 18 and October 25, 1777, thirty-three Braunschweig-Wolfenbüttel prisoners taken at Bennington were hired out by private citizens upon petition to the Massachusetts Council.

27. Colonel von Gall to Wilhelm IX, September 22, 1778, Relationes Gall, fol. 86.

28. Colonel von Gall to Wilhelm IX, July 24, 1778, ibid., fol. 84.

29. "July 13, 1778," Thomas Cole, Orderly Book, LC.

30. For a similar argument, see Huck, "Soldaten gegen Nordamerika," 220.

31. On reports from Braunschweig-Wolfenbüttel units about efforts to persuade Convention soldiers to work for wages and to desert, see ibid., 218.

32. For the original German text of the 1778 pamphlet translated here, see ibid., 218–19.

33. Quoted in ibid., 219.

34. Ibid., 220.

35. Ibid., 226.

36. "Briefe, Berichte, Journale, Listen," StA Marburg, Best. 4h, Nr. 3108, fol. 111.

37. Bense, "Marschroute," fols. 12–12v.

38. Quoted in Huck, "Soldaten gegen Nordamerika," 227.

39. Ibid.

40. John Hawkins to Theodoric Bland, June 3, 1779, Virginia Historical Society, Mss1 B6108a, sec. 63.

41. Bense, "Marschroute," fol. 13.

42. Colonel von Gall to Wilhelm IX, September 20, 1779, Relationes Gall, fols. 101–102v.

43. Ibid., fols. 101–102.

44. Huck, "Soldaten gegen Nordamerika," 229.

45. For these numbers, see ibid.

46. Colonel Lenz to Wilhelm IX, April 13, 1781, StA Marburg, Best. 4h, Nr. 3111, fols. 4–5; Colonel Lenz to Wilhelm IX, August 28, 1781, ibid., fols. 6–6v.

47. Colonel Lenz to Wilhelm IX, June 10, 1782, ibid., fols. 28–29. See chap. 10 for more details.

48. General von Riedesel to Karl Wilhelm of Braunschweig-Wolfenbüttel, June 6, 1781, NdsStA Wf, 38B Alt 256, fol. 84v. While officers were exchanged once the soldiers of the Convention Army were declared prisoners of war in April 1781—one lieutenant colonel counted for seventy-two rank and file—the average dragoon or musketeer had to wait until the war ended in 1783 to be released from captivity. There apparently was an exchange, however, in the summer of 1782 between American soldiers held in Canada and men from the former Convention Army. Huck, "Soldaten gegen Nordamerika," 233.

49. Colonel Lenz to Wilhelm IX, August 28, 1782, StA Marburg, Best. 4h, Nr. 3111, fol. 8; Colonel Lenz to Wilhelm IX, August 24, 1782, ibid., fols. 38–39v.

50. Mersereau, *Advertisement.*

51. Major Päusch to Wilhelm IX, January 1781, StA Marburg, Best. 4h, Nr. 3106, fol. 123.

52. General Washington to the Council of the State of Massachusetts, May 19, 1778, PFC, ser. 7E, item 85, ser. I.

53. *Virginia Gazette,* July 24 and August 21, 1779.

10. Continuity and Change, 1779–1783

1. Richard Peters to Thomas Bradford, October 5 and October 9, 1779, Bradford Papers, box 22, folder 7. Of course, British prisoners of war also worked in Philadelphia. War Office to Thomas Bradford, November 2 and 3, 1779, ibid., folder 9.

2. "State of the Prisoners of War at Philadelphia," October 11, 1779, ibid., box 26, folder 6.

3. "State of the Prisoners of War in Philadelphia," February 3, 1780, ibid., box 25, folder 2. See the appendix for an explanation of the numbers for the captives from the *Molly* and *Triton.*

4. "Memoir des Corporal Justus Eggert," Oberösterreichisches Landesarchiv Linz. On Eggert, see also Krüll, "Aus dem Tagebuch"; and Eggertt, "Bericht." See also Städtler, *Die Ansbach-Bayreuther Truppen,* 109. Eggert's journal, however, contains a number of distorted facts.

5. Popp, "Geschichte," 195–96.

6. Colonel von Gall to Wilhelm IX, March 30, 1780, Relationes Gall, fols. 104–107.

7. "Verordnung gelegentlich der in Kriegs-gefangenschaft gerathenen Mannschaft," December 21, 1781, StA Nürnberg, Rep. 116, Tit. XXIX, Bd. III, 2, Nr. 23.

8. Hannah Morman, "New Gaol," to Thomas Bradford, August 18, 1779, Bradford Papers, box 22, folder 5.

9. Döhla, "Marschroute," 519.

10. William A. Atlee to Thomas Bradford, December 21, 1778, Bradford Papers, box 21, folder 7.

11. Secretary at War Gen. Lincoln, War Office, to Congress, July 10, 1782, PCC, item 149, 1:497.

12. "Report by Committee in Congress," July 11, 1782, PCC, item 27, 171.

13. Ibid., 463, 475.

14. Altogether, twenty-one officers from the Regiments Voit von Salzburg and von Seybothen accompanied the prisoners into captivity. From the Regiment Voit von Salzburg: Captains von Ellrod, von Stain, and von Koeniz; Lieutenants von Marschall, von Trecksel, von Prechtel, Dechsel, Baumann, von Fabrice, Halbmeier, and Hofmann; and Regimental Surgeon Rapp. From the Regiment von Seybothen: Major von Beust; Captains von Quesnoy and von Metsch; Lieutenants von Kruse, von Reitzenstein, von Ciriacy, von Lindemeyer, Wein[hart], and Graeb[ner]. Prechtel, "Beschreibung," 517.

15. Ibid., 526.

16. Ibid., 571.

17. Döhla, "Marschroute," 502–503. Baily's name is often spelled "Bayly" or "Bailey."

18. Ibid., 505–506.

19. On this march, see also Chilton, "Journey," 200–203.

20. Popp, "Geschichte," 224–25.

21. Döhla, "Marschroute," 474.

22. Ibid., 460.

23. Like Lancaster, Winchester had been an important garrison town during the Seven Years' War. Miles, "Winchester Hessian Barracks," 41.

24. On British and German prisoners of war in Maryland, particularly Frederick and Fort Frederick, see also Gull, "Captor's Conundrum" and "Hessians."

25. Popp, "Geschichte," 235–36.

26. Döhla, "Marschroute," 496.

27. Popp, "Geschichte," 242–43.

28. General Heath had asked Congress in April 1778 to remove the Convention troops from Boston. "Address to Henry Laurens, President of Congress," April 1778, PFC, ser. 7E, item 85, ser. I.

29. Colonel von Gall to Wilhelm IX, October 30, 1778, Relationes Gall, fols. 93–94.

30. Ibid., fols. 95–96v.

31. Quoted in Huck, "Soldaten gegen Nordamerika," 225.

32. Ibid., 226.

33. Bense, "Marschroute," fol. 15.

34. Silas Condit, Morris Town, to Thomas Bradford, July 7, 1780, Bradford Papers, box 23, folder 7. The men's names were Conrad Hobinglet and Heinrich Blömenhofer.

35. The data listed here contains information on only thirty-one men and women released by Bradford and John Beatty between 1779 and 1781. Statistically, this number is too small to draw wider conclusions. Only eight or nine men—the names are difficult to read—were German prisoners of war. Six men

were likely British prisoners of war. In addition, five black male prisoners and one black female prisoner were also listed. Seven men were parolees—some of them loyalists. One girl, "a child of a British prisoner," was listed as an apprentice to a Walter Stephen in Philadelphia. Information for another soldier is unclear. "American Securities for British Prisoners, 1779–1781," ibid., American Naval Prisoners' Paroles and Bonds for Their Delivery, vol. 2.

36. For these and the following exchange rates, see table C-1 on currency depreciation in McCusker, *How Much Is That?*, 354–55.

37. Of course, such data does not take into account the skills that those soldiers might have possessed. A day laborer was probably cheaper to hire than, for example, a highly trained gunsmith. We do not know whether it was skills or inflation that necessitated a $400 deposit in June 1781 for Conrad Michaelis, a prisoner of war captured at Trenton in 1776.

38. Archibald Ritchie, Virginia, to Thomas Bradford, October 31, 1779, Bradford Papers, box 22, folder 8.

39. Döhla, "Marschroute," 486.

40. Ibid., 469.

41. Popp, "Geschichte," 230, 233.

42. Ibid., 512.

43. "Memoir des Corporal Justus Eggertt," Oberösterreichisches Landesarchiv Linz.

44. Bowie, *Ancient Barracks*, 16; Bowie, "German Prisoners," 187–88.

45. "Walnut Street Prison," n.d., Bradford Papers, box 7, folder 12. See also Condie, "Plan, Construction &c."; Sellin, "Philadelphia Prisons," 326–29.

46. Listed were 17 noncommissioned officers, a drummer, and 144 common soldiers. The prisoners came from the Regiments von Loßberg, von Knyphausen, Rall, von Donop, Landgraf, von Bose, Erbprinz, and von Bünau, the grenadiers, the artillery, and the *Jäger*. A number of prisoners came from Ansbach-Bayreuth units, the Hessen-Hanau artillery and infantry, and Braunschweig-Wolfenbüttel troops.

47. "Return of the German Prisoners of War in the New Gaol at Philadelphia," December 11, 1780, Bradford Papers, box 26, folder 8.

48. "Return of the Number of Prisoners of War Deceas'd in the New Gaol Philadelphia's from the First to the Last April, 1781," ibid., folder 9.

49. "Board of War," November 25?, 1781, PCC, item 148, vol. 2, 469–71.

50. Sergeant Philipp Rauthe, Hessian Prisoner of War in New Gaol, to Col. John Mitchell, Adjutant Quartermaster General, August 17, 1780, Bradford Papers, box 23, folder 8.

51. William A. Atlee to Thomas Bradford, December 8, 1780, ibid., folder 10.

52. See below for more on these events in 1782.

53. General von Loßberg to Friedrich II, August 10, 1782, Relationes Loßberg, fols. 37v–38. Wolff also appears on a list of twelve German prisoners of war at Lancaster compiled on November 6 and 20, 1779. PFC, ser. 9, vol. 27. See also "Report on Treatment in American Captivity, Sergeant Wolff and Private Dippel," February 24, 1783, BHQ, no. 7000.

54. Döhla, "Marschroute," 456.

55. Popp, "Geschichte," 216–18, 221–22, 231–32.

56. Barton, "Revolutionary Prisoners," 30.

57. It seems that County Lieutenant John Smith prevented such action. John Smith to Governor Harrison, May 21, 1783, in *CVSP*, 3:487.

58. "A System on Which Provisions Are to Be Issued," in Glass, *Winchester, Virginia,* 236–38. Following the final ratification of the Articles of Confederation in 1781, Congress established posts for the secretary at war (Benjamin Lincoln), the secretary of foreign affairs (Robert R. Livingston), and the superintendent of finance (Robert Morris).

59. Döhla, "Marschroute," 485.

60. James Wood to Benjamin Lincoln, January 5, 1782, PCC, item 149, vol. 1, 125. Wood's father founded Winchester in 1744. Hofstra and Mitchell, "Town and Country," 628.

61. Major Claiborne to Timothy Pickering, December 23, 1781, MNR, no. 24752.

62. Wood noted from Winchester at the end of December that about "a Third of the Prisoners" were "dispersed over the Country" seeking food and work. James Wood to Governor Harrison, December 27, 1781, in *CVSP,* 2:673.

63. Markets near prisoner-of-war camps were common. In England, for instance, large camps, mostly for seamen, regularly saw merchants coming to the buildings to peddle their goods during the Seven Years' War, the American War of Independence, and the French Revolutionary and Napoleonic Wars. In these exchanges, merchants often took whatever the prisoners manufactured. Inside the prisons, the captives often established a secondary market in which soldiers could buy and sell goods traded in from the outside. Lloyd, *History,* 104, 201.

64. Döhla, "Marschroute," 465, 475–81, 538–39.

65. Major von Scheer from the Hessen-Kassel Regiment von Bose also reported frequently about insufficient or rotten rations. At one time, Scheer even petitioned Congress. "Journal des Infanterie-Regiments von Trümbach," StA Marburg, Best. 10e, Nr. I/7, 224–25.

66. Döhla, "Marschroute," 508–509.

67. Ibid., 513, 515.

68. Ibid., 462.

69. Colonel Voit von Salzburg to Adjutant General von Schlammersdorf, January 20, 1782, HAV, fols. 395–96.

70. Margrave Karl Alexander to Colonel Voit von Salzburg, June 18, 1782, ibid., fols. 430–31; Adjutant General von Schlammersdorf to Colonel Voit von Salzburg, March 18, 1783, ibid., fol. 399; Adjutant General von Schlammersdorf to Voit von Salzburg, March 30, 1782, ibid., fols. 414–15.

71. Döhla, "Marschroute," 485–86.

72. Ibid., 505.

73. Meyer, "Tagebucheinträge."

74. Colonel Voit von Salzburg to Adjutant General von Schlammersdorf, May 5, 1782, HAV, fols. 419–21.

75. Ibid.

76. Prechtel, "Beschreibung," 557.

77. Döhla, "Marschroute," 510–11.

78. Popp, "Geschichte," 249–50.

79. Margrave Karl Alexander to Colonel Voit von Salzburg, July 30, 1782, HAV, fols. 440–41; Colonel Voit von Salzburg to Margrave Karl Alexander, August 3, 1782, ibid., fols. 434–37; Colonel Voit von Salzburg to Adjutant General von Schlammersdorf, October [26?], 1782, ibid., fols. 456–58.

80. Döhla, "Marschroute," 543–44. Not every soldier received a blanket. Döhla's Company von Quesnoy, for instance, was only given eight.

81. Colonel Voit von Salzburg to Margrave Karl Alexander, December 15, 1782, HAV, fols. 469–70. However, Voit von Salzburg did not receive permission from British headquarters to send the prisoners their pay in cash. Instead, he received an "Assignation" for £5,000 sterling to be paid out in Lancaster.

82. Prechtel, "Beschreibung," 606; Colonel Voit von Salzburg to Adjutant General von Schlammersdorf, April 3, 1783, HAV, fols. 499–500; "Return of Deficient Clothing of Ansbach Troops in Chester County," March 15, 1783, DLAR, film 24, roll 20, frame 249. The missing items were worth about £3,000 in Pennsylvania currency. See also "List of Waggoners Who Stopped in Chester County and Did Not Arrive in Lancaster with British Goods," March 25, 1783, ibid., frame 291.

83. Döhla, "Marschroute," 546–47.

84. Ibid., 553.

85. Colonel Voit von Salzburg to Margrave Karl Alexander, July 28, 1782, HAV, fols. 432–33.

86. "Massachusetts Council, Resolve," January 6, 1778, PFC, ser. 7E, item 82, boxes 29–31, 133.

87. "Return of Guards, Albemarle Barracks, Col. Taylor's Regiment and the Militia," April 8, 1780, Library of Virginia, Accession no. 28960; "Return of Guards, Albemarle Barracks, Col. Crockett's Western Battalion," July 1, 1780, ibid.

88. Browne et al., *Archives of Maryland*, 41:377, 45:662, 48:72, 121, 138, 140, 204, 207.

89. Döhla, "Marschroute," 538.

90. Popp, "Geschichte," 230–32. For similar comments, see Döhla, "Marschroute," 475–76. See also McIlwaine, *Journals*, 3:312, for information on a lack of guards in Winchester in March 1781.

91. Asa Douglas, Barrington, to the Massachusetts Council, January 1, 1778, PFC, ser. 7E, item 85, ser. I.

92. "Resolves of Congress Regarding Prisoners of War," January 13, 1780, PCC, item 183, 2–16; Springer, *America's Captives*, 26.

93. "An Act for the Disposing of Such Prisoners as Have Been or Hereafter May Be Taken by the Land or Sea Forces of This State," March 18, 1780, PCC, item 74, 1–4.

94. Springer, *America's Captives*, 15.

95. War Office to Thomas Bradford, October 26, 1779, Bradford Papers, box 22, folder 8.

96. Timothy Pickering, War Office, to Thomas Bradford, October 6, 1779, ibid., folder 7.

97. See, for instance, the letters of October 23 and 25, 1779, ibid., folder 8.

98. John Beatty to Thomas Bradford, November 4, 1779, ibid., folder 9. Beatty succeeded Elias Boudinot in this office. In 1780, Beatty was succeeded by Abraham Skinner. See "Board of War," March 31, 1780, PCC, item 147, vol. 4, 297.

99. Secretary at War Lincoln had sent out orders for the removal of German prisoners of war from Winchester to Frederick on December 12, 1781. He hoped that the militia would turn out "with spirit" because of the "idea of being freed from the trouble of guarding them" in the future. Benjamin Lincoln to the County Lieutenants of Frederick, Va., December 12, 1781, in *CVSP*, 2:653. Holmes also operated a merchandise store in Winchester that imported dry

goods and circulated them to regional consumers and smaller retail stores in the region. Hofstra and Mitchell, "Town and Country," 641.

100. Colonel Joseph Holmes to Colonel William Davies, January 6, 1782, in *CVSP*, 3:9.

101. Inhabitants of Winchester to Congress, PCC, item 149, vol. 1, 133. See also Dixon, "Divided Authority," 184.

102. Lt. Colonel North to Benjamin Lincoln, January 6, 1782, PCC, item 149, vol. 1, 129.

103. Popp, "Geschichte," 234.

104. Döhla, "Marschroute," 492.

105. Benjamin Lincoln to Congress, January 16, 1782, PCC, item 149, vol. 1, 121.

106. Governor Harrison to Colonel John Smith, in McIlwaine, *Official Letters*, 3:146.

107. In exchange for Havana, Cuba, Spain had ceded Florida to the British in the Treaty of Paris (1763). Yet it had already gained all of French Louisiana west of the Mississippi in the Treaty of Fontainebleau (1762).

108. Burgoyne, *Third English-Waldeck Regiment*, 106.

109. On these events, see Reid, "Waldeckische Truppen."

110. Burgoyne, *Third English-Waldeck Regiment*, 111. Among these captives were forty-nine common soldiers.

111. This would result in a total of 264 or 265 Waldeck prisoners at the end of September 1779. These numbers, however, might be inaccurate. Colonel von Hanxleden, for instance, reported a total of only 238 prisoners of war for 1779, including 206 common soldiers. Burgoyne listed a total of 221 Waldeck prisoners of war for 1779 after extensive research in various records. It is not entirely clear whether the men captured on the Amite River and at Fort Bute were included in these lists and calculations. "Return of December 7, 1779," StA Marburg, Best. 118a, Nr. 974, fol. 112; Burgoyne, *Third English-Waldeck Regiment*, 117–23, 135.

112. *HETRINA*, 5:7–10. It is not entirely clear whether all remaining prisoners of war were indeed exchanged in 1782. Burgoyne lists several deserters in Havana for March and April of that year. Burgoyne, *Third English-Waldeck Regiment*, 224.

113. "Report from Pensacola," March 20, 1779, StA Marburg, Best. 118a, Nr. 974, fol. 87v; "Return," March 19, 1779, ibid., fol. 89.

114. Burgoyne, *Third English-Waldeck Regiment*, 242.

115. Only two diaries have survived from this unit, the journals of Field Surgeon Philip Waldeck and Corporal Steuernagel. Burgoyne, *Eighteenth Century America*; M. Burgoyne, *Hessian Letters*.

116. "Schreiben des Waldeckschen Feldpredigers, Hrn [Philip] Waldeck, aus Pensacola in Westflorida, 18. März 1779," in Schlözer, *Briefwechsel*, vol. 5, issue 26, Nr. 16. The German term used here is *Spanerde*, "humus."

117. "Report from Pensacola," May 8, 1779, StA Marburg, Best. 118a, Nr. 974, fol. 93.

118. Lord George Germain to General Clinton, July 7, 1780, PRO CO 5/100, fol. 3.

119. "Report and Return from Pensacola," November 11, 1779," StA Marburg, Best. 118a, Nr. 974, fols. 100–102; *HETRINA*, 5:7–10.

120. "Report from Pensacola," November 6, 1779, StA Marburg, Best. 118a, Nr. 974, fols. 100–101; "Return," November 6, 1779," ibid., fol. 102; Colonel von Hanxleden to Court Secretary Frensdorff, November 6, 1779, ibid., fol. 104; Colonel von Hanxleden to Friedrich Karl August, December 7, 1779, ibid., fols. 108v–109.

121. Colonel von Haxleden to Court Secretary Frensdorff, December 7, 1779, ibid., fols. 115–17; "Report from Pensacola," December 22, 1779, ibid., fol. 120v; "Report from Pensacola," February 16, 1780, ibid., fol. 130v; "Report from Fort George," June 7, 1780, ibid., fols. 132–32v.

122. "Report from Fort George," August 4, 1780, ibid., fols. 148–49; "Return," July 18, 1780, ibid., fol. 143; "Return," August 4, 1780, ibid., fol. 152.

123. Burgoyne, *Third English-Waldeck Regiment*, 188–91.

124. "Report from Fort George," October 30, 1780, StA Marburg, Best. 118a, Nr. 974, fol. 159.

125. Lowell, *Hessians*, 253.

126. Lieutenant Colonel Horn to Friedrich Karl August, May 20, 1781, StA Marburg, Best. 118a, Nr. 975, vol. 1, fols. 34–35v.

127. Lt. Andreas Brumhard to his uncle from New Orleans, May 22, 1780, ibid., Nr. 972, vol. 1, fols. 143–44v. Brumhard's uncle was Court Secretary Frensdorff.

128. "Return of the Waldeck Rgt., Prisoners, Killed and Wounded" (probably December 15, 1779), ibid., fol. 177.

129. Lt. Karl Heinrich Strubberg to Court Secretary Frensdorff from Kingston, Jamaica, June 28, 1781, ibid., vol. 2, fols. 173–74v.

130. Lt. Andreas Brumhard to his uncle from Kingston, Jamaica, June 30, 1781, ibid., fols. 176–76v; Lt. Karl Heinrich Strubberg to Friedrich Karl August, June 30, 1781, ibid., fol. 178.

131. Lt. Karl Heinrich Strubberg to Court Secretary Frensdorff, Jamaica, September 4, 1781, ibid., fols. 182v–83v.

132. Lt. Karl Heinrich Strubberg to Court Secretary Frensdorff, Jamaica, October 15, 1781, ibid., fols. 191–92. See also Strubberg's and Brumhard's letter of November 16, 1781, from Jamaica and January 4, 1782, from New York, ibid., fols. 195–97.

133. As stated above, Burgoyne lists an additional twenty-six deserters in Cuba for March and April 1782; *Third English-Waldeck Regiment*, 224.

134. Lt. Andreas Brumhard to his uncle from New York, June 18, 1782, StA Marburg, Best. 118a, Nr. 972, vol. 2, fol. 247v.

135. "Return of the Prisoners in Cuba," January 5, 1782, ibid., vol. 2, fol. 213; "Return of the Prisoners Still in Havana," January 6, 1782, ibid., fol. 200.

136. Carp, "Origins," 369. See also Jillson and Wilson, *Congressional Dynamics*, 111.

137. In Congress, this loosely organized group included northerners such as Alexander Hamilton, James Wilson, Thomas Smith, Samuel Atlee, Joseph Montgomery, George Clymer, and Richard Peters. Southern nationalists in Congress were James Madison, Daniel Carroll, and Hugh Williamson. Robert Morris was appointed superintendent of finance on February 20, 1781. The Articles of Confederation, adopted in 1777, were finally ratified in 1781. Jillson and Wilson, *Congressional Dynamics*, 242–45.

138. Ibid., 249.

139. Ward, *Department of War*, 11; "Diary," December 5, 1781, *Papers RM*, 3:332–33.

140. Barton, " Revolutionary Prisoners," 30.

141. *JCC*, 16:47–52.

142. Casino, "Elizabethtown."

143. "Diary," May 1, 1782, *Papers RM*, 5:30. Present were Benjamin Lincoln, Robert Livingston (secretary of foreign affairs), Charles Thomson (secretary of Congress), General Henry Knox, and Gouverneur Morris (Robert Morris's assistant and, together with Knox, negotiator at Elizabethtown).

144. Springer, *America's Captives*, 36. See also George Washington to Moses Rawlings, December 12, 1781, in Fitzpatrick and Matteson, *Writings of George Washington*, 23:383–84.

145. Present at the May 6 meeting were Robert Morris, Elias Boudinot (former commissary general of prisoners), Samuel Atlee (colonel in the army and brother of William A. Atlee, commissary of prisoners in Lancaster), John Rutledge (former governor of South Carolina), Benjamin Lincoln, Gouverneur Morris, and Brigadier General Moses Hazen (commander of a Continental regiment stationed in Lancaster).

146. "Diary," May 6, 1782, *Papers RM*, 5:116–17; "Diary," July 10, 1782, ibid., 5:557; *JCC*, 22:274–76. For the congressional resolve of June 5, 1782, following this report and recommendations, see *JCC*, 22:316–17. The bounty was $8, and the recruits could be counted against the state quotas. All new German recruits would be under General Washington's control.

147. "Report of Committee on Prisoners," May 15, 1782, PCC, item 28, 67–68.

148. *JCC*, 22:321, 372–73. See also Springer, *America's Captives*, 37.

149. Ibid., 38.

150. *JCC*, 22:343–47.

151. "Draft for Resolve," July 3, 1782, PCC, item 149, vol. 1, 477; *JCC*, 22:372–73.

152. *JCC*, 22:373–74. See also Springer, *America's Captives*, 38.

153. Jillson and Wilson, *Congressional Dynamics*, 240–54; Carp, "Origins," 365–69, 380–89. Carp also noted that America's "localistic perspective" was simply too powerful to be overcome.

154. *JCC*, 22:316–18.

155. George Washington to Benjamin Lincoln, April 27, 1782, PCC, item 149, vol. 1, 309–12. Congress, however, as the resolves of June 5, 1782, showed, did not follow Washington's suggestions. German recruits in the Continental Army would be added to state quotas. See also "Diary," May 1, 1782, *Papers RM*, 5:91n. One reason for this decision might have been the opposition of such delegates as Arthur Middleton of South Carolina. His notes for a speech against Washington's proposal stated: "With power to hire foreign Troops—this Democracy by rotation might be converted into perpetual Aristocracy." "Notes for Speech in Congress, Arthur Middleton," May 15?, 1782, *LDC*, 18:518. Conservative delegates from the Deep South such as Middleton knew that the nationalists' plans pointed toward a centralized government. In 1782 and 1783, they often voted together with New England delegates against the nationalists. See also Jillson and Wilson, *Congressional Dynamics*, 200, 244–46.

156. Preprinted discharges for German prisoners of war, discussed and authorized by James Wilson, Robert Morris, and Benjamin Lincoln, stated: "Know all

men . . . that _____ of _____ Regiment _____ a native of Germany and late a prisoner of war to the United States of America, has signified a Desire to become a free Citizen of the said States." The soldiers then had to swear: "I the above-named _____ do hereby solemnly swear and declare, that I will bear faith and true Allegiance to the United States of America, and that I will demean myself as a good Subject of the same, So help me god!" "Diary," July 11, 1782, *Papers RM*, 5:562–63; "Instructions of Robert Morris and Benjamin Lincoln on the Liberation of German Prisoners," ibid., 5:563; "Proposals to German Prisoners at Reading," July 30, 1782, BHQ, no. 5159.

157. See Ober, "Classical Greek Times," 13; Stacey, "Age of Chivalry," 37; Parker, "Early Modern Europe," 55; Hohrath, "'In Cartellen,'" 163–69.

158. See also chap. 4 on these issues.

159. Foster, *Captors' Narrative*, 2, 14–18; Haefeli, "Ransoming New England Captives," 113–27; Steele, "Surrendering Rites," 142–45; Steele, "When Worlds Collide," 24.

160. To the prisoners in Reading, Morris sent a close ally from the newly established Marine Department, James Read. "Diary," July 27, 1782, *Papers RM*, 6:31; "Diary," August 12, 1782, ibid., 6:168; "Instructions of Morris and Lincoln," ibid., 5:563n.

161. On October 23, 1776, Congress had resolved that Hazen's regiment was to be "recruited to its full complement in any of the thirteen United States and that this regiment cannot be said to belong to any particular state." *JCC*, 6:900. See also ibid., 4:78; Commissioners to Canada to Moses Hazen, May 6, 1776, *LDC*, 3:630n.

162. See, for instance, "Recall of Prisoners Farmed Out," June 7, 1782, Bradford Papers, box 24, folder 10.

163. The reference to the "Turkish nation" almost certainly alluded to the mistreatment, enslavement, and mass killings of enemy fighters in the wars of the Habsburg and Holy Roman Empires with the Ottoman Empire. On the fate of prisoners of war in these conflicts, see Kroener, "Der Soldat als Ware," 286–87.

164. "Abschrift des Brief der Gefangenen aus Philadelphia," July 28, 1782, Relationes Loßberg, fols. 39–40. See also PRO CO 5/107, fols. 238–44v.

165. Bense, "Marschroute," fols. 15v–16. For certificates for a number of German indentured prisoners from the former Convention Army, see, for instance, MNR, nos. 31716, 31731, 31734, 31741, 31744, 31748, 31751.

166. "Ordres aus dem engl. Hauptquartier," StA Marburg, Best. 4h, Nr. 3153, fols. 140–42. See also BHQ, nos. 6705, 9722. For a summary of Vaupel's and other prisoners' reports, see General von Loßberg to Friedrich II, January 17, 1783, Relationes Loßberg, fols. 91–92v.

167. "A Return of Prisoners Received and Discharged, Philadelphia," November 1, 1781–July 11, 1782, Bradford Papers, box 26, oversized folder 6. On Mount Hope and the prisoners there, see Bodle and Schenck, "John Jacob Faesch"; Miles, "Iron Master"; Schwalm, "Composite List." A list of the thirty-five prisoner-laborers at Mount Hope can be put together through the reports and letters in Relationes Loßberg; PRO T 38/814, pt. 3, pos. 8; and BHQ, nos. 7174, 8236, 9722. See also "Return of the German Prisoners," Bradford Papers, box 26, folder 8; and the respective entries in *HETRINA*, vols. 4 and 6.

168. "Return of Prisoners Received and Discharged," Bradford Papers, box 26, oversized folder 6; "Return of the German Prisoners," ibid., folder 8.

169. Jacob Faesch to Samuel Hodgdon, November 29, 1782, MNR, no. 21734; BHQ, no. 7920.

170. BHQ, no. 7174. The prisoners of war made good money at Faesch's ironworks. They received 3 shillings 6 pence in Pennsylvania currency for a cord of wood and 4 shillings 5 pence per day for other labor. Ibid., no. 8236.

171. Ibid., nos. 7174, 7920.

172. A total of $2,640 for thirty-three soldiers is recorded in Morris's accounts. Robert Morris to Congress, May 15, 1783, PCC, item 137, vol. 2, 432–39; "Certificate," March 13, 1783, MNR, no. 31713.

173. BHQ, no. 7920.

174. "Receipt for Two German Prisoners," March 11, 1783, MNR, no. 20719.

175. "Relationes des hochfürstl. Heßischen Corps," StA Marburg, Best. 4h, Nr. 3105, fols. 150–51v; BHQ, no. 7174. Only the English version of this letter could be found.

176. BHQ, nos. 8236, 9722. Peter eventually paid 75 Spanish dollars in ransom on his own.

177. *JCC*, 24:243.

178. General von Loßberg to Friedrich II, May 16, 1783, Relationes Loßberg, fol. 125.

179. In the most basic terms, indentured servants had a debt, most often a ship passage, paid by another person in exchange for their labor for a specified period, usually between three and seven years. See, for instance, Eltis, *Coerced and Free Migration*; Palmer, *Worlds of Unfree Labour*; Salinger, *"To Serve."*

180. Jacob Faesch to Samuel Hodgdon, May 16, 1783, MNR, no. 21669.

181. For a copy of Faesch's announcement, see General von Loßberg to Friedrich II, June 16, 1783, Relationes Loßberg, fol. 151.

182. On this mission, see General von Loßberg to Friedrich II, July 12, 1783, ibid., fols. 158–58v; "Relationes des hochfürstl. Heßischen Corps," StA Marburg, Best. 4h, Nr. 3105, fol. 159.

183. General von Loßberg to Friedrich II, July 24, 1783, Relationes Loßberg, fols. 171–72.

184. Quoted in Uhlendorf, *Revolution*, 555, 572–74.

185. BHQ, no. 8120; General von Loßberg to Friedrich II, July 12, 1783, Relationes Loßberg, fol. 159.

186. Friedrich II to General von Loßberg, September 5, 1783, Relationes Loßberg, fol. 166; Friedrich II to General von Loßberg, October 9, 1783, ibid., fol. 177.

187. PRO T 38/814, pt. 3, pos. 8.

188. General von Loßberg to Friedrich II, August 10, 1783, Relationes Loßberg, fol. 173.

189. The sources often contradict each other or provide varying numbers. As best as can be ascertained from the sources, Faesch hired thirty-five German prisoners of war in April 1782. He returned two of them on March 11, 1783. "Receipt for Two German Prisoners," March 11, 1783, MNR, no. 20719. Five of the men were apparently able to pay their own ransom, and twenty-four were redeemed by Lieutenant Ungar, on order of General von Loßberg. PRO T 38/814, pt. 3, pos. 8; BHQ, no. 8236. However, one of these men, Heinrich Schultheis, also appears to have paid his own ransom. According to Loßberg's report on August 10, 1783, only twenty-two men returned from Mount Hope. Relationes Loßberg,

fol. 173. This means that between four and six men from the group at Mount Hope did not return to British lines. Faesch, however, also wrote on March 13, 1783, that one of his German prisoners, probably Corporal Röder, had successfully escaped. MNR, no. 21667. On August 13, 1783, he also told Samuel Hodgdon, a friend and the deputy commissary general for military stores, that six of his prisoner-laborers had chosen to stay. Ibid., no. 21642. See also Bodle and Schenck, "John Jacob Faesch," 81, 84n.

190. Döhla, "Marschroute," 513–14.

191. Prechtel, "Beschreibung," 568.

192. Döhla, "Marschroute," 530–31. Döhla also noted here that German prisoners of war who were married to American women were allowed to go free upon payment of a ransom.

193. Ibid., 534. On these recruits, see also Prechtel, "Beschreibung," 580.

194. Döhla, "Marschroute," 533.

195. Ibid.

196. Prechtel, "Beschreibung," 585; Döhla, "Marschroute," 540.

197. Obrist Lieutenant von Scheer to General von Loßberg, May 28, 1783, Relationes Loßberg, fols. 137–38.

198. Nourse, "Accounts of Receipts and Expenditures," January 1, 1782–June 30, 1783, PCC, item 137, vol. 2, 635–36, and vol. 3, 337.

199. United States Department of the Treasury, *Statements of Receipts and Expenditures*, 7. Neither number gives information about how many soldiers actually served as indentured servants, paid the ransom on their own, or were recruited.

200. "Namentliches Verzeichnis," NdsStA Wf, 38B Alt 260, fol. 92.

201. PRO HCA 32/453/17.

202. Bense also mentions the men from the *South Carolina*: "Some of our [soldiers] enlisted on a privateer which was captured at once after leaving Philadelphia and was brought to New York." "Marschroute," fol. 16.

203. "Ordres aus dem engl. Hauptquartier," StA Marburg, Best. 4h, Nr. 3153, fols. 142–42v. On the enlistment of German prisoners on this frigate, see "Motion by David Ramsay," October 2, 1782, PCC, item 36, vol. 2, 389; *JCC*, 23:632, 703; BHQ, no. 5899. See also the report of one of the officers who interrogated the soldiers in Kapitain von Eschwege to Wilhelm IX, January 14, 1783, StA Marburg, Best. 4h, Nr. 3110, fols. 78–79v.

204. The *Pennsylvania Gazette* on January 1, 1783, printed a British report that complained that German prisoners were compelled to sign up with Captain John Joyner of the *South Carolina* to avoid being "sold by the rebels."

205. Christian Karl von Eschwege to William IX of Hessen-Kassel, January 14, 1783, StA Marburg, Best. 4h, Nr. 3110, fols. 78–79v.

206. Lewis, *Neptune's Militia*, 91–94.

11. Release and Return

1. General Washington to General Carleton, April 21, 1783, PRO CO 5/109, fols. 275–77.

2. Prechtel, "Beschreibung," 613–15.

3. Döhla, "Marschroute," 569.

4. Popp, "Geschichte," 252–59.

5. Döhla, "Marschroute," 571–73.

6. "List of Hessian Prisoners," January 6–7, 1777, PFC, ser. 9, vol. 190; "A List of Hessian & Waldeck Prisoners of War Recd. July 1778 from Wm Atlee Esq Lancaster & Sent Forwards to be exchanged," HSP, AM 620; "List of Hessian & Waldeck Prisoners of War Sent from Lancaster July 13 Recd in Philad July," ibid.; "List of Hessian & Waldeck Prisoners of War Sent from Lancaster July 29 & Recd," ibid.; "Monatliche Listen, Regiment Rall," October 1783, StA Marburg, Best. 15, Nr. 252; Kirchenbuch Fürstenhagen, 1754, Landeskirchliches Archiv Kassel.

7. Döhla, "Marschroute," 577. It is possible that Döhla was speaking here about Colonel Hazen's regiment, which recruited extensively among German prisoners of war and was stationed for some time in Lancaster.

8. Ibid., 579.

9. Ibid., 581.

10. Ibid., 585–86.

11. Colonel Voit von Salzburg to Adjutant General von Schlammersdorf, May 20, 1783, HAV, 503–504.

12. On June 29, 1783, Döhla wrote from Long Island, back from captivity, "I started to write for Adjutant von Streit. I had to write three regimental rosters, one for Colonel von Seybothen, one for Major Beust, and one for [Streit]." Döhla, "Marschroute," 591.

13. Ibid., 457.

14. Ibid., 486.

15. For an example of a successful escape, see Colonel Voit von Salzburg to Margrave Karl Alexander, September 12, 1782, HAV, fols. 445–47, where Voit von Salzburg reports that six common soldiers under leadership of Corporal Hilpert ran away from Frederick and arrived safely in New York.

16. Döhla, "Marschroute," 485, 502 (and, similarly, 517–18); Städtler, *Die Ansbach-Bayreuther Truppen*, 168.

17. Döhla, "Marschroute," 511–12.

18. This number corresponds with the number of common soldiers given in the official muster rolls and rosters as preserved in PRO T38/812, no. 2. Döhla probably prepared at least some of these lists for his company and regiment.

19. "Pro Memoria zur Desertion und Vermögen der Deserteure und Invalidenkasse vom Aug. 1786," StadtA Ansbach, AM 995.

20. Döhla, "Marschroute," 568.

21. See PRO T38/812, no. 2. Each list shows changes in a company over a six-month period, usually from December (Christmas) until June and from July to December.

22. "Liste der im Month Martii 1777 nach America abmarchirten Hochfürstl. Brandenburgischen Trouppen, und der bis 1782 incl. nachgesandten Recouten, ingleichen der inzwischen abgegangenen Mannschaften, dann wie solche mit den 19ten Nov: effective bestanden," NYPL, Bancroft Collection, no. 75.

23. For slightly different numbers—a total of 2,386 soldiers—from Erhard Städtler, see table 1.

24. Sikora, *Disziplin und Desertion*, 260.

25. For details, see chap. 8.

26. Huck, "Soldaten gegen Nordamerika," 204.

27. Ibid., 233–34; "Namentliches Verzeichnis," NdsStA Wf, 38B Alt 260.

28. Huck, "Soldaten gegen Nordamerika," 234–35.

29. Ibid., 254–56.

30. Annual desertion rates differ from average desertion rates. The latter is the total number of soldiers who deserted in a unit, with no regard to time frame; the former is the number of soldiers who deserted over the course of a year. Sikora, "Das 18. Jahrhundert," 90.

31. Ingrao, *Hessian Mercenary State*, 158.

32. Ingrao took his numbers from a random sample of 1,465 soldiers selected from the *HETRINA*. Ibid., 159.

33. Atwood, *Hessians*, 256. Taking into account only Atwood's 18,970 men who served in North America, Ingrao's 2,949 soldiers who deserted would result in a desertion rate of 15.5 percent.

34. "Rapport des Regiments von Bose," Relationes Loßberg, fols. 133–34. Not all 365 soldiers stayed in captivity; 13 men (9 common soldiers) went to New York on parole.

35. In this regiment, 33 soldiers (9 percent) died between October 19, 1781, and May 28, 1783; a vast majority of those troops, 30 men, were common soldiers.

36. On this unit, see also Hildebrand, "Das Regiment Erbprinz."

37. "Rapport Regiment Erbprinz," May 28, 1783, Relationes Loßberg, fols. 135–36v.

38. Sikora, "Desertion," 119.

39. Miles, *Hessians*, ii–iii, 1–2.

40. Ibid., 37–38.

41. Ibid., 5–6.

42. Kiddoo, "'Of Revolutionary Memory.'" Four of these 182 men died before the war was over, and one Ansbach-Bayreuth officer, who had married a woman from Lancaster, Catherine Schenkmayer, eventually returned home with the troops. An important source for this compilation was the diary of Jacob Engelbrecht, the son of Johann Engelbrecht, a private in the Regiment von Seybothen who deserted on May 13, 1783—just as the former captives had left Frederick on their march to New York. Jacob was a tailor and later became the mayor of Frederick. Beginning in 1818, at the age of twenty-one, he started recording and commenting on events and people in his hometown. The memory of his father, it seems, never left him. On May 12, 1853, he notes in the diary: "This day it is 70 years that the German Troops left Frederick for Germany—those who had been taken prisoners at Yorktown, Va., at the surrender of Lord Cornwallis." Quoted in ibid., 46.

43. From the Regiment Erbprinz, 47 men were located; from the Regiment von Bose, 36 men; from both Ansbach-Bayreuth regiments, 47 men; from Braunschweig-Wolfenbüttel, 22 men; from Hessen-Hanau, 15 men; from other German, *Jäger*, and artillery units, 15 men. Ibid., 44.

44. Ibid., 46, 69; Städtler, *Die Ansbach-Bayreuther Truppen*, 167.

45. See chap. 10.

46. Kiddoo, "'Of Revolutionary Memory,'" 48, 71.

47. Ibid., 73.

48. See chap. 1.

49. Ibid., 63.

50. "Verabschiedung unentbehrlicher," StadtA Bayreuth, Nr. 23285; Rainsford, "Transactions," 417. According to a letter from Lord Barrington in the British War Office to General Howe, the deserters from Ochsenfurt who were returned to the troops were Peter Nitzell, Johann Ch. Dorrer, Johannes Kolb,

Johann Maiar, Johann Georg Greenbeg, Johann [Hudricke/Heydenreich?], and Johann Tizemann. Lord Barrington to General Howe, June 6, 1777, BHQ, no. 572.

51. Margrave Karl Alexander to Colonel Voit von Salzburg, January 4, 1783, HAV, fols. 475–76.

52. Adjutant General von Schlammersdorf to Colonel Voit von Salzburg, January 9, 1783, ibid., fol. 481. Voit von Salzburg blamed desertions among his captured troops, before or after May 1783, entirely on the American revolutionaries who had offered the former prisoners in Frederick "citizenship in the United States." Colonel Voit von Salzburg to Margrave Karl Alexander, June 1, 1783, ibid., fols. 506–508.

53. Merz, *Hessians*, xi.

54. Döhla, "Marschroute," 598–99.

55. Prechtel, "Beschreibung," 632.

56. Hall, *Heritage Remembered*, 16–27.

57. Ibid., 20–21.

58. The letters were preserved by Hetterich and his descendants. They are now in the Nova Scotia Archives in Halifax and were used by E. Foster Hall for *Heritage Remembered*. Hetterich's parents, Gerda and Leonhard, may have taken advantage of the special mail service that was established by Margrave Karl Alexander in 1777 when his men left for North America; see chap. 1.

59. In an earlier letter, Hetterich had told his family about a "sweetheart," probably his future wife, Eleanor. The couple had two daughters, Elizabeth and Eleanor.

60. The family home had burned down in 1782 or 1783 and had to be rebuilt. Ibid., 19.

61. Ibid., 24.

62. In 1788, Christian von Molitor, an Ansbach-Bayreuth officer who also had stayed behind, told Conrad Hetterich in a letter that he had met "more than twelve discharged men from our regiment" in New York, and "all have their good income." Ibid., 26.

63. Adjutant General von Schlammersdorf to Voit von Salzburg, March 18, 1782, HAV, 399–402; Margrave Karl Alexander to Voit von Salzburg, March 28, 1782, ibid., 410–11.

64. "Memorial from Christian von Molitor," August 10, 1783, BHQ, no. 8684. See nos. 8558 and 8497 for the discharge and land petitions of Field Surgeon Friedrich Arnold and Field Chaplain Wagner.

65. General Carleton to Governor Parr, Nova Scotia, July 20, 1783, ibid., no. 8485; General Carleton to Governor Parr, Nova Scotia, August 6, 1783, ibid., no. 8651–52.

66. Merz, *Hessians*, 156–58.

67. Hall, *Heritage Remembered*, 26.

68. Merz, *Hessians*, 156–58.

69. BHQ, no. 8876.

70. "General Abstract of Men, Women, & Children on the New Townships on the River St. Laurence, Beginning at Nr. 1. Lake St. Francis and Running Upwards," DLAR, film 423, reel 85, no. 21828, 40; "Return of the Disbanded Men from the German Troops Settled in the Township Nr. 5, Bay of Quinte," October 4, 1784, ibid., 78.

71. Atwood, *Hessians*, 256; Merz, *Hessians*, 1–2.

72. Merz, *Hessians*, xii.

73. Döhla, "Marschroute," 640, 650, 656.

74. Ibid., 680–82, 687–88.

75. Ibid., 683–84.

76. Ibid., 689–90.

77. Ibid., 685.

78. Ibid., 708–709.

79. Margaretha Barbara Meyer, Gerabronn, to Carl Wilhelm Friedrich Meyer, Ansbach, November 23, 1783, in Meyer, "Tagebucheinträge."

80. On Meyer and his service after the American War of Independence, see Meyer, *Carl Wilhelm Friedrich Meyer*, 145–221.

81. In 1803, following the *Reichsdeputationshauptschluß* (German mediatization), the Landgraviate of Hessen-Kassel became the Electorate of Hesse. For designations such as "old American," used by the veterans themselves and obviously hinting at the importance and meaning of this war for their life and personality, see "Bewilligte Pensionen," StA Marburg, Best. 12c, Nr. 181. Many petitions listed here were simply signed *"Ein alter Amerikaner"*—"An old American." Veteran officers or their widows could not receive pensions.

82. "Auszug aus dem Protokoll des Kriegsministerium," March 26, 1831, StA Marburg, Best. 12a, Nr. 489; "Antwort des Kriegs-Ministeriums auf Anfrage der Ständeversammllung in Kassel zu Pensionsbestimmungen und der Vorgang vom 10. Juni 1831," ibid. The Staatsministerium (State Ministry) decided on October 19, 1831, that all veterans older than 80—those men were 25 years old in 1776—and anyone who had served during the entire war were to receive 3 *Thaler*. Those who were at least 78 years old but not yet 80 received between 2½ *Thaler* (common soldiers, not wounded) and 3 *Thaler* (noncommissioned officers). Those younger than 78 years received between 2 *Thaler* (common soldiers, not wounded) and 2⅔ *Thaler* (noncommissioned officers). "Sitzung des Staats-Ministeriums unter Vorsitz des Kurprinzen Friedrich Wilhelm," October 19, 1831, ibid.

83. The State Ministry in Hesse decided on December 5, 1831, that all widows were eligible for pensions, even those who had married veterans only after the payments were announced. Payments were dependent only on the level of need, not the date or place of the marriage. Thus a number of very old veterans were suddenly considered very desirable husbands. "Vorbereitende Sitzung des Staatsministeriums," December 5, 1831, ibid.

84. "Bericht des provisorischen Vorstandes des Kriegs-Ministeriums, General-Major Friedrich Wilhelm von Loßberg," June 6, 1831, ibid.

85. "Bericht des provisorischen Vorstandes des Kriegs-Ministeriums," June 12, 1831, ibid.

86. "Namenslisten von noch lebenden Teilnehmern," StA Marburg, Best. 12a, Nr. 490.

87. "Bewilligte Pensionen," StA Marburg, Best. 12c, Nr. 181; "Namenslisten," Best. 12a, Nr. 490. Later, veterans of the Dutch war in the 1780s—Hessen-Kassel and Ansbach-Bayreuth again sent subsidy troops—were also granted pensions.

88. "Beschluß des Kriegsministeriums unter von Loßberg," April 19, 1831, StA Marburg, Best. 12b, Nr. 177.

89. "Bewilligte Pensionen," StA Marburg, Best. 12c, Nr. 181.

90. Ibid. Johannes Battenberg's pension was granted.
91. "Namenslisten," StA Marburg, Best. 12a, Nr. 490. The Regiment von Ange-lelly was the old Regiment Rall, captured at Trenton in 1776.
92. "Bewilligte Pensionen," StA Marburg, Best. 12c, Nr. 181.
93. On the *Landschaft* in Brandenburg-Kulmbach, see chap. 2.
94. "Acta die Bestimmungen über die Fränkische Invaliden Cassa und deren Rechnungswesen betr.," GStA PK, II. HA., Nr. 36; "Acta, die im Bayreuthsch. Fürstenthum etablierte Wohltätigkeits- oder Invaliden Cassa betr.," ibid., Nr. 37.
95. "Abrechnung der beiden Invalidenkassen in Ansbach und Bayreuth," December 30, 1796, ibid., Nr. 36; "Rechnungsabschluss über Einnahmen und Ausgaben der Kgl. Pr. Bayr. Militär-Invaliden-Cassa vom 1. Juni 1793 bis März 1794," ibid., Nr. 37. On August 26, 1798, the two *Cassa* merged.
96. Stadt- und Policeydirektor Schnitzlein to Geh. Legationsrath Nagler, April 21, 1806, GStA PK, I. HA. Rep. 44C, Nr. 443.
97. "Gesuch einiger Soldaten," April 24, 1806, ibid.
98. Stadt- und Policeydirektor Schnitzlein to Immediatskommission, April 26, 1806, ibid.
99. Immediatskommission to Bayreuther Kammer, April 29, 1806, ibid.
100. Bayreuther Kammer to Immediatskommission, May 5, 1806, ibid.
101. Immediatskommission to Ansbacher Kammer, Erster Senat der Kriegs- und Domainen Kammer, May 17, 1806, ibid.
102. Umgelds-Controlleur Riss to Geh. Legationsrath Nagler, May 21, 1806, ibid.

Epilogue

1. "Instructions to Commissioners," October 29, 1783, PCC, item 116, 1–5; "Resolves by Congress on Treaties of Amity and Commerce," May 7, 1784, ibid., 5–13. This is the letter book kept by the joint commissioners Adams, Franklin, and Jefferson. For the original documents, see PCC, item 86.
2. "Depesche, Graf von der Goltz," December 2, 1784, GStA PK, I. HA. Rep. 11, Nr. 21a 1.5. (Amerika), fols. 1–1v. The first contacts between Prussia and the American revolutionaries were established in 1776. In 1777, Silas Deane and Benjamin Franklin already wanted to send a plenipotentiary to Berlin.
3. "Depesche, Baron von Thulemeier," February 20, 1784, ibid., fol. 2v.
4. Gebhard Werner von der Schulenburg to Departement der Auswärtigen Angelegenheiten, March 8, 1784, ibid., fols. 5–6v; "Traité d'amitié et de Commerce conclu entre S. M. le Roi de Suede et les Etats Unis de l'Amerique," ibid., fols. 8–12v.
5. "Classification of Treaty Provisions," *TJP*, 7:476.
6. "Outline," ibid., 7:478.
7. "Draft of a Model Treaty," ibid., 7:486, art. 23.
8. Ibid., 7:486–87, art. 24.
9. Ibid., 7:490, n. 36.
10. For the draft of this treaty, see Baron von Thulemeier to Departement der Auswärtigen Angelegenheiten, December 10, 1784, GStA PK, I. HA. Rep. 11, Nr. 21a 1.5. (Amerika), fols. 36–48v.
11. American Commissioners to Baron von Thulemeier, November 10, 1784, *TJP*, 7:490–91.

12. Baron von Thulemeier to Departement der Auswärtigen Angelegenheiten, December 10, 1784, fol. 43. See also *TJP*, 7:491; "Memorandum," November 10, 1784, PCC, item 116, 103–104.

13. For a similar interpretation, see Ranlet, "In the Hands of the British," 731. For a different interpretation, stating that this treaty was less important for defining international law because it was only a bilateral agreement, see Oeter, "Die Entwicklung des Kriegsgefangenenrechts," 49. The same proposals for a treaty of amity and commerce were sent to Portugal and Tuscany at the end of 1784. "Second Report to Congress [American Commissioners]," December 15, 1784, PCC, item 116, 138–40.

14. John Adams to Baron von Thulemeier, February 13, 1785, *TJP*, 7:465; Thomas Jefferson to Elbridge Gerry, ibid., 8:142–44.

15. "A Treaty of Amity and Commerce between His Majesty the King of Prussia and the United States of America," GStA PK, I. HA. Rep. 11, Nr. 10. See also Nrn. 11 and 12. Schulenburg considered the treaty to have been "sorted out" in April 1784. Gebhard Werner von der Schulenburg to Departement der Auswärtigen Angelegenheiten, April 13, 1784, GStA PK, I. HA. Rep. 11, Nr. 21a 1.5. (Amerika), fol. 72v. In 1799, the treaty was renewed after brief negotiations. Ibid., Nr. 13.

16. Gebhard Werner von der Schulenburg to Friedrich II, December 24, 1784, GStA PK, I. HA. Rep. 11, Nr. 21a 1.5. (Amerika), fols. 61–61v. See also Baron von Thulemeier to American Commissioners, December 10, 1784, PCC, item 116, 142–44.

17. The Lieber Code of the U.S. Army during the Civil War stated that prisoners of war were not to be killed or punished for their killings in combat. Moreover, private individuals could not take prisoners of war, and all prisoners of war were captives of the government. Only the government could release prisoners, and they could not be ransomed by private persons. Finally, prisoners had to be fed "plain and wholesome food" and be "treated with humanity." Friedman, *Law of War*, 1:167–72.

18. Revolutionaries claimed that the British took American prisoners of war from England to the East Indies between 1776 and 1783. Warren, *History*, 3:35–36.

19. Thomas Jefferson to Jean Nicolas Démeunier, June 26, 1786, *TJP*, 10:61–62.

20. Friedman, *Law of War*, 1:172.

Appendix

1. The article was reprinted as "Return of the Hessian Troops Taken at Trenton," *Pennsylvania Gazette*, June 11, 1777. At the same time, Osborn's official return for the Regiments von Loßberg, von Knyphausen, and Rall in December 1776 listed 1,541 soldiers, including 1,253 rank and file. But this return also counted all soldiers from these units who had remained behind in New York and elsewhere for various reasons. "Raport des Troupes Hessoises en solde de Sa Majesté Brittannique du 28me de Decembre 1776," PRO CO 5/94, fol. 390. The official journal of the Regiment von Knyphausen stated that 200 soldiers escaped by crossing Assunpink Creek "in mortal danger." LB Ks, 4° Ms. Hass. Nr. 163, fols. 36–37. In a letter to Friedrich II, General von Heister spoke of 292 men who had escaped at Trenton. General von Heister to Landgrave Friedrich II, January 5,

1777, Relationes Heister, fol. 470v. Atwood, *Hessians*, 95, lists three officers and seventeen Hessian soldiers who were killed that day in battle.

2. Stephen Moylan to Robert Morris, December 27, 1776, PCC, item 78, vol. 15 (M), 155; General Washington to Robert Morris & Committee, December 27, 1776, PCC, item 152, vol. 3, 406. In this return, 32 common soldiers were listed for the Hessen-Kassel artillery, 206 for the Regiment von Loßberg, 258 for the Regiment von Knyphausen, and 244 for the Regiment Rall. Atwood, *Hessians*, 95, lists 919 prisoners from another return from General Washington, but this number also included Colonel Rall and Major von Dechow, who had both died of their wounds received during the battle. Taken together, the individual reports from the three Hessen-Kassel regiments listed 940 soldiers in American captivity for December 1776, including 787 rank and file. However, these numbers include the soldiers who were taken prisoner in the weeks and months before the Battle of Trenton. "Monatliche Listen des Füsilierregiments Loßberg," StA Marburg, Best. 15, Nr. 250, fol. 33; "Monatliche Listen vom Infanterie-Regiment von Knyphausen," ibid., Nr. 120, fol. 19.

3. General von Heister to Friedrich II, January 5, 1777, Relationes Heister, fol. 471.

4. "Summarischer Extract," ibid., fol. 530; "Ausführliche Relation," ibid., fols. 530–51. Barth, Doernemann, and Schwalm, "Trenton Prisoner List," is based on a copy of Müller's report in the Library of Congress and contains a transcription and translation of the lists.

5. Benjamin Lincoln, Bennington, to the Massachusetts Council, August 18, 1777, PFC, ser. 7E, item 85, 63–65.

6. Numerous problems, for instance, arise because the returns had different purposes. See the brief overview for three of the available returns in Knepper, "Convention Army," appendix 2, 273.

7. "State of the British, German, and American Army on October 17, 1777," PFC, ser. 7E, item 14; "Liste de la Force du Corps des Troupes Allemandes, le Jour de la Convention le 17me d'Octobre 1777," ibid. See also James Wilkinson's "Statement of Facts Relative to the Convention of Saratoga," n.d., PCC, item 57, roll 70, 106. It is not clear how many Canadians were counted in these returns.

8. "A General Return of His Britannic Majesty's Forces under Lieut. General Burgoyne Which Surrendered to the American Army Commanded by Major General Gates at Saratoga on the 17th October 1777," PFC, ser. 7E, item 14. It is not clear how many servants were included in these numbers. For the British, Wilkinson listed 2,139 rank and file. The regimental journal of the Regiment von Specht provided similar numbers. In this case, the German staff surrendered with 27 men and 5 officers, the dragoons with 33 men and 2 officers, the grenadiers with 262 men and 9 officers, the Battalion von Barner with 175 men and 6 officers, the Regiment von Rhetz with 402 men and 17 officers, the Regiment von Riedesel with 444 men and 13 officers, and the Regiment von Specht with 397 men and 17 officers. The Hessen-Hanau Regiment Erbprinz sent 509 men and 19 officers into revolutionary hands, and the artillery sent 72 men and 3 officers. Altogether, the return in Specht's journal accounted for 2,322 men and 91 officers who surrendered at Saratoga. "Auszug aus dem Journal von der Braunschweig'schen Brigade des Obersten Specht vom 17ten October bis 9ten Novbr: 1777," NYPL, Bancroft Collection, no. 77, fol. 205. This return, however, does not differentiate ranks beyond "officers" and "men." Subtracting the

number of sergeants, drummers, and fifers in Wilkinson's return from the total of 2,322 "men" in this return, we reach a total of 2,022 common German soldiers in revolutionary hands after Saratoga. For the Braunschweig-Wolfenbüttel contingent among General Burgoyne's men, as Stephan Huck found out in a report from General von Riedesel, 1,327 common soldiers surrendered on October 17, 1777. Including officers, musicians, drummers, staff, and servants, a total of 1,795 Braunschweig-Wolfenbüttel military personnel laid down their arms at Saratoga. Huck, "Soldaten gegen Nordamerika," 204.

9. Knepper, "Convention Army," appendix 2, 273. It remains unclear how many soldiers listed in these categories were included in the returns quoted above. Wilkinson's and Specht's returns seem to point toward 2,022 common German soldiers who surrendered at Saratoga. Burgoyne's return presented 1,792 common soldiers, but also listed 188 servants who may or may not have been included in other returns. Kingston's total of 2,198 seems not to have included any servants, only officers, noncommissioned officers, staff members, drummers and fifers, and surgeons.

10. "State of the Prisoners of War at Philadelphia," October 11, 1779, Bradford Papers, box 26, folder 6.

11. "Monatliche Listen vom Infanterie-Regiment von Knyphausen," StA Marburg, Best. 15, Nr. 120, fol. 17.

12. PRO CO 5/183–84, fols. 199, 202v.

13. Burgoyne, *Third English-Waldeck Regiment*, 106.

14. Ibid., 111.

15. "Return," December 7, 1779, StA Marburg, Best. 118a, Nr. 974, fol. 112; Burgoyne, *Third English-Waldeck Regiment*, 117–23, 135.

16. Unless specifically noted otherwise, these numbers include the soldiers captured at Gloucester.

17. "Return of the Killed, Wounded & Missing, September 28–October 19, 1781," PRO CO 5/103, fol. 291; "State of the Army under Cornwallis on October 18, 1781," ibid., fol. 293. This return was meant to ascertain the number of soldiers who were sick and fit for duty among Cornwallis's army. The siege and campaign had a devastating effect on the British and German troops. The two Ansbach-Bayreuth regiments, which had arrived in Virginia only a few months before, counted 118 sick soldiers among their rank and file in October 1781, with only 718 men fit for duty. The Hessen-Kassel Regiment Erbprinz had 135 sick and only 232 fit for duty.

18. "General Return of Prisoners Taken at Yorktown," October 19, 1781, MNR, no. 31603. According to these numbers, the two Ansbach-Bayreuth infantry regiments went into captivity with 909 common soldiers, the Hessen-Kassel Regiment Erbprinz with 367, the Hessen-Kassel Regiment von Bose with 274, and the Ansbach-Bayreuth and Hessian *Jäger* with 75. "General Return of Prisoners Surrendered at Yorktown," October 19, 1781, MNR, no. 31604. These numbers, however, also include several captured wagoners and other camp followers. According to this return, the Ansbach-Bayreuth regiments went into captivity with 948 common soldiers, the Regiment Erbprinz with 425, the Regiment von Bose with 271, and the *Jäger* with 68. However, there could be problems with the latter list. Among the Ansbach-Bayreuth troops, for instance, only 32 sergeants were listed, but there were 60 officers and staff members, including 32 lieutenants, a surprisingly large number.

19. The number of Ansbach-Bayreuth and Hessian *Jäger* captured on this day varies greatly in different returns. The British counted 53 captured *Jäger*, including 47 common soldiers. The American return for October 19, 1781, counted 84 *Jäger*, including 75 common soldiers. For the entire campaign and siege, then, the American return reported 73 captured *Jäger*, including 68 common soldiers. That the *Jäger* usually fought independently in small groups or embarked on special reconnaissance missions during the campaign, and thus were often far removed from any oversight, might have contributed to these diverging numbers. Of course, there was also ample reason for the British to downplay the numbers of captured soldiers. "Return of the Killed, Wounded & Missing," PRO CO 5/103, fol. 293; "General Return of Prisoners Taken at Yorktown," MNR, no. 31603; "General Return of Prisoners Surrendered at Yorktown," ibid., no. 31604.

20. From the Regiment Voit von Salzburg (Ansbach), 541 men went into captivity, and from the Regiment von Seybothen (Bayreuth), 536 men. Christoph L. von Reitzenstein to Margrave Karl Alexander, October 21, 1781, HAV, 358–59; "Extract aus dem Serenissimo erstatteten Rapport [d.d.] Yorktown d. 21. Oktober 1781," StA Bamberg, C 18/I Coll. Spiess. Fasc. 26, fol. 13. These numbers include all officers, staff members, noncommissioned officers, and rank and file. The British counted a total of 909 common soldiers for the Ansbach-Bayreuth troops on October 18, 1781. "Return of the Killed, Wounded & Missing," PRO CO 5/103, fol. 293. American returns counted 948 captured Ansbach-Bayreuth common soldiers. "General Return of Prisoners Taken at Yorktown," MNR, no. 31603; "General Return of Prisoners Surrendered at Yorktown," ibid., no. 31604.

21. "Monatliche Listen des Regiments Erbprinz," October 1781, StA Marburg, Best. 15, Nrs. 13–15, fol. 22v. Apparently this number also included the wounded and those who died in American captivity. On October 18, 1781, the British counted a total of 447 men for this regiment, including 367 common soldiers. "Return of the Killed, Wounded & Missing," PRO CO 5/103, fol. 293. According to the American return for the entire campaign, however, 484 men were captured from the Hessen-Kassel Regiment Erbprinz, including 425 common soldiers. "General Return of Prisoners Taken at Yorktown," MNR, no. 31603; "General Return of Prisoners Surrendered at Yorktown," ibid., no. 31604.

22. "Monatliche Listen des Infanterieregiments von Bose," October 1781," StA Marburg, Best. 15, Nrn. 246–48, fol. 32. This list was signed by Major von Scheer in American captivity on December 2, 1781. For this unit, the British listed 344 men on October 18, 1781. The American return for the entire campaign recorded 349 prisoners. The British return listed 274 of those soldiers as common soldiers, while the American return listed 271 common soldiers. "General Return of Prisoners Taken at Yorktown," no. 31603; "Return of the Killed, Wounded & Missing," PRO CO 5/103, fol. 293. The journal of the Regiment von Bose counted 367 captive soldiers from this unit, including 281 common soldiers. "Journal des Infanterie-Regiments v. Trümbach (ab 1778 v. Bose)," StA Marburg, Best. 10e, Nr. I/7, 219.

$\mathcal{B}ibliography$

Manuscript Collections

Bayerisches Hauptstaatsarchiv, Munich (Germany), Abteilung IV: Kriegsarchiv
   HS 580/1: Johann Ernst Prechtel, "Beschreibung derer vom 7. Mart: 1777 bis 9. December: 1783 in Nord-America mitgemachten Feld-Züge."
   HS 1053: Acta, die ad Serenissimum . . . erstattete unterthänigst Rapports, höchst Ihroselben in Königl: Großbrittani: Subsidien überlaßenen Infanterie Regiments hierauf ertheilte gnädigst Ordres und Resolutiones, de Anno 1777 usque 1783.

David Library of the American Revolution, Washington Crossing, Pa.
   Film 24: Pennsylvania Division of Archives and Manuscripts, Records of Pennsylvania's Revolutionary Governments, 1775–1790.
   Film 57: British Headquarters (Sir Guy Carleton, Lord Dorchester) Papers, 1724–1808.
   Film 423: Papers of Sir Frederick Haldimand.

Geheimes Staatsarchiv Preußischer Kulturbesitz, Berlin (Germany)
   I. HA. Rep. 11: Auswärtige Beziehungen, Akten und Staatsverträge.
   I. HA. Rep. 44C: Militaria. Immediatskommission zur Übergabe des Fürstentums Ansbach-Bayreuth an Bayern.
   II. HA. General-Direktorium. Fränkisches Departement. IV. Militaria.

Historical Society of Pennsylvania, Philadelphia
   AM 620: Hessian, Waldeck, British Prisoners of War, 1776–1779.
   AM 639: Letters, Prisoners of War (Thomas Bradford Letterbook).
   AM 6093: Charles Swift Riché Hildeburn Collection, 1760–1777.
   Collection 1676: Bradford Family Papers.
   William Henry Papers.
   Papers of Christopher Marshall, 1709–1797.

Landes- und Murhardsche Bibliothek der Stadt Kassel (Germany)
   2° Ms. Hass. Nr. 185: Journal des hessischen Corps in Amerika unter dem General von Heister, 1776–1777 (Abschrift).

335

2° Ms. Hass. Nr. 247: Aktenstücke, Correspondenzen und Aufzeichnungen den Amerikanischen Feldzug und die Theilnahme der Brigade von Mirbach an denselben betr.

4° Ms. Hass. Nr. 163: Journal des Regiments von Knyphausen, Febr. 19, 1776 bis Oct. 16, 1783. Geführt und aufgestellt von Lieutenant Ritter.

4° Ms. Hass. Nr. 169: Journal des hochlöblichen Füselier Regiments von Alt-Loßberg. Geführt durch den Regiments-Quartier Meister Heusser, vom Ausmarsch aus der Garnision Rinteln an, bis zur Zurückkunft des gedachten hochlöblichen Regiments aus Amerika.

4° Ms. Hass. Nr. 188: Geschichte des hochlöblichen Fusilier-Regiments von Loßberg in Form eines Tagebuchs angefangen, 1776–1778 (von Jacob Piel).

4° Ms. Hass. Nr. 216: Tagebuch des Hauptmanns Wiederholdt 1776 bis 1780.

8° Ms. Hass. Nr. 46/1: Tagebuch des Grenadiers Johannes Reuber. Eingefügt Bericht eines Anderen über die Belagerung Gibraltars 1782 und die Eroberung von Mannheim 1795, von Reubers Hand geschrieben.

Tgb. Nr. 77/76: Notizbuch des Captain d'Armes Jeremias Kappes aus dem Amerikanischen Feldzug, 1776–1778.

Landeskirchliches Archiv der Evangelischen Kirche von Kurhessen-Waldeck, Kassel (Germany)
Kirchenburch Fürstenhagen.

Library of Congress, Washington, D.C.
Elias Boudinot Papers.
Thomas Cole, Orderly Book.
Records of Colebrooke, Nesbitt, Colebrooke & Franks.
Peter Force Collection.
Series 7E, item 12: Elias Boudinot Papers.
Series 7E, item 13–14: Horatio Gates Papers.
Series 7E, item 82: Massachusetts Council
Series 7E, item 83: Massachusetts General Court
Series 7E, item 85: Massachusetts. Revolutionary War, Letters.
Series 8D, item 86: Minutes, Lancaster County, Committee of Safety.
Series 9: Miscellaneous Manuscripts.
Joshua Mersereau Papers.
George Washington Papers.

Library of Virginia, Richmond
Accession no. 28960: James Wood Papers, 1777–1783.

Maryland State Archives, Annapolis
Maryland State Papers, Rainbow Series.

Moravian Archives, Bethlehem, Pa.
Bethlehem Diary.
Hebron Diary.
LeA: Lebanon (Quitopehiu, Hebron).

National Archives and Records Administration, Washington, D.C.
  RG 93: War Department Collection of Revolutionary War Records.
  RG 217: Records of the Accounting Officers of the Department of the Treasury.
  RG 360: Papers of the Continental Congress, 1774–1788.

The National Archives/Public Record Office, Kew, England
  CO: Colonial Office Papers.
  HCA: Records of the High Court of the Admiralty and Colonial Vice-Admiralty Courts.
  HO: Home Office Papers.
  SP: State Papers.
  T: Treasury Papers.
  WO: War Office Papers.

New York Public Library, New York
  George Bancroft Collection, 1606–1872.
      No. 47: Marschroute und Beschreibung der merkwürdigsten Begebenheiten nach, in und aus Amerika von Johann Conrad Döhla in Zell, für Johann Adam Holper in Münchberg, 1811.
      No. 65: Ansbach Papers.
      No. 66: Ansbach Papers.
      No. 75: Ansbach Papers.
      No. 77: Brunswick Papers.

Niedersächsisches Staatsarchiv Wolfenbüttel (Germany)
  VI Hs 5, Nr. 23: Fragment eines Tagebuchs über die braunschweigischen Truppen im amerikanischen Kriege.
  VI Hs 11, Nr. 248: Reisebeschreibung Erste Division der Fürstl: braunschweigischen Trouppen nach America, gesammlet von Julius Friedrich Wasmus.
  VI Hs 18, Nr. 7: Marschroute von Braunschweig bis America Nebst den Vorschehnissen & Gegebenheiten der Herzoglich Braunschweigischen Troppen die 1. Division [von Johann Bense].
  38B Alt 256: General von Riedesels Berichte an den regierenden Herzog zu Braunschweig, nebst Anlagen, 1781–1782.
  38B Alt 260: Namentliches Verzeichnis aller vom Herzogl. Braunschweigischen Corps in America vor dem Feind gebliebenen, an Wunden oder Krankheit gestorbenen, desertierten, oder auf sonstige Art abgegangenen Officiers, Unterofficiers, Gemeine und Knechte.

Oberösterreichisches Landesarchiv Linz (Austria)
  Herrschaftsarchiv Weinberg, Bd. 182, Fasz. aa: Memoir des Corporal Johann Justus Eggertt.

Pfarramt St. Georgen, Bayreuth (Germany)
  Hochzeitsbuch der Kirche St. Georgen.

Private Collections

Dr. Robert Arnholdt, Würzburg (Germany): Geschichte des Nordamerikanischen Krieges besonders was die beiden Bayreuthisch und Ansbachischen Regimenter anbelangt: Von einem bei dem Bayreuthischen
Regiment von Seyboth gestandenen Soldaten aufgezeichnet namens
Stephan Popp von 1777 bis 1783.

Dr. Adolf Lang, Ahnatal (Germany): Tagebuch und Briefe [von Johann
Christoph Döhlemann].

Meyer Family, Rügland (Germany): Tagebucheinträge und Briefe, sowie
Briefe der Familie und anderer Bekannter [von Carl Wilhelm Friedrich Meyer].

Staatliche Bibliothek (Schlossbibliothek) Ansbach (Germany)

Ms. Hist. 485a: Gesang bey dem Abmarsch der Hochfürstlich Brandenburg-
Anspach-Baireuthischen Auxiliar-Truppen nach Amerika, Anno 1777.

Staatsarchiv Bamberg (Germany)

C 18/1: Coll. Spiess. Fasc. 26: Die in grossbritannischen Sold nach Amerika
überlasssenen Hochfürstl. Brandenburg. Kriegsvölker.

Staatsarchiv Marburg (Germany)

Best. 4h: Politische Akten nach Philipp d. Großen, 1567–1821. Kriegssa-
chen.

Nr. 3098: Relationes vom Nord-Amerikanischen Krieg unter General von Heister.

Nr. 3099: Relationes vom Nord-Amerikanischen Krieg unter General von Knyphausen.

Nr. 3102: Relationes vom Nord-Amerikanischen Krieg unter General von Loßberg.

Nr. 3105: Relationes des hochfürstl. Heßischen Corps in America von 1776–1783. Geführt durch den [späteren] Obristen
Bauermeister.

Nr. 3106: Journal von der Campagne in America. Tom VII: Berichte
des Majors Päusch.

Nr. 3108: Journal von der Campagne in America. Tom. V: Briefe,
Berichte, Journale, Listen des hessen-hanauischen Infanterie
Regiments Erbprinz.

Nr. 3110: Journal von der Campagne in America. Tom. VIII: Berichte
der Offiziere des I. Bat. des hessen-hanauischen Infanterie Regiments an den Erbprinzen.

Nr. 3111: Journal von der Campagne in America. Tom IX: Berichte
des Oberst Lenz.

Nr. 3152: Ordrebuch von der Campagne in America. Regiment Erbprinz aus Hessen-Hanau.

Nr. 3153: Ordres aus dem engl. Hauptquartier (1782) u. Bericht
über die Vernehmung der aus amerikanischer Kriegsgefang-
eschaft befreiten hessen-hanauischen Soldaten.

Best. 10c: Maß- und Rangierbücher.

Best. 10e: Kriegstagebücher, 1776–1783.

    Nr. I/7: Journal des Infanterie Regiments von Trümbach (ab 1778 von Bose).

    Nr. I/19: Relationes aus Amerika vom Hessen-Hanauischen Infanterie Regiment unter Oberst Wilhelm Rudolf v. Gall.

    Nr. I/23: Tagebuch eines Grenadiers im I. Bataillon des Hessen-Hanauischen Infanterie Regiments Erbprinz.

Best. 12: Kurhessisches Kriegsministerium und Vorbehörden, 1813–1867.

    12a, Nr. 489: Akten, betr. die Bestimmungen wegen Zahlung der Pensionen an Amerikaner-Krieger u. Witwen von solchen.

    12a, Nr. 490: Namenslisten von noch lebenden Teilnehmern an den nordamerikanischen Feldzügen sowie deren Witwen, mit detaillierten Angaben zu den sozialen Verhältnissen.

    12b, Nr. 177: Pensionsgesuche von kurhessischen Soldaten, die am amerianischen Krieg teilgenommen haben, jetzt aber in den abgetretenen Gebietsteilen wohnen.

    12c, Nr. 181: Bewilligte Pensionen für die im amerikanischen Krieg gedienten Unteroffiziere und Soldaten.

Best. 15: Truppenteile, Garnisonen, Festungen.

    Nr. 13–15: Monatliche Listen, Regiment Erbprinz.

    Nr. 120: Monatliche Listen, Regiment von Knyphausen.

    Nr. 246–48: Monatliche Listen, Regiment von Bose.

    Nr. 250: Monatliche Listen, Regiment von Loßberg.

    Nr. 252: Monatliche Listen, Regiment Rall.

Best. 118a: Waldeckisches Kabinett.

    Nr. 951: General-Kontobuch über Soll und Haben der Offiziere und Mannschaften des dritten englisch-waldeckischen Soldregiments.

    Nr. 972: Berichte vom dritten englisch-waldeckischen Regiment an den Fürsten und Frensdorff.

    Nr. 974: Berichte des Kommandeurs des dritten englisch-waldeckischen Soldregiments in Amerika, Oberstleutnant (dann Obersten) Johann Ludwig Wilhelm von Hanxleden.

    Nr. 975: Korrespondenz des Fürsten und Frensdorffs mit dem Oberstleutnant v. Horn vom dritten englisch-waldeckischen Soldregiment in Amerika.

Staatsarchiv Nürnberg (Germany)

    Film D1: Musterlisten der Ansbach-Bayreuther Truppen (aus PRO T38/812).

    Rep. 105: Verträge mit benachbarten Reichsständen—Verträge mit England.

    Rep. 107/III, Nr. 118: Grundliste der löbl. Hauptmann von Tritschlerischen Compagnie, welche den 22ten Novembr. 1783 errichtet worden.

    Rep. 107/III, Nr. 120: Grundliste der hochfürstl. brandenburg-ansbachischen Hauptmann von Güß'schen Compagnie vom 1. Januar 1746.

    Rep. 116: Brandenburg-Ansbachische Ausschreiben und Verordnungen.

Rep. 165a, Nr. 1551: Acta, die wegen des Abmarsches der hochfürstl. in königl. Großbrittanischen Dienst und Sold überlassenen Trouppen, dann deren Verpflegung zu Ketteldorf, bestritten werdener Kosten btr.

Rep. D 12/2, Nr. 482: March Ruthen für Georg Adam Stang, Haudtboist.

Rep. D 12/2, Nr. 485: Wortgetreue Abschrift des Tagebuchs eines Soldaten, der unter der Ansbach. Brigade den Zug nach Amerika mitmachte, den 8. März 1777 bis 19. Oktober 1781 (von Johann Ernst Prechtel).

Rep. D 12/2, Nr. 487: Acta, die verschiedene Gnaden Ertheilungen, an die in königl. Großbrittann. Sold nach America abgegangene hiesige Hochfürstl. Trouppes betr.

Staatsarchiv Würzburg (Germany)
Domkapitel Protokolle, 1777.
Lichtbildsammlung 337: Ochsenfurter Ratsprotokoll 1777.
Militärsachen Nr. 95: Akt der Würzburger geh. Kanleiz betr. den fürstlich-ansbach'schen und bayreuth'schen Truppentransport nach Großbritannien betr.
Militärsachen Nr. 97: Akt der Würzburger Geh. Kanzlei betr. den zum fürstlich ansbach'schen nach England abgegangenen Trouppentransport für die dabei darunter befindlichen Catholiquen abgegebenen Ex-Jesuiten Franz. Piret betr.

Stadtarchiv Ansbach (Germany)
AM 994–96: Enrollement, 1742–1782.

Stadtarchiv Bayreuth (Germany)
Hist. 15: Urkunden und Acta des Historischen Vereins von Oberfranken zu Bayreuth die amerikanische Expedition der brandenburger Truppen betr. (Abschriften).
Nr. 23285: Verabschiedung unentbehrlicher der Landschaft und Nachlässe für die Landschaft.
Nr. 28197: Enrollierungs-Geschäfte.

Universitätsbibliothek Bayreuth (Germany)
Historischer Verein Oberfranken
B150: Gesang bei dem Abmarsch der Hochfürstlich Brandenburg-Anspach-Baireuthischen Auxiliartruppen nach America. Anno 1777.
Ms. 112: Tagebuch aus dem amerikanischen Freiheitskrieg. 1777–1783. (Abschrift) [von Johann Conrad Döhla].
Ms. 115: Grundliste des Hochfürstl. Husaren-Corps (zu Ansbach) d.d. 1. Januar 1773.
Ms. 188: Tagebuch eines Ansbacher Soldaten aus dem nordamerikanischen Freiheitskriege von 1777–1783 [von Johann Ernst Prechtel].

Van Pelt Library, Rare Books and Manuscripts, University of Pennsylvania, Philadelphia
J. G. Rosengarten Collection.

Virginia Historical Society, Richmond
    Mss1 B6108a: Bland Family Papers.

Zentralarchiv der Evangelischen Kirche von Hessen und Nassau, Darmstadt
    (Germany)
    Kirchenbuch Fürstenhagen.

Published Primary Sources

Allen, Ethan. *A Narrative of Col. Ethan Allen's Captivity from the Time of His Being Taken by the British, near Montreal, on the 25th Day of September, in the Year 1775, to the Time of His Exchange, on the 6th Day of May, 1778: Containing His Voyages and Travels.* Early American Imprints, Series I: Evans, no. 16181. Boston: Draper and Folsom, 1779.

Auerbach, Inge, and Otto Fröhlich. *Hessische Truppen im amerikanischen Unabhängigkeitskrieg (HETRINA): Index nach Familiennamen.* 6 vols. Marburg: Archivschule Marburg, 1972–87.

Bader, P. C. "Extracts From the Records of the Moravian Congregation at Hebron, Pennsylvania, 1775–1781." *Pennsylvania Magazine of History and Biography* 18 (1894): 449–63.

Baxter, James Phinney, ed. *The British Invasion from the North: Digby's Journal of the Campaigns of Generals Carleton and Burgoyne from Canada, 1776–1777.* New York: Da Capo Press, 1970.

Boudinot, Elias. *Journal of Events in the Revolution.* 1894. Reprint, New York: New York Times and Arno Press, 1968.

Boudinot, J. J., ed. *The Life, Public Services, Addresses, and Letters of Elias Boudinot.* New York: Da Capo Press, 1971.

Boyd, Julian P., et al., eds. *The Papers of Thomas Jefferson.* 30 vols. Princeton: Princeton University Press, 1950–2000.

Browne, William H., et al., eds. *Archives of Maryland.* 72 vols. Baltimore: Maryland Historical Society, 1883–1972.

Bucks County, den 14ten December, 1776: Der Fortgang der brittischen und hessischen Truppen durch Neu-Jersey ist mit solcher Verwüstung und Ausgelassenheiten begleitet gewesen. Early American Imprints, Series I: Evans, no. 42997. Philadelphia: s.n., 1776.

Burgoyne, Bruce E., ed. *The Ansbach-Bayreuth/Prechtel Diaries.* Dover, Del.: B. E. Burgoyne, 1989.

———, ed. *Diaries of a Hessian Chaplain and the Chaplain's Assistant: Excerpts from Two Diaries Showing Religious Influences among the Hessians during the American Revolution.* Pennsauken, N.J.: Heritage Books, 1990.

———, ed. *Eighteenth Century America: A Hessian Report on the People, the Land, the War as Noted in the Diary of Chaplain Philipp Waldeck, 1776–1780.* Bowie, Md.: Heritage Books, 1995.

———, ed. *A Hessian Diary of the American Revolution.* Norman: University of Oklahoma Press, 1990.

———, ed. *A Hessian Officer's Diary of the American Revolution.* Bowie, Md.: Heritage Books, 1994.

Burgoyne, Bruce E., et al., eds. *The Diary of Lieutenant von Bardeleben and Other von Donop Regiment Documents.* Bowie, Md.: Heritage Books, 1998.

————, eds. *Hessian Chaplains: Their Diaries and Duties*. Bowie, Md.: Heritage Books, 2003.

Burgoyne, Marie E., ed. *Hessian Letters and Journals and a Memoir*. Translated by Bruce E. Burgoyne. Westminster, Md.: Heritage Books, 2006.

Burnett, Edmund C., ed. *Letters of Members of the Continental Congress*. 8 vols. Washington, D.C.: Carnegie Institution of Washington, 1921–36.

Doblin, Helga, and Mary C. Lynn. "A Brunswick Grenadier with Burgoyne: The Journal of Johann Bense, 1776–1783." *New York History* 66, no. 4 (1985): 433–46.

————, eds. *An Eyewitness Account of the American Revolution and New England Life: The Journal of J. F. Wasmus, German Company Surgeon, 1776–1783*. New York: Greenwood Press, 1990.

Döhla, Johann Conrad. "Amerikanische Feldzüge, 1777–1783." *Jahrbuch der Deutsch-Amerikanischen Historischen Gesellschaft von Illinois* 17 (1917): 9–358.

Duane, William, ed. *Extracts from the Diary of Christopher Marshall: Kept in Philadelphia and Lancaster, during the American Revolution, 1774–1781*. Albany: J. Munsell, 1877.

Eggertt, Justus. "Bericht des Leutnants Johann Justus Eggertt." In *Berichte aus der Neuen Welt: Die Vereinigten Staaten von Amerika zwischen Unabhängigkeits- und Bürgerkrieg aus (ober)österreichischer Sicht*, edited by Siegfried Haider, 14–30. Linz: Landesverlag, 2000.

Ferguson, James E., et al., eds. *The Papers of Robert Morris, 1781–1784*. 8 vols. Pittsburgh: University of Pittsburgh Press, 1973–84.

Fisher, Sara. "'A Diary of Trifling Occurrences,' Philadelphia, 1776–1778." *Pennsylvania Magazine of History and Biography* 82 (1958): 411–65.

Fitzpatrick, John C., and David M. Matteson, eds. *The Writings of George Washington: From the Original Manuscript Sources, 1745–1799*. 39 vols. Washington, D.C.: U.S. Government Printing Office, 1931–44.

Force, Peter, ed. *American Archives: Consisting of a Collection of Authentick Records, State Papers, Debates, and Letters and Other Notices of Publick Affairs, the Whole Forming a Documentary History of the Origin and Progress of the North American Colonies*. 4th and 5th ser. 9 vols. Washington, D.C.: M. St. Clair Clark and Peter Force, 1837–53.

Ford, Worthington C., et al., eds. *Journals of the Continental Congress, 1774–1789*. 34 vols. Washington, D.C.: U.S. Government Printing Office, 1904–37.

Friedman, Leon, ed. *The Law of War: A Documentary History*. 2 vols. New York: Random House, 1972.

Geisler, Adam F. *Geschichte und Zustand der königlich grosbrittannischen Kriegsmacht von den frühesten Zeiten bis an's Jahr 1784: Wie auch Verzeichnisse einiger Deutscher in diesem Kriege rühmlichst zur Hülfe gewesener Offiziere*. Dessau: Buchhandlung der Gelehrten, 1784.

Gerland, Otto. "Aus dem Tagebuch eines hessischen Feldpredigers im amerikanischen Krieg." 2 pts. *Hessenland* 6 (1894): 72–76; 7 (1894): 87–91.

Gräf, Holger, et al., eds. *Krieg in Amerika und Aufklärung in Hessen: Die Privatbriefe (1772–1784) an Georg Ernst von und zu Gilsa*. Marburg: Hessisches Landesamt für geschichtliche Landeskunde, 2010.

Hanger, George Baron Coleraine. *The Life, Adventures and Opinions of Col. George Hanger*. 2 vols. London and Philadelphia: G. & R. Waite, 1801.

Heisey, John W. "Extracts from the Diary of the Moravian Pastors of the Hebron Church, Lebanon, 1755–1814." *Pennsylvania History* 34 (1967): 44–63.

Jones, S. Shepard, et al., eds. *Documents on American Foreign Relations.* New York: Simon and Schuster, 1938.

Junghans, F. W. "Der amerikanische Feldzug der Hessen nach dem Tagebuch des Grenadiers Johannes Reuber von Niedervellmar, 1776–1783." *Hessenland* 8 (1894): 155–57, 167–68, 183–86.

Kestler, Stefan. "Geschichte des Nordamerikanischen Krieges besonders was die beiden Bayreuthisch und Ansbachischen Regimenter anbelangt von einem bei dem Bayreuthischen Regiment von Seyboth gestandenen Soldaten aufgezeichnet namens Stephan Popp von 1777 bis 1783." *Archiv für Geschichte und Altertumskunde von Oberfranken* 81 (2001): 317–54.

Köster, Heinrich Martin, ed. *Die Neuesten Staatsbegebenheiten mit historischen und politischen Anmerkungen.* 6 vols. Frankfurt a. M.: Barrentrappische Buchhandlung, 1776–82.

Krause, Heinz, ed. *Das Tagebuch des Sockenstrickers Johann Valentin Asteroth aus Treysa (1776–1831): Übertragen und kommentiert von Heinz Krause.* Treysa: Stadtgeschichtlicher Arbeitskreis e. V. Schwalmstadt, 1992.

Krauseneck, J. C. *Die Werbung für England: Ein ländliches Lustspiel in einem Aufzuge.* Augsburg, 1777.

Krüll, Georg. "Aus dem Tagebuch eines ewigen Soldaten." *Mitteilungen des Oberösterreichischen Landesarchiv* 9 (1968): 291–97.

Linn, John B., et al., eds. *Pennsylvania Archives.* 1st and 2nd ser. Harrisburg and Philadelphia: Joseph Severns and Clarence M. Bush, 1852–79.

McIlwaine, H. R., ed. *Journals of the Council of the State of Virginia.* 5 vols. Richmond: Division of Purchase and Printing, 1931–67.

———, ed. *Official Letters of the Governors of the State of Virginia.* 3 vols. Richmond: Virginia State Library, 1926–1929.

Mersereau, Joshua. *Advertisement Urging the Apprehension of Prisoners of War.* Early American Imprints, Series I: Evans, no. 16347. Boston: s.n., 1779.

Palmer, William Pitt, et al., eds. *Calendar of Virginia State Papers and Other Manuscripts, 1652–1781, Preserved in the Capitol at Richmond.* 11 vols. Richmond: R. F. Walker, 1875–93.

Popp, Stephan. "Popp's Journal, 1777–1783." Edited by J. G. Rosengarten. *Pennsylvania Magazine of History and Biography* 26 (1902): 25–41, 245–54.

Quynn, William R., et al., eds. *The Diary of Jacob Engelbrecht.* 2 vols. Frederick, Md.: Historical Society of Frederick County, 2001.

Rainsford, Charles. "Transactions as Commissary for Embarking Foreign Troops in the English Service from Germany: With Copies of Letters Relative to It; For the Years 1776–1777." In *Collections of the New York Historical Society for the Year 1879,* 313–543. New York: Printed for the Society, 1880.

Scheer, George F., ed. *Private Yankee Doodle: Being a Narrative of Some of the Adventures, Dangers, and Sufferings of a Revolutionary Soldier.* Boston: Little, Brown and Co., 1962.

Schiller, Friedrich von. *Kabale und Liebe: Ein bürgerliches Trauerspiel in fünf Aufzügen.* Munich: DTV, 1997.

Schlözer, August Ludwig, ed. *Briefwechsel meist historischen und politischen Inhalts.* 10 vols. Göttingen: Vandenhoeck, 1776–82.

Schmitt, Thomas. "J.G. Theis in Wissen—Begebenheiten auf der Reise nach America. Anno 1777. Erlebnisse eines Wisseners im amerikanischen Unabhängigkeitskrieg. Eine text- und sachkritische Volltext-Transkription." *Heimatjahrbuch des Kreises Altenkirchen* 45 (2002): 256–63.

Smith, Paul Hubert, et al., eds. *Letters of Delegates to Congress, 1774–1789.* 25 vols. Washington, D.C.: Library of Congress, 1976–2000.

Specht, Johann Friedrich. *The Specht Journal: A Military Journal of the Burgoyne Campaign.* Translated by Helga Doblin. Edited by Mary C. Lynn. Westport, Conn.: Greenwood Press, 1995.

Thacher, James. "Diary of the American Revolution." In *America Rebels: Narratives of the Patriots,* edited by Richard M. Dorson, 276–87. New York: Pantheon, 1953.

Tilden, Robert J. "The Doehla Journal." *William and Mary Quarterly,* 2nd ser., 22, no. 3 (1942): 229–74.

Treaty and Convention, for the Sick, Wounded and Prisoners of War of the Land Forces of His Majesty the King of Great-Britain, and of His Most Christian Majesty. Early American Imprints, Series I: Evans, no. 15353. Philadelphia: John Dunlap, [1777].

Tustin, Joseph P., ed. *Diary of the American War: A Hessian Journal.* New Haven: Yale University Press, 1979.

Uhlendorf, Bernhard A., ed. *Revolution in America: Confidential Letters and Journals, 1776–1784.* New Brunswick: Rutgers University Press, 1957.

United States Department of the Treasury. *Statements of the Receipts and Expenditures of Public Monies, during the Administration of the Finances by Robert Morris, Esq., Late Superintendant; with Other Extracts and Accounts from the Public Records, Made Out by the Register of the Treasury.* Early American Imprints, Series I: Evans, no. 23922. Philadelphia: Childs and Swaine, 1791.

Vattel, Emer de. *The Law of Nations; or, Principles of the Law of Nature Applied to the Conduct and Affairs of Nations and Sovereigns; A Work Tending to Display the True Interest of Powers.* Northampton, Mass.: Thomas M. Pomroy for S. & E. Butler, 1805.

Waldenfels, Freiherr Werner von, ed. *Tagebuch eines Bayreuther Soldaten, des Johann Conrad Döhla, aus dem Nordamerikanischen Freiheitskrieg von 1777 bis 1783: Mit einem Vorwort von W. Frhr. v. Waldenfels.* Bayreuth: Druck von L. Ellwanger vorm. T. Burger, 1913.

Secondary Sources

Abell, Francis. *Prisoners of War in Britain, 1756–1815: A Record of Their Lives, Their Romance, and Their Sufferings.* London: Oxford University Press, 1914.

Anderson, Fred. *Crucible of War: The Seven Years' War and the Fate of Empire in British North America, 1754–1766.* New York: Alfred A. Knopf, 2000.

———. *A People's Army: Massachusetts Soldiers and Society in the Seven Years' War.* Chapel Hill: University of North Carolina Press, 1984.

Anderson, M. S. *War and Society in Europe of the Old Regime, 1618–1789.* Montreal: McGill-Queen's University Press, 1998.

Anderson, Olive. "The Treatment of Prisoners of War in Britain during the American War of Independence." *Bulletin of the Institute of Historical Research* 28, no. 77 (1955): 63–83.

Andrews, Melodie. "'Myrmidons from Abroad': The Role of the German Mercenary in the Coming of American Independence." Ph.D. diss., University of
Houston, 1986.

Armitage, David, and Michael J. Braddick, eds. *The British Atlantic World, 1500–
1800.* Houndmills: Palgrave Macmillan, 2002.

Asche, Matthias, et al., eds. *Krieg, Militär und Migration in der Frühen Neuzeit.* Berlin: LIT Verlag, 2008.

Atwood, Rodney. *The Hessians: Mercenaries from Hessen-Kassel in the American Revolution.* New York: Cambridge University Press, 1980.

Auerbach, Inge. "Die Festung Ziegenhain: Der Soldatenhandel mit Amerika,"
In *Hessen: Geschichte und Politik,* edited by Bernd Heidenreich, 216–22. Stuttgart: Kohlhammer, 2000.

———. *Die Hessen in Amerika, 1776–1783.* Marburg: Hessische Historische Kom-
mission, 1996.

———. "Die hessischen Soldaten und ihr Bild von Amerika, 1776–1783." *Hessisches Jahrbuch für Landesgeschichte* 35 (1985): 138–58.

———. "Marburger im amerikanischen Unabhängigkeitskrieg." *Zeitschrift des Vereins für hessische Geschichte und Landeskunde* 87 (1978): 321–35.

Bailyn, Bernard. *Atlantic History: Concept and Contours.* Cambridge, Mass.: Harvard University Press, 2005.

Baker, Norman. *Government and Contractors: The British Treasury and War Supplies,
1775–1783.* London: Athlone Press, 1971.

Barth, Richard C., William Doernemann, and Mark Schwalm. "The Trenton
Prisoner List." *Journal of the Johannes Schwalm Historical Association* 3, no. 1
(1985): 1–22.

Barton, Lewis. "The Revolutionary Prisoners of War in Winchester and Frederick
County." In *Men and Events of the Revolution in Winchester and Frederick County,
Virginia,* edited by Garland R. Quales, 30–54. Winchester: Winchester–Fred-
erick County Historical Society, 1975.

Bell, Catherine M. *Ritual: Perspectives and Dimensions.* New York: Oxford University Press, 1997.

Bellinger, Andréa, and David J. Krieger, eds. *Ritualtheorien: Ein einführendes
Handbuch.* 2nd ed. Wiesbaden: Westdeutscher Verlag, 2003.

Berbig, Johannes. *Revolte in Ochsenfurt: Deutsches Blut für englische Pfunde.* Leipzig:
Köhler & Voigtländer, 1940.

Berger, Carl. *Broadsides and Bayonets: The Propaganda War of the American Revolution.* Philadelphia: University of Pennsylvania Press, 1961.

Best, Geoffrey. *Humanity in Warfare: The Modern History of the International Law of
Armed Conflicts.* London: Columbia University Press, 1980.

———. *War and Law since 1945.* New York: Oxford University Press, 1994.

Bezzel, Oskar. "Ansbach-Bayreuther Miettruppen im nordamerikanischen Freiheitskrieg, 1777–1783." *Zeitschrift für bayerische Landesgeschichte* 8 (1935):
185–214, 377–424.

———. *Die Haustruppen des letzten Markgrafen von Ansbach-Bayreuth unter preus-
sischer Herrschaft.* Munich: C. H. Beck, 1939.

Bischof, Günter, and Rüdiger Overmans, eds. *Kriegsgefangenschaft im Zweiten Weltkrieg: Eine vergleichende Perspektive.* Ternitz-Pottschach: G. Höller, 1999.

Black, Jeremy. *A Military Revolution? Military Change and European Society, 1550–
1800.* Atlantic Highlands, N.J.: Humanities Press, 1991.

———. *Rethinking Military History*. New York: Routledge, 2004.

Blumenthal, Walter H. *Women Camp Followers of the American Revolution*. Philadelphia: G. S. MacManus, 1952.

Bodle, Wayne. *The Valley Forge Winter: Civilians and Soldiers in War*. University Park: Pennsylvania State University Press, 2002.

Bodle, Wayne, and Helen R. Schenck. "John Jacob Faesch at Mount Hope, 1770–1809." Unpublished manuscript, 1990.

Böhm, Uwe-Peter. *Hessisches Militär: Die Truppen der Landgrafschaft Hessen-Kassel, 1672–1806*. Beckum: Deutsche Gesellschaft für Heereskunde, 1986.

———. *Uniformen der deutschen Kontingente im Amerikanischen Unabhängigkeitskrieg, 1776–1783, Nach Fritz Kredel*. Eichenzell: Selbstverlag der Gesellschaft für hessische Militär- und Zivilgeschichte, 2006.

Böhme, H. G. *Die Wehrverfassung in Hessen-Kassel im 18. Jahrhundert bis zum Siebenjährigen Krieg*. Kassel: Bärenreiter, 1954.

Bonnell, Victoria E., and Lynn Hunt, eds. *Beyond the Cultural Turn: New Directions in the Study of Society and Culture*. Berkeley: University of California Press, 1999.

Bourdieu, Pierre. *Distinction: A Social Critique of the Judgement of Taste*. Translated by Richard Nice. Cambridge, Mass.: Harvard University Press, 1984.

———. "The Forms of Capital." In *Handbook for Theory and Research for the Sociology of Education*, edited by John G. Richardson, 241–58. New York: Greenwood Press, 1986.

———. *Outline of a Theory of Practice*. Translated by Richard Nice. Cambridge: Cambridge University Press, 1977.

———. "Social Space and Symbolic Power." *Sociological Theory* 7, no. 1 (1989): 14–25.

Bowie, Lucy Leigh. *The Ancient Barracks at Fredericktown: Where Hessian Prisoners Were Quartered during the Revolutionary War*. Frederick: Maryland State School for the Deaf, 1939.

———. "German Prisoners in the American Revolution." *Maryland Historical Magazine* 40 (1945): 185–200.

Bowman, Larry G. *Captive Americans: Prisoners during the American Revolution*. Athens: Ohio University Press, 1976.

———. "The New Jersey Prisoner Exchange Conferences, 1778–1780." *New Jersey History* 97, no. 3 (1979): 149–58.

Boyd, Georg Adams. *Elias Boudinot: Patriot and Statesman, 1740–1821*. Princeton: Princeton University Press, 1952.

Bradburn, Douglas. *The Citizenship Revolution: Politics and the Creation of the American Union, 1774–1804*. Charlottesville: University of Virginia Press, 2009.

Breiter, Helmuth. "Auf den Spuren eines hessischen Soldaten im amerikanischen Unabhängigkeitskrieg." *Kassel: Jahrbuch Landkreis Kassel* (1977): 33–37.

Brewer, John. *The Sinews of Power: War, Money, and the English State, 1688–1783*. 1st Harvard ed. Cambridge, Mass.: Harvard University Press, 1990.

Brinck, Andreas. *Die deutsche Auswanderungswelle in die britischen Kolonien Nordamerikas um die Mitte des 18 Jahrhunderts*. Stuttgart: Franz Steiner, 1993.

Burgoyne, Bruce E. *The Third English-Waldeck Regiment in the American Revolutionary War*. Bowie, Md.: Heritage Books, 1999.

Burrows, Edwin G. *Forgotten Patriots: The Untold Story of American Prisoners during the Revolutionary War*. New York: Basic Books, 2008.

Butterfield, Lyman H. "Psychological Warfare in 1776: The Jefferson-Franklin Plan to Cause Hessian Desertions." *Proceedings of the American Philosophical Society* 94 (1950): 233–41.

Canstein, Benno. *Der waldeckisch-englische Subsidienvertrag von 1776: Zustandekommen, Ausgestaltung und Erfüllung.* Arolsen: Selbstverlag des Waldeckischen Geschichtsvereins, 1989.

Carp, E. Wayne. "Early American Military History: A Review of Recent Work." *Virginia Magazine of History and Biography* 94 (1986): 259–84.

———. "The Origins of the Nationalist Movement of 1780–1783: Congressional Administration and the Continental Army." *Pennsylvania Magazine of History and Biography* 107, no. 3 (1983): 363–92.

Casino, Joseph J. "Elizabethtown, 1782: The Prisoners-of-War Negotiations and the Pawns of War." *New Jersey History* 102, no. 1–2 (1984): 1–35.

Chilton, Harriet. "Journey of the Yorktown Prisoners to Winchester, Virginia and Frederick, Maryland." *Daughters of the American Revolution Magazine* 115, no. 3 (1981): 200–203.

Citino, Robert M. "Military Histories Old and New: A Reintroduction." *American Historical Review* 112, no. 4 (2007): 1070–90.

Cohen, Sheldon S. *Yankee Sailors in British Gaols: Prisoners of War at Forton and Mill, 1777–1783.* Cranbury: University of Delaware Press, 1995.

Colley, Linda. *Captives.* New York: Pantheon Books, 2002.

Condie, Thomas. "Plan, Construction, &c. of the Jail, and Penitentiary House of Philadelphia." *Philadelphia Monthly Magazine* 1, no. 2 (1798): 97–101.

Condit, William W. "Christopher Ludwick: Patriotic Gingerbread Baker." *Pennsylvania Magazine of History and Biography* 81 (1957): 365–90.

Conway, Stephen. *The War of American Independence, 1775–1783.* New York: E. Arnold, 1995.

Cramer, William S. "From Hessian Drummer to Maryland Ironmaker." *Journal of the Johannes Schwalm Historical Association* 3, no. 1 (1985): 23–36.

Curtis, Edward E. *The Organization of the British Army in the American Revolution.* New Haven: Yale University Press, 1926.

Dabney, William M. *After Saratoga: The Story of the Convention Army.* Albuquerque: University of New Mexico Press, 1954.

Dallhammer, Werner. *Ansbach: Geschichte einer Stadt.* Ansbach: Hercynia, 1993.

Dandridge, Danske B. *American Prisoners of the Revolution.* Charlottesville, Va.: Michie, 1911.

Davis, Natalie Zemon. *Fiction in the Archives: Pardon Tales and Their Tellers in Sixteenth-Century France.* Stanford: Stanford University Press, 1987.

Dederer, John M. *War in America to 1775: Before Yankee Doodle.* New York: New York University Press, 1990.

Demos, John. *The Unredeemed Captive: A Family Story from Early America.* New York: Knopf, 1994.

Dippel, Horst. *Germany and the American Revolution, 1770–1800.* Translated by Bernhard A. Uhlendorf. Chapel Hill: University of North Carolina Press, 1977.

Dixon, Martha W. "Divided Authority: The American Management of Prisoners in the Revolutionary War, 1775–1783." Ph.D. diss., University of Utah, 1977.

Doyle, Robert C. *The Enemy in Our Hands: America's Treatment of Prisoners of War from the Revolution to the War on Terror.* Lexington: University Press of Kentucky, 2010.

―――. *Voices from Captivity: Interpreting the American POW Narratives.* Lawrence: University Press of Kansas, 1994.

Ducrey, Pierre. "Kriegsgefangene im antiken Griechenland: Forschungsdiskussion 1968–1998." In *In der Hand des Feindes: Kriegsgefangenschaft von der Antike bis zum Zweiten Weltkrieg,* edited by Rüdiger Overmans, 63–81. Cologne: Böhlau, 1999.

Duffy, Christopher. *Siege Warfare: The Fortress in the Early Modern World, 1494–1660.* 2 vols. London: Routledge, 1979.

Eckhardt, Wilhelm A. "Hessisches Truppen im Amerikanischen Unabhängigkeitskrieg." In *Miszellen und Vorträge,* edited by Wilhelm A. Eckhardt, 106–15. Marburg: Trautvetter & Fischer, 1995.

Eelking, Max von. *Die deutschen Hülfstruppen im nordamerikanischen Befreiungskriege 1776 bis 1783.* 1863. Reprint, Kassel: Hamecher, 1976.

Elias, Norbert. *Über den Prozess der Zivilisation: Soziogenetische und psychogenetische Untersuchungen.* 2 vols. Basel: Zum Falken, 1939.

Elster, Otto. *Geschichte der stehenden Truppen im Herzogtum Braunschweig-Wolfenbüttel.* Vol. 2, *Von 1714–1806.* Leipzig: M. Heinsius, 1901.

Elting, John, ed. *Military Uniforms in America: The Era of the American Revolution, 1755–1795.* San Rafael: Presidio Press, 1974.

Eltis, David, ed. *Coerced and Free Migration: Global Perspectives.* Stanford: Stanford University Press, 2002.

Endres, Rudolf. "Ansbach-Bayreuth zwischen Preußen und Bayern." *Franken unter einem Dach* 9 (1986): 27–33.

Evans, Melvern, Jr. "Lancaster Borough: Host to British and Hessian Prisoners of War, 1775–1784." *Journal of the Lancaster County Historical Society* 89, no. 4 (1985): 144–51.

Ferling, John. *Almost a Miracle: The American Victory in the War of Independence.* New York: Oxford University Press, 2007.

Fetter, Frank W. "Who Were the Foreign Mercenaries of the Declaration of Independence?" *Pennsylvania Magazine of History and Biography* 104, no. 4 (1980): 508–13.

Fickert, Wilhelm. *Geldwesen, Kaufkraft und Maßeinheiten im Bereich des Fürstentums Kulmbach-Bayreuth.* Neustadt a.d. Aisch: Selbstverlag der Gesellschaft für Familienforschung in Franken, Nuremberg, 1989.

Fischer, David Hackett. *Washington's Crossing.* New York: Oxford University Press, 2004.

Fischer, Joachim. "Eiserngespartes aus America, 1776–1783." In *Aus Geschichte und ihren Hilfswissenschaften: Festschrift für Walter Heinemeyer,* edited by Hermann Bannasch and Hans-Peter Lachmann, 741–56. Marburg: Elwert, 1979.

―――. "Wer Alles hat in Hanau 1776 bis 1786 am Soldatenhandel nach Amerika verdient?" *Neues Magazin für hanauische Geschichte* 9, no. 4 (1990): 333–46.

Flory, William E. S. *Prisoners of War: A Study in the Development of International Law.* Washington, D.C.: American Council on Public Affairs, 1942.

Fogleman, Aaron S. *Hopeful Journeys: German Immigration, Settlement, and Political Culture in Colonial America, 1717–1775.* Philadelphia: University of Pennsylvania Press, 1996.

Foster, William H. *The Captors' Narrative: Catholic Women and Their Puritan Men on the Early American Frontier.* Ithaca: Cornell University Press, 2003.

France, John. *Western Warfare in the Age of the Crusades, 1000–1300.* Ithaca: Cornell University Press, 1999.

Franklin, H. Bruce. "The POW/MIA Myth." In *The Lessons and Legacies of the Vietnam War,* edited by Walter L. Hixson, 189–210. New York: Garland, 2000.

Frevert, Ute, ed. *Militär und Gesellschaft im 19. und 20. Jahrhundert.* Stuttgart: Klett-Cotta, 1997.

———, ed. *Vertrauen: Historische Annäherungen.* Göttingen: Vandenhoeck & Rupprecht, 2003.

Friedman, Yvonne. *Encounter between Enemies: Captivity and Ransom in the Latin Kingdom of Jerusalem.* Leiden: Brill, 2002.

Fuchs, Thomas. "Idee und Wirklichkeit des hessen-kasselischen Militärstaates." *Zeitschrift des Vereins für hessische Geschichte und Landeskunde* 106 (2001): 19–35.

Games, Alison. "Atlantic History: Definitions, Challenges, and Opportunities." *American Historical Review* 111, no. 3 (2006): 741–57.

———. "Introduction, Definitions, and Historiography: What Is Atlantic History?" *Organization of American Historians Magazine of History* 18, no. 3 (2004): 3–7.

———. *Migration and the Origins of the English Atlantic World.* Cambridge, Mass.: Harvard University Press, 1999.

Gennep, Arnold van. *Les rites de passage: Étude systématique des rites.* Paris: Nourry, 1909.

———. *The Rites of Passage.* Translated by Monica B. Vizedom and Gabrielle L. Caffé. Chicago: University of Chicago Press, 1960.

Gordon, John P. "Barracks in Lancaster: The First Ten Years." *Journal of the Lancaster County Historical Society* 99 (1997): 80–92.

Grady, Robert F. "The Evolution of Ethical and Legal Concern for the Prisoner of War." Ph.D. diss., Catholic University of America, 1970.

Gräf, Holger, et al., eds. *Adliges Leben am Ausgang des Ancien Régime: Die Tagebuchaufzeichnungen des Georg Ernst von und zu Gilsa.* Marburg: Hessisches Landesamt für geschichtliche Landeskunde, 2010.

Greene, Jack P., and Philip D. Morgan, eds. *Atlantic History: A Critical Appraisal.* Oxford: Oxford University Press, 2009.

Greene, Katherine Glass. *Winchester, Virginia, and Its Beginnings, 1734–1814: From Its Founding by Colonel James Wood to the Close of the Life of His Son, Brigadier-General and Governor James Wood, with the Publication for the First Time of Valuable Manuscripts.* Strasburg, Va.: Shenandoah Publishing House, 1926.

Grenier, John. *The First Way of War: American War Making on the Frontier, 1607–1814.* Cambridge: Cambridge University Press, 2005.

Gull, P. Kirby. "A Captor's Conundrum: The Management of German Prisoners after Yorktown; A Maryland Perspective." *Journal of the Johannes Schwalm Historical Association* 7, no. 3 (2003): 34–41.

———. "Hessians at Fort Frederick: A Story Revisited." *Journal of the Johannes Schwalm Historical Association* 8 (2005): 45–50.

Haefeli, Evan. "Ransoming New England Captives in New France." *French Colonial History* 1 (2002): 113–27.

Haffner, Gerald O. "The Treatment of Prisoners of War by the Americans during the War of Independence." Ph.D. diss., Indiana University, 1952.

Hagemann, Karen. "Militär, Krieg, und Geschlechterverhältnisse: Untersuchungen, Überlegungen und Fragen zur Militärgeschichte der Frühen Neuzeit." In *Klio in Uniform? Probleme und Perspektiven einer modernen Militärgeschichte der Frühen Neuzeit*, edited by Ralf Pröve, 35–88. Cologne: Böhlau, 1997.

Hagist, Don N. "The Women of the British Army during the American Revolution." *Minerva: Quarterly Report on Women and the Military* 13, no. 2 (1995): 29–85.

Hale, J. R. *War and Society in Renaissance Europe, 1450–1620*. Baltimore: Johns Hopkins University Press, 1986.

Hall, E. Foster. *Heritage Remembered: The Story of Bear River*. 2nd ed. New Minas, N.S.: Kentville, 1998.

Heinritz, J. G. "Versuch einer Geschichte der älteren Militair-Verfassung im Fürstenthume Bayreuth, besonders der Bürger-Miliz." 2 pts. *Archiv für Geschichte und Altertumskunde des Ober-Main-Kreises* 1, no. 1 (1831): 98–119; 1, no. 2 (1832): 70–83.

Heisey, John W. "Extracts from the Diary of the Moravian Pastors of the Hebron Church, Lebanon, 1755–1814." *Pennsylvania History* 34 (1967): 44–63.

Hell, Klaus. "Von der Aushebung entbehrlicher über Konskription und Auslosung dienstpflichtiger zur Anwerbung Freiwilliger im Militärwesen des Fürstbistums Münster von 1763 bis 1786." *Westfälische Zeischrift* 149 (1999): 57–100.

Henderson, Rodger C. *Community Development and the Revolutionary Transition in Eighteenth-Century Lancaster County*. New York: Garland, 1990.

Higginbotham, Don. "The Early American Way of War: Reconnaissance and Appraisal." *William and Mary Quarterly*, 3rd ser., 44 (1987): 230–73.

———. "War and State Formation in Revolutionary America." In *Empire and Nation: The American Revolution in the Atlantic World*, edited by Eliga Gould and Peter S. Onuf, 54–71. Baltimore: Johns Hopkins University Press, 2005.

———. *The War of American Independence: Military Attitudes, Policies, and Practice, 1763–1789*. New York: Macmillan, 1971.

Hildebrand, Erich. "Das Regiment Erbprinz von Hessen-Kassel im Amerikanischen Unabhängigkeitskrieg." *Zeitschrift des Vereins für hessische Geschichte und Landeskunde* 90 (1985): 183–211.

———. "Trenton 1776: Die Schuldfrage in Neuer Sicht." *Zeitschrift des Vereins für hessische Geschichte und Landeskunde* 87 (1978): 297–320.

Hofstra, Warren R., and Robert D. Mitchell. "Town and Country in Backcountry Virginia: Winchester and the Shenandoah Valley, 1730–1800." *Journal of Southern History* 59 (1993): 619–46.

Hohrath, Daniel. "'In Cartellen wird der Werth eines Gefangenen bestimmet': Kriegsgefangenschaft als Teil der Kriegspraxis des Ancien Régime." In *In der Hand des Feindes: Kriegsgefangenschaft von der Antike bis zum Zweiten Weltkrieg*, edited by Rüdiger Overmans, 141–70. Cologne: Böhlau, 1999.

Holle, J. W. "Die politische Verfassung des Fürstenthums Bayreuth unter Markgraf Friedrich (1735–1763)." *Archiv für Geschichte und Altertumskunde des Ober-Main-Kreises* 3, no. 3 (1847): 109–20.

Hollenberg, Günter. "Landstände und Militär in Hessen-Kassel." *Hessisches Jahrbuch für Landesgeschichte* 34 (1984): 101–29.

Holton, Woody. *Forced Founders: Indians, Debtors, Slaves, and the Making of the American Revolution in Virginia*. Chapel Hill: University of North Carolina Press, 1999.

Howard, Michael. "Constraints on Warfare." In *The Laws of War: Constraints on Warfare in the Western World*, edited by Michael Howard, George J. Andreopoulos, and Mark R. Shulman, 1–11. New Haven, Conn.: Yale University Press, 1994.

Huck, Stephan. "Soldaten gegen Nordamerika: Lebenswelten braunschweiger Subsidientruppen im Amerikanischen Unabhängigkeitskrieg." Ph.D. diss., Universität Potsdam, 2009.

———. "Verkauft und Verraten?" In *Brücken in eine neue Welt: Auswanderer aus dem ehemaligen Land Braunschweig*, edited by Herzog August Bibliothek, 201–14. Wiesbaden: Herzog August Bibliothek, 2000.

Ingrao, Charles W. "'Barbarous Strangers': Hessian State and Society during the American Revolution." *American Historical Review* 87, no. 4 (1982): 954–76.

———. *The Hessian Mercenary State: Ideas, Institutions, and Reform under Frederick II, 1760–1785*. New York: Cambridge University Press, 1987.

———. "Kameralismus und Militarismus im deutschen Polizeistaat: Der hessische Söldnerstaat." In *Stände und Gesellschaft im Alten Reich*, edited by Georg Schmidt, 171–97. Wiesbaden: Franz Steiner Verlag, 1989.

Jillson, Calvin, and Rick K. Wilson. *Congressional Dynamics: Structure, Coordination, and Choice in the First American Congress, 1774–1789*. Stanford: Stanford University Press, 1994.

Jones, Kenneth S. "Karl Friedrich Führer: Prisoner, Patriot, Publisher." *Journal of the Johannes Schwalm Historical Association* 3, no. 3 (1987): 2–21.

Kaiser, Erich. "Nachschub für die hessischen Regimenter in Amerika: Das Rekrutendepot in der Festung Ziegenhain." *Zeitschrift des Vereins für hessische Geschichte und Landeskunde* 86 (1976): 185–200.

———. "Rebellion im Rekrutendepot Ziegenhain: Aufsässiger Nachschub für die hessischen Amerikaregimenter 1775–1784." *Schwälmer Jahrbuch 1977* (1977): 20–26.

Kapp, Friedrich. *Der Soldatenhandel deutscher Fürsten nach Amerika: Ein Beitrag zur Kulturgeschichte des achtzehnten Jahrhunderts*. Berlin: Franz Dunker, 1864.

Karsten, Peter. *Law, Soldiers, and Combat*. Westport, Conn.: Greenwood Press, 1978.

Katcher, Philip R. N. *Encyclopedia of British, Provincial, and German Army Units, 1775–1783*. Harrisburg, Pa.: Stackpole Books, 1973.

Keegan, John. *The Face of Battle*. New York: Viking Press, 1976.

Keen, Maurice H. *The Laws of War in the Late Middle Ages*. London: Routledge, 1965.

Kennedy, Michael V. "The Home Front during the War for Independence: The Effect of Labor Shortages on Commercial Production in the Mid-Atlantic." In *A Companion to the American Revolution*, edited by Jack P. Greene and J. R. Pole, 332–41. Malden, Mass.: Blackwell, 2004.

Kertzer, David I. *Ritual, Politics, and Power*. New Haven, Conn.: Yale University Press, 1988.

Kessler, Charles H. *Lancaster in the Revolution*. Lititz, Pa.: Sutter House, 1975.

Ketchum, Richard M. *Saratoga: Turning Point of America's Revolutionary War*. New York: Henry Holt, 1997.

Kiddoo, Nancy Rice. "'Of Revolutionary Memory': German Mercenaries Who Immigrated to Western Maryland." *Journal of the Pennsylvania German Society* 23, no. 2 (1989): 43–80.

Kipping, Ernst. *The Hessian View of America, 1776–1783*. Monmouth Beach, N.J.: Philip Freneau Press, 1971.

———. *Die Truppen von Hessen-Kassel im Amerikanischen Unabhängigkeitskrieg, 1776–1783.* Darmstadt: Wehr und Wissen Verlagsgesellschaft, 1965.

Knepper, George W. "The Convention Army, 1777–1783." Ph.D. diss., University of Michigan, 1954.

Knight, Betsy. "Prisoner Exchange and Parole in the American Revolution." *William and Mary Quarterly,* 3rd ser., 48, no. 2 (1991): 201–22.

Kocka, Jürgen, ed. *Sozialgeschichte im Internationalen Überblick: Ergebnisse und Tendenzen der Forschung.* Darmstadt: Wissenschaftliche Buchgesellschaft, 1989.

Krammer, Arnold. *Nazi Prisoners of War in America.* New York: Stein and Day, 1979.

———. *Prisoners of War: A Reference Handbook.* Westport, Conn.: Praeger Security International, 2008.

Kroener, Bernhard. "Kriegsgurgeln, Freireuter und Merodebrüder: Der Soldat des Dreißigjährigen Krieges. Täter und Opfer." In *Der Krieg des Kleinen Mannes: Eine Militärgeschichte von unten,* edited by Wolfram Wette, 51–67. Munich: Pieper, 1992.

———. "Der Soldat als Ware." In *Krieg und Frieden im Übergang vom Mittelalter zur Neuzeit: Theorie—Praxis—Bilder,* edited by Patrice Veit and Heinz Duchhardt, 271–95. Mainz: Verlag Philipp von Zabern, 2000.

———. "Soldat oder Soldateska? Programmatischer Aufriß einer Sozialgeschichte militärischer Unterschichten in der Ersten Hälfte des 17. Jahrhunderts." In *Militärgeschichte. Probleme—Thesen—Wege,* edited by Manfred Messerschmidt et al., 100–23. Stuttgart: Deutsche Verlags-Anstalt, 1982.

———. "Vom 'Extraordinari Kriegsvolck' zum 'Miles Perpetuus': Zur Rolle der bewaffneten Macht in der europäischen Gesellschaft der Frühen Neuzeit; Ein Forschungs- und Literaturbericht." *Militärgeschichtliche Mitteilungen* 43 (1988): 141–88.

Kroener, Bernhard, and Ralf Pröve, eds. *Krieg und Frieden: Militär und Gesellschaft in der Frühen Neuzeit.* Paderborn: Ferdinand Schöningh, 1996.

Kroll, Stefan, and Kersten Krüger. *Militär und ländliche Gesellschaft in der Frühen Neuzeit.* Münster: LIT Verlag, 2000.

Lee, Wayne E. *Crowds and Soldiers in Revolutionary North Carolina: The Culture of Violence in Riot and War.* Gainesville: University Press of Florida, 2001.

———. "Early American Ways of War: A New Reconnaissance, 1600–1815." *Historical Journal* 44, no. 1 (2001): 269–89.

———. "Restraint and Retaliation: The North Carolina Militias and the Backcountry War of 1780–1782." In *War and Society in the American Revolution: Mobilization and Home Fronts,* edited by John Resch and Walter Sargent, 163–90. DeKalb: Northern Illinois University Press, 2007.

Lemisch, Jesse. "Listening to the Inarticulate: William Widger's Dream and the Loyalties of American Revolutionary Seamen in British Prisons." *Journal of Social History* 3, no. 1 (1969): 1–29.

Lewis, James A. *Neptune's Militia: The Frigate* South Carolina *during the American Revolution.* Kent, Ohio: Kent State University Press, 1999.

Lindsey, William R. "Treatment of American Prisoners of War during the Revolution." *Emporia State Research Studies* 22, no. 1 (1973): 5–32.

Lipp, Anne. "Diskurs und Praxis: Militärgeschichte als Kulturgeschichte." In *Was ist Militärgeschichte?,* edited by Thomas Kühne and Benjamin Ziemann, 211–27. Paderborn: Ferdinand Schöningh, 2000.

Lloyd, Clive L. *A History of Napoleonic and American Prisoners of War, 1756–1816.* Woodbridge, Suffolk: Antique Collectors Club, 2007.

Lochner, Horst, and Henry J. Retzer. "Ansbach-Bayreuther Truppen in Amerika (1777–1783): Der 1. Nachschub in der Darstellung eines Teilnehmers." *Archiv für die Geschichte von Oberfranken* 82 (2002): 295–310.

Losch, Philipp. *Soldatenhandel.* Kassel: Bärenreiter, 1933.

Lowell, Edward J. *The Hessians and the Other German Auxiliaries of Great Britain in the Revolutionary War.* 2nd ed. 1884. Reprint, Williamstown: Corner House, 1975.

Luh, Jürgen. *Kriegskunst in Europa, 1650–1800.* Cologne: Böhlau, 2004.

Lynn, John A. *Battle: A History of Combat and Culture.* 2nd paperback ed. Cambridge, Mass.: Westview, 2004.

Mann, Kristin. "Shifting Paradigms in the Study of the African Diaspora and of Atlantic History and Culture." *Slavery and Abolition* 22, no. 1 (2001): 3–21.

Martin, James K., and Mark E. Lender. *A Respectable Army: The Military Origins of the Republic, 1763–1789.* Arlington Heights, Ill.: H. Davidson, 1982.

Mauch, Christof. "Images of America, Political Myths, Historiography: 'Hessians' in the War of Independence." *Amerikastudien* 48, no. 3 (2003): 411–23.

Mayer, Holly A. *Belonging to the Army: Camp Followers and Community during the American Revolution.* Columbia: University of South Carolina Press, 1996.

Maza, Sarah. "Stories in History: Cultural Narratives in Recent Works in European History." *American Historical Review* 101, no. 5 (1996): 1493–1515.

McCusker, John J. *How Much Is That in Real Money? A Historical Commodity Price Index for Use as a Deflator of Money Values in the Economy of the United States.* 2nd ed. Worcester, Mass.: American Antiquarian Society, 2001.

Meranze, Michael. *Laboratories of Virtue: Punishment, Revolution, and Authority in Philadelphia, 1760–1835.* Chapel Hill: University of North Carolina Press, 1996.

Merz, Johannes H. *The Hessians of Nova Scotia.* Hamilton: German Canadian Historical Book Publishing, 1994.

Metzger, Charles M. *The Prisoner in the American Revolution.* Chicago: Loyola University Press, 1971.

Meyer, Luise. *Carl Wilhelm Friedrich Meyer (1754–1817): Brandenburg-ansbachischer Stabsfourier in Amerika und Amtmann von Mainbernheim.* Ansbach: Meyer, 1979.

Miles, Lion G. *The Hessians of Lewis Miller.* Lyndhurst, Ohio: Johannes Schwalm Historical Association, 1983.

———. "The Iron Master and the Hessians." *Journal of the Johannes Schwalm Historical Association* 2, no. 1 (1981): 17–30.

———. "The Winchester Hessian Barracks." *Winchester–Frederick County Historical Society Journal* 3 (1988): 19–63.

Miller, Kenneth J. "Dangerous Guests: Enemy Captives and American National Identity in Revolutionary Lancaster, Pennsylvania, 1760–1783." Ph.D. diss., University of California at Davis, 2006.

Mintz, Max M. *The Generals of Saratoga: John Burgoyne and Horatio Gates.* New Haven, Conn.: Yale University Press, 1990.

Möller, Hans-Michael. *Das Regiment der Landsknechte: Untersuchungen zu Verfassung, Recht und Selbstverständnis in deutschen Söldnerheeren des 16. Jahrhunderts.* Wiesbaden: Franz Steiner, 1976.

Montgomery, Norton L. "Early Furnaces and Forges of Berks County, Pennsylvania." *Pennsylvania Magazine of History and Biography* 8 (1884): 56–81.

Muir, Edward. *Ritual in Early Modern Europe.* New York: Cambridge University Press, 1997.

Münkler, Herfried, and Johannes Kunisch. *Die Wiedergeburt des Krieges aus dem Geist der Revolution: Studien zum bellizistischen Diskurs des ausgehenden 18. und beginnenden 19. Jahrhunderts.* Berlin: Duncker & Humblot, 1999.

Müssel, Karl. "Bayreuth 1769: Die obergebirgische Residenzstadt im Jahre der Vereinigung der brandenburgischen Fürstentümer in Franken unter Markgraf Alexander." *Jahrbuch des Historischen Vereins für Mittelfranken* 95 (1991): 243–56.

Neimeyer, Charles. *America Goes to War: A Social History of the Continental Army.* New York: New York University Press, 1996.

Neisser, George. "Items of History of York, Pa., during the Revolution." *Pennsylvania Magazine of History and Biography* 44 (1920): 309–24.

Nöding, Arnulf S. "'Min Sicherheit si Din': Kriegsgefangenschaft im christlichen Mittelalter." In *In der Hand des Feindes: Kriegsgefangenschaft von der Antike bis zum Zweiten Weltkrieg,* edited by Rüdiger Overmans, 99–117. Cologne: Böhlau, 1999.

Nowosadtko, Jutta. *Krieg, Gewalt und Ordnung: Eine Einführung in die Militärgeschichte.* Tübingen: Edition Diskord, 2002.

———. "Ordnungselement oder Störfaktor? Zur Rolle der stehenden Heere innerhalb der frühneuzeitlichen Gesellschaft." In *Klio in Uniform? Probleme und Perspektiven einer modernen Militärgeschichte der Frühen Neuzeit,* edited by Ralf Pröve, 5–34. Cologne: Böhlau, 1997.

Ober, Josiah. "Classical Greek Times." In *The Laws of War: Constraints on Warfare in the Western World,* edited by Michael Howard, George J. Andreopoulos, and Mark R. Shulman, 12–26. New Haven, Conn.: Yale University Press, 1994.

Oeter, Stefan. "Die Entwicklung des Kriegsgefangenenrechts: Die Sichtweise eines Völkerrechtlers." In *In der Hand des Feindes: Kriegsgefangenschaft von der Antike bis zum Zweiten Weltkrieg,* edited by Rüdiger Overmans, 41–59. Cologne: Böhlau, 1999.

Oltmer, Jochen, ed. *Kriegsgefangene im Europa des Ersten Weltkriegs.* Paderborn: Schöningh, 2006.

Ousterhout, Anne M. *A State Divided: Opposition in Pennsylvania to the American Revolution.* Westport, Conn.: Greenwood Press, 1987.

Overmans, Rüdiger. "'In der Hand des Feindes': Geschichtsschreibung zur Kriegsgefangenschaft von der Antike bis zum Zweiten Weltkrieg." In *In der Hand des Feindes: Kriegsgefangenschaft von der Antike bis zum Zweiten Weltkrieg,* edited by Rüdiger Overmans, 1–39. Cologne: Böhlau, 1999.

———, ed. *In der Hand des Feindes: Kriegsgefangenschaft von der Antike bis zum Zweiten Weltkrieg.* Cologne: Böhlau, 1999.

Overton, Albert G., and J. W. W. Loose. "Prisoner-of-War Barracks in Lancaster Used during the Revolutionary War: An Unusual Discovery." *Journal of the Lancaster County Historical Society* 84, no. 3 (1981): 131–34.

Palmer, Colin A. *The Worlds of Unfree Labour: From Indentured Servitude to Slavery.* Aldershot: Ashgate Variorum, 1998.

Pancake, John S. *This Destructive War: The British Campaign in the Carolinas, 1780–1782.* Tuscaloosa: University of Alabama Press, 1985.

Parker, Geoffrey. *The Army of Flanders and the Spanish Road, 1567–1659: The Logistics of Spanish Victory and Defeat in the Low Countries' Wars.* New York: Cambridge University Press, 1972.

―――. "Early Modern Europe." In *The Laws of War: Constraints on Warfare in the Western World*, edited by Michael Howard, George J. Andreopoulos, and Mark R. Shulman, 40–58. New Haven, Conn.: Yale University Press, 1994.

―――. *The Military Revolution: Military Innovation and the Rise of the West, 1500–1800.* 2nd ed. New York: Cambridge University Press, 1996.

Pencak, William. *Jews and Gentiles in Early America, 1654–1800.* Ann Arbor: University of Michigan Press, 2005.

Peters, Jan. *Ein Söldnerleben im Dreissigjährigen Krieg: Eine Quelle zur Sozialgeschichte.* Berlin: Akademie Verlag, 1993.

―――. "Wegweiser zum Innenleben? Möglichkeiten und Grenzen popularer Selbstzeugnisse der Frühen Neuzeit." *Historische Anthropologie* 1 (1993): 235–49.

―――. "Zur Auskunftsfähigkeit von Selbstsichtzeugnissen schreibender Bauern." In *Ego-Dokumente: Annäherung an den Menschen in der Geschichte*, edited by Winfried Schulze, 175–90. Berlin: Akademie, 1996.

Phifer, Mike. "Campaign to Saratoga." *Military Heritage* 2, no. 1 (2000): 40–51.

Pohlmann, Cornelia. *Die Auswanderung aus dem Herzogtum Braunschweig im Kräftespiel staatliche Einflussnahme und öffentlicher Resonanz, 1720–1897.* Stuttgart: Franz Steiner, 2002.

Preser, Carl. *Der Soldatenhandel in Hessen: Versuch einer Abrechnung.* Marburg: N. G. Elwert, 1900.

Pröve, Ralf. *Militär, Staat und Gesellschaft im 19. Jahrhundert.* Munich: Oldenbourg, 2006.

―――. *Stehendes Heer und städtische Gesellschaft im 18. Jahrhundert: Göttingen und seine Militärbevölkerung 1713–1756.* Munich: Oldenbourg, 1995.

―――. "Zum Verhältnis von Militär und Gesellschaft im Spiegel gewaltsamer Rekrutierungen." *Zeitschrift fur Historische Forschung* 22, no. 2 (1995): 191–223.

Ranlet, Philip. "In the Hands of the British: The Treatment of American POWs during the War of Independence." *Historian* 62, no. 4 (2000): 731–57.

Rees, John. "'The Multitude of Women': An Examination of the Numbers of Female Camp Followers with the Continental Army." *Minerva: Quarterly Report on Women and the Military* 14 (1996): 1–47.

Rehm, Thomas. "Niedervellmar." *Topographisch-Statistische Nachrichten von Niederhessen* 2, no. 3 (1795): 312–14.

Reichardt, Carl. "Ein waldeckischer Feldprediger im amerikanischen Freiheitskriege." *Geschichtsblätter für Waldeck und Pyrmont* 41 (1949): 44–65; 42 (1950): 5–30.

Reid, Gisela M. "Waldeckische Truppen im Amerikanischen Unabhängigkeitskrieg." *Geschichtsblätter für Waldeck* 71 (1983): 217–86.

Retzer, Henry J. "Hessian Prisoners of War Taken on Staten Island in 1776." *Journal of the Johannes Schwalm Historical Association* 5, no. 3 (1995): 54–55.

―――. "Philipp Theobald, Hanau Regiment Chaplain—Maine Physician." *Journal of the Johannes Schwalm Historical Association* 6, no. 2 (1998): 39–44.

Rice, Howard C., et al. *The American Campaigns of Rochambeau's Army, 1780, 1781, 1782, 1783.* 2 vols. Princeton: Princeton University Press, 1972.

Richter, Daniel K. *Facing East from Indian Country: A Native History of Early America.* Cambridge, Mass.: Harvard University Press, 2001.

Rodgers, Daniel T. "Republicanism: The Career of a Concept." *Journal of American History* 79, no. 1 (1992): 11–38.

Rosas, Allan. *The Legal Status of Prisoners of War: A Study in International Humanitarian Law Applicable in Armed Conflicts.* 2nd ed. Turku: Institute for Human Rights at Abo Akademi University, 2005.

Royster, Charles. *A Revolutionary People at War: The Continental Army and American Character, 1775–1783.* 3rd ed. Chapel Hill: University of North Carolina Press, 1986.

Rüpke, Jörg. "Kriegsgefangene in der römischen Antike: Ein Problemskizze." In *In der Hand des Feindes: Kriegsgefangenschaft von der Antike bis zum Zweiten Weltkrieg,* edited by Rüdiger Overmans, 83–98. Cologne: Böhlau, 1999.

Ryerson, Richard Alan. *The Revolution Is Now Begun: The Radical Committees of Philadelphia, 1765–1776.* Philadelphia: University of Pennsylvania Press, 1978.

Salay, David L. "Arming for War: The Production of War Material in Pennsylvania for the American Armies during the Revolution." Ph.D. diss., University of Delaware, 1977.

Salinger, Sharon V. *"To Serve Well and Faithfully": Labor and Indentured Servants in Pennsylvania, 1682–1800.* New York: Cambridge University Press, 1987.

Schaffel, Kenneth. "The American Board of War, 1776–1781." *Military Affairs* 50, no. 4 (1986): 185–89.

Schlenkrich, Elke, and Helmut Bräuer. "Armut, Verarmung, und ihre öffentliche Wahrnehmung: Das sächsische Handwerk des ausgehenden 17. und 18. Jahrhunderts." In *Stadt und Handwerk in Mittelalter und früher Neuzeit,* edited by Karl Kaufhold and Wilfried Reininghaus, 93–117. Cologne: Böhlau, 2000.

Schmidt, Georg. *Stände und Gesellschaft im Alten Reich.* Wiesbaden: Franz Steiner Verlag, 1989.

Schmitt, Albert R. "'The Hessians and Who?' A Look at the Other Germans in the American War of Independence." *Yearbook of German-American Studies* 18 (1983): 41–61.

Schulze, Winfried. "Ego-Dokumente: Annäherung an den Menschen in der Geschichte." In *Ego-Dokumente: Annäherung an den Menschen in der Geschichte,* edited by Winfried Schulze, 11–30. Berlin: Akademie, 1996.

Schumann, Günter. *Die Markgrafen von Brandenburg-Ansbach: Eine Bilddokumentation zur Geschichte der Hohenzollern in Franken.* Ansbach: Selbstverlag des Historischen Vereins für Mittelfranken, 1980.

Schwalm, Mark A. "A Composite List of German Prisoners of War Held by the Americans, 1779–1782." *Journal of the Johannes Schwalm Historical Association* 2, no. 1 (1981): 4–15.

Schwoerer, Lois G. *"No Standing Armies!" The Antiarmy Ideology in Seventeenth-Century England.* Baltimore: Johns Hopkins University Press, 1974.

Scott, Samuel F. "Foreign Mercenaries, Revolutionary War, and Citizen-Soldiers in the Late Eighteenth Century." *War & Society* 2, no. 2 (1984): 41–58.

Seehase, Hagen. "Die hessischen Truppen im Amerikanischen Unabhängigkeitskrieg." *Zeitschrift des Vereins für hessische Geschichte und Landeskunde* 103 (1998): 135–72.

Selesky, Harold E. "Colonial America." In *The Laws of War: Constraints on Warfare in the Western World,* edited by Michael Howard, George J. Andreopoulos, and Mark R. Shulman, 59–85. New Haven: Yale University Press, 1994.

Selig, Robert A. "George Washington's German Allies: Das Deutsche Königlich-Französische Infanterie Regiment von Zweybrücken or Royal Deux-Ponts." *Journal of the Johannes Schwalm Historical Association* 7, no. 3 (2003): 42–52.

———. "A German Soldier in America, 1780–1783: The Journal of Georg Daniel Flohr." *William and Mary Quarterly*, 3rd ser., 50, no. 3 (1993): 575–90.

———. "Hessians Fighting for American Independence? German Deserters Recruited for Lauzun's Legion in America, 1780–1782." *Journal of the Johannes Schwalm Historical Association* 7, no. 4 (2004): 39–51.

Selig, Robert A., and David Curtis Skaggs, eds. *Treatise on Partisan Warfare.* New York: Greenwood Press, 1991.

Sellin, Thorsten. "Philadelphia Prisons of the Eighteenth Century." *Transactions of the American Philosophical Society* 43, no. 1 (1953): 326–31.

Sener, Samuel M. *The Lancaster Barracks: Where the British and Hessian Prisoners Were Detained during the Revolution.* 1896. Reprint, Harrisburg, Pa.: Harrisburg Publishing Co., 1989.

Sikora, Michael. "Das 18. Jahrhundert." In *Armeen und ihre Deserteure: Vernachlässigte Kapitel einer Militärgeschichte der Neuzeit*, edited by Michael Sikora and Ulrich Bröckling, 86–111. Göttingen: Vandenhoeck & Ruprecht, 1998.

———. "Desertion und nationale Mobilmachung: Militärische Verweigerung, 1792–1813." In *Armeen und ihre Deserteure: Vernachlässigte Kapitel einer Militärgeschichte der Neuzeit*, edited by Michael Sikora and Ulrich Bröckling, 112–40. Göttingen: Vandenhoeck & Ruprecht, 1998.

———. *Disziplin und Desertion: Strukturprobleme militärischer Organisation im 18. Jahrhundert.* Berlin: Duncker & Humblot, 1996.

———. "Söldner—Historische Annäherung an einen Kriegertypus." *Geschichte und Gesellschaft* 29, no. 2 (2003): 210–38.

Slagle, Robert O. "The Von Loßberg Regiment: A Chronicle of Hessian Participation in the American Revolution." Ph.D. diss., American University, 1965.

Slaski, Eugene R. "The Lehigh Valley." In *Beyond Philadelphia: The American Revolution in the Pennsylvania Hinterland*, edited by John B. Frantz and William Pencak, 46–66. University Park: Pennsylvania State University Press, 1998.

Smith, Clifford N. *Annotated Hessian Chaplaincy Record of the American Revolution, 1776–1784: Christenings, Marriages, Deaths.* McNeal, Ariz.: Westland, 1994.

Sowers, Gladys Bucher. "Hessian Prisoners and Their Employers in the Lebanon Township Area." *Lebanon County Historical Society* 18, no. 4 (2002): 1–70.

Speer, Lonnie R. *Portals to Hell: Military Prisons of the Civil War.* Mechanicsburg, Pa.: Stackpole Books, 1997.

Sprenger, Bernd. *Das Geld der Deutschen: Geldgeschichte Deutschlands von den Anfängen bis zur Gegenwart.* Paderborn: Ferdinand Schöningh, 1991.

Springer, Paul J. *America's Captives: Treatment of POWs from the Revolutionary War to the War on Terror.* Lawrence: University Press of Kansas, 2010.

Stacey, Robert C. "The Age of Chivalry." In *The Laws of War: Constraints on Warfare in the Western World*, edited by Michael Howard, George J. Andreopoulos, and Mark R. Shulman, 27–39. New Haven, Conn.: Yale University Press, 1994.

Städtler, Erhard. *Die Ansbach-Bayreuther Truppen im Amerikanischen Unabhängigkeitskrieg, 1777–1783.* Nuremberg: Kommisionsverlag Die Egge, 1956.

Starkey, Armstrong. *European and Native American Warfare in North America, 1675–1815.* Norman: University of Oklahoma Press, 1998.

————. *War in the Age of Enlightenment, 1700–1789.* Westport, Conn.: Praeger, 2003.

Steele, Ian K. *Betrayals: Fort William Henry and the "Massacre."* New York: Oxford University Press, 1990.

————. "Surrendering Rites." In *Hanoverian Britain and Empire: Essays in Memory of Philip Lawson,* edited by Stephen Taylor et al., 137–57. Woodbridge, Suffolk: Boydell Press, 1998.

————. "When Worlds Collide: The Fate of Canadian and French Prisoners Taken at Fort Niagara, 1759." *Journal of Canadian Studies* 39, no. 3 (2005): 9–39.

Stephens, Thomas R. "'In Deepest Submission': The Hessian Mercenary Troops in the American Revolution." Ph.D. diss., Texas A&M University, 1998.

Strathmann, Gabriele. *Das ehemalige Herzogtum Braunschweig unter dem Aspekt der Auswanderung—bei besonderer Berücksichtigung der westlichen Landkreise Holzminden und Gandersheim—von 1750 bis 1900: Motive, Verlauf und Folgen der Auswanderungsbewegung.* Braunschweig: Appelhans, 2003.

Strickland, Matthew. *War and Chivalry: The Conduct and Perception of War in England and Normandy, 1066–1217.* Cambridge: Cambridge University Press, 1996.

Suck, Friedrich, and Holger Hamecher. *Mirabeau, Schlieffen und die nach Amerika verkauften Hessen: Zwei zeitgenösische Pamphlete zum "Soldatenhandel" für den Amerikanischen Unabhängigkeitskrieg.* Kassel: Hamecher, 1991.

Taaffe, Stephen R. *The Philadelphia Campaign, 1777–1778.* Lawrence: University Press of Kansas, 2003.

Tallett, Frank. *War and Society in Early Modern Europe, 1495–1715.* New York: Routledge, 1992.

Taylor, Peter K. *Indentured to Liberty: Peasant Life and the Hessian Military State, 1688–1815.* Ithaca: Cornell University Press, 1994.

Titus, James. *The Old Dominion at War: Society, Politics, and Warfare in Late Colonial Virginia.* Columbia: University of South Carolina Press, 1991.

Turner, Eunice H. "American Prisoners of War in Great Britain, 1777–1783." *Mariner's Mirror* 45, no. 3 (1959): 200–206.

Turner, Victor W. "Liminalität und Communitas." In *Ritualtheorien: Ein einführendes Handbuch,* edited by Andréa Bellinger and David J. Krieger, 2nd ed., 247–60. Wiesbaden: Westdeutscher Verlag, 2003.

————. *The Ritual Process: Structure and Anti-Structure.* Chicago: Aldine Publishing Co., 1969.

Venables, Robert W. "'Faithful Allies of the King': The Crown's Haudenosaunee Allies in the Revolutionary Struggle for New York." In *The Other Loyalists: Ordinary People, Royalism, and the Revolution in the Middle Colonies, 1763–1787,* edited by Joseph S. Tiedeman, Eugene R. Fingerhut, and Robert W. Venables, 131–60. Albany: State University of New York Press, 2009.

Voigtländer, Lutz. *Die preußischen Kriegsgefangenen der Reichsarmee 1760/1763.* Duisburg: Gilles und Francke Verlag, 1995.

Volm, M. H. *The Hessian Prisoners in the American War of Independence and Their Life in Captivity.* Charlottesville: n.p., 1937.

Ward, Harry M. *The Department of War, 1781–1795.* Pittsburgh: University of Pittsburgh Press, 1962.

Warren, Mercy Otis. *History of the Rise, Progress and Termination of the American Revolution: Interspersed with Biographical, Political and Moral Observations*. 3 vols. 1805. Reprint, New York: AMS Press, 1970.

Watt, Gavin K. *Rebellion in the Mohawk Valley: The St. Leger Expedition of 1777*. Toronto: Dundurn, 2002.

Wehler, Hans-Ulrich. *Vom Feudalismus des Alten Reiches bis zur defensiven Modernisierung der Reformära, 1700–1815*. 3rd ed. 5 vols. Munich: Beck, 1996.

Weigley, Russell F. *The Partisan War: The South Carolina Campaign of 1780–1782*. Columbia: University of South Carolina Press, 1970.

Wekhrlin, Wilhelm Ludwig, ed. *Chronologen: Ein Periodisches Werk*. 12 vols. Frankfurt a. M. und Leipzig: Felßeckerische Buchhandlung, 1779–81.

Wette, Wolfram. *Der Krieg des Kleinen Mannes: Eine Militärgeschichte von unten*. Munich: Pieper, 1992.

Wilhelmy, Jean-Pierre. *Les mercenaires allemands au Québec, 1776–1783*. Québec: Septentrion, 1997.

Wilson, Peter H. *German Armies: War and German Politics, 1648–1806*. Bristol, Pa.: UCL Press, 1998.

———. "The German 'Soldiertrade' of the Seventeenth and Eighteenth Centuries: A Reassessment." *International History Review* 18 (1996): 757–92.

———. "Social Militarization in Eighteenth-Century Germany." *German History* 18, no. 1 (2000): 1–39.

———. "Violence and the Rejection of Authority in Eighteenth-Century Germany: The Case of the Swabian Mutinies in 1757." *German History* 12, no. 1 (1994): 1–26.

Winter, Martin. *Untertanengeist durch Militärpflicht? Das preußische Kantonsystem in brandenburgischen Städten im 18. Jahrhundert*. Bielefeld: Verlag für Regionalgeschichte, 2005.

Wokeck, Marianne S. *Trade in Strangers: The Beginnings of Mass Migration to North America*. University Park: Pennsylvania State University Press, 1999.

Wolf, Edwin, and Maxwell Whiteman. *The History of the Jews of Philadelphia from Colonial Times to the Age of Jackson*. 2nd ed. Philadelphia: Jewish Publication Society of America, 1975.

Wood, Gordon S. *The Radicalism of the American Revolution*. New York: Knopf, 1991.

Wood, Jerome H. *Conestoga Crossroads: Lancaster, Pennsylvania, 1730–1789*. Harrisburg: Pennsylvania Historical and Museum Commission, 1979.

Wright, John W. "Sieges and Customs of War at the Opening of the Eighteenth Century." *American Historical Review* 39, no. 4 (1934): 629–44.

Ziegler, Karl-Heinz. "Die Bedeutung von Hugo Grotius für das Völkerrecht: Versuch einer Bilanz am Ende des 20. Jahrhunderts." *Zeitschrift für Historische Forschung* 23, no. 3 (1996): 355–71.

Zottl, Christian Michael. "'Die Hungrigen schreiben selten Geschichte, und Historiker sind selten hungrig.' Mikrohistorische Aspekte der Alltagsernährung städtischer Unterschichten in der deutschen Frühen Neuzeit: Urbane Siedlungen im Vergleich." *Concilium Medii Aevi* 8 (2005): 53–106.

Index

361

British 26th Regiment of Foot, 121,
126, 128, 138
British Treasury, 167
Brumhard, Andreas, 223, 224
Budin, Conrad, 254
Buford, Abraham, 94
Burgoyne, John, 95, 101, 104, 106–
107, 171, 185, 186, 204, 277
Burrows, Edwin, 173
Butland, James, 205

Campbell, John, 218
Campbell, William, 94–95
Camp followers, 72–73, 165, 201
Canada: German auxiliaries in, 93;
land grants in, 256–57; postwar
settlement in, 258–60; prisoner-
laborers in, 89
Canary, Charles, 254
Canton system, 9, 37, 50–52, 64
Capital, defined, 284n19
Capture, versus surrender, 93
Carleton, Guy, 174, 242, 259
Carpenter, Emanuel, 230
Carroll, Daniel, 320n137
Cartel agreements, 91, 171; in
American Revolution, 175–77;
in European warfare, 85–87,
175; negotiations for, 176–77;
Spain and, 222. *See also* Prisoner
exchanges
Cassa, 264–65
Casualty lists: Ansbach-Bayreuth
troops, 249*t*; Braunschweig-
Wolfenbüttel troops, 238–39,
239*t*, 251; Company von Quesnoy
troops, 248*t*; Hessen-Kassel
troops, 251
Catherine II (Russia), 20
Charitable and disability funds,
264–65
Charles III (Spain), 220
Charleston siege, 108, 112
Charlottesville prison camp, 120,
193–97, 195*f*, 214
Chester County militia, 216
Chivalry, 81–82
Ciriacy, Andreas Gottlieb von, 202,
244
Citizen armies, 3, 34–35
Civilians, legal status of in warfare,
87–88

Claiborne, Richard, 210
Clark, George Rogers, 220
Cleve, Heinrich Urban, 250
Clinton, Henry, 20, 92, 108, 112, 168,
174, 212
Clymer, George, 98–99, 320n137
Cole, Thomas, 190, 192
Comet (privateer), 96
Commissary general of prisoners,
125, 168, 215; deputies of, 140;
problems involving, 139
Company rosters, 61, 293n1
Company Tritschler von Falckenstein.
See Ansbach-Bayreuth Company
Tritschler von Falckenstein
Company von Dechow. *See* Hessen-
Kassel Company von Dechow
Company von Quesnoy. *See* Ansbach-
Bayreuth Company von Quesnoy
Condit, Silas, 205
Congress: commissionary general of
prisoners and, 139; in delay of
Convention Army parole, 185–86;
instruction on prison policy from,
126–27; nationalist movement in,
225–26, 320n137, 321n155; policy
on recruitment, ransom and
indenture of prisoners, 227–28;
prisoner desertions encouraged
by, 100, 143, 192–93; prisoner
exchanges and, 176, 177–78, 226;
in prisoner-of-war administration,
138, 215; on prisoner-of-war
conventions, 270–71; prisoner
provisioning and, 131, 167, 168,
169, 225; prisoner recruitment
and, 140, 182–83, 200; prisoner
treatment and, 119
Congress's Executive Committee: on
prisoner housing, 117; victory
parade and, 98–100
Connecticut Assembly, 121
Connecticut colony, 121, 123, 132
Conrade, Leopold, 66
Conscription, 3, 37, 46–55;
exemptions from, 46–48, 51; in
maintenance of social order, 51;
mercantilist principles in, 47–48
Continental Army: organization of,
90; prisoner exchanges and, 171–
72, 175; recruitment of prisoners
by, 140–41, 200, 225, 227, 229,

objections to, 231–32; at
Mount Hope furnace, 232–34;
postwar, 234–35; recruitment as
preferable to, 237
Infantry units, 57–58
Ingrao, Charles, 52, 59, 183, 251
Ireland, 88–89
Iron forges, 153, 154
Isaac, Melchior, 150

Jäger troops, 16, 57, 93, 164, 249,
293n8
Jefferson, Thomas, 268, 269, 271, 272
Joyner, John, 324n204
Juliat, Gustav, 182
Just War theory, 83–84, 87

Kabale und Liebe (Schiller), 26
Kalneck, Jacob, 259
Kammeramtmann, 263
Kantonsystem, 9, 37, 50–52, 64
Kapp, Friedrich, 22, 29
Kappes, Jeremias, 56, 62, 71, 293n1
Karl Alexander (Ansbach-Bayreuth),
23, 25, 48, 49, 67, 211, 256;
assistance to soldiers' families by,
55, 60; Ochsenfurt mutiny and,
16, 17, 53–55; recruitment and,
37–38; rumored will of, 265–66;
territories of, 285n3
Karl I (Braunschweig-Wolfenbüttel),
20, 24–25, 41, 66
Karl Wilhelm Ferdinand
(Braunschweig-Wolfenbüttel),
28–29
Kastenamtmann, 262–63
Keen, Maurice, 82
Kingston, Robert, 278
Kitz, Johannes, 148
Klein, Wilhelm, 182
Kleinschmidt, Karl Wilhelm, 181–83,
312n56
Klosteramtmann, 263
Kniewaßer, Georg, 202
Knoll, Adam, 202, 244
Knox, Henry, 125, 226, 321n143
Knyphausen, Wilhelm von, 148, 158,
178, 179, 182
Koch, Barthold, 58
Koernich, Wolf, 285n4
Kolb, Johannes, 255–56, 326n50
Kolb, Kunigunda, 256

Kompaniewirtschaft, 39
Koselleck, Reinhart, 28
Krauseneck, Johann, 26
Kreuth, Bayreuth, 48
Kucher, Christopher, 161
Kühn, Johannes, 61–62
Kulmbach, Bayreuth, 48
Kümmel, Heinrich, 45

Lafayette, Marie-Joseph Gilbert du
Motier, Marquis de, 108
Lahe, Eleanora, 255
Lancaster Committee of Inspection,
127, 128, 131, 134, 145
Lancaster Committee of Observation
and Correspondence, 201
Lancaster Committee of Safety, 126,
131–32, 157
Lancaster County, Penn.: German
immigration to, 133–34; prisoner
employment in, 136; trades and
occupations in, 133
Lancaster prison camp, 120; British
agents in provisioning, 128–29;
congressional instruction
concerning, 126, 127; design of,
134, 136, 137f; enlargement of,
135–36; food shortage at, 146;
German provisioning of, 147–49;
as model site, 134; overcrowding
in, 146; prisoner control in,
134–35; prisoner dispersal from,
159; prisoner-laborers at, 131–32,
148; prisoner resistance at,
156–57; prisoner trades at, 151t,
306n18; reimbursement requests
from, 131; removal of officers
from, 128
Lancaster Town Committee, 149–50
Landau, Valentin, 234
Land grants, 256–57
Landschaft, in Ansbach-Bayreuth, 48
Lange, Heinrich, 206, 307n51
L'arbre des batailles (Bonet), 83
Laurens, Henry, 141
Lauwaldt, Adam, 257
Lebanon prison camp:
accommodations in, 159–60;
Moravian church and, 160–61;
prisoner-laborers in, 153–54;
shortages at, 162
Lee, Arthur, 32, 35